D0193320

The Election After Reform

DISCARD

A CAMPAIGN FINANCE INSTITUTE BOOK

The Campaign Finance Institute is a non-partisan, non-profit institute affiliated with the George Washington University that conducts objective research and education, empanels task forces and makes recommendations for policy change in the field of campaign finance. Statements of the Campaign Finance Institute and its Task Forces do not necessarily reflect the views of CFI's Trustees or financial supporters. For further information, visit the CFI web site at www.CampaignFinance Institute.org.

The Election After Reform

Money, Politics, and the Bipartisan Campaign Reform Act

Edited by
Michael J. Malbin

ROWMAN & LITTLEFIELD PUBLISHERS, INC.
Lanham • Boulder • New York • Toronto • Oxford

ROWMAN & LITTLEFIELD PUBLISHERS, INC.

Published in the United States of America
by Rowman & Littlefield Publishers, Inc.
A wholly owned subsidary of The Rowman & Littlefield Publishing Group, Inc.
4501 Forbes Boulevard, Suite 200, Lanham, Maryland 20706
www.rowmanlittlefield.com

P.O. Box 317, Oxford OX2 9RU, UK

Copyright © 2006 by The Campaign Finance Institute

Cover newspaper headlines, excerpts, and images: "Donors use loopholes to avoid finance law," "The Swift Boat TV Ad Furor," and "Campaign reform works so far" reproduced with the permission of *The Post-Standard*. "Bush denounces outside attack ads" reproduced with the permission of *The Chronicle-Telegram*. "Ad spending in presidential contest triples that of 2000" reproduced with the permission of *Gettysburg Times*. "Campaign law mess" reproduced with the permission of *Placerville Mountain Democrat*. David Broder image and syndicated column excerpt reproduced with permission from David Broder.

All rights reserved. No part of this publication may be reproduced, stored in a retrieval system, or transmitted in any form or by any means, electronic, mechanical, photocopying, recording, or otherwise, without the prior permission of the publisher.

British Library Cataloguing in Publication Information Available

Library of Congress Cataloging-in-Publication Data

The election after reform : money, politics, and the Bipartisan Campaign Reform Act / edited by Michael J. Malbin.
    p.   cm.— (Campaigning American style)
Includes bibliographical references and index.
ISBN-13: 978-0-7425-3869-6 (cloth : alk. paper)
ISBN-10: 0-7425-3869-9 (cloth : alk. paper)
ISBN-13: 978-0-7425-3870-2 (pbk. : alk. paper)
ISBN-10: 0-7425-3870-2 (pbk. : alk. paper)
    1. Campaign funds—United States.   2. Campaign funds—Law and legislation—United States.   3. United States. Bipartisan Campaign Reform Act of 2002.   I. Malbin, Michael J.   II.   Series.
JK1991.E54   2006
324.7'80973—dc22   2005030131

Printed in the United States of America

♾ ™ The paper used in this publication meets the minimum requirements of American National Standard for Information Sciences—Permanence of Paper for Printed Library Materials, ANSI/NISO Z39.48-1992.

Contents

Figures and Tables

FIGURES

TABLES

Acknowledgments

The Election After Reform is the second Campaign Finance Institute book about the federal law known officially as the Bipartisan Campaign Reform Act of 2002. We are grateful to the Carnegie Corporation, the Joyce Foundation, the Pew Charitable Trusts, the Smith Richardson Foundation, and the Stuart Family Foundation for their generous support of CFI's research.

This research could not have happened without a lot of hard work from CFI's graduate and undergraduate student research assistants. Paul Zummo, Margaret Teng Fu, Erin Ryan, and Jonathan Vaupal labored for many months to create the database of presidential campaign contributors relied on in chapter 11. Paul Zummo also contributed significantly to most of CFI's analyses of these databases once they were created. Zummo, Todd Andrews, and Mitchell Killian worked on political parties, candidates, soft money donors, and political action committees. Allison Garcimonde prepared the manuscript and bibliography.

On CFI's full-time staff, Erika Starr oversaw the book production process. (Renée Legatt and Jehanne Schweitzer did so for Rowman & Littlefield.) Brendan Glavin is responsible for the computer systems and campaign finance databases that make CFI go. The book cover design is by Betsy Rubinstein of In·Form.

Before this manuscript went through revisions, CFI held a public conference in January 2005 based on drafts of some of the book's chapters. In addition to chapter authors, the participants (with the titles they then held) were Jack Oliver, National Finance Vice Chair of Victory 2004 for the Republican National Committee; Jackson Dunn, Finance Vice Chair of the Democratic National Committee; Ellen Malcolm, President of America Coming Together; Mike Russell of Creative Response Concepts; Lois Murphy, a Democratic congressional candidate from Pennsylvania; Don McGahn, General Counsel of the National Republican Congressional Committee; and Bob Bauer of Perkins Coie, who represents both the Democratic Senatorial and Democratic Congressional Campaign Committees. The participants all provided valuable insights, which can be read or seen in streaming video on the CFI website. These insights were used for revisions. If we missed anything, that remains the authors' responsibility. Finally, the chapter on the presidential election campaign (chapter 11) was also published as an article in the *Election Law Journal* (vol. 5, no. 1, January 2006). We are grateful to the journal's anonymous peer reviewers for their helpful comments.

Michael J. Malbin
The Campaign Finance Institute

1

Assessing the Bipartisan Campaign Reform Act

Michael J. Malbin

We may as well begin in the middle. The following statements appeared in *Newsweek*, the *Denver Post*, and the *Washington Post* during the last few weeks of the 2004 U.S. election campaign:

- *Newsweek, September 20, 2004:* "This was supposed to be the year Big Money would be driven out of presidential politics—or at least wrestled under control. Don't kid yourself. The McCain-Feingold campaign-reform law may have succeeded in drying up the political parties' soft money slush funds. But that money—and more—has simply found a new home in the murkier world of 527s" (Hosenball, Isikoff, and Bailey 2004).
- *The Denver Post, October 31, 2004:* "The McCain-Feingold campaign finance reform law—much debated and ballyhooed—has been an ineffectual speed bump in the chase of money after politicians. The so-called reforms have done nothing at all to alleviate the influence of big money in politics and very well may have exacerbated it . . . It is time to admit that McCain-Feingold has been a near-total bust" (David Harwood 2004).
- *Senators John McCain and Russell Feingold in the Washington Post, October 23, 2004:* "The McCain-Feingold law was never about reducing money in politics. Its goal was to reduce the corrupting influence of unlimited 'soft money' contributions to the political parties, usually solicited by federal candidates and officeholders . . . Ending the practice of the president, party leaders, and members of Congress soliciting huge donations from corporations, unions, and wealthy individuals improved the system. And, despite predictions to the contrary, the parties have thrived in the new hard-money world" (McCain and Feingold 2004).

1

These disagreements were hardly new. It took six years for Congress to pass McCain-Feingold—more formally known as the Bipartisan Campaign Reform Act of 2002 (BCRA, pronounced "Bikra"). In some ways, rereading the intense debates before the law's passage made me feel as if I were reading the children's tale, *Goldilocks and the Three Bears*. One set of critics was saying the law would do too much, another too little. From those who said "too much" we heard the law would undermine political parties, weaken free speech, curtail competition, and strengthen special interest groups. From those who said "too little," as well as those who said "foolishly futile," we heard that major donors would readily find their way around the new rules, producing wasted effort but no major change. Sometimes a critic would even say "too much" and either "too little" or "futile" in the same speech. But then the Goldilocks analogy began to break down because the law's supporters—including the lead sponsors, Sen. McCain, Sen. Feingold, Rep. Shays, and Rep. Meehan—never did declare it "just right." They claimed the law would shift politics incrementally in the right direction— "sort of right," not "just so." Even that point is still disputed, as the opening quotations make clear.

These claims and counterclaims should not be understood as technical disputes of interest only to campaign finance junkies. BCRA's two main subjects—political party soft money and corporate or labor funding for certain election-related advertising—seem at first glance to be self-contained. But by regulating them, the law promised (or threatened, depending upon one's perspective) to affect just about every aspect of public life in the United States. Here is a short list of subjects that supporters and opponents have plausibly claimed BCRA will affect:

- The role of political parties in federal elections;
- The balance of power between Democrats and Republicans;
- The health of state and local parties;
- The political influence of independent advocacy organizations;
- The frequency and content of political advertising;
- The competitive status of incumbents and challengers;
- The relative influence of large and small donors;
- The relationships between public officials and donors;
- The content of the legislative and governing agenda; and, ultimately,
- The speech, political participation, and civic engagement of individual citizens.

The legislative battle for BCRA was so intense because, as this list shows, the stakes were so high. Participants were divided over matters of principle. They were also divided by their perceptions of their own and their respective parties' self-interests.

SUMMARY OVERVIEW

This book will not settle all disputes over BCRA. We will be satisfied to understand how the law worked in its first cycle and to draw broader implications from that experience. It is the second book produced by teams of political scientists assembled by the nonpartisan Campaign Finance Institute to assess this new law. The goal of the first book, published before BCRA's first election, was to predict how political organizations and actors were likely to react and adapt to this major change (Malbin 2003). After one election, it is time to test theories with facts. Many of the political scientists who contributed to this volume also contributed to the last one. We hold different views about BCRA's wisdom but share common perspectives about how to research its impact. Our goal is not merely to look at the law's direct or short-term impact on money in a single election but to begin answering questions about its longer term effects on the political system.

To give a short preview of the pages that follow, here are the authors' main conclusions:

- On the first or simplest level, the law seems to have accomplished its basic objectives without the negative consequences most often mentioned during the advance debate.
  - By restoring the 1974 legal concept that all contributions to federal candidates, parties, and their agents should be subject to limits, BCRA prevented public and party officials from using soft money contributions to the parties as a loophole for unlimited contributions.
  - Despite the loss of soft money, which made up about half of their income from 1999–2002, the parties were remarkably resilient—raising more money and playing a more significant role in the 2004 elections than even BCRA's supporters had predicted.
  - Part of this resilience came from one of the major "good news" political stories of 2004: a marked increased in small (under $200) contributions to the parties and presidential candidates.
  - In addition, the law did not simply move the major donors' money from one pocket to another: most of the soft money donors in the elections before BCRA especially the major corporate donors apparently did *not* put their former soft money contributions into some other form of election spending.
  - Moreover these 2004 results seem *not* to have come at the expense of robust, open, and nearly ubiquitous political speech.
  - Finally, in response to the concern that BCRA would alter the prospects for incumbents or challengers, the authors found BCRA's impact on congressional elections and presidential primaries overwhelmed by larger forces in favor of congressional incumbents and presidential front-runners.
- On a more complex level, however, the impact on political party committees was uneven, and the increasing role of nonparty organizations will need to be followed closely.
  - Political party committees were not all equal in 2004. The two parties' national committees did extremely well in support of their presidential candidates, raising more hard money in 2004 than hard and soft money

combined in 2002 or 2000. In contrast, the four congressional campaign committees did not do as well. The two House campaign committees made up most of the soft money they lost but did not quite close the gap; the two Senate committees had an even more disappointing year, increasing their hard money but leaving a significant gap in their total receipts.

o As for the impact of the soft money ban on donors and nonparty advocacy organizations, even though most of the former soft money donors did not put their money back into politics, large gifts from megadonors let new political committees which had the tacit support of the political parties (the so-called 527 committees) pick up much of the slack.

o Finally, even though there was a great deal of vigorous public debate in 2004, it is important to monitor whether the law advantages individuals or organizations with some kinds of resources over others. Some have suggested, for example, that the law will favor polarizing ideological organizations over business or labor groups. Others have said the opposite. Both cannot be right.

• These complex countercurrents suggest, therefore, that it is premature to treat the experience of 2004 as if it were the last word. Campaign finance laws are not yet stable, particularly with respect to independent advocacy organizations. Even if the law were stable, we cannot yet know whether the 2004 experience was a by-product of that year's election climate. The 2004 election was dominated by a closely fought presidential election with heightened voter interest and turnout. A different environment will produce different incentives for those donors who participated, perhaps leading some to scale back or sit out the next election. At the same time, shifts in either the legal environment or issue agenda could bring back some former soft money donors who sat out 2004. We are in a position to speculate how this might play out but not yet to foresee how it will.

The authors of this volume begin sorting out these layers in the chapters to follow. But before we turn to their analyses, we need a proper introduction to the law and its context.

THE BIPARTISAN CAMPAIGN REFORM ACT

The main provisions in BCRA prohibited unlimited soft money contributions to national political parties for any purpose and to state parties for "federal election activity." The law also prohibited corporate or labor union funding of certain "electioneering" ads and required disclosure of individual financing for electioneering. But these provisions make no sense in isolation. Soft money and electioneering are technical terms that grew within an older system of law. BCRA is best understood as an attempt to patch and repair the older system because it had sprung major leaks. Specifically, BCRA is an attempt to restore meaningful contribution limits and disclosure to federal campaign finance law.

The older law traces back mainly to the Federal Election Campaign Act (FECA) Amendments of 1974 (Public Law 93-443). FECA enacted a fairly comprehensive regulatory system that included:

- A broad system of disclosure for all receipts and spending on federal elections;
- Limits on the amounts of contributions to federal candidates and political parties;
- A continuation of preexisting bans on contributions and expenditures by corporations and labor unions, which under FECA were permitted to establish separate funds (political action committees called PACs) governed by contribution limits;
- Limits on the amount a party could spend in cooperation with a candidate to help the candidate win; and
- Partial public financing for presidential primary candidates and full public funding in the general election for candidates who agree to limit their spending in return for taking the public money.

The 1974 law's constitutionality was challenged immediately. In the 1976 landmark case of *Buckley v. Valeo* (424 U.S. 1 [1976]), the Court upheld all of these provisions, while overturning others that would have imposed mandatory spending limits on all federal candidates, contribution limits on candidates who give to their own campaigns, and limits on independent spending. The *Buckley* Court also interpreted the law in a way that was to have important consequences later. In the course of upholding disclosure and interpreting "independent spending," the Court indicated that it had a problem with the law's potential reach. FECA had brought within the scope of federal regulation all spending "intended to influence the outcome" of a federal election. This formulation had two problems, according to the Court: it was potentially too broad, and it was vague. People who participate in politics deserve clear definitions of what the law would and would not allow. Without these, the justices feared some potential speakers would avoid public discussion of issues just to be sure they steered clear of potential election law penalties. In judicial terms, the lack of a clear boundary could have a "chilling effect." To avoid this, the Court read a "bright line" test into FECA, interpreting it only to cover speech that advocated a candidate's election or defeat with such words of "express advocacy" as "vote for," "vote against," or the equivalent.

For some years after *Buckley,* the country had in place a system with strong disclosure, contribution limits, and partial public funding of presidential elections. The pieces functioned more or less as intended for several elections. During the 1980 and 1984 elections, virtually all spending on the presidential election fit within FECA's boundaries (Alexander 1983; Alexander and Haggerty 1987).

But then the system began to erode. The Federal Election Commission (FEC), which administers the law, had said that national political parties could raise money without concern for federal contribution limits as long as the money was spent for "nonfederal election" activities. Originally understood to allow unlimited contributions for capital expenditures and other party-building activities, the term nonfederal by the mid-1990s had come to mean any activity that did not "expressly advocate" the election or defeat of a federal candidate. That is, the interpretation the Court devised to create a bright line for disclosure and independent spending to protect speech about issues came to be the standard others used for spending by the political parties. An activity could be deemed nonfederal even if it was a paid advertisement featuring and praising (or attacking) a candidate during the height of an election campaign, so long as the advertisement did not contain words of express advocacy. This interpretation allowed the parties to accept unlimited corporate, labor union, and individual contributions (soft money) to pay for nonfederal activities central to federal election campaigns, including advertising. For independent nonparty organizations—spurred by favorable FEC and lower court decisions in the 1990s—the broadened use of express advocacy had an equally powerful effect. Long-established federal laws—dating back to the Tillman Act of 1907 (34 Stat. 864) and Taft Hartley Act of 1947 (61 Stat. 136)—had prohibited corporations and labor unions from contributing or spending money to influence federal elections. But if an advertisement did not contain words of express advocacy, a corporation or labor union could spend unlimited amounts to pay for the ad, and the ad's sponsors would not have to disclose where the money came from or how they spent it.

The practical implications of these interpretations were dramatically noticeable during the election of 1996. President Clinton's lawyers realized they could use party soft money to pay for nonfederal advertising that featured the President. But this did not remain only a Democratic story for long, as Republicans imitated the Democrats, raising soft money in large chunks to advertise their candidate too. By end of 1996, soft money raised by the six major national Democratic and Republican party committees had more than tripled, from $86 million in 1991–1992 to $262 million in 1995–1996. Nonparty organizations also were breaking new ground in 1995–1996, led by the AFL-CIO. Interest groups and advocacy organizations on the right and left were learning from each other, as candidate-specific "issue ads" mushroomed. Although less money was involved for the nonparty groups than for parties, the amounts were substantial and—unlike the party money—the funding sources could stay hidden, with no public disclosure. With these two changes, the part of the 1996 campaign that was outside of FECA's limits was almost as large as the part inside (Alexander 1999). Express advocacy—a phrase offered by the Court before FECA's first election as a reasonable rough-cut attempt to fit the law within constitutional bounds—had become the vehicle political entrepreneurs were using to bring a functional end to much of FECA.

BCRA's overriding purpose was to restore what had once been in effect under FECA. The new law sought, first, to restore meaningful contribution limits (as well as spending limits for publicly funded presidential campaigns) by prohibiting the unlimited soft money for national political parties that in effect had become end runs around the old system. BCRA accomplished this by placing limits on all contributions to national party committees and protecting against new end runs by restricting contributions to state and local parties for what the law describes as "federal election activities."

The law's second major purpose was to bring back corporate and labor spending restrictions, as well as disclosure, to electioneering speech by all persons other than candidates and parties. The definition of electioneering was meant to draw a bright line that would include more messages than the express advocacy test while satisfying the Court's concerns about vagueness. Under the BCRA definition, a communication is considered electioneering if it (1) is conveyed by a broadcast, cable, or satellite communication; (2) is broadcast to a market of at least 50,000 people in the relevant electorate; (3) names or identifies a federal candidate; and (4) airs within sixty days of a general election or thirty days of a primary.

Additional BCRA provisions increased FECA's contribution limits for individuals, which had not been adjusted since 1974 and had therefore lost two-thirds of their real value to inflation. The new limits increased the maximum individual contribution to candidates from $1,000 to $2,000 per election; increased the aggregate limit on the total amount an individual could give to all candidates, parties, and political committees combined; and indexed those limits to adjust for future inflation. Special, variable contribution limits were also introduced for candidates who faced wealthy, self-funded candidates. Finally, the new law codified electronic disclosure on the Internet. (A more detailed summary of the law is provided in appendix 1, at the end of this book.)

Of course, Congress does not generally have the last word about a law's meaning. FECA's history makes clear that the law in practice is the law as it is interpreted by the courts and the Federal Election Commission. BCRA's constitutionality, like FECA's, was challenged immediately. On December 10, 2003, the Supreme Court decided—with a 5-4 split on most of the important issues relating to soft money and electioneering—to uphold virtually all of BCRA's important provisions, except for one that would have made it hard for political parties to make unlimited "independent expenditures." (For a summary of the Court's decision in *McConnell v. Federal Election Commission*, 540 U.S. 93 [2003], see appendix 2.) Whether this may be modified in the future, however, remains open as of this writing. On January 23, 2006, the Supreme Court remanded the case of *Wisconsin Right to Life, Inc. v. Federal Election Commission*, 546 U.S. _____ (2006), saying that it would hear an "as applied" challenge to its earlier facial support of the electioneering provision in *McConnell*. After a new lower court decision on the facts in this case, it will be reheard by a Supreme Court that will have two new members, and without one of the narrow *McConnell* majority.

The Federal Election Commission's regulations to implement the law's soft money, electioneering, and other provisions have also been highly controversial, with potentially major effects on the law's meaning in practice. (The regulations and controversies are summarized in appendices 3 through 5.) The law's main sponsors challenged nineteen of the FEC's regulations in the case of *Shays v. Fed-*

eral Election Commission. In September 2004 the U.S. District Court for the District of Columbia overturned fifteen of those nineteen regulations. As of this writing, the FEC is in the process of appealing the decision concerning five regulations and rewriting others. The regulations therefore may change for 2006, but the ones summarized in the appendix were in effect for 2004.

HOW TO ASSESS MOVING TARGETS

We said earlier that assessing BCRA's impact would be straightforward on some levels but complex on others. Like any regulatory statute of significance, the law is not self-enforcing, and its interpretations are contested. Laws gain their effect by altering the thoughts and decisions of flesh-and-blood human beings. BCRA (like FECA and other campaign finance laws) works primarily by constraining those who are, or work for, or give money to candidates, political parties, or anyone else who communicates directly with others about politics. These people and organizations have different goals from those who wrote and lobbied for BCRA. Candidates, party leaders, and their consultants or other agents generally participate in elections to win. They will do whatever they can, within the law, to serve that objective. Once a law passes they will adjust their own tactics, shift their organizational structure, or find space within the law to reach their goal. Of course, not all actors will be equally able to adapt to all laws. The ability to adapt will depend upon the actors' own resources and constraints as well as the law. As people adapt, laws will shift over time in their practical consequences, favoring some organizations or some paths of action over others. The fact that this occurs does not by itself signal a law's failure. It is an inevitable process that occurs over time and leads to an equally inevitable need to readjust the laws.

Moreover, campaign finance laws make up only part of the legal, political, technological, and economic context shaping the decision strategies of parties, candidates, interest groups, and consultants. The people who are reacting and adapting to BCRA are reacting simultaneously to every aspect of their environment that will affect their ability to reach their objectives. The issue environment in some years will favor some approaches over others. The economics and technology of communications will shift participants' assessments about how best to raise and spend money. In a multifaceted world, therefore, we cannot assume that if a particular practice changed *after* a new law took effect, the law *caused* the change or that the change will continue if the political environment shifts again.

For example, there was an apparent shift by some organizations between 1996 and 2004 toward putting a smaller percentage of their resources into television advertising and more into voter mobilization. This looks on the surface as if it might have been a reaction to BCRA's electioneering rules, which focused on radio and television ads. But the process began before BCRA and seems more of a reaction to the cost of television and to the fact that most voters had made up their minds early. Together, these made voter mobilization more cost-efficient for these organizations than it would be in a different context. But the context might change again, either because the national agenda changes or because of shifts in the economics of advertising.

Therefore, because adaptation is a process that occurs over time, and because laws and the people who operate under them will react differently as other parts of the political context change, we are bound to know more about BCRA after two or three elections than after one. Nevertheless, we are not jumping the gun by offering an assessment now. While our conclusions cannot be the last word, one election does take us beyond speculation. We now have seen BCRA work at least once. We may not know everything, but we know more than we did.

PREVIEW OF THE BOOK

The main political arguments over the impact of BCRA, as evidenced by the quotations that opened this chapter, are (1) whether the law harmed the political parties and (2) whether the soft money that used to go to the parties simply changed locations, without a significant change in effect. Accordingly, the ten chapters that follow begin with three on political parties—a national overview, one on congressional parties, and one on state parties. The nonparty soft money story of 2004 is addressed by the next two chapters. One is about 527 committees. The other is about ongoing interest groups and advocacy organizations, with the first part of the latter chapter focusing on what happened to the former soft money donors.

After soft money, the next major set of questions is about the impact of BCRA's rules for candidate-specific broadcast advertising. These are addressed in the final two-thirds of the chapter about ongoing interest groups, as well as in two separate chapters on the air war and ground war. The book ends with three chapters on candidates' campaigns—two on congressional elections and one on a presidential election.

Political Parties

Overview

In the first of the party chapters (chapter 2), Anthony Corrado shows that the national parties responded to the loss of soft money by redoubling their fundraising efforts for hard money (i.e., money within federal contribution limits). As a result, the parties raised more hard money in 2003–2004, the first election cycle under BCRA, than hard and soft money combined in either of the previous two cycles when soft money made up about half of the parties' total receipts. The Republican National Committee (RNC) raised slightly more hard money in 2004 than hard and soft money combined in 2000. The Democratic National Committee (DNC) did even better, with one-and-a-half times as much hard money in 2004 as hard and soft combined in 2000. Even more remarkably, the DNC—for the first time in recent memory—raised more than the RNC ($394 million to $392 million), thus defying predictions that the new law initially would favor the GOP. Unitemized contributions from donors who give less than $200 in a calendar year went from $59 million to $166 million for the DNC and from $91 million to $157 million for the Republicans. Donors at the high end ($20,000–$25,000) also increased their hard money giving, but the above $25,000 donors who previously had dominated soft money giving were no longer part of the mix. In short, Corrado argues, the parties "demonstrated their capacity for adapting to changes in the regulatory and political environment. At the end of the first election under BCRA, the national party organizations were stronger, not weaker."

Hill Committees

But the national party committees were not uniformly of equal strength. As Diana Dwyre and Robin Kolodny note (chapter 3), the congressional campaign committees did not make up so quickly for all of the soft money they lost. The two House committees raised slightly less than their past years' combined hard and soft money, while the two Senate committees fell well short of their previous combined totals. However, all four committees raised much more hard money than they had in the past, with increases coming in the amounts from both large and small donors. One source of increased hard money contributions were the contributions from the campaign committees of incumbent House Members to the Democratic Congressional Campaign Committee (DCCC) and National Republican Congressional Committee (NRCC), which were 44 percent higher in 2003–2004 ($42 million) than in 2001–2002 ($29 million).

The removal of soft money funded advertising does *not* appear to have brought about a major change in the congressional committees' spending patterns. The parties were able to concentrate their hard money independent spending in much the same way as they once did their soft money efforts. In Senate elections, $38 million in independent spending concentrated on twelve races, with a maximum of $8.3 million spent in Florida. In the House, $80 million of independent spending concentrated on thirty races. That is an average of $1.3 million per candidate in targeted races, with the party actually outspending the candidates in seven Democratic and ten GOP contests.

State Parties

Under the old regime pre-BCRA, the national committees would transfer to state parties much of the soft money they raised at the national level. The state parties would then spend most of the transferred money on shared activities to help federal candidates. With no soft money at the national level, and therefore no transfers, some were concerned that the state parties would suffer. But according to Raymond La Raja (chapter 4), the state parties raised and spent about the same amount of money reportable to the Federal Election Commission in 2004 as in 2000, minus the transfers. In itself, that is not so surprising. Perhaps more significant was that once you remove spending for broadcast advertising, Republican state parties in 2004 spent more on their other activities and Democratic state parties about the same amount as they had in 2000. In other words, the soft money spent on advertising essentially was "pass-through" money, with its absence apparently not having a major effect on the remaining activity (including grassroots voter mobilization and administration) or on the financial health of the state parties.

What Happened to Soft Money? 527s and Other Groups

The parties may have done well without soft money, but what happened to the former soft money donors? According to the press accounts quoted earlier, the soft money moved to a new location. But according to Steve Weissman and Ruth Hassan (chapter 5), this is only half true. Federally active 527 committees raised and spent about $424 million during the 2004 cycle, which is about $273 million more than comparable 527s raised in the 2002 cycle, before BCRA. The increase, therefore, equals less than half of the political party soft money that BCRA banned. Moreover, the authors' analysis of all individual contributions to 527 committees of $5,000 or more shows that most of the former soft money donors did not give to 527s. So the 527s did not replace party soft money. Even so, the 527s were a major force.

These were not merely continuations of the established 527s active in past elections, many of which were associated with long-standing advocacy organizations that also have hard money PACs. Some of the most active 527s in 2004— America Coming Together (ACT), The Media Fund, and Progress for America—were new organizations legally independent of the parties but nourished by their tacit support. Their dependence on megadonors has been well documented. Two dozen individual donors gave $2 million or more to 527s in 2004, accounting by themselves for more than half of the $5,000 + individual contributions raised by all of the 527s combined. (This does not include contributions by corporations or labor unions.) Less well noticed are the contributors just behind the megadonors. The number of individuals who gave $100,000 or more to a 527 quadrupled from 66 to 265 between 2002 and 2004. The presence of such a cadre of large donors suggests a strong potential for future growth.

Ongoing Interest Groups

While much of the growth among 527s was among new committees, the focus of chapter 6 (by Robert Boatright, Mark Rozell, Clyde Wilcox, and this author) is about ongoing interest groups and advocacy organizations. To answer whether former soft money donors kept their money in the campaign finance system as a whole, this chapter begins from a list of all former organizational soft money donors (and individual donors employed by them) instead of beginning with current spenders. It examines all corporations and other organizations that gave (or whose employees individually gave) at least $100,000 in soft money in both the 2000 and 2002 election cycles. Collectively, these organizations and their employees accounted for nearly half of the parties' soft money in each of these two cycles. The vast majority of these regular soft money donors—corporations and their employees—did *not* "replace" their former soft money contributions, either by increasing their hard money giving to candidates and parties or by giving more money to 527 committees. The corporations least likely to have replaced their money were the largest publicly held corporations. We speculate that this is because most of the major donors from large corporations were responding to requests from party leaders and other officeholders rather than pursuing an urgently felt political agenda. The organizations that did increase their participation in 2004 were labor unions and the very few privately held corporations owned by the top megadonors to the new 527s. The other independent issue and ideological groups supporting the major 527s in 2004 tended not to have been party donors in the past.

Air Wars and Ground Wars: Interest Groups and Campaign Strategies

The second major set of provisions in BCRA regulated broadcast electioneering ads—increasing disclosure and prohibiting corporate and labor funding for ads that name or identify candidates within sixty days of a general election or thirty days of a primary. We wanted to know whether these provisions reduced the total amount of broadcast advertising, shifted its timing, or caused political actors to move resources away from broadcast ads to other forms of political communication and mobilization. Our answers for 2004 appear in two separate chapters and part of a third chapter.

TV Advertising

Michael Franz, Joel Rivlin, and Kenneth Goldstein ask (in chapter 7) whether BCRA significantly affected the amount or content of political advertising in 2004. The answer largely is no. About twice as many advertisements relating to the election aired in 2004 as in 2000. For federal elections, advertising was highly targeted: fewer than half of all Americans lived in a media market in which a single advertisement was broadcast in during 2004, but those who lived in competitive states or districts found their airwaves flooded. Interest group advertising went up substantially between 2000 and 2004, and a greater percentage of the ads appeared earlier (before BCRA's sixty-day window) in 2004 than 2000. The preceding chapter about ongoing interest groups (chapter 6) presents material that supplements the findings in chapter 7 by using the same data set for a more detailed analysis of advertising by nonparty groups in three election cycles. Taken together, the chapters show that BCRA affected the funding, timing, and sponsorship of interest group advertising more than its amount, content, or targeting.

The advertising chapter (chapter 7) also tests a provision in BCRA that aimed to reduce the negative tone of campaigning—requiring candidates to "stand by" their ads by appearing in them personally. The authors find little change in the percentage of positive or negative advertising by candidates, parties, or interest groups. In short, they conclude, with respect both to content and frequency: "Advertising in post-BCRA America is largely the same as in pre-BCRA America." This should not be a surprise from a careful reading of BCRA's language, which only regulates specific sources of funding within specific time periods. It may be disheartening to those who expected a major change in the tone or amount of advertising but should reassure those who were concerned that the law would be a substantial threat to robust speech and debate.

Ground War

The increase in advertising in 2004 certainly did *not* come at the expense of other forms of campaigning. David Magleby and Kelly Patterson note in chapter 8 that the renewed emphasis in campaigning on personal contact, targeted mail, and phone banks has been evident since 1998. However, the authors suggest that BCRA helped accelerate the process. Because BCRA excludes these activities from the definition of electioneering, they remain the main source of late election season activity open to be funded by corporations and labor unions. For most of the major players in 2004, ground war strategies were "presidency centered." The authors describe several techniques the party and 527 committees used: microtargeting, coordination, multiple waves of direct mail followed by telephoning, and Internet-based communications. In a three-wave panel survey of registered voters in battleground and nonbattleground states, the authors found that 27 percent of the respondents in battleground states had been reached, compared to only 9 percent in the nonbattleground states. With tactics becoming ever more sophisticated, they predict that "the lessons learned in 2004 will shape the ground war in future cycles."

The final third of the earlier chapter on ongoing interest groups (chapter 6) complements these findings with a discussion of organizations on which that chapter's authors have been conducting ongoing case studies. Many of the case study organizations made tactical adjustments *consistent* with what one would expect from the new electioneering rules (less television, more voter mobilization, and more cooperative activity within coalitions). However, our interviews showed that most of these adjustments began before BCRA, were not particularly caused by it, and could easily shift once again in a different political context.

Congressional and Presidential Candidates

Congressional Elections

The final section of the book considers BCRA's effects on candidates' campaigns. BCRA raised the limit on individual contributions to candidates from $1,000 to $2,000. This doubling of the limit, Gary Jacobson points out in his chapter about congressional elections (chapter 9), recaptured only about half of the value the maximum contribution had lost to inflation since 1974. However, Jacobson says, "the flow of campaign funds is so thoroughly dominated by the strategic considerations that shape congressional campaign finance" that BCRA's substantive effects on congressional elections "were swamped by other, far more fundamental considerations." The most basic of these are, first, that few House elections are competitive and, second, that people tend not to give money to candidates who do not have a chance. Incumbents can raise money. So can many candidates who are running for an open seat. But few challengers have a chance and therefore, few raise any money. Because even fewer House races were competitive in 2004 than in the recent past, in part because of redistricting, donors concentrated on the presidential election and competitive Senate races. The high level of independent spending by the parties in House races (see chapter 3) did nothing to make races more competitive, since the spending was concentrated in only a few districts that were already the most competitive. "The principal effect seems to have been to increase the already grossly lopsided distribution of campaign resources," Jacobson writes. This situation is not likely to change without more fundamental changes than BCRA was intended to supply.

Millionaires' Amendment

One BCRA provision that was expected to apply to only a few races in any given year was the "Millionaires' Amendment." Under this provision a candidate with a self-financed opponent may be able, under certain circumstances, to accept higher contributions from individuals than would be permitted under the normal contribution limit. According to Jennifer Steen (chapter 10), ninety-three candidates were eligible in 2004 to raise money under increased contribution limits (eighty-five candidates in primaries and eight in general elections), but only a few raised significant amounts from donors who gave more than $2,000. The amendment had a noticeable impact on Senate races in Illinois and Florida. In other races, any effects were more subtle. One negative consequence some had feared was that the amendment would help incumbents who faced wealthy challengers. It turns out that only one incumbent took advantage of the increased limits in 2004.

Presidential Candidates

The final chapter, by this author, is about presidential financing. It focuses on the nomination period. Because both major party candidates accepted full public funding for the general election, as has every major party candidate since 1976, the interesting questions for the general election period are discussed in earlier chapters on parties and interest groups.

Under FECA, candidates may receive public matching funds ($1 for the first $250 from each contributor) in return for adhering to a spending limit. Even before BCRA, participation in the public matching fund system had become questionable. The spending limit is too low and inflexible for current campaign realities, particularly for a candidate running against someone who opts out. BCRA did not change the presidential system's matching funds or spending limit, but it did increase the maximum individual contribution from $1,000 to $2,000. In other words, BCRA did not alter the deteriorating benefit-risk calculations for candidates but did make it easier to raise the top dollar contributions that had become the backbones of most presidential campaigns. We expected, therefore, that more candidates would reject public funding in 2004 and would come to depend on $2,000 contributions.

The advance expectation was partly right. The three candidates with the most money (George W. Bush, John Kerry, and Howard Dean) opted out so they could go over the spending limit. But they also raised record amounts from donors who gave $200 or less. On the face of it, this seems to confound previous expectations about major donors. However, as the monthly data and narrative in chapter 11 make clear, all of the 2004 presidential candidates except Dean depended on large contributions and donor networks (e.g., Bush's "Rangers" and "Pioneers") until the nomination contest was settled in early March. The situation raises major policy questions that go beyond BCRA. Unless the public funding system is modified, the chapter argues that the only presidential candidates likely to stand a chance in the future will be those who can afford to opt out because they are (1) personally wealthy, (2) incumbents or front-runners well tapped into loyal networks of major donors, or (3) factional candidates who are able to build intense followings. Other kinds of underdog candidates may not have the wherewithal to keep their campaigns viable even until the early primaries.

The chapter ends with recommendations from a Campaign Finance Institute (CFI) Task Force to (1) increase the spending limit, (2) provide candidates with a way out of the limit if an opponent opts out, and (3) adjust the public matching funding formula to favor small donors. Whether one agrees with these recommendations or with Gary Jacobson's comments in an earlier chapter about competition in congressional elections, they underline that BCRA—whatever its merits or flaws—was designed as an incremental solution to specific problems. It was not meant to be the last word about campaign finance, just as this book cannot be the last word about BCRA.

CONCLUSIONS AND QUESTIONS FOR THE FUTURE

The short-term effects of the Bipartisan Campaign Reform Act of 2002 seem clear. Abolishing party soft money for federal elections put officeholders and federal candidates out of the business of asking for unlimited party contributions. Surprisingly, the absence of soft money did *not* hurt the major parties' overall fundraising totals in 2004, especially the national party committees that spent heavily to support presidential candidates. Among nonparty organizations, concern felt about the presidential race helped stimulate megadonations from a few former soft money donors to 527 committees. The increase in 527 money equaled less than half of the value of party soft money. Even so, the overwhelming majority of party soft money donors—especially the corporate donors—did *not* increase their 527 giving or hard money giving to make up for the soft money that BCRA took out of the system. Finally, the sections of the law on electioneering had a modest effect on the timing and funding for political advertising. However—and acknowledging that there may be individual stories to the contrary—it is hard from our vantage point to see any systematic effect on the amount, content, diversity, or intensity of political speech.

Although BCRA's short-term effects are clear, the future is less so. The massive increase in hard money contributions in 2004 occurred during a polarized election in which national security issues commanded the voters' attention. We do not know whether the next few elections will raise equally compelling issues. One could argue the point both ways: Supreme Court nominations could potentially be polarizing, particularly among policy elites, but it is also possible that no issue will polarize potential donors as strongly as the issues of 2004. We will have to track the results through additional cycles to know how much the parties' success depended upon temporary issues as opposed to a strengthened organizational capacity that will be sustained.

The issue climate will also affect nonparty committees, as will the legal climate and future communications technology. We assume that some divisive policy issues will continue to motivate ideological megadonors who gave to the 527 committees, but it would be surprising if the top givers gave as much in a mid-term election as they did in a presidential year. Beyond that, we can imagine nonparty committees developing along any of several different lines. Let us also assume that the law (as interpreted) remains stable, with no limit on the size of contributions to 527 committees. (Changing the law would obviously expand the possible outcomes.) If large 527 committees become increasingly identified with the major parties, the 527s could conceivably attract contributions from former soft money donors who were reluctant to give in 2004. As another possibility, more adventurous major donors might give to "one-shot" organizations designed to make quick advertising hits in specific elections—much as the Swift Boat veterans did in 2004—while smaller donors may increase their giving to organizations that rely on the Internet, such as MoveOn.org. To a significant extent, the latter organizations have developed and will continue to develop on a track independent of BCRA. Or, to imagine the opposite scenario, the parties could continue to increase their importance as a vehicle of choice for smaller donors if the parties continue to build on their ongoing organizational advantages to sustain future fundraising.

In short, BCRA's future impact in a dynamic political environment necessarily must be somewhat unknowable. The question is what one should make of that. One argument often made against just about any reform is that no matter what you try to do, the results are unpredictable and often perverse. But even though long-term consequences cannot be *known* right away, it is wrong to think we are clueless. Most of the predictions the scholars in this volume made before 2004 about BCRA have so far proven accurate. Analysis is not just opinion, and prediction is not just a guess. We offer the next ten chapters as a testament.

I

THE POLITICAL PARTIES
POST-BCRA

2

Party Finance in the Wake of BCRA: An Overview

Anthony Corrado

Political party committees were the organizations most directly affected by the Bipartisan Campaign Reform Act (BCRA). Because the law was principally designed to address the problems associated with unlimited contributions to national party committees, commonly known as "soft money," many of its major provisions were focused on party financing. In addition to prohibiting national party committees from raising or spending soft money, the law required all party committees, including state and local organizations, to finance any federal election activities, including any broadcast ads that promote, support, attack, or oppose a federal candidate, with federally regulated, hard money funds.[1] The new rules even eliminated the exemption contained in the original provisions of the 1974 Federal Election Campaign Act (Public Law 93-443), which allowed national party committees to use unlimited contributions to finance building construction and maintenance costs. The law also increased party contribution limits, codified provisions for party independent expenditures on behalf of candidates, and established a new category of federally regulated state or local party funding known as "Levin money."

In short, BCRA required significant changes both in the ways parties raise money and in the ways parties finance their electioneering efforts in support of federal candidates. Its direct effects on party financing were greater than those of any other campaign finance regulation adopted in the past century, with the possible exception of the 1907 Tillman Act (34 Stat. 864) ban on corporate contributions.[2]

In an effort to assess the principal effects of the new law, this chapter presents an overview of national party committee financing in the wake of BCRA. The discussion focuses on the central issues raised in the debate on BCRA and gives particular attention to the financial activities of the Democratic National Committee (DNC) and Republican National Committee (RNC). While the activity in one election cycle is not enough to gauge the eventual consequences of this reform, the 2004 experience highlights how the parties have responded to the new rules and offers indications of how they are likely to conduct their financial activities in the future.[3]

QUESTIONS

Would the parties be weakened under BCRA? This was a central question throughout the congressional deliberations, legal challenges, and regulatory proceedings associated with the law's passage. Those engaged in the debate generally agreed that parties have a vital and salutary effect on the political system, and most were advocates of strong party organizations. But they disagreed as to the parties' potential capacity to raise funds under BCRA's constraints and drew varying conclusions from recent patterns in party finance.

The major issue raised in the BCRA debate concerned the role of party committees in national elections. Would the parties continue to play an important role in campaign funding without soft money? Would they be able to replace a substantial portion of their former soft money receipts and, if so, over what period of time? The national party committees certainly faced a sizable task in replacing the combined $495 million of soft money receipts that they raised in each of the two previous election cycles. To compensate for this loss completely, the Democrats would need to more than double the $213 million of hard money they raised in 2000, while the Republicans would have to up their total of $362 million by almost 70 percent. By contrast, between the 1996 and 2000 presidential election cycles, the national parties had increased their combined hard money resources by only $77 million, with the Democratic committees, which began with a much smaller base, increasing their hard money funds by $47 million, or 28 percent, and the Republican committees increasing theirs by $30 million, or 9 percent. Some analysts argued that the national parties would not be able to compensate wholly for the loss of soft money and that they would be required to reduce their activities and organizational efforts in federal campaigns (La Raja 2002, 2003c; Milkis 2003). Others contended that the parties would have an incentive to invest more effort into hard money fundraising, especially with regard to the solicitation of small donors, and, as a result, would strengthen their grassroots organizational support by involving larger numbers of party members in their fundraising activities (Green 2003; Mann and Ornstein 2004; Mann 2004).

A second, and related, issue concerned the effect of BCRA on interparty competition. Since the adoption of the Federal Election Campaign Act (FECA) in 1974, the Republican national party committees had been more successful in raising hard dollars than their Democratic counterparts. The Republicans benefited from continuing investments in direct mail fundraising over a long term, which had provided the party with a broad base of active small donors. Accordingly, many analysts expected that under BCRA's hard money regime the Republicans would hold a substantial financial advantage over the Democrats. In the two elections immediately preceding the adoption of the new law, the Republicans raised significantly more hard money than the Democrats, and the Democrats had become increasingly dependent on soft money to remain competitive. In the 2000 cycle, the Republicans raised $149 million more in hard money contributions than the Democrats; in 2002, $191 million more. In these same elections, the Democratic national party committees raised more than half of their total receipts from soft dollars. These patterns led some analysts to argue that the Democrats would be seriously disadvantaged under the new rules, with some observers going so far as to claim that it would prove to be a "Democratic Party suicide bill" (Gitell 2003). Others maintained that the Democrats would rise to the occasion and raise the monies needed to wage meaningful campaigns. The Democrats, they contended, would at least have the resources needed to compete where party spending might matter most—in battleground presidential general election states and the relatively small number of competitive Senate and House contests. Thus, the question of whether the Democrats would be able to raise enough money to compete financially remained open, particularly given the expected financial disparity between the parties and the fact that party committees would have the option of spending unlimited amounts of hard money on independent expenditures in key contests.

Experts also differed in their assessments of the effects of BCRA on party campaigning and party integration. From 1996 to 2002, national party committees on both sides of the aisle relied increasingly on soft money funded electioneering tactics as their principal means of candidate support. While the parties continued to spend hard dollars on candidate contributions and coordinated expenditures that were limited by law, most of their electioneering resources were devoted to candidate-specific issue advocacy advertisements and voter mobilization programs conducted jointly by national and state party organizations, both activities that could be financed in large part with soft money. BCRA's ban on soft money prohibited national parties from continuing such activities. Consequently, some analysts predicted that the law would discourage coordination among federal and nonfederal party organizations and thereby reduce the party-building initiatives that had been advanced in recent years (La Raja 2003b, 2003c; Milkis 2003). Others noted that the new law would give parties a stronger incentive to pursue independent expenditures as a principal means of candidate support (Malbin 2004). This approach would allow party committees to spend unlimited amounts of hard money on behalf of a candidate, so long as the party did not coordinate its efforts with the candidate. It would thus encourage less interaction between parties and their candidates. Advocates of BCRA countered these arguments with claims that the parties' growing reliance on soft money fundraising and the advent of issue-advocacy advertising had done little to promote party grassroots development (Krasno and Sorauf 2003). They further noted that the national committees could still use hard dollars to assist state and local committees and work with their affiliates to build stronger party organizations.

NATIONAL PARTY ADAPTATION AND RESPONSE

The 2004 election cycle was not the first in which national party committees were forced to respond to changes in campaign finance law. During the past three decades, the parties have had to adjust to changes in the regulatory environment on more than one occasion and have demonstrated a notable capacity to adapt to new rules in both intended and unintended ways.

In the 1970s, national party committees had to adjust to the fundraising and spending restrictions imposed by FECA, which required national party committees to finance their campaign efforts with monies raised in limited amounts from restricted sources. The parties responded by recruiting thousands of individual donors through direct mail and telemarketing programs and embarked on a period of financial growth in which national party committee receipts rose from less than $60 million in 1976 to more than $400 million in 1984.

In the mid-1980s, parties again altered their financial strategies to capitalize on regulatory rulings that permitted the expanded use of soft money, or nonfederal funding. In this "mixed system" of hard and soft money fundraising, national party revenues rose from $425 million in 1988 to more than $1 billion in 2002. Soft money fundraising alone jumped from $45 million in 1988 to $496 million in 2002, growing from about 11 percent of total national committee revenues in 1988 to more than 40 percent in 2002.

The parties, however, faced a more formidable challenge in adapting to BCRA. BCRA did increase the individual limit on party contributions, allowing an individual to give up to $25,000 per year to a single national party committee (as opposed to $20,000 under FECA) and up to $57,500 in aggregate contributions to party committees in each two-year election cycle (as opposed to an aggregate individual contribution limit under the old law of $50,000 every two years for all federal contributions, including donations to candidates and political action committees called PACs). But the higher limit offered the parties an opportunity to reclaim only a minor portion of former soft money funds. For example, in the 2000 election cycle, the national party committees received a combined $39.3 million of soft money from about 3,900 individual donors who each gave at least $1,000 but less than $60,000. They received $135.6 million of soft money from 429 individual donors who each gave more than $60,000. Even if none of these 429 donors made hard money contributions in 2000 and each of them gave the $57,500 maximum in the 2004 cycle, the parties' maximum total receipts would only be $24.7 million in the 2004 cycle, which would represent a decline of more than $110 million from this small group alone. The parties also raised a total of $280.3 million in soft money contributions from corporations, labor unions, and other organizations, almost all of which would now be prohibited by law (Rogers 2001).

The revenue implications of BCRA were obvious, and both parties began to enhance their hard money fundraising infrastructures and reorient their financial strategies months before the law took effect. The DNC, facing the prospect of a much better funded Republican opposition, began their efforts even before the McCain-Feingold bill was approved by Congress. The DNC used a portion of its soft money funds in 2002 to pay for the construction of a new party headquarters. In addition to providing the party with a modern headquarters facility, this action reduced the committee's overhead costs. It ended the DNC's need to spend more than a million dollars every election cycle leasing office space, while at the same time, because the costs were prepaid, freed the committee from future mortgage payments. The committee also invested about $15 million into new computer technology to retool its direct mail and Internet fundraising programs, as well as millions to build a centralized voter contact list, informally known as "Demzilla," containing information on more than 150 million potential voters (Associated Press 2003; Cillizza 2003a; Farhi 2004a).

Both national parties also increased investments in small donor solicitation programs and announced new donor programs designed to take advantage of BCRA's higher contribution limit. In March of 2002, DNC chairman Terrence McAuliffe announced an ambitious plan to replace soft dollars by raising $100 million in direct mail donations (as compared to $31 million in 2000) and $12 million in online contributions (as compared to $2 million in 2000) (Lane and Edsall 2002). In addition, the DNC formed the "Presidential Trust Fund" to attract $25,000 gifts, pledging to deposit donations of this amount into the Trust for exclusive use in supporting the party's 2004 presidential nominee (Associated Press 2003; Edsall and VonDrehle 2003).

The DNC and RNC also modified their networked fundraising efforts to accommodate the new rules. In recent years both parties had worked to develop networks of volunteer fundraisers, sometimes called "bundlers" in campaign finance parlance, to help raise money for party coffers. In advance of the 2004 election, both parties revised their fundraising network programs, or established new ones, to enhance their capacity to attract hard dollar contributions. The DNC, for example, established an elite "Patriots" program for party supporters. To qualify as a "Patriot," an individual was required to raise at least $100,000 for the party during the 2004 election cycle. The DNC also established a more select "Victory 2004 Trustees" program, consisting of individuals able to raise $250,000 for the party between May 1 and July 1 of the election year (Kaplan 2004). By the time of the 2004 national party convention, the DNC had recruited at least 17 Trustees and 188 Patriots (Democratic National Committee 2004c).

The RNC continued to rely on many of its established donor programs, including its long-standing Republican Eagles program and Team 100, which began in 1988 as a vehicle for recruiting $100,000 soft money donors and was now converted to a program for individuals willing to give the maximum contribution of $25,000 in each of the four years of a presidential election cycle (Van Natta and Broder 2000; Justice 2004a). The Republicans also sought to build from President Bush's strong personal fundraising base by creating a group of volunteer fundraisers known as "Super-Rangers." This group was an extension of the successful "Rangers" fundraising effort established by the Bush presidential committee, which consisted of volunteer fundraisers, each of whom was responsible for raising $200,000 for the campaign. The Super-Rangers consisted of an elite group of Rangers and other Bush fundraisers who, in addition to their efforts on behalf of the presidential campaign, were charged with raising at least $300,000 for the party committee (Kaplan 2004). By July of 2004, 62 individuals had already achieved Super-Ranger status; by November, 104 individuals had qualified for this group (Edsall 2004d; 2004a).

PARTY FUNDRAISING

Establishing the requisite infrastructure and outreach programs to solicit contributions nationally is only part of a successful party fundraising effort. Individuals also have to be willing to give. At times in the past, the national parties, especially the DNC, had invested resources into hard money fundraising efforts without realizing a major return in response (Corrado 1994). But the 2004 election cycle was defined by a number of factors that led to a political environment that proved especially conducive to party fundraising.

The deep partisan polarization within the electorate offered fertile ground for party fundraising appeals. Even before the election year was underway, the Democrats were unified by the lingering dissatisfaction with the outcome of the controversial 2000 presidential race and the aggressive partisan politics exhibited by the Republicans in the 2002 election cycle. Republicans rallied in support of the President as he led efforts to confront the threat of terrorism and directed the war in Iraq. By the time the voters began going to the polls in Iowa and New Hampshire, public opinion on the President's overall performance was fairly evenly divided, with Democrats and Republicans expressing sharply contrasting views on most of the key issues facing the nation, ranging from the state of the economy to the conduct of the war in Iraq. These partisan attitudes intensified throughout the election cycle, strengthened by the high levels of voter interest in the close presidential race and citizen perceptions of the contest as an important election, with high stakes for the future direction of the nation's foreign and domestic priorities.

The parties also benefited from their investments in improved technology. Both parties used highly sophisticated, computerized direct mail and telemarketing programs to target prospective contributors. These efforts identified likely donors not only by such standard measures as past contribution activity and demographic information, but also by sophisticated "data mining" models that culled cultural and lifestyle information that was used to build donor profiles on the basis of such personal information as magazine subscriptions, personal vehicle ownership, and consumer buying habits (Farhi 2004a). More important, the growth of the Internet as a means of conducting a variety of everyday financial transactions made it easy for partisan supporters to contribute to the party of their choice. The DNC and RNC worked to promote this move to online contributions by constructing email lists of millions of party supporters who could be solicited for donations in a highly efficient manner at minimal cost.

This combination of factors constituted a powerful mix, creating a context that one national party leader described as "a perfect storm" for party fundraising (Farhi 2004c). It produced strong donor incentives, an unprecedented surge in party contributions, and historic levels of individual participation in party funding. As a result, both parties raised record sums of money, and many of the problems anticipated at the time BCRA was adopted failed to emerge.

By the end of the 2004 election, the national party committees had raised more money in hard dollars *alone* than they raised in hard and soft dollars *combined* in any previous election cycle. In all, the national party committees collected more than $1.2 billion, or about $164 million more than they received in hard and soft money in the 2000 election cycle, and $222 million more than they received in the 2002 cycle. This total included almost $56 million in leftover presidential primary campaign monies transferred to the parties by Bush ($26 million) and Kerry ($29.6 million). Even if these monies are excluded, party fundraising rose by more than $100 million from the 2000 cycle. Both parties were thus able to make up for the loss of soft money with new hard dollar contributions.

As in the past, the Republicans led the Democrats, but by nowhere near the margin that most analysts expected. The Republicans raised $657.1 million compared to $576.2 million by the Democrats. In the 2000 cycle, the Republicans had raised $611.5 million compared to the Democrats' $458.1 million. The Democrats thus narrowed the gap by a substantial amount. In dollar terms, the gap in the amounts reported by the two national parties was the smallest in more than two decades. The last election cycle in which the Democratic national committees were less than $90 million behind their Republican counterparts was in 1978. In that cycle, the Republican national committees took in a mere $59 million, but they still outspent the Democrats, who raised a total of $14 million, by a margin of four-to-one.

It is important to note, however, that a strict comparison of the finances of the national party committees in the 2004 election cycle with receipts in previous cycles is complicated by changes in party structure that took place in response to BCRA. Prior to the 2004 cycle, the RNC included certain nonfederal party organizations, such as the Republican Governors Association and Republican state leadership organizations within their Republican National State Elections Committee (RNSEC), the party's principal nonfederal (soft money) operation. The Republican Governors Association conference was also included in the RNC's soft money accounts. In advance of the 2004 election, the Republican Governors Association was reorganized as a Section 527 organization independent of the RNC, so that its finances would not be affected by the soft money ban imposed on the national committee. (The Democratic Governors Association had operated as an independent Section 527 organization for a number of years prior to 2004 for political reasons unrelated to BCRA.) Similarly, the Republican State Leadership Committee operated as a Section 527 organization independent of any national party committee. In the 2004 cycle, the Republican Governors Association raised and spent $34 million, according to reports filed with the IRS covering all of 2003 and 2004. (The Democratic Governors Association reported $24 million in receipts and expenditures.) The Republican State Leadership Committee raised and spent $10.7 million. Since the finances of these committees were reported by the RNC as part of the aggregate amount received in the RNSEC account, separate disclosure reports detailing the finances of these particular entities were not filed with the FEC in past years. Consequently, the finances of these committees in past cycles, which are included in the Republican soft money totals for past cycles, are not readily available. If the funds raised by these committees in 2004 are considered in calculations of national committee funding, the gap between the two parties is wider than that suggested by the totals reported by the national party committees but still smaller than in any previous election cycle in at least a decade.

Democratic national party committees increased their total hard money receipts by almost $365 million compared to the 2000 cycle, while the Republican committees increased their hard money by $295 million. Moreover, for the first time since the beginning of the modern campaign finance era in 1974, the DNC led the RNC in fundraising. The Democrats' principal national committee raised $394.4 million in the 2004 cycle, or about $2 million more than the RNC. This achievement was especially noteworthy, given the committee's failure to keep pace with RNC hard money fundraising in the past. In the 2000 cycle, for example, the RNC raised about $89 million more than the DNC in hard money donations to go with a $30 million advantage in soft money gifts. In the 2002 cycle, the RNC surpassed the DNC by more than $100 million in hard dollars alone. But in 2004, the combination of strong anti-Bush sentiments among the Democratic faithful and a renewed emphasis on small dollar donors helped the DNC more than triple its hard money fundraising total as compared to the 2000 cycle, which was the committee's best previous hard money fundraising cycle ever. After

Table 2.1   National Party Committee Fundraising ($ *millions*)

Committee	2000			2002			2004	
	Hard	*Soft*	*Total*	*Hard*	*Soft*	*Total*	*Hard*	*Total*[a]
DNC	124.0	136.6	260.6	67.5	94.6	162.1	394.4	394.4
DSCC	40.5	63.7	104.2	48.4	95.1	143.5	88.7	88.7
DCCC	48.4	56.7	105.1	46.4	56.4	102.8	93.2	93.2
Democrats	212.9	245.2	458.1	162.3	246.1	408.4	576.2	576.2
RNC	212.8	166.2	379.0	170.1	113.9	284.0	392.4	392.4
NRSC	51.5	44.7	96.1	59.2	66.4	125.6	79.0	79.0
NRCC	97.3	47.3	144.6	123.6	69.7	193.3	185.7	185.7
Republicans	361.6	249.9	611.5	352.9	250.0	602.9	657.1	657.1
Total	574.5	495.1	1,069.6	515.2	496.1	1,011.3	1,233.2	1,233.2

Source: Federal Election Commission data. Totals are adjusted for transfers among committees, particularly in soft money accounts, and thus may vary slightly from the sums reported individually by committees.

[a]The 2004 Democratic totals include $29.6 million in excess primary funds transferred from the Kerry for President Committee ($23.6 million to the DNC, $3 million to the DSCC, and $3 million to the DCCC). The Republican totals include $26 million in excess primary funds transferred from the Bush-Cheney '04 presidential committee ($24 million to the RNC, $1 million to the NRSC, and $1 million to the NRCC).

the election in November, the DNC held a surplus of almost $10 million, a stark contrast to its position four years earlier, when it ended the election cycle in debt.

Furthermore, the DNC demonstrated impressive fundraising momentum, gaining ground on its Republican counterpart throughout the election year. At the end of 2003, the RNC led the DNC in fundraising by a margin of more than two-to-one, with the RNC garnering $107.8 million and the DNC, $43.8 million. In the first half of 2004, the RNC remained ahead, but by a narrower margin, raising $111.6 million during this period as opposed to the DNC's $81.6 million. From July 1 through November of 2004, the DNC burst ahead, raising $279.4 million to $173.0 million for the RNC.

All of the national party committees significantly increased their hard money receipts as compared to previous election cycles, but the congressional committees did not manage to replace all of their former soft money resources. In this regard, their financial results were more in line with preelection predictions, although they too achieved notable success in hard money fundraising. The Democratic Senatorial Campaign Committee (DSCC) and Democratic Congressional Campaign Committee (DCCC) were the most dependent on soft money of all the national party committees, raising more than 57 percent of their combined funds in the 2000 cycle and 61 percent in the 2002 cycle from unlimited donations. It is therefore not surprising that they had a more difficult time making up for their lost soft money revenues. In all, the DSCC increased its hard money receipts from $40 million in the 2000 cycle and $48 million in 2002 to almost $89 million in 2004. But total DSCC receipts were down in comparison to 2000, when the committee raised $104.2 million including soft money, and 2002, when it raised a total of $143.5 million. The DCCC raised over $93 million in the 2004 cycle, including a $10 million loan. The committee's $83 million in contributions compared to $48 million in hard money donations in the 2000 cycle and $46 million in 2002. But total committee receipts (including soft money) were down in comparison to the 2000 cycle, when the committee raised $105 million in all, and the 2002 cycle, when the committee took in a total of $103 million.

The National Republican Senatorial Committee (NRSC) and National Republican Congressional Committee (NRCC) were less dependent on soft money than the Democratic competitors. These committees raised about 40 percent of their combined funds from soft money sources in the 2000 and 2002 cycles. The NRCC was the better performer of these two committees in 2004, raising $186 million as opposed to almost $145 million in hard and soft money combined in the 2000 cycle. It was the sole congressional committee to best its 2000 fundraising performance. The NRCC did not, however, replace all of its funds compared to the 2002 cycle, when it raised almost $193 million, or about $8 million more than it did in the 2004 cycle. NRCC hard money receipts continued, however, to show a steady—and impressive—upward climb, rising from $97 million in the 2000 cycle to $124 million in 2002 to $186 million in 2004. In contrast, the NRSC was the worst performing of the national party committees, raising about $79 million, or about $10 million less than the DSCC. The committee did increase its hard money resources from about $52 million in the 2000 cycle to

$59 million in 2002 and to $79 million in 2004, but the rate of the growth did not match that of any of the other congressional committees.

The parties' success in adapting to BCRA and increasing their hard money resources was largely the result of an unprecedented surge in the number of party donors, particularly in the number of small donors. Although final contributor information has not been released by all of the national committees, the available information indicates that both parties significantly expanded their bases of donor support and involved more individuals in the financing of party activity than ever before in the nation's history. The scale of the increase in donor partic- ipation was historic by any standard.

This growth in party support was evident by the beginning of the election year. The RNC, benefiting from the President's heightened support in the aftermath of 9/11 and building from the party's gains in the 2002 midterm elections, added more than one million new donors to its rolls by the beginning of the 2004 elec- tion year. This expansion of party support surpassed the growth experienced during the Reagan administration, when the Republicans added almost 854,000 donors in the course of eight years (*USA Today* 2003). The DNC also began to expand its donor list, increasing its number of direct mail donors from 400,000 in the 2000 cycle to more than one million (Democratic National Committee 2004a). As a result, $32 million of the DNC's $44 million in total 2003 receipts came from small donations. This $32 million represented an 85 percent increase in small donor funds, as compared to the amount raised from such contributions in 1999 (Democratic National Committee 2004a).

The congressional committees also succeeded in expanding their donor bases. By the end of the spring primary season, committees on both sides of the aisle had recruited hundreds of thousands of new donors. The NRSC and NRCC recruited a combined total of more than 700,000 new donors before June (Edsall 2004b; Carney 2004b). The DCCC added 230,000 new donors, more than double the 100,000 new donors it recruited in the entire 2002 election cycle (Carney 2004b). The DSCC at the time did not release specific numbers but noted that its donor base had "increased significantly" (Democratic Senatorial Campaign Committee 2004a, 2004b).

This sharp rise in the number of new contributors early in the cycle proved to be a harbinger of things to come. As public opinion on the war in Iraq became more divided, and the presidential election began to take shape with the emer- gence of John Kerry as the Democratic challenger, party support continued to expand, as hundreds of thousands of individuals expressed their political views by contributing to their party's cause. In the first four months of 2004, the DNC posted 35 million pieces of fundraising mail, which exceeded the amount of fundraising mail posted by the committee in the entire decade of the 1990s (Democratic National Committee 2004d). By the end of the election in Novem- ber, the DNC had completely revitalized its once relatively moribund direct mail program. Starting with 400,000 direct mail donors after the 2000 election, the DNC added 2.3 million more, bringing its total direct mail donor base to 2.7 million, a seven-fold increase from 2000 (Democratic National Committee 2004b). In addition, the DNC had 4 million donors make contributions via the

Internet (McAuliffe 2004). As a result, the committee easily surpassed its goals for small donor fundraising and online contributions. In all, the committee reported raising more than $248 million in small donations as of December 2004, which represented an extraordinary increase over the $35 million in small donations that the party reported receiving in the 2000 election cycle (Democratic National Committee 2004b).

While the RNC did not release final figures on its new donors or fundraising patterns, it is clear that the committee also experienced a flood of new small donor gifts. One measure of the committee's success in attracting small donors is the number of unitemized (less than $200) contributions that it reported on its FEC disclosure filings. Unitemized contributions are contributions that sum to $200 or less for any donor in a given year. Such donations do not have to be itemized on FEC disclosure reports, hence the nomenclature. According to an analysis conducted by the FEC, the RNC reported $157.1 million in unitemized receipts by the end of the election in the 2004 cycle as opposed to $91.1 million in the comparable period in the 2000 cycle (Federal Election Commission 2005b). This represents an increase of almost 75 percent in small donor contributions. (The comparable numbers for unitemized DNC receipts were $165.8 million in the 2004 cycle, up from $59.5 million in the 2000 cycle.)

While much of the growth in party receipts was a result of the increase in small donor fundraising, the national party committees did collect substantial amounts from their large donor solicitation programs, which made an important contribution to the national parties' overall financial success. According to a postelection analysis of party contributions conducted by the FEC, the RNC and DNC raised a total of $104.2 million in individual contributions of the maximum permissible amount ($25,000 per year per committee), with the RNC garnering $60.9 million from such gifts and the DNC, $43.4 million (Federal Election Commission 2004b). In the comparable period in the 2000 cycle, the two committees raised a total of $23.7 million of hard money from individual contributions of the maximum permissible amount (at the time $20,000 per committee per year), with the RNC collecting $12.7 million in such gifts and the DNC, $11.0 million.

Simple division of these aggregate amounts by the size of a maximum party donation in each election cycle reveals that the RNC and DNC received at least 4,168 maximum contributions in the 2004 cycle and 1,185 maximum hard money gifts in the 2000 cycle. The RNC received at least 2,434 maximum contributions in the 2004 cycle and 633 in the 2000 cycle. The DNC received at least 1,734 in 2004 and 552 in 2000. Since BCRA increased the annual limit on individual gifts to a national party committee by $5,000, these 4,168 maximum donations translate into $20.8 million in additional hard dollar receipts that can be attributed to the change in the contribution limit.

PARTY EXPENDITURES

Armed with ample coffers, the national party committees were able to spend substantial sums of money in support of their candidates. Generally, the parties followed the basic strategic approach employed in other recent election cycles: they concentrated their expenditures in battleground presidential election states and a relatively small number of Senate and House races, while allocating only minor sums to party activities in states that were not venues for targeted federal contests. The DNC and RNC also followed past patterns in concentrating their expenditures on the presidential race, leaving spending in the congressional races to the Hill committees.

Beyond these general approaches, party spending varied significantly from the patterns established in the past. While some of these changes were related to BCRA, most of the differences were due to the particular dynamics of the 2004 presidential race, as well as major innovations in the way parties participate in presidential elections. One of these innovations, the use of independent expenditures, was an anticipated change. The other, which can be called "hybrid spending," was not.

After the passage of the 1974 FECA and the implementation of the presidential public funding system, direct candidate support in presidential general election campaigns was financed principally through the public funding grant received by each of the major party nominees, along with a limited amount of party coordinated spending financed with hard money funds. FECA rules specifically prohibited party committees from making independent expenditures that directly advocated the election or defeat of a presidential candidate. Yet, parties did find ways of supplementing their limited coordinated spending, primarily by supporting candidates through indirect means of support, such as expenditures on generic party activities, including voter registration and mobilization programs, most of which could be funded with soft dollars. In the 1996 election, the parties also began to use a mix of hard and soft money to finance issue advocacy advertisements in direct support of their presidential nominees. This tactic quickly became the preferred alternative of both party committees, since monies spent on issue ads were not subject to spending restrictions. In both 1996 and 2000 the parties spent more on issue advocacy advertisements than they spent on coordinated communications.

BCRA ended the soft money expenditures of national party committees but made no change in the limits on party coordinated expenditures. Thus, in 2004, the DNC and RNC were permitted to spend $16.2 million apiece in coordination with their presidential nominees. BCRA did, however, expand the parties' capacity to spend money in direct support of a federal candidate by codifying rules that recognize the national party committees' ability to make independent expenditures on behalf of candidates. Under BCRA's original provisions, a party committee was required to choose at the time of a candidate's nomination whether it would assist that candidate through limited coordinated expenditures or unlimited independent expenditures. But the Supreme Court struck down this provision (Section 213 in the statute) in *McConnell v. Federal Election Commission* (540 U.S. 93, 199-205 [2003]), thus opening the possibility that a party might engage in both forms of support in a postnomination campaign. The rules promulgated by the FEC to implement BCRA allowed parties to make coordinated and/or independent expenditures in support of a candidate, provided that the party abided by the coordination rules to ensure that the independent expenditures were "independent." The new regulations also dropped the pre-BCRA regulatory provision that prohibited independent expenditures in presidential general election contests (see 69 Fed. Reg. 63919).

The parties made the most of the new regulatory environment, spending money both in coordination with and independent of the presidential candidates. The parties also waited until the general election to begin this spending. Although the DNC and RNC did spend money throughout the election year on generic activities such as voter registration, volunteer organization, and voter mobilization, they made no coordinated or independent expenditures until after the national conventions. In 1996 and 2000, the parties had begun spending funds much earlier, launching issue advocacy advertising campaigns in support of their prospective nominees by early summer. But these efforts, particularly the RNC's advertising in 1996 in support of Robert Dole and the DNC's advertising in 2000 in support of Al Gore, were designed to help candidates constrained by the public funding expenditure limit to weather the "bridge period" between the effective end of the primaries (the point at which a putative nominee has clearly emerged) and the start of the formal general election period. In 2004, such party assistance was not needed, since Bush and Kerry had opted out of the primary matching funds program and were raising unprecedented sums of money in the months leading up to the party conventions. During the preconvention period, Kerry also benefited from tens of millions of dollars of spending by Democratic-oriented 527 groups, which minimized the need for party assistance. Consequently, the national committees could conserve their monies for use in the final election.

The DNC and RNC spent more money on direct candidate support in the 2004 presidential race than in any previous presidential contest. In addition to the $16 million in coordinated expenditures made by each party, the committees carried out major advertising campaigns financed through independent expenditures. Overall, the two national committees spent a combined $138.7 million on independent expenditures, all focused on the presidential race. Most of this sum, more than $120 million, was spent by the DNC. From the time of Kerry's nomination at the end of the July, the DNC maintained a relatively steady stream of independent advertising, primarily consisting of negative advertising against President Bush. The committee averaged about $9 million in spending per week, beginning in the first week of August, and spent more than twice the amount the Kerry campaign spent on paid media during the course of the general election.

DNC spending was especially important in August, when the Bush campaign held a major financial advantage over Kerry. During this month, the Kerry campaign, due to its end of July convention, was already operating off of the $75 million presidential public funding grant, while the Bush campaign was still free to spend unlimited amounts during the weeks before the Republican convention at the end of August. The DNC was therefore responsible for carrying the Democratic message in August and spent $35 million on paid media doing so. In comparison, the Bush campaign spent about $33 million on paid media during this month, while the Kerry campaign spent a mere $406,000.

The DNC, however, chose to broadcast negative advertisements against President Bush throughout August, rather than ads directly promoting Kerry or responding to the charges contained in the ads sponsored by the Swift Boat Veterans for Truth (SBVT), which attacked Kerry's record of service in Vietnam. The SBVT ads were initially broadcast in only seven markets, with fewer than 100 spots aired each day, as part of a relatively modest $500,000 media buy (Nielsen Monitor-Plus and The University of Wisconsin Advertising Project 2004; Edsall 2004e). But the attacks received widespread media coverage, multiplying their exposure, and thus had a greater effect on the public discourse in the campaign than the DNC media, which failed to effectively address the issues raised by the group.

The RNC devoted $18.3 million to independent expenditures in support of President Bush in the period after the Republican convention. Thus it spent substantially less in this way than the Democrats. The primary reason for the disparity is that the Republicans pursued an innovative tactic, unforeseen by either the Kerry campaign or analysts of the new law. This new form of financing consisted of campaign advertisements jointly funded by the presidential campaign and the RNC in an "allocated" or "hybrid" manner. The initial advertisements financed in this way, which were broadcast in September, featured President Bush and included generic party messages about the party's agenda or principles, as well as mention of the Republican "leaders in Congress" (Sidoti 2004a). The Republicans contended that such ads, which combined a message of support for the President with a generic party message, could be financed in an allocated manner with the cost divided between the presidential campaign and the party committee. Further, they reasoned that such allocated generic party spending did not count against the party's coordinated spending limit or constitute a contribution to the publicly funded presidential nominee. At the time these ads were initiated, neither the party nor the presidential campaign committee submitted an advisory opinion request to the FEC seeking guidance as to whether this practice was permissible under federal law.

The Republicans chose the hybrid spending approach over the independent expenditure approach because it allowed the presidential campaign to exercise more control over the content of party advertising, since the party did not have to act independently of the presidential campaign. It was also a highly creative way of reducing the severity of the spending caps imposed on both publicly funded candidates and party coordinated expenses. In effect, the tactic allowed the presidential campaign to stretch its limited public money and spend far more than the amount allowed under the public funding expenditure limit. From the party's perspective, it allowed the RNC to spend far more in coordination with a candidate than the amount allowed under the coordinated spending limit.

Not to be outdone, the DNC and the Kerry campaign soon followed suit and developed jointly financed hybrid advertisements of their own (Sidoti 2004b; *New York Times* 2004b). By the end of the general election campaign, the RNC had reported $45.8 million in generic hybrid expenditures to the FEC. The DNC did not specify its hybrid spending in its FEC reports, but an analysis conducted after the election estimated that the DNC devoted about $24.0 million to this type of spending (Devine 2005; FEC 2005b). Party funds were thus used to augment expenditures by the presidential campaigns with about $70 million worth of paid media advertising.

Contrary to most preelection expectations, the financial role of the national parties did not diminish in 2004. In fact, the DNC and RNC spent record sums on direct candidate support in the presidential race. Moreover, in the presidential general election, the party committees actually outspent the candidates. In all, the DNC spent $160 million in support of Kerry, or twice the amount given to the Kerry campaign in public funding. The RNC spent $80 million in direct support of Bush, an amount slightly greater than the sum Bush received in public funding. In contrast, in 2000 the national parties spent $13.7 million apiece in coordinated funds in support of the presidential nominees. In addition, the parties spent at least $59 million on issue advocacy advertising funded largely with soft money (Corrado 2002). The 2000 total, about $86 million, was less than 40 percent of the $240 million total spent by the national committees in 2004.

Beyond this direct candidate support, both parties also mounted extensive, highly sophisticated, volunteer-intensive voter outreach and mobilization efforts. These efforts were particularly noteworthy, not only because they constituted an important component of party activity in 2004, but also because it was this aspect of party operations that some observers thought would be the most likely to suffer the loss of soft money under BCRA. In recent elections, the parties financed their voter outreach efforts primarily with soft money. Thus, it was anticipated that this aspect of party electioneering might be reduced significantly under BCRA's hard money regime (La Raja 2003b, 2003c; Milkis 2003; Cochran 2001; Clymer 2001).

The parties' willingness to invest resources in these voter turnout programs was based on the experience of the 2000 presidential election, which highlighted

Table 2.2   National Party Committee Expenditures in 2004 (*$ millions*)

	Contributions	Coordinated Expenditures	Independent Expenditures	Generic Ads	Total Candidate Support
DNC	0.0[a]	16.1	120.4	24.0	160.5
DSCC	0.7	4.4	18.7	—	23.8
DCCC	0.4	2.4	36.9	—	39.7
Democrats	1.1	22.9	176.0	24.0	224.0
RNC	0.2	16.1	18.3	45.8	80.4
NRSC	0.8	8.4	19.4	—	28.6
NRCC	0.5	3.2	47.3	—	51.0
Republicans	1.6	27.7	85.0	45.8	160.0
Total	2.7	50.6	261.0	69.8	384.5

Source: Based on Federal Election Commission data as of March 14, 2005. Totals may not add up due to rounding.

[a]The DNC made only $7,000 in contributions to candidates.

the importance of turning out and counting every vote. It was also spurred by the experience in the 2002 election, wherein the Republicans developed a "72-Hour Program" that was credited with increasing Republican turnout and producing victories in a number of important congressional contests. Both parties therefore began the 2004 cycle with the intention to emphasize person-to-person voter contact programs.

In this regard, the RNC had an advantage over the DNC, since it began the election cycle with a head start. In the 2002 cycle, the Republicans had invested $50 million into voter registration and the 72-Hour Program (Edsall and Grimaldi 2004). In 2004, they continued to build on this base and further refined their voter identification and contact methods. At the start of the election year, the Republicans announced a goal of registering three million new Republican voters, and in one week in March alone, deemed "National Voter Registration Week," registered more than one million (Sweeting 2004; Republican National Committee 2004b).

The party also decided to focus its efforts on turning out its partisan base and concentrating on prospective Republican supporters, or "soft" voters, who were not currently registered or had not voted in the previous presidential race, instead of focusing most of its resources on undecided voters. This strategic decision was based on the assumption, supported by opinion research, that more than 90 percent of likely voters or registered partisans had already made their decision as to whether or not they would support President Bush for reelection. It was grounded on party research that highlighted the inefficiency of an approach relying on traditional phone banks and direct mail programs to turn out voters in traditionally Republican precincts. This research indicated that only 15 percent of all Republican voters—and an even smaller share of soft Republican voters—lived in precincts that voted Republican by 65 percent or more (Edsall and Grimaldi 2004). The RNC thus relied on sophisticated microtargeting programs based on commercial databases and survey research to identify prospective supporters outside of these traditional Republican strongholds, including those living in primarily Democratic neighborhoods. These efforts produced a broad base of potential contacts. According to Bush campaign strategist Matthew Dowd, this targeting quadrupled the number of Republican voters who could be reached through direct mail, phone banks, and knocking on doors (Edsall and Grimaldi 2004). The party developed an extensive person-to-person, colleague-to-colleague, largely volunteer voter contact program to reach these new voters, spending a total of $125 million on this effort, or three times the amount allocated for voter contact in the 2000 campaign (Balz and Edsall 2004).

The Democrats also increased their investments in voter contact and mobilization, even as pro-Democratic 527 groups such as America Coming Together, Voices for Working Families, and the New Democratic Network were spending tens of millions of dollars to conduct voter registration and outreach programs that were designed to increase Democratic turnout. Like the RNC, the DNC emphasized person-to-person contact methods and identified prospective supporters with computerized targeting programs. But unlike the RNC, the Democrats tended to focus on city precincts and other Democratic strongholds, while the pro-Democratic 527 groups placed more effort on rural areas and suburban precincts. In all, the DNC invested $80 million into its field operation, an increase of 166 percent over the amount spent on such operations in 2000 (Democratic National Committee 2004b). The party organized 233,000 volunteers to form the backbone of its efforts and made eleven million person-to-person, door-to-door contacts with voters, as well as thirty-eight million telephone calls to prospective supporters in battleground states (Democratic National Committee 2004b).

Thus, the parties sponsored a substantial amount of activity in the 2004 election. The DNC and RNC each spent a total of more than $200 million in connection with the presidential race, with the DNC spending more on advertising ($160 million) than field operations ($80 million), and the RNC emphasizing field operations ($125 million) over advertising ($80 million). While the parties engaged in more activity independent of candidates than in the past, there was still a substantial amount of coordinated activity. Most important, the parties made major gains in their organizational development, at least in targeted areas of the nation, and developed viable programs for promoting grassroots participation.

LOOKING AHEAD

National party financing in the first election conducted under BCRA proved to be more dynamic and vigorous than most observers anticipated. Will these committees continue to thrive in the future? Although major challenges remain, the prospects for future party success are very encouraging, and the parties are likely to continue to play a prominent role in federal electioneering for some time to come.

In the 2006 election cycle, the parties will again face the problem of raising the monies needed to wage meaningful campaigns without access to soft money. They will face the additional burden of having to raise funds without the public excitement and partisan intensity that accompanies a presidential campaign. It is therefore likely that national committee receipts will decline, as is typical in a midterm election cycle. But the parties are now in a better position to maintain their financial support than they were four years ago and should continue to operate for some time in a political environment conducive to party fundraising.

The national committees will begin the next election cycle with the largest donor bases ever recruited in party history. The central challenge they will face is finding ways to retain these donors and keep them actively involved in party funding. If the general experience of most organizations with direct mail contributors is taken as a basis for judging party prospects, it is likely that these committees will experience some attrition in donor support. The party organizations' success in minimizing the rate of attrition will be a key to their continuing financial success. This task will be complicated by the competition for dollars created by the leading 527 committees—should they follow through on their stated intentions of continuing their efforts in future elections—since these groups will be making appeals to many of those who gave to the parties in 2004. The parties thus will need to be responsive to donors and put forward clear messages that provide individuals with strong incentives to continue to invest in party politics, rather than the initiatives of more specialized organized groups.

Party prospects should also be buoyed by a political environment characterized by polarized partisan attitudes. A second narrowly decided presidential race did little to resolve the partisan divide within the electorate. Nor did it resolve the divisions of opinion on such key issues as the war in Iraq, tax cuts, health care, and budget priorities. With a debate over Social Security reform and the prospect of at least one Supreme Court nomination looming in the next Congress, the parties should have an issue agenda favorable to partisan appeals.

Finally, the Internet and other technologies will continue to offer parties a means of soliciting contributions at minimal cost. Both parties have developed email lists containing contact information for millions of individuals, which will provide them with opportunities to solicit contributions through narrowly targeted and personalized messages. Party websites will receive even greater use as portals for collecting contributions. Individuals interested in supporting a party will find it easy to do so by making a donation with only a few clicks of a mouse.

In 2004, the national party organizations once again demonstrated their capacity for adapting to changes in the regulatory and political environment. At the end of the first election under BCRA, the national party organizations were stronger, not weaker.

NOTES

1. BCRA sets forth a specific statutory definition of the activities that constitute "federal election activity" for purposes of the act. In general, federal election activity is defined as including: (1) voter registration activity within 120 days of a federal election; (2) voter registration, get-out-the-vote activity, or generic campaign activity conducted in connection with an election in which a federal candidate appears on the ballot (regardless of whether a state or local candidate also appears on the ballot); (3) any public communication that refers to a clearly identified candidate for federal office that promotes or supports, or attacks or opposes, a candidate for federal office, regardless of whether the communication expressly advocates a vote for or against a candidate; and (4) services provided during any month by an employee of a state, district, or local party committee who spends more than 25 percent of compensated time during that month on activities in connection with a federal election (see 2 U.S.C. §431[20]).

2. The adoption of the Tillman Act, which banned corporate contributions in federal elections, including any election in connection with the selection of electors for the office of President and Vice President, had a major effect on Republican Party fundraising at the time but no significant effect on the Democratic Party. In 1904, the RNC collected an estimated $2.35 million, including as much as $1.53 million from corporations. The DNC relied on contributions from a few wealthy individuals for most of its $700,000 in funding at the time and did not accept corporate or trust contributions in 1904 at the insistence of its presidential nominee, Judge Alton Parker. In 1908, without corporate contributions, the RNC raised an estimated $1.65 million, including the funds sent directly to selected state party committees. The DNC collected $629,000 that year (*New York Times* 1912b; *New York Times* 1912a; Alexander 1971; Pollack 1926; U.S. Senate Committee on Privileges and Elections

1912–1913). The author thanks Heitor Gouvêa of Boston College for sharing his research on party fundraising in the early twentieth century.

3. Unless otherwise noted, all of the data on party finances included in this chapter are based on the information contained in national party committee disclosure reports as summarized and reported by the Federal Election Commission.

3

The Parties' Congressional Campaign Committees in 2004

Diana Dwyre and Robin Kolodny

One central purpose of the Bipartisan Campaign Reform Act of 2002 (BCRA) was to end soft money financing of political parties at the national level. The effect of eliminating soft money was widely debated by practitioners and academics before passage of BCRA and immediately after. Indeed, one of the arguments made by some who questioned the legislation when it was being debated in Congress and those who challenged the law before the Supreme Court was that banning party soft money would weaken the political parties, a development considered negative by most (La Raja 2003c; Dwyre and Farrar-Myers 2001; McConnell 2003). As one might expect in politics, the potential negative consequences were wildly exaggerated. In *Life After Reform* (2003), we argued that the political parties would adapt to the new post-BCRA landscape.

However, there are important differences in the success the congressional campaign committees had compared to the two national committees (NCs), as reported by Corrado in chapter 2. While the parties' congressional campaign committees (CCCs) found ways to increase their hard money receipts to offset their soft money losses in the 2004 cycle, they were not able to meet or exceed their previous overall fundraising levels as the Republican National Committee (RNC) and Democratic National Committee (DNC) both did. And while all six national party committees used independent expenditures to help candidates in competitive races instead of soft money issue advocacy advertisements, the independent expenditures undertaken by the CCCs were far less effective than those undertaken by the RNC and DNC. It turns out that candidates for Congress (and their affiliated campaign committees) needed soft money donors more than candidates for the White House. Thus, eliminating party soft money hampered the CCCs more than the NCs in 2004.

At the outset, it is important to note that while the Supreme Court's decision (*McConnell v. Federal Election Commission* 540 U. S. 93 [2003]) on the constitutionality of BCRA upheld most of the original law, one "small" change had a great effect on potential CCC behavior. The court struck down the original provision in BCRA that would have forced national party committees to choose whether they would make coordinated expenditures or independent expenditures on behalf of a candidate—one or the other, but not both. The original intent was to respond to previous court rulings (specifically in *Colorado II: Federal Election Commission v. Colorado Republican Federal Campaign Committee,* 533 U.S. 431 [2001]), which said that parties could both coordinate with and be independent of their candidates in elections. BCRA's authors felt that ruling should be changed in the legislation. However, the Court upheld the findings of *Colorado II* (see appendix 2).

The party committees had been very concerned with how the restrictive provision would have affected their activities, as the language regarding simultaneous monitoring of all party committees working on national elections seemed unruly. Once it was clear that the party committees could both coordinate and spend independently of their candidates, independent expenditures were adopted as the logical venue for party spending in the absence of issue advocacy ads paid for in part with millions of dollars of soft money. Much of this chapter discusses the implications of the independent expenditure path. The restrictions imposed by independent expenditures made effective electoral strategies difficult for the CCCs. We will consider whether independent expenditures are helpful to the democratic process and the implications for our system if independent expenditures continue to be employed as the dominant electoral assistance from the CCCs to their candidates. Ultimately, the elimination of soft money donations and issue advocacy expenditures curtailed CCC participation in the 2004 elections.

WHAT HAS CHANGED? RESOURCES

Before the committees could spend any money, they had to raise it. As Anthony Corrado notes in chapter 2, the parties' national committees, the DNC and the RNC, were able to compensate for the loss of soft money with hard money in 2004. Indeed, they exceeded everyone's fundraising expectations, including their own. However, as Corrado's tables also make clear, the parties' House and Senate campaign committees tell a somewhat different story (see chapter 2, table 2.1). None of the Hill committees were able to compensate for the loss of soft money with hard money. Both senatorial committees, the Democratic Senatorial Campaign Committee (DSCC) and the National Republican Senatorial Committee (NRSC), witnessed a significant loss of total receipts compared to the 2000 and 2002 election cycles. The House campaign committees, the Democratic Congressional Campaign Committee (DCCC) and the National Republican Congressional Committee (NRCC), did a little better without soft money than their

Senate counterparts. The NRCC surpassed its 2000 totals, but it fell short of its 2002 combined receipts. It is important to remember that 2002 was a special fundraising year because all party committees were staging a "run" on soft money, in anticipation of its end as a result of BCRA (Federal Election Commission 2002; Dwyre and Kolodny 2003). The DCCC raised almost as much hard money in 2004 as it raised in hard and soft money in 2000 and 2002, having greater success than its senatorial counterpart.

Even though the CCCs failed to keep up with their combined hard and soft money fundraising of pre-BRCA days, the hard money fundraising increases are still quite significant: from $48 million to $89 million for the DSCC, from $46 million to $93 million for the DCCC, from $59 million to $79 million for the NRSC, and from $124 million to $186 million for the NRCC. Clearly, the dire prediction that the parties had maximized their hard money resources prior to BCRA was off the mark. The parties are doing better than expected with hard money only, with all six committees raising more hard money in the 2003–2004 cycle than in previous cycles. The DNC especially raised record amounts of hard money for the 2004 election, almost three times more hard money than it raised in the last presidential election year, 2000. Where did this new hard money come from?

New Donors

The amounts collected from individual contributors rose significantly over past election cycles for two reasons: higher individual contribution limits (both to candidates and to party committees) and vigorous new donor prospecting. The individual hard money contribution limit was increased by BCRA for donations both to candidates and political party committees. Prior to the new law, an individual could give $20,000 in hard money to all national party committees per year ($40,000 per two-year election cycle). After passage of BCRA, an individual could give $25,000 per election cycle per party committee, with an aggregate total of $57,500 per election cycle to all national party committees and political action committees (PACs). Moreover, these limits are, for the first time, indexed to inflation, so that they will increase from one election cycle to the next. The new aggregate limit for individual contributors (to all sources—parties, candidates, and PACs) increased from $25,000 per calendar year to $95,000 per two-year cycle, also indexed to inflation. The higher limits made it possible to raise more hard money from already generous donors. Indeed, the proportion of hard money receipts from large donors to the CCCs increased significantly, as did the number of contributions reaching the higher maximum limit (Federal Election Commission 2005b). The _proportion_ of the _hard_ money the committees received in contributions of $200 or less also declined across the four committees, even though the _amount_ of money raised in small contributions doubled. The seeming paradox is explained by the absence of soft money: almost all of the soft money in 2000 and 2002 came in amounts greater than $25,000, so the proportion of the parties' full receipts from large contributions (hard and soft money combined in 2000 and 2002 versus hard money alone in 2004) was actually lower in 2004.

Smaller contributions made up a much larger portion of the parties' total receipts even though they were a smaller portion of the hard money portion alone.

All party committees also began aggressive prospecting of new donor lists because it was clear that simply getting more money out of previous donors was not going to compensate for the loss of soft money. Early in the cycle, the NRCC invested a significant amount in telemarketing firms to expand their hard-dollar donor base (Cillizza 2003c), and by early 2004, the committee claimed 500,000 new donors (Bolton 2004d). However, the NRCC already had an effective small donor strategy, and the 2004 activities can be seen as a normal extension of their existing programs (McGahn 2005). All party committees engaged in direct mail fundraising as well. The expanded fundraising appeals to individuals paid off, and the increased contribution limits seem to have made a difference. Figure 3.1 shows the national party committees' hard money receipts from individual contributors over the last three election cycles. Once again, the national committees, the DNC and RNC, showed the greatest jump in receipts, with the DNC making the largest gains.

Members of Congress

One of the consequences not intended by the authors of BCRA was the increased importance of individual Members of Congress as fundraisers for both

Figure 3.1 National Party Receipts from Individual Contributors (Hard Money Only), 2000–2004

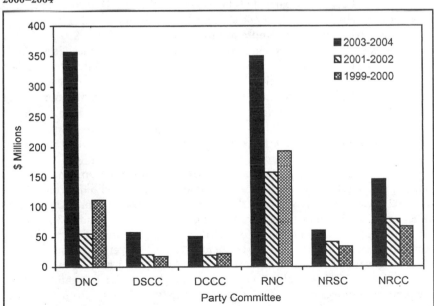

Source: FEC, "Party Financial Activity Summarized for the 2004 Election Cycle," News Release, March 2, 2005.

the party committees and for other candidates. While Members have always had the opportunity to form leadership PACs and contribute to the party committees through their personal campaign committees, giving by Members of Congress has accelerated in recent years (Bedlington and Malbin 2003). Of great importance is the increase in the amount individuals can donate to the campaigns of Members of Congress from $1,000 (constant since 1974) per person per election to $2,000 (indexed for inflation) in BCRA, starting in the 2004 election cycle. Since we know that individual donors are motivated more by their personal connection to candidates than to the broader concept of party majorities (Francia et al. 2004), it is not a surprise that members would have an easier time raising money for elections than the party committees. Moreover, as the 2003–2004 DCCC Chairman Rep. Robert Matsui (D-CA) pointed out, "Money from members is particularly important, because there [are] no costs of fundraising. . . . When a member gives a dollar, that entire dollar is spent on candidates, whereas with direct mail, there's the cost of stamps and printing" (Carney 2004b). And the law allows candidates to transfer unlimited amounts from their campaign accounts to a party committee (Federal Election Commission 2004a).

House CCCs

In early summer 2004, the CCCs revealed their plans to use Members as a central funding source. The DCCC proved particularly aggressive in this cycle, declaring that 186 safe incumbents were sitting on a total of $87 million in their campaign accounts (Billings 2004; Carney 2004b). Accordingly, the DCCC expected Members to pay party dues between $70,000 and $400,000, depending on their seniority, committee posts, leadership roles, and fundraising history. The average contribution by House Members to the DCCC was $20,000 in the previous cycle, so their efforts represent a significant increase. Indeed, the DCCC at one point said it expected its own Members to fund one-third of its budget for the 2003–2004 election cycle (Carney 2004b). The real percentage ended up much lower as the committee raised more than expected from other sources, but the total amount coming from Members increased from $12.1 million to $18.3 million. By contrast, the NRCC's Member dues were modest—ranging from $6,000 to $25,000 (Bolton 2004a)—yet the total went up from $13.9 million to $19.4 million (see table 3.1).

Our data show that the proportion of money given from Members' personal campaign committees (PCCs) to the party committees indeed did increase from the 2002 cycle, particularly among the Democrats. House Members gave both a larger proportion of donations from their PCCs to the parties and a larger absolute amount. When looking at the total House Member contributions to all party committees, we find that House Members gave 88.7 percent of that money to their congressional campaign committees (the DCCC and NRCC) in 2002 and 89.5 percent in 2004 (see table 3.1). Further, the absolute total amount given to the party committees increased 43.7 percent in 2004 over 2002 (from $29.3 million to $42.1 million). Broken down by party and committee type, we see that

Table 3.1 Legislators' Giving to Parties and Candidates ($ millions)

Candidate	PCC to All Party Committees	Percent Increase PCC to All Party	PCC to Party CCCs	Percent of PCC Total Party Giving to CCCs	Percent Increase or Decrease to Party CCCs	PCC to Candidates	Percent Increase PCC to Candidates	Number of Leadership PACs	Leadership PAC Contributions	Percent of Leadership PAC to Candidates
HOUSE										
2002										
Dem	$14.1	—	$12.1	85.8	—	$ 3.9	—	35	$ 5.8	—
Rep	15.3	—	13.9	90.8	—	2.4	—	68	10.1	—
Total	29.3	—	25	88.7	—	6.3	—	103	15.9	91
2004										
Dem	20.3	44.0	18.3	90.1	51.2	4	2.6	48	5	—
Rep	21.8	42.5	19.4	89.0	39.6	2.9	20.8	85	15.8	—
Total	42.1	43.7	37.7	89.5	45.0	6.9	9.5	133	20.8	83
SENATE										
2002										
Dem	3.6	—	1.6	44.4	—	0.15	—	22	4.9	—
Rep	2.3	—	1.9	82.6	—	0.32	—	29	4.3	—
Total	5.9	—	3.5	59.3	—	0.47	—	51	9.2	79
2004										
Dem	11.3	213.9	8.0	70.8	400.0	0.16	6.6	36	4.7	—
Rep	4.9	113.0	3.2	65.3	68.4	0.13	−59.0	28	6.8	—
Total	16.2	174.6	11.2	69.1	220.0	0.29	−38.0	64	11.5	66

Source: Compiled from FEC data.

House Republicans donated 42.5 percent more to the NRCC in 2004 than in 2002, and House Democrats donated 44.0 percent more to the DCCC. This meant that Member contributions were now almost at parity by party, with Republicans giving $19.4 million to the NRCC in 2004 and Democrats giving $18.3 million to the DCCC. At a minimum, it seems the Democrats succeeded in duplicating the Republicans' success at exacting Member contributions to CCCs in the House. We believe that this will have significant implications for the internal operations of the House, as campaign contributions from Members become an important way to gauge Members' suitability for leadership and committee positions.

House Members also gave 9.5 percent more to other House candidates out of their PCCs. Though giving from Democrats to candidates was almost flat (around $3.9 million in each cycle), while Republicans gave 20.8 percent more, Republicans still gave less than the Democrats in dollars (up to $2.9 million this cycle). More Members had active leadership PACs in 2004 than in 2002, but the increase was greater for Republicans. Not surprisingly, the bulk of leadership PAC contributions went to candidates directly (91 percent in 2002, 83 percent in 2004). After all, one purpose of leadership PACs is to launch a bid for or solidify a leadership position in Congress. Making donations to Members who will be grateful later (rather than to the collectivized CCC) is a rational strategy for Members with these PACs. Moreover, there are limits on contributions from a Member's PAC to a party but no such limit on contributions from a Member's campaign committee to the party committees.

Senate CCCs

The senatorial campaign committees did not have formalized dues, but the DSCC's chairman, Sen. Jon Corzine (D-NJ), did ask Senate Democrats to give $50,000 from their own campaign committees or PACs and to raise an additional $100,000 for the party; Senate Democratic leaders were expected to write a $100,000 check and to raise $250,000 more "through events, phone calls, Internet fundraising, and the like" (Carney 2004b). The DSCC also sponsored "call-a-thons" that brought Senators together to dial for dollars on behalf of the party (Carney 2004b). The amount of money given from Senators' personal campaign committees to the party committees increased an astonishing 175 percent from 2002 but from a lower base than the House. Most of the increase came from the Democrats who more than tripled their contributions to party committees from $3.6 to $11.3 million (see table 3.1). Two exceptional donations from Member PCCs account for a significant portion of the increase: one for $2.5 million from New York Senator Charles Schumer and one for $1 million from Nevada Senator Harry Reid. Senatorial giving to candidates from PCCs actually declined slightly from Republicans but held steady for Democrats, though the amounts are not significant. The amount Senators gave to the party committees from their personal campaign committees is less than the donations they made to candidates directly through Leadership PACs, a distinct difference from the

House figures where donations from PCCs were higher than Leadership PAC donations. Senatorial leadership PAC donations to parties and candidates increased 25 percent overall (from $9.2 million in 2002 to $11.5 million in 2004), though all of that gain was from Republicans; Senate Democrats actually gave less through their leadership PACs (see table 3.1).

Big-name Senators helped the DSCC raise funds as well. Senator John Edwards (D-NC) organized a matching-funds drive for the DSCC, in which he pledged that he and other Democratic Senators would match the DSCC's online fundraising in May 2004, up to $50,000 (Carney 2004b). NRSC chairman George Allen (R-VA) pressed GOP Senators with a strong dose of peer pressure. He used what he called a "Team Ball" tracking system to keep track of what Senators did for the party and for their fellow Senators and GOP candidates, and then he shared that information with the Senate Republican Conference (Carney 2004b). Additionally, all party leaders were working hard to persuade retiring Members to be as generous as they could. Democrats especially stood to benefit, since they had more Senators retiring. Indeed, *Roll Call*'s Paul Kane called this excess campaign money "the closest thing the party committees have to soft money" (Kane 2004a).

In the House, departing Members did not prove to be much of a source of funds to either party committees or candidates. Of the thirty-one Members not running for reelection, thirteen were running for higher office and made either trivial or no donations. The remaining seventeen Members only contributed 2.5 percent of the overall total contributed by all Members to the party from their PCCs. Indeed, there were only three retiring Members (all of them Republicans) who made significant donations: Dunn (WA-8) $386,550; Greenwood (PA-8) $315,000; and Schrock (VA-2) $221,000. In the Senate, hopes of a windfall were not realized. Of the eight retiring Senators, two gave nothing, Campbell (R-CO) and Graham (D-FL); and three gave less than $30,000, Miller (D-GA), Fitzgerald (R-IL), and Edwards (D-NC). The only three departing Senators to give significant amounts to the parties or candidates were Nickles (R-OK) $465,706 total, Breaux (D-LA) $254,978, and Hollings (D-SC) $273,500.

The presidential candidates' campaigns and recent former candidates for federal office also donated significant funds to the congressional campaign committees. The Kerry-Edwards campaign transferred $6 million to the Democratic CCCs ($3 million each to the DSCC and the DCCC), while Bush-Cheney '04 donated $2 million split evenly between the NRSC and NRCC (Kane 2004b). Most of this money from the presidential nominees was excess primary funds. Earlier in the cycle, Al Gore also made a significant transfer to the Democratic committees, $1 million each to the two Democratic CCCs and $4 million to the DNC (Cillizza 2004b).

The indexing of contribution limits to both Members and party committees will probably mean that both the average contribution and the proportion of large contributions going to the CCCs will continue to rise. Perhaps this is as it should be, since the $25 contribution buys so much less than it did in 1974, but it seems to us that the CCCs will remain as dependent on a small number of wealthy contributors as they were under soft money rules. The main difference will be that though Members will still be responsible for bringing significant money to the parties (what BCRA was trying to stop), it will come indirectly through increased hard money contributions to their own campaigns that are then transferred to the parties instead of directly through large soft money contributions made to the parties.

High (and Not-So-High) Dollar Fundraising

The CCCs also relied heavily on "old tricks" used in the past to take advantage of the increase in individual contribution limits to the party committees. The NRSC started the "Majority Makers" program, which required a $25,000 donation. These donors were invited to a private reception at Majority Leader Bill Frist's Washington area home to meet with President George W. Bush (Theimer 2004). The DSCC's "Majority Council" requested $25,000 donations from the personal funds of "allied lobbyists and consultants," not just PAC contributions, promising them meetings in Washington with Senate Democratic leaders every month or so (Bolton 2004c).

The parties also worked to find new contributors. For example, a wealthy Washington, D.C., real estate developer sponsored a relatively low-dollar fundraiser at his elegant D.C. home and invited about seventy-five of his business associates and friends, most of whom were first-time political donors (Carney 2004b). All of the Hill committees brought in more with small-dollar fundraising using the Internet, direct mail, and events. For example, while the NRCC had long had a well-developed and lucrative direct mail program, the DCCC sent out almost 20,000 pieces of mail, doubling its mail efforts in 2004 and bringing in over $1 million per month (Carney 2004b).

Joint Fundraising Committees

Joint fundraising committees, also referred to as "victory funds," were first used in the 2000 election. In 2000, joint fundraising committees were another vehicle for raising soft money, whereby a candidate would ask a donor for "the maximum individual contribution to the candidate account, a hard money contribution to the party, and a soft money contribution with the understanding that the soft money raised through the candidate's victory fund would be spent in that candidate's contest" (Magleby 2002a). House and Senate candidates and their parties continued to use joint fundraising committees after passage of BCRA but without the soft money component. In the 2003–2004 election cycle through June 30, 2004, the DSCC had received $3,920,102 and the NRSC $157,961 in proceeds from joint fundraising committees (Federal Election Commission 2004c). At that point in the election, the joint fundraising committees were helping to make up for the lower rate of direct contributions from Senators to candidates. The House committees had not received any funds from joint committees at that time. Although no longer a vehicle for soft money fundraising, joint fundraising committees are a means for party fundraising that can help the CCCs make up for the loss of soft money. As we noted earlier, it is easier for incumbents to raise money from individual contributors than it is for the party committees (Francia et al. 2004), making joint fundraising committees a potentially significant source of party funds.

PARTY SPENDING POST-BCRA

Prior to BCRA, political party committees used four main spending vehicles to help candidates: direct contributions (limited-hard money), coordinated expenditures (limited-hard money), independent expenditures (unlimited-hard money), and issue advocacy (unlimited-soft/hard money mix). BCRA eliminated the fourth type of spending. This meant that independent expenditures, if the parties could raise sufficient hard money, were now the best option for helping candidates in competitive races because they could spend unlimited amounts in this manner. The only constraint would be independence—the candidate must not have any knowledge of, or consent to, the electioneering activities the party engaged in on his or her behalf.

Contributions and Coordinated Spending

House party campaign committees' direct donations and coordinated spending followed the same patterns as in the past, especially with the House committees. However, the senatorial campaign committees contributed more directly to candidates. BCRA raised the direct contribution limit from party committees to senatorial candidates from $17,500 to $35,000 [U.S. Code, Title 2, Chapter 14, Sec. 441a(h)]. House and Senate campaign committees approximately doubled their direct contributions to candidates in 2003–2004 over the amounts they gave in the previous two cycles (Federal Election Commission 2004b).

However, that does not account for senatorial party coordinated spending on behalf of candidates. Because of the need to mix hard money with soft money under the old fundraising rules (Dwyre and Kolodny 2002), the senatorial committees decided not to spend coordinated money in recent pre-BCRA elections. Indeed, there was little left in the parties' coffers for hard money coordinated expenditures after devoting large sums of hard money to the hard-soft money mixes that were spent on issue advocacy advertising through the state party committees. That was certainly not the case in the post-BCRA 2004 election, with tremendous increases in coordinated expenditures by the DSCC and NRSC. As figure 3.2 shows, the DSCC spent about twenty-four times more on coordinated expenditures in 2003–2004 than it had in 2001–2002, and the NRSC spent about nineteen times more than in the previous cycle (Federal Election Commission 2005b). The House campaign committees spent about the same amount of coordinated expenditures on behalf of candidates, reflecting a slight decline in the number of competitive races.

Figure 3.2   Party Coordinated Expenditures, 2000–2004

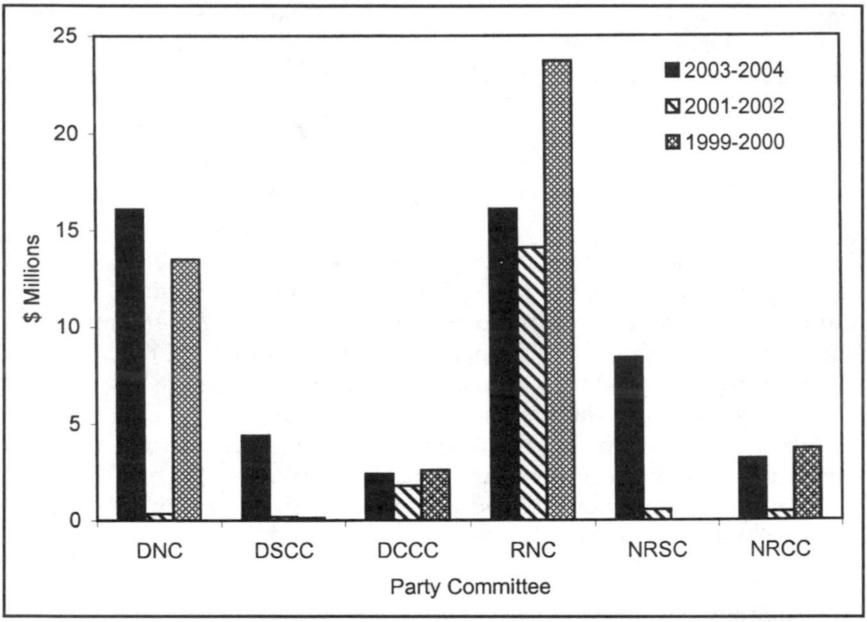

Source: FEC, "Party Financial Activity Summarized for the 2004 Election Cycle," News Release, March 2, 2005.

Independent Expenditures

The greatest increases in House and Senate party committee spending were in the form of independent expenditures (IEs). IEs are hard money expenditures spent for or against a candidate without the candidates' knowledge or consent. Unlike the issue ads paid for with mixes of party soft and hard money prior to the passage of BCRA, independent expenditure communications may expressly advocate the election or defeat of a specific candidate. The party committees used independent expenditure money directly for electioneering instead of soft money matched with hard money for issue advertising. All four committees report dramatic increased spending compared to that of previous cycles, indicating that independent expenditure spending was the parties' preferred mode of spending (in reality, the only available mode) in this first post-BCRA election cycle. Figure 3.3 shows the dramatic increases in independent expenditure spending by the congressional campaign committees.

The two senatorial committees spent roughly the same amount as each other ($18.7 million for the DSCC and $19.4 million for the NRSC), while the NRCC outspent the DCCC by $10 million ($47.2 million by the NRCC to $36.9 million by the DCCC). This extraordinary spending was tightly targeted around a handful of competitive races and focused mostly on express electioneering on television and through direct mail.

On the Senate side, the total of $38 million dollars in independent expendi-

Figure 3.3   Party Independent Expenditures, 2000–2004

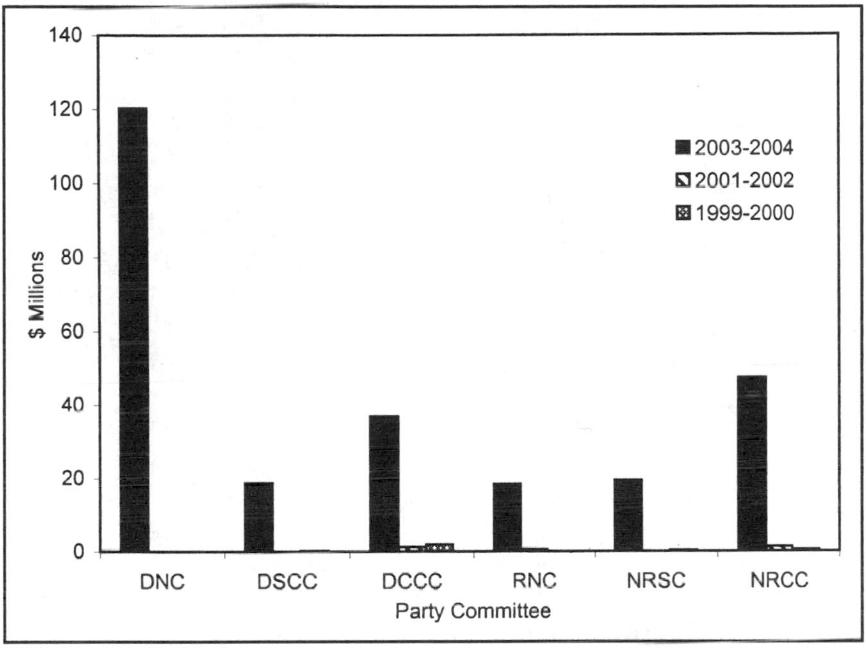

Source: FEC, "Party Financial Activity Summarized for the 2004 Election Cycle," News Release, March 2, 2005.

tures was made in twelve races. Table 3.2 lists the senatorial IEs. Each party committee spent at least a million dollars in eight of these races. Several were extraordinarily expensive undertakings (such as the $8.3 million spent in Florida through party IEs) that help give us a sense of what soft money/hard money issue advocacy spending must have been like. An analysis of the available data on how the IEs were spent shows that the great bulk of it was spent on television advertising. The next greatest expenditure was for polling (see more on the importance of this below), followed by almost identical small expenditures on direct mail and phone banks.

On the House side, we find that the combined IEs of over $80 million were concentrated in about thirty races. This exceptional concentration of spending in a handful of races meant that some of the most competitive races found the CCCs outspending the candidates they were helping. Table 3.3 shows the party commitment to U.S. House races by adding coordinated and independent expenditures and dividing that total by candidate spending to find how CCC spending compared to candidate spending. We see that the Democratic Party outspent its candidate in seven House races, while the GOP did so in ten. Democrats won two of these seven races, Republicans five out of ten.

The picture is also startling when looking at absolute amounts of money spent. Republicans spent over $3 million in Washington's 8th congressional district race (the Democrats spent over $2 million in the same race, making it the race with

Table 3.2 Senate Races with Party Independent Expenditures in 2004 (*$ millions*)

State	Candidate	Party	I/C/O	W/L	Gen. %	Party Ind. Exp.	Party Coord. Exp.	Candidate Exp.
AK	Knowles, Tony	Dem	C	L	46	3.05	0.15	5.70
	Murkowski, Lisa	Rep	I	W	49	1.82	0.32	5.27
CA	Boxer, Barbara	Dem	I	W	58	0.00	2.80	14.50
	Jones, Bill	Rep	C	L	38	0.14	0.39	6.93
CO	Coors, Peter	Rep	O	L	47	1.99	0.50	7.73
	Salazar, Ken	Dem	O	W	51	2.30	0.45	9.56
FL	Castor, Betty	Dem	O	L	48	3.73	1.91	11.14
	Martinez, Mel	Rep	O	W	49	4.68	1.95	12.20
GA	Isakson, John H	Rep	O	W	58	0.00	0.16	7.87
	Majette, Denise L	Dem	O	L	40	0.00	0.33	1.91
KY	Bunning, Jim	Rep	I	W	51	0.05	0.47	6.04
	Mongiardo, Daniel	Dem	C	L	49	0.87	0.41	3.07
LA	John, Chris	Dem	O	L	29	1.65	0.18	4.57
	Kennedy, John N	Dem	O	L	15	0.00	0.00	1.89
	Vitter, David	Rep	O	W	51	1.35	0.50	6.99
NC	Bowles, Erskine B	Dem	O	L	47	2.53	1.47	13.28
	Burr, Richard	Rep	O	W	52	2.45	1.11	12.75
OK	Carson, Brad R	Dem	O	L	41	2.32	0.58	6.05
	Coburn, Thomas A	Rep	O	W	53	2.33	0.61	2.94
SC	Demint, James W	Rep	O	W	54	2.13	0.47	8.85
	Tenenbaum, Inez M	Dem	O	L	44	3.86	0.24	5.99
SD	Daschle, Thomas A	Dem	I	L	49	0.94	0.15	19.74
	Thune, John R	Rep	C	W	51	3.26	0.00	14.13
WA	Murray, Patty	Dem	I	W	55	0.00	0.00	11.34
	Nethercutt, George	Rep	C	L	43	0.02	0.71	7.65

Source: Compiled from FEC data.

Table 3.3 Party Commitment to House Races: Independent and Coordinated Expenditures, as Percent of Candidate Spending

	>100%	75–100%	50–75%	25–50%	Total
Democrats	7	3	8	8	26
Republicans	10	4	9	8	31
Total	17	7	17	16	57

Source: Compiled from FEC data.

the most party independent expenditures—a total of $6.1 million, which includes outside group independent expenditures as well). Table 3.4 shows that sixty-one candidates' races found their party spending $500,000 or more in IEs. These numbers sound fantastic but did they represent a big change over past behavior?

The Problem of Independence

The party committees could spend IEs before BCRA (since *Colorado II*), so why didn't they? Why had they chosen issue advocacy instead? First, issue ads could be paid for with a mix of soft and hard money, and at that time, the parties believed that it was not possible to raise the same amount of money using only hard money (small donor) techniques. However, that hurdle has not proven so large. Second, running issue ads through state parties allowed the CCCs to avoid two other mandates: disclosure of activity to the Federal Election Commission and noncoordination. Without centralized disclosure, previous issue advocacy advertisements were harder to estimate and identify. BCRA leaves the parties with no alternative but disclosure.

The coordination problem is an interesting one. Technically the state parties ran issue advocacy even though they were guided by the CCCs. However, because the issue ads did not count as candidate support under the old law, there was no barrier to coordination. Now, the CCCs are running IEs as well as coordinated expenditure campaigns, but they must be separate efforts. The *Hill* newspaper reported that at the NRCC "the Republicans who handle independent expenditures are cordoned off from the rest of the campaign committee" (Savodnik 2004). One consequence of this independence is that the parties make redundant outlays for polls before they will make any meaningful IE investment in television ads or mail. Don McGahn, general counsel of the NRCC, confirmed this problem along with the redundant overhead costs associated with maintaining separate office space (McGahn 2005). It will be interesting to analyze what proportion of IEs is spent on real campaign efforts rather than on the research required to make these appeals. In the end, we will probably find that less spending actually benefited candidates under independent expenditures than it would have under the old soft money issue advocacy party spending. The effort to avoid coordination between candidates and their parties is the least attractive aspect of IEs for the parties (and why they must wish they could have unlimited coordinated expenditures instead!). Another consequence of independence is the possibility that the parties make campaign decisions that work against the candidate's best interests. If the candidate therefore has to campaign against the party trying to help him or her, money is wasted, and the voters are shortchanged by having less meaningful discourse.

Campaign Strategizing Using IEs

The CCCs were in mostly uncharted water this cycle. Faced with eventual disclosure, the parties leaked their plans to the media, thus signaling to the cam-

Table 3.4 House Party Spending Compared to Candidate Spending in Races with More Than $500,000 in Party Spending ($ millions)

State	District	Candidate	Party	I/C/O	W/L	Gen. %	Party Independent Exp.	Party Coordinated Exp.	Total Ind. & Coord. Exp.	Candidate Exp.	Party: Candidate Ratio
AZ	1	Renzi, Richard George	R	I	W	59	1.60	0.06	1.67	2.18	0.76
AZ	1	Babbitt, Paul J Jr	D	C	L	36	1.13	0.03	1.16	1.26	0.92
AZ	7	Beauprez, Robert L	R	I	W	55	0.54	0.07	0.61	2.90	0.21
CA	20	Ashburn, Roy	R	O	L	47	2.00	—	2.00	1.08	1.86
CO	3	Walcher, Gregory E	R	O	L	47	2.52	—	2.52	1.55	1.63
CO	3	Salazar, John T	D	O	W	51	1.87	0.04	1.91	1.60	1.20
CO	4	Musgrave, Marilyn N	R	I	W	51	0.98	0.07	1.05	3.15	0.33
CT	2	Simmons, Robert R	R	I	W	54	1.61	0.07	1.69	2.42	0.70
CT	2	Sullivan, James M	D	C	L	46	1.27	0.07	1.34	1.05	1.27
GA	12	Barrow, John J	D	C	W	52	1.14	0.03	1.17	1.81	0.64
GA	12	Burns, O Maxie	R	I	L	48	0.68	0.07	0.75	2.77	0.27
IL	8	Crane, Philip M	R	I	L	48	1.23	0.41	1.64	1.58	1.04
IL	8	Bean, Melissa L	D	C	W	52	0.88	0.04	0.92	1.55	0.59
IN	8	Hostettler, John N	R	I	W	53	0.65	—	0.65	0.48	1.35
IN	9	Sodrel, Michael E	R	C	W	49	1.95	0.07	2.03	1.51	1.34
IN	9	Hill, Baron P	D	I	L	49	0.78	0.04	0.82	1.43	0.57
KS	3	Moore, Dennis	D	I	W	55	0.69	0.06	0.75	2.35	0.32
KS	3	Kobach, Kris	R	C	L	44	0.61	0.07	0.68	1.19	0.57
KY	3	Northup, Anne M	R	I	W	60	0.63	0.07	0.70	3.32	0.21
KY	3	Miller, Tony	D	C	L	38	0.62	0.04	0.65	1.20	0.54
KY	4	Clooney, Nick	D	O	L	44	1.99	0.04	2.03	1.43	1.42
KY	4	Davis, Geoffrey C	R	O	W	54	1.84	0.07	1.91	2.68	0.71
LA	3	Tauzin, Wilbert J II	R	O	R	32	2.61	0.03	2.64	0.77	3.43
LA	3	Melancon, Charles J	D	O	R	24	1.81	0.03	1.83	1.05	1.74
LA	7	Mount, Willie L	D	O	R	25	0.93	0.00	0.94	0.72	1.31
LA	7	Boustany, Charles W	R	O	R	39	0.80	0.05	0.85	1.65	0.51
MN	6	Kennedy, Mark R	R	I	W	54	0.69	0.07	0.76	2.31	0.33
MN	6	Wetterling, Patty	D	C	L	46	0.50	0.05	0.55	1.92	0.29

State	District	Name	Party		W/L						
NC	11	Keever, Patricia	D	C	L	45	0.48	0.02	0.50	1.20	0.42
NE	1	Fortenberry, Jeffrey	R	O	W	54	0.55	0.07	0.62	1.16	0.53
NM	1	Romero, Richard M	D	C	L	46	1.25	0.03	1.28	1.99	0.64
NM	1	Wilson, Heather A	R	I	W	54	1.01	0.07	1.09	3.33	0.33
NV	3	Gallagher, Tom	D	C	L	40	0.77	0.03	0.79	2.16	0.37
NV	3	Porter, Jon C Sr	R	I	W	54	0.44	0.07	0.51	2.61	0.20
NV	1	Manger, William	R	C	L	44	0.56	0.07	0.63	1.38	0.46
NV	27	Higgins, Brian M	D	O	W	51	1.02	0.17	1.19	1.32	0.90
NV	27	Naples, Nancy A	R	O	L	49	0.86	0.07	0.93	1.56	0.60
PA	6	Gerlach, Jim	R	I	W	51	1.95	0.07	2.02	2.19	0.92
PA	6	Murphy, Lois	D	C	L	49	1.43	0.02	1.45	1.89	0.77
PA	8	Fitzpatrick, Michael	R	O	W	55	2.27	0.07	2.34	1.00	2.35
PA	8	Schrader, Virginia	D	O	L	43	1.42	0.05	1.46	0.54	2.69
PA	13	Brown, Melissa M	R	O	L	41	0.79	0.04	0.83	1.91	0.44
PA	13	Schwartz, Allyson	D	O	W	56	0.80	0.04	0.83	4.52	0.18
SD	AL	Diedrich, Larry Will	R	C	L	46	1.49	0.16	1.65	0.96	1.72
SD	AL	Herseth, Stephanie M	D	I	W	53	1.03	0.11	1.15	1.65	0.70
TX	1	Gohmert, Louis B	R	C	W	61	1.38	0.07	1.45	1.77	0.82
TX	1	Sandlin, Max	D	I	L	38	0.53	0.07	0.60	1.66	0.36
TX	2	Poe, Ted	R	C	W	55	1.87	0.07	1.94	1.45	1.34
TX	2	Lampson, Nicolas	D	I	L	43	1.07	0.07	1.14	2.32	0.49
TX	17	Wohlgemuth, Arlene M	R	C	L	47	1.69	0.07	1.77	2.55	0.69
TX	17	Edwards, Chet	D	I	W	51	1.49	0.07	1.56	2.63	0.60
TX	19	Neugebauer, Randy	R	I	W	58	0.46	0.07	0.53	2.16	0.25
TX	32	Frost, Martin	D	I	L	44	1.11	0.07	1.19	4.64	0.26
TX	32	Sessions, Pete	R	I	W	54	0.75	0.07	0.82	4.42	0.19
UT	2	Swallow, John	R	C	L	43	1.00	0.09	1.10	1.45	0.76
UT	2	Matheson, Jim	D	I	W	55	0.66	0.06	0.72	1.98	0.36
VA	2	Drake, Thelma	R	O	W	55	0.54	—	0.54	0.81	0.67
WA	5	Barbieri, Donald K	D	O	L	40	0.80	0.06	0.87	1.63	0.53
WA	5	Mcmorris, Cathy	R	O	W	60	0.71	0.07	0.78	1.47	0.53
WA	8	Reichert, Dave	R	O	W	52	3.66	0.07	3.73	1.55	2.41
WA	8	Ross, Dave	D	O	L	47	2.37	0.04	2.41	1.43	1.68

Source: Compiled from FEC data.

paigns they were trying to help while maintaining the required independence. All summer the media reported large reservations of television time at cheaper advance rates. The Associated Press reported just after Labor Day that the DCCC had already reserved $20 million of television airtime for about three dozen seats and that the NRCC had reserved $10 million in about a dozen districts (Espo 2004). Throughout the cycle, news of CCC activity fluctuated. On September 28, *Roll Call* proclaimed "DCCC Expands Beneficiary List" (Whittington 2004) but by the 30th declared "Once-Touted Races Neglected" (Cillizza 2004c). Even now we do not have the full sense of IE activity by the parties.

In any given race, the IE strategy was contingent on a number of variables, specifically the candidates' changing poll numbers and decisions made by the presidential candidates and outside groups, which helped determine the price of media in certain markets. An example will illustrate the point. The Philadelphia area was unique in 2004, with the CCCs eyeing four House races: PA-6, PA-8, PA-13, and PA-15. The U.S. Senate race was not considered competitive enough to warrant IE money, though the candidates' purchase of time affected the price. Only the Sixth District found a vulnerable incumbent facing a strong challenger—the other three were open seat races. In the Sixth District, which was newly drawn in 2001, Republican incumbent Jim Gerlach repeated his 51 percent margin from 2002. In 2004, Gerlach was opposed by Lois Murphy, an attorney who formerly headed Pennsylvania NARAL Pro-Choice America. The contrast between the two candidates was quite stark ideologically, and the incumbent again seemed quite vulnerable. Both parties and a wide spectrum of groups participated in this race, especially buying television time. The NRCC spent $1,946,464 in independent expenditures, and the DCCC spent $1,432,496 (Federal Election Commission 2005b).

The Eighth District, held by popular and moderate Republican incumbent Jim Greenwood since 1992, was expected to be uncompetitive, but Greenwood announced his intention to retire at the end of the 108th Congress in mid-July to become the president of a major biotechnology lobbying firm (Mullins 2004b). His departure set off a fevered search for a Republican nominee and a close examination of the Democratic candidate Ginny Schrader. Thus, what was predicted to be a noncompetitive, low-profile race became instantly competitive, especially since the eventual Republican nominee, Mike Fitzpatrick, was a conservative, pro-life Republican waging a campaign in a district that gave Al Gore its vote in 2000. The race became so critical that the NRCC spent $2,270,296 in independent expenditures and the DCCC spent $1,418,944, according to an FEC press release (January 3, 2005). As in the Sixth District, the Eighth District now had a pro-life Republican man facing a pro-choice Democratic woman. As a result both districts were saturated with television and mail from parties, interest groups, and the candidates themselves.

The open seats in the Thirteenth and Fifteenth Districts were thought to be competitive in the summer, and the NRCC and DCCC bought television time in advance without indicating which race it would be used for. The committees were unsure in August which of the four races would be worthy of investment, especially in the wake of Greenwood's retirement. Ultimately, both parties scrapped their plans to spend any money on television in the Thirteenth and Fifteenth Districts, finding the party of the retiring incumbent to be favored in both instances. The CCCs had the flexibility to adjust their IE strategy without having "wasted" any money on the reserved airtime. Yet this flexibility did not come cheap. As circumstances changed, the CCCs continued to spend more on polling and other research to help them determine which of these contests should get independent expenditure advertising.

Party Orchestrated Activities

Much of what parties have done in recent years to help them win elections is what we call "party orchestrated activities" (Kolodny and Dwyre 1998). Parties do not only act directly to promote candidates. In response to the party's direction and guidance, that is, to its orchestration, party members and allied groups often make efforts to help the party's preferred candidates win. For example, labor unions have long been an integral part of Democratic get-out-the-vote efforts, and the unions follow the party's lead in deciding which races to target. Parties used a variety of methods to get others to help them reach their electoral goals throughout the 1990s and early 2000s (Kolodny and Dwyre 1998). After passage of BCRA, some of these changed or were stepped up, and new methods have been developed.

For instance, House Majority Leader Tom DeLay (R-TX) introduced STOMP (Strategic Task Force to Organize and Mobilize People) in 2001 to enhance GOP House candidates' field operations. STOMP dispatches volunteers (e.g., Hill staffers, lobbyists, and college students) to targeted House races to do door-to-door and other GOTV activities close to Election Day. During the 2001–2002 election cycle, STOMP was paid for with soft money from the NRCC and the RNC, but now these party-orchestrated efforts must be paid for with hard money (Cillizza 2004c). While the NRCC no doubt funded some STOMP activities with its hard money resources in 2004, some STOMP efforts were bankrolled by individual House Members. For instance, Congressman Wally Herger (R-CA) paid for transportation, lodging, and food for a number of college students from his northern California District to travel to Washington state to work on a number of targeted House races during the last week of the election.

It is difficult to track the exact level of such grassroots efforts, but it is clear that the NRCC continued its STOMP activities in 2004. In fact, Senate Republicans started a project named "Special Teams" in 2004 that was modeled after STOMP. Senate Republican Conference Chairman Rick Santorum (R-PA) coordinated the Special Teams project to maximize turnout by working to send 750 volunteers to six states with close Senate contests (Preston and Kane 2004). These Senate GOP Special Teams were paid for with money raised by a joint fundraising committee sponsored by the NRSC and state party committees. Individual contributors who donated the maximum amount ($57,500) to the Special Teams committee were promised a private reception with GOP Senate leaders, and PACs (up to $45,000) and GOP Senators were asked to fund the program as well (Preston and Kane 2004). As with STOMP, the money is used to provide transportation, food, and lodging for unpaid volunteers.

CONCLUSION

It is clear that BCRA did not cripple the parties. Indeed, the parties proved quite robust, finding new ways to raise funds and creative ways to spend them. Independent expenditures allowed the parties to invest massive sums in races they felt could benefit from their presence. Yet independent spending was costly for the CCCs, for they had to spend precious hard money to figure out how best to allocate their expenditures. Thus BCRA rules that allow for unlimited independent, but not coordinated, spending may mean that the level of spending by party committees in congressional elections will not go down. Unlike the situation with soft money, however, the amount spent on each race will be disclosed.

That per-race spending by the parties is so high is not a result of their robust fundraising, but an artifact of the shrinking number of competitive congressional races. Parties can continue to invest at about the same level they did per race as long as the pool of opportunity contests remains small. The challenge for congressional parties will be to continue raising small-to-modest hard money contributions, especially in midterm election cycles, to cultivate the resources needed if competition expands. While the CCCs could not entirely compensate for the loss of soft money in 2004, they collected more hard money than observers predicted. Can the expansion of the parties' donor base continue? Early reports of fundraising for the 2005–2006 cycle indicate that the parties can continue to improve on their fundraising performance. Nevertheless, we will need to witness more election cycles before we can conclude that political parties successfully adapted to the post-BCRA environment.

4

State and Local Political Parties

Raymond J. La Raja

The Bipartisan Campaign Reform Act of 2002 (BCRA) had at least several important effects on parties in the states. First, the law made state parties switch almost completely toward hard money financed operations in federal elections. A provision in the law, which allowed some soft money spending for federal election activity, was hardly exploited. Nevertheless, state parties raised roughly the same amount in 2004 as in 2000 for federal or shared party activities, once you take out the money the national committees used to transfer to the states. Second, the state parties no longer sponsor television advertising in federal campaigns. The ban on national party soft money and soft money transfers has effectively eliminated this state party activity. (Spending for other activities reported to the Federal Election Commission [FEC] went up for Republican state parties and stayed about even for Democrats.) Finally, the new law appears to have given an initial advantage to Republican state parties in 2004. These parties raised and spent more money in federal elections than Democrats, particularly on voter mobilization activities. The Democratic lag might be due in part to their past reliance on soft money and their decision to pursue an outside strategy using 527 organizations in battleground states. This chapter explores these changes at the state level using spending data from the Federal Election Commission.

THE SETTING

The 2004 elections were extraordinary for the emphasis both parties put on turnout operations in the states. Polls showed that most voters were already decided about their choice for president. The election outcome would rely heavily on which party could deliver their voters to the polls. Past conventional wisdom had been that Democrats enjoy an advantage in generating turnout. But as early as 2001, Republicans were already preparing to deploy a massive voter operation for the presidential election in 2004. Karl Rove, Kenneth Mehlman, and Republican National Committee (RNC) staff had been working closely with Republicans in the states to marry sophisticated voter targeting technology with traditional shoe leather canvassing in neighborhoods (Keen and Bendetto 2004; Postman 2004). The strategy of the GOP was to erect a dense network of partisan volunteers through state and county party staff. These volunteers would be responsible for tapping into personal networks of friends and neighbors for Election Day turnout.

Democrats also recognized that field operations in the states could make the difference in the 2004 elections. Being the out party, however, they lacked the unity prior to the presidential nomination to start building a formidable ground campaign before 2004. BCRA was also part of the reason for Democrats' delay. The complexity of the statutes regulating intraparty coordination led some Democrats to wonder if they would even implement the same kind of state party field organizations they had in the past. Above all, Democratic party activists worried that the loss of soft money from national party coffers, which had supported many state operations, would put them at a significant disadvantage relative to hard money rich Republicans. Given these concerns, Democratic partisans chose to pursue a dual strategy to ensure that sufficient resources would be deployed in battleground states. Some experienced political operatives from Democratic-leaning groups, such as Ellen Malcolm of EMILY's list and Steven Rosenthal, former political director of the AFL-CIO, joined to start an organization called Americans Coming Together (ACT) (see chapter 5). The plan was to make this organization the centerpiece of an intense voter mobilization strategy for Democrats. Simultaneously, Democratic state parties would kick-start their traditional field operations as best they could under the new campaign finance rules. Even though the Democratic supporters hedged their strategy by deploying a party and outside approach, there were risks involved. Conceivably, partisans might work at cross-purposes in fielding two major turnout operations that could not coordinate activities.

The intensive efforts to build ground operations in the states appeared to bring dividends to both parties. John Kerry received an additional 6.8 million Democratic votes over Gore's totals in 2000. The Bush team, however, added 10.5 million votes to their totals. The Republicans countered the intense focus of Democrats in their traditional urban areas by generating huge margins in exurban and rural areas (Edsall and Grimaldi 2004). Which approaches most helped Republicans generate voters is still a question to be explored in future research, but the amounts that Republican state and national committees spent on field operations certainly suggests that the GOTV (get-out-the-vote) effort was formidable.

BACKGROUND ON CAMPAIGN FINANCE LAWS
AFFECTING STATE PARTIES

When reformers sought to end the flow of soft money in federal elections, they understood the law's reach had to extend to the operations of state political parties. It seemed clear that a party ban at the national level would simply encourage party operatives to channel funds through state parties. Thus, they drew statutes intended to minimize the possibility of an "end run" that would keep soft money flowing into federal campaigns. However, the statutes could not simply federalize state campaign finance laws. Only a small percentage of elections in the United States are for federal offices, so there had to be some accommodation to the state-based regulatory systems. The solution was to define a segment of campaigning called "federal election activity." Any party activity that fell within federal election activity would have to be financed under the federal rules contained in BCRA.

Federal election activity in the law includes voter registration (120 days prior to an election in which a federal candidate appears on the ballot), voter identification, GOTV, and public communications that promote, attack, support, or oppose a federal candidate. State parties must use federal funds to pay for these election activities, even if these same activities are geared toward helping candidates lower down on the ballot. In 2004, just over one-third of state party spending (a total of almost $400 million) reported to the FEC was counted as federal election activity under the new guidelines.[1] The parties spent the balance on maintaining headquarters, staff expenses, fundraising, and other administrative functions. Some of these administrative expenses can still be paid for with a portion of soft money so long as they do not fall under the definition of federal election activity.[2] These hard and soft funds for administration are reported to the FEC. However, it is important to keep in mind that state parties may also spend money solely for state elections, which does not have to be reported to the FEC. The analysis in this chapter is based on the hard and soft money reported to the FEC, except where noted. Thus, the reader should keep in mind that I report a subset of state party spending, which does not include money that parties might spend separately to influence state and local elections.[3]

To ease the transition to the new campaign finance system, the limits on contributions to state parties for federal election activity were raised from $5,000 to $10,000. In addition, donors now have higher aggregate limits on total political contributions allowable for federal elections, so the competition for hard money among parties and candidates would be attenuated. To encourage grassroots activity, Senator Carl Levin (D-MI) successfully attached an amendment to BCRA that would allow state and local party committees to use soft money from donors who could not otherwise contribute under federal law (corporations, labor unions) so long as (1) state law permitted, (2) the money was raised from donors who gave $10,000 or less to each state or local committee, and (3) each party committee raised the money on its own (no transfers). It was hoped that this change accommodated state rules so that grassroots activity in states would not be diminished under new federal rules. Few parties, however, took advantage of the Levin Amendment to raise soft money for the 2004 elections.

The new regulations raised a host of intriguing questions about how parties in the states might respond. Prior to BCRA, state parties received infusions of soft and hard money from national committees to spend on candidate-specific issue ads and other campaign activity. BCRA effectively ended the national committee transfers of soft money. Not only would states miss out on national party soft money, they faced a legal regime that compelled them to raise political funds for federal election activity under federal rather than state rules. Would they participate in federal elections as much as in the past given that soft money financing was constrained? To what extent would national committees continue to support state parties with hard money transfers in lieu of the soft money transfers?

Another set of questions concerned how state parties spent their available money. Would BCRA encourage them to change the mix of campaign activities? In the past, state parties sponsored soft money advertising. How much of this would cease, and would these funds be invested instead in voter contacts?

Finally, a third set of questions dealt with the partisan implications of BCRA. The conventional wisdom was that Republicans were in better shape to make this transition than Democrats. Would Republicans outspend Democrats in the states?

To give a preview, I found that state parties spent about as much in federal elections as they did in previous elections, *minus* the spending on advertising. The national parties did not transfer as much money to the states in 2004 as in the previous election because, lacking soft money, they had no incentive to fund ads through the state parties. For this reason, state parties did not sponsor ads in federal elections in 2004. Instead, Republican spending at the state level surged for mobilization and grass roots, while Democratic state party spending on these activities diminished slightly. It appears, in fact, that Republicans outspent the Democrats at both the national and state level, particularly on voter contact operations. These findings are consistent with anecdotal accounts about intensive Republican ground campaigns in many states, which gave President Bush higher margins of victory than in his first election.

THE TRANSITION FROM FECA TO BCRA

BCRA created considerable uncertainty among state party officials, at least initially, about what they could do in the 2004 elections. Under the Federal Election Campaign Act (FECA), the state parties kept two sets of books: federal and nonfederal. The parties were allowed before BCRA to use money from both accounts to pay for organizational activities that influenced both federal and nonfederal elections simultaneously. State parties, however, did not have unlimited discretion in how they could combine soft and hard money. Under accounting guidelines issued by the Federal Election Commission, they were compelled to spend a minimal threshold of hard money whenever they spent soft money. Typically, the hard-soft money ratio reflected the ratio of federal to nonfederal candidates on the ballot (though these ratios varied depending on the campaign activity). Under BCRA, however, state parties may no longer spend soft money for activities defined as "federal election activity," *unless* these funds are raised under federal contribution limits or with the exceptions allowed by the Levin Amendment. As a consequence, parties must now keep no fewer than three sets of books if they want to exploit all the features of the new law: federal, Levin Amendment funds, and nonfederal. The first two accounts allow state parties to spend money on federal election activity. The nonfederal account is for state and local elections only. State parties, however, may spend some nonfederal money for administration and election work that does not fall under the definition of federal election activity.

This brief but complex description of party accounting under a federal system suggests that the process has never been easy, even before BCRA was introduced. The parties adapted and learned how to work under FECA. After a few elections they should have a better understanding of how to operate under BCRA. One indication that parties struggled with the new law is that they barely used the Levin fund accounts. According to the FEC, state and local parties spent only $2.8 million in Levin funds, even though total state spending almost exceeded $400 million dollars. The accounting rules for Levin funds seemed too onerous: state and local parties would have to create special Levin fund accounts for soft money capped uniquely at $10,000, raise all the Levin funds on their own (without transfers from other party committees), and spend only soft money from Levin accounts for federal election activity. To avoid breaking the law and to maximize spending flexibility, the state and local parties federalized their operations as much as possible. In practice, this meant they raised and spent mostly hard money. Only 17 percent of state party spending reported to the Federal Election Commission was financed with soft money, and all of this was allocated purely to administrative expenses as described earlier, rather than for federal election activity. This percentage does not include soft money that may have been spent solely for state elections. The decline in soft money spending is an astonishing change from 2000 when 62 percent of state party activity reported to the FEC was financed with soft money. At that time, soft money could be used not only for shared administrative expenses but also for other shared items BCRA now defines as federal election activities (including registration, get-out-the-vote, or public communication that mentions a federal candidate without expressly advocating the candidate's election or defeat).

Figure 4.1 shows that the major political parties spent just $67 million in soft money in the 2004 federal elections—all of it at the state level—compared with $562 million in the 2000 election cycle, which included both national committee soft money spending ($238 million) and state party soft money spending ($324 million). The $67 million reflects the soft money that state parties can continue to spend to pay for the nonfederal portion of shared federal and nonfederal administrative expenses that do not fall into the category of federal election activ-

Figure 4.1   **Federal and Nonfederal Spending for Political Parties, 2000 vs. 2004**

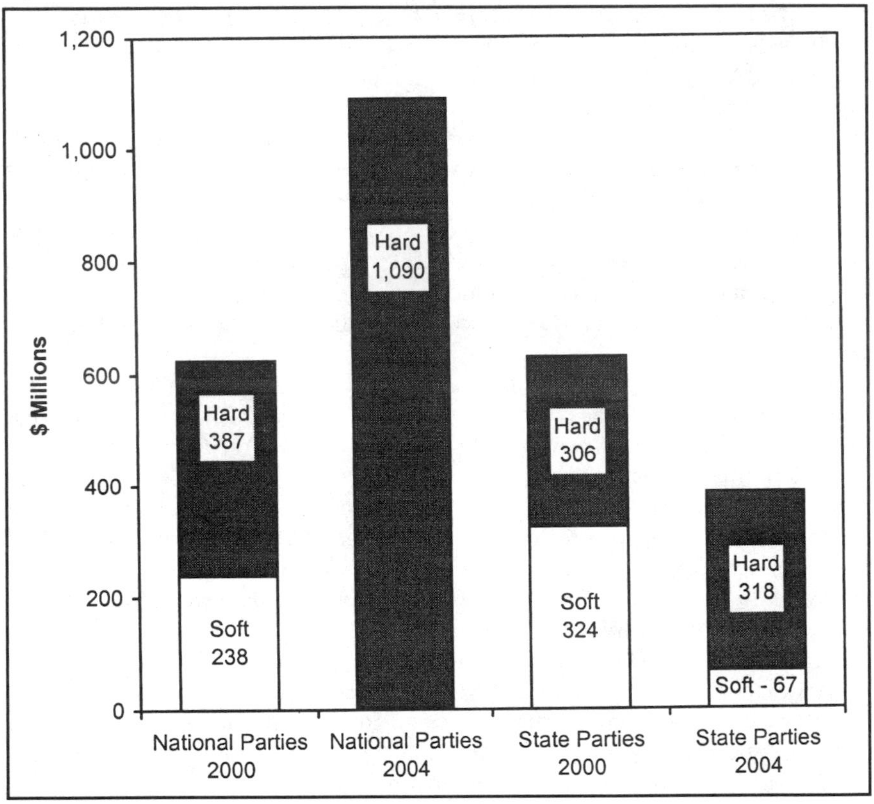

Source: Federal Election Commission.

ity. If they wanted to spend additional soft money for federal election activity, they would have to raise it under the Levin Amendment provisions, which they chose not to do in the 2004 elections. Instead, state parties focused on hard money spending for federal elections. State party hard money spending in federal elections increased slightly from $306 million in 2000 to $318 million in 2004. In contrast, national committee hard money spending soared from $387 million to $1,090 million. These data show that BCRA virtually eliminated soft money spending for any activity that might be construed as part of federal elections. The minimal amount of soft money spent by state parties was for party-based campaigning and organizational tasks that did not fall under BCRA's definition of federal election activity.

The state parties, however, continued to raise and spend soft money for their state elections, not all of which is reported to the FEC. According to the Center for Public Integrity, the parties in the states (including legislative campaign committees and state central committees) collected $445 million directly from donors, not counting transfers from other party committees. This sum was $128 million more than they raised directly in 2000 (Armendariz and Pilhofer 2005). Some of this $445 million went toward defraying administrative expenses that was reported to the FEC as soft money (the $67 million reported above). It is unclear how much of the $445 money was soft money under BCRA's definition. Any contributions not meeting BCRA's source limits (no corporate or union contributions) and size limits ($10,000) would constitute soft money. The Center for Public Integrity did not report how much of the $445 million was soft or hard money, but their findings suggest that many donors fall outside the hard money limits of BCRA.

In previous elections, state parties benefited from transfers of soft and hard money from the national committees. Under BCRA, however, national committees could not raise or spend soft money for their own accounts or on behalf of state parties. State parties could continue to receive hard money transfers from national committees, but these funds could not be mixed with soft money funds for federal election activity. In fact, state parties could only spend soft money they raised for basic administrative tasks, unless this soft money was collected under the Levin Amendment rules for federal election activity. One question was whether state parties would be able to spend as much money in federal elections on their own with the new restrictions in place, especially without soft money transfers from the national committees.

Figure 4.2 shows that both sets of state parties spent less money in the 2004 federal elections than in 2000. Again, these sums represent *only* the money reported to the FEC. The difference between 2004 and 2000 in these reported sums can largely be accounted for by the decline in transfers from national committees to state parties for spending on broadcast advertising for federal candidates.[4] In 2004, for example, Republican state party spending was $196 million compared with $312 million in 2000. In 2000, however, the Republicans had spent $98 million on advertising through the state parties.[5] If this sum is subtracted from the 2000 total, then Republican state party spending without advertising would have been $214 million in 2000. Thus, Republican state party spending that is unrelated to advertising declined slightly from $214 million in 2000 to $196 million in 2004. The Democrats, in contrast, spent $129 million less than they spent in the 2000 election. Again, using the same calculation to deduct advertising expenditures, Democratic state party spending without advertising in 2000 would have been $179 million in 2000 ($318 million total minus $139 million on advertising). Thus, Democratic state party spending (nonadvertising) increased slightly from $179 million to $189 million between 2000 and 2004.

While Democrats increased their spending in 2004 that was unrelated to advertising, Republicans still outspent them slightly by $7 million. As I explain later, these small spending differences between the state parties obscure important differences in their capacity to raise hard money, since Democrats relied heavily on transfers from national-level committees while Republicans were able to raise much of the money on their own.

Figure 4.2 does not include spending by local parties because it remains so

Figure 4.2　Party Spending, National and State, 2000 vs. 2004

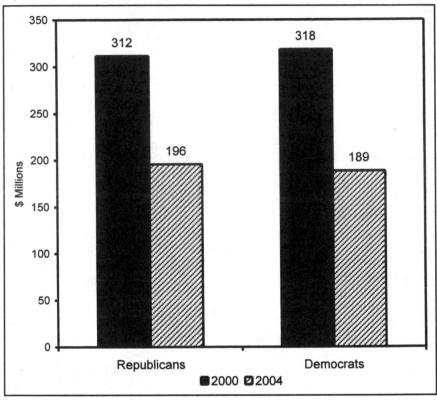

Source: Federal Election Commission.

insignificant relative to committees at higher levels. In fact, local committee spending barely exceeds 1 percent of total party spending before or after BCRA. In 2004, Republican local parties reported spending just $6.3 million for federal elections while Democratic local parties spent only $2.6 million. These sums increased slightly for Republican local committees, which spent only $4 million in the 2000 elections. But the 2004 figure is a slight decline for Democratic committees, which spent $2.9 million in 2000. Few of these committees took advantage of the Levin fund provisions to raise and spend soft money. Of the total sums spent by local parties, Levin expenditures amounted to just $483,000 for Republican committees and $160,000 for Democratic committees. Thus, BCRA appeared to have only minor, if any, effects on increasing local party spending.

To what extent were state parties able to raise their own funds? According to the Center for Public Integrity (CPI), overall fundraising for state parties declined from $802 million in 2000 to $735 million in 2004. These data include the finances of campaign committees run by party leaders in the state legislatures, as well as the state central committees; they also include transfers from other committees ($290 million) as well as direct contributions ($445 million). The CPI data suggest that large institutions stepped into the breach left behind by the national committees, which could no longer transfer soft money, especially for the Democrats. The Kerry campaign affiliates (e.g., Citizen Soldier Fund), for example, contributed roughly $11 million to state parties.[6] The Democratic Governor's Association was a close second, supplying over $9 million. In addition, two unions, AFSCME and the Service Employees International Union (SEIU) gave $4.9 million and $4.7 million, respectively. Republicans appeared to rely less on large institutions than on wealthy individuals, such as Richard and Elisabeth DeVos, Jr., who gave $2.3 million and Jay VanAndel who gave $2 million, divided equally between the Michigan and Florida Republican parties. Based on campaign finance records in the states it is difficult to parse how much of state party money came in increments that exceeded the federal hard money limits; thus, it is hard to assess whether BCRA affected the amounts of soft money raised by state parties.

Using data reported to the FEC, however, it is possible to assess whether state parties were able to finance federal elections on their own with hard money as much as they had in previous elections. Since the FEC does not publish data on *receipts* that distinguish between hard money contributions versus transfers, my estimates are derived by simply subtracting all hard money transfers from how much hard money the state parties *spent*. This calculation provides a rough measure of hard money that state parties raised from contributions rather than through transfers from national committees. In short, it indicates whether the parties "held their own" between 2000 and 2004, not including the help of party transfers.

Table 4.1 suggests that Republican state parties did better raising hard money for federal elections in 2004, while Democratic parties have not made any gains. In 2004, Republican parties received only $51 million in hard money transfers

Table 4.1   Funds Raised by State Parties for Spending Reported to the FEC (*$ millions*)

	2000	2004	% change from 2000
Republicans			
State Party Spending Reported to the FEC	$312	$196	−37%
Minus: National Committee Transfers	187	51	−73%
Difference: Est. Funds Raised by State Parties	124	145	17%
Democrats			
State Party Spending Reported to the FEC	$318	$189	−41%
Minus: National Committee Transfers	228	66	−71%
Minus: Kerry Campaign Committee Transfers	—	40	—
Difference: Est. Funds Raised by State Parties	91	82	−9%

Source: Federal Election Commission.

Notes: National Committee transfers in 2000 included both federal and nonfederal dollars but only federal in 2004. State committee receipts include nonfederal funds in both cycles.

from the national committees, compared with $187 million in 2000, when the national parties could give both soft and hard money transfers. Subtracting the transfers in each cycle, I estimate that Republican state committees raised $145 million on their own in 2004, an increase of 17 percent over the $124 million they raised in the 2000 elections. Much of this success could be attributed to a concerted effort, early on, by the Bush reelection team to encourage major donors to contribute to state parties rather than 527s (Mullins 2004a).

In contrast, fundraising actually appeared to decline for Democratic state parties, at least as it applies to federal election activity reported to the FEC. In 2000, Democratic state parties received a massive infusion of $228 million in transfers from the national committees (both hard and soft money), while they only received $66 million in 2004 (hard money only). Subtracting out transfers from total spending implies that the state parties raised about $91 million in the 2000 elections on their own for activity related to federal elections. In 2004, they raised only $82 million while receiving $66 million in transfers from the national committees and an unprecedented $40 million in transfers from the Kerry presidential campaign. Overall, Democratic state parties made little progress improving their hard money fundraising even though BCRA was crafted to help state parties boost hard money income by increasing the contribution limits from $5,000 to $10,000 and raising individual aggregate contributions. In 2004, Democratic organizations, in aggregate, raised 9 percent less for their federal accounts compared with 2000, while Republican state organizations raised 17 percent more. Democratic state organizations in nonbattleground states fared much worse than other state parties, particularly where state laws allowed soft money.

How can one account for these party differences? As mentioned previously, Democratic partisans divided their campaign efforts. Many were simultaneously channeling money for voter contact activity and advertising through 527 organizations as well as state parties. It appears that the Democratic state parties may have suffered from this competition with outside organizations. Republicans, in contrast, appeared to focus more of their financial activity within the party structure.

Another possible explanation for the relatively poor Democratic performance is that the "federalizing" of campaign finance hurt Democrats in the states more than Republicans. Data from previous elections have shown that Democratic committees have been more reliant on soft money than Republican committees. While state parties may continue to spend some soft money for activities, BCRA greatly restricts its uses for any campaigning that might be construed as federal election activity.

Thus, it appears that spending restrictions, such as soft money caps, have made it more difficult for Democrats to keep pace with Republicans in the states, at least in the short term. For several election cycles, Republican parties have invested in direct mail fundraising operations, which take time to bear fruit. The Democrats may plausibly catch up soon given the success of low-cost Internet fundraising in the last election cycle. However, the Republican state parties are currently in a better position to take advantage of a campaign finance system that encourages hard money donations, given their more extensive donor lists.

The future success of Democratic state parties may hinge on whether the potential pool of major Democratic donors is large enough for these committees to compete effectively against the aggressive tactics of the national parties, presidential committees, and 527 organizations.

HOW DID STATE PARTIES SPEND FUNDS?

One hope of BCRA was to shift the party emphasis from advertising to more spending on grassroots and voter contacts. If soft money was no longer available for ads, then the assumption was that political parties would invest more money in the ground campaign. Even before passage of BCRA, David Magleby and his team of scholars observing tightly contested congressional elections noted that political parties and interest groups have been moving in the direction of emphasizing more voter contacts rather than relying so much on television advertising (Magleby 2002b). BCRA may have spurred this trend although it is difficult to determine the independent effect of this new law on party grassroots activity.

As for media activity, the data in figures 4.3a and 4.3b show dramatically that BCRA eliminated advertising by state political parties mentioning federal candidates. Republican state parties spent $97 million on such media advertising in

Figure 4.3a Republican State Party Spending, 2000 vs. 2004

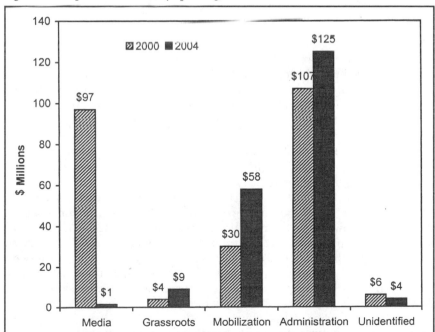

Figure 4.3b Democratic State Party Spending, 2000 vs. 2004

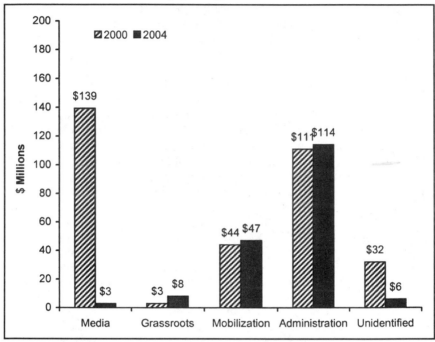

Source: Federal Election Commission.

2000 but a scant $1.3 million in 2004 (figure 4.3a). Democrats invested $139 million in 2000 but only accounted for $3.2 million state-based advertising in 2004 (figure 4.3b). In short, state parties are no longer in the business of advertising in federal elections. The elimination of soft money "issue ads" that supported or opposed federal candidates was a clear goal of BCRA, and it appears that it succeeded.

Did the disappearance of candidate-specific advertising translate into more spending in the ground campaign? For Republicans, it did. They increased their spending on mobilizing voters from $30 to $58 million for a net gain of $28 million. They also increased spending by $4.6 million on grassroots activity, such as volunteer-based rallies and handing out campaign paraphernalia (or "chum"), which includes lawn signs, bumper stickers, and pins. The Democrats kept pace with spending in their ground campaign of 2000, spending $46.6 million in 2004, which is roughly the same as the previous election. Their spending on lawn signs, bumper stickers, and other party hoopla increased from $3.0 to $8.4 million. While Democrats held to previous levels of spending in these categories, these data show that the Republican state parties were able to outspend Democrats on mobilization and grass roots combined by more than $12 million. The Republican surge in 2004 is especially salient given that they were *outspent* by Democrats in these two voter contact categories in 2000 ($34 million to $47 million).

These findings correspond to postelection comments by party operatives that Republicans outperformed Democrats in mobilizing voters, which was long thought to be an advantage for Democrats. However, these figures do not take into consideration the significant efforts by Democratic-leaning 527 organizations to get voters to the polls. The data from this analysis and that of chapter 5 show that the parties pursued different strategies in 2004. Democrats tended to rely more on outside groups, while Republicans beefed up their operations through the political parties. The Republican loss of state party advertising under BCRA translated into gains in voter mobilization in 2004. For Democrats, the gains were slight.

The spending on administration suggests that Republican state party operations may be a bit larger than Democratic organizations, but not by much. Republican operations spent roughly $125 million on administration and overhead while Democrats spent about $114 million. Administrative costs for Republicans increased by almost $20 million, which may be related to the increased costs of fundraising in pursuit of hard money.[7] The Democratic state parties increased their spending slightly from $111 million to $114 million. The apparent stability of Democratic operations is plausibly an artifact of the data, since the numbers from 2000 showed $31 million in "unidentified" expenditures. If these unidentified sums were mostly related to administrative costs, then the Democrats spent considerably less on administration and overhead in 2004 than in 2000. Overall, however, it appears that both sets of state parties maintained their operations at similar levels to the previous presidential cycle. The GOP state organizations expanded their operations while Democratic organizations either stayed the same or lost some ground.

TARGETING OF PARTY EXPENDITURES

As in previous election cycles, party funds are spent primarily in battleground states. Table 4.2 shows that the top five spenders among Republican state parties were Florida, California, Pennsylvania, Ohio, and Minnesota, in that order. These states accounted for one-third of all funds spent by the fifty Republican parties (and reported to the FEC). On the Democratic side, the five biggest spenders were Florida, Michigan, California, Ohio, and Pennsylvania. These also accounted for one-third of all state party spending. The concentration of funds in just a few states has not changed much since 2000. In that election year Democrats spent 30 percent of their funds in just five states, while Republicans spent roughly 40 percent. The median spending level for Republican state parties in 2004 was greater than for Democrats ($2.9 million versus $2.4 million). While these differences are not large, it is interesting to note that the Republicans, who have spread spending more in 2004 than in 2000, made gains in the popular vote for the presidential election. Unlike the 2000 elections, George W. Bush won the popular vote in the 2004 elections. Democrats, in contrast, concentrated their

Table 4.2   Highest State Party Spenders Reported to the FEC, 2004

	Rank	State	Expenditures ($ millions)
Republicans			
	1	FL	$ 23.3
	2	CA	$ 15.7
	3	PA	$ 10.2
	4	OH	$ 9.7
	5	MN	$ 9.3
Top 5 Total			$ 68.1
50 state total			$201.9
% top 5			34%
50 state avg			$ 4.0
50 state median			$ 2.9
Democrats			
	1	FL	$ 15.8
	2	MI	$ 15.6
	3	CA	$ 12.3
	4	OH	$ 11.4
	5	PA	$ 10.2
Top 5 Total			$ 65.3
50 state total			$190.8
% top 5			34%
50 state avg			$ 3.8
50 state median			$ 2.4

Source: Federal Election Commission.

funds more in 2004, and their candidate fared worse in the percentage of the popular vote.

While the Democrats spent about the same amount as Republicans in Ohio and Pennsylvania, they were overwhelmed by Republican spending in Florida. Here, Republicans spent $23.3 million compared to Democratic spending of $15.8 million. The party differences may account, in part, for the relatively poor results in Florida for Democrats. It is important to keep in mind, however, that Democratic-leaning 527 organizations were active in all of these states. For this reason, it is quite possible that pro-Democratic spending exceeded pro-Republican spending in all of these states. On the other hand, Democratic 527s were hampered by their inability to coordinate their efforts with the state party organizations and presidential candidates. The organizational dilemma on the Democratic side may have made grassroots spending less efficient than for Republicans.

It is not clear why the California Republican Party spent so much money in the 2004 election, given that this was not a battleground state. The Bush reelection team may have been hoping to diminish the vote margins in the state so that the president would win the popular vote. Or some of these funds may have been related to the gubernatorial recall election in 2003. The Republicans had high hopes for taking Minnesota, which accounts for the $9.3 million that was spent in that state (the Minnesota Democrats spent about $7 million). The Democrats, in contrast, were worried about losing Michigan where they invested $15.6 million through the state party—about the same amount they spent in Florida. Republican state party spending was only $7 million in this state, suggesting that they did not seriously think they could win the electoral votes, even though they forced the Democrats to spend a lot here.

CONCLUSION

Based on this analysis of party expenditures, it appears that BCRA led to three critical changes for parties in the states. First, these parties underwent a radical transition in federal elections from funding based on a mix of soft and hard money to one that is based overwhelmingly on hard money. Less than 17 percent of money reported to the FEC by state parties was soft money, compared to 62 percent in 2000. By this measure, BCRA was phenomenally successful at getting soft money out of federal political campaigns, even at the state level where parties might have availed themselves of opportunities to use soft money. There is no guarantee, however, that the situation will remain this way in future elections as state parties become more familiar with BCRA and discover easier methods to use soft money. In the 2004 elections, it appears the parties made a decision to focus mainly on raising and spending hard money to avoid any confusion about what they could do with their funds. The definition of federal election activity was sufficiently broad to discourage parties from concentrating on raising soft money.

The dearth of party soft money may also be related to the supply side of the equation. Many donors appeared wary of giving soft money to state parties in this first election cycle, particularly corporate donors (Riskind 2004). But among those ready and willing, the parties faced competition from 527 organizations. Indeed, on the Democratic side, partisan donors were cued to give soft money to 527 organizations rather than state parties. As mentioned in chapter 5, party leaders like Bill Clinton encouraged this partition when meeting with major donors. As donors and political committees adapt to BCRA, this partition may break down, with state parties drawing soft money again for federal election activity through Levin accounts or learning how to use nonfederal accounts to pursue federal election objectives.[8] In 2004 Levin funds accounted for only a very small fraction of total state party spending. Most parties decided these funds were too complicated to administer, and there was a sense that such funds were not nearly as useful as hard money since they had to be applied solely to volunteer generic campaign activity.[9]

A second dramatic change under BCRA was the disappearance of candidate-specific ads in federal elections by state political parties. In the 2000 cycle, state parties spent an estimated $236 million on such ads but only $4 million on any kind of broadcast media activity in 2004 (La Raja 2003a). By eliminating national party soft money, BCRA effectively ended the decade-long practice of state parties using national party transfers to air election-related advertising. Instead, national parties kept their hard dollars to run independent advertisements, either as coordinated or independent expenditures (see chapter 3). One important consequence of the ban on national party soft money is that political spending in federal elections is now concentrated heavily at the national level. The shift from state to national party spending is primarily a function of national committees choosing to pay directly for political advertising with hard money in 2004 rather than funnel soft money to state parties for this purpose as occurred in 2000.

While state parties are no longer venues for federal election-related advertising, they continue to be engaged in other aspects of federal election activity at levels similar to those in 2000. Both parties at the state level increased their hard money spending to support campaign activities. It is clear, however, that Republicans pulled ahead in 2004, which marks the third significant effect of BCRA. Republicans at the state level appear more robust under the hard money system produced by the new campaign finance law. Not only did Republicans increase their hard money fundraising by almost 17 percent, they spent an additional $43 million in 2004 on voter mobilization and grass roots compared with 2000. In contrast, Democratic activity in these same areas declined by $7 million since the previous election.

The fact that Democrats found the transition to BCRA somewhat more difficult is not surprising since they relied previously on soft money more heavily than Republicans. Moreover, Democratic national committees tended to invest less in the past in building their state parties than Republicans. As a result, in 2004 the Democratic state parties started from a weaker position. They also started preparations later than Republicans since they were the out party conducting a highly contested nomination. BCRA may also have contributed to the delay. Given the complexity of the law, some Democrats were not even sure they would be running voter mobilization campaigns out of the state party, even in key battleground states like Pennsylvania and Florida. By the time state parties began to muster their field organizations for the 2004 election, much of the talent and money had already been recruited by the 527 organizations (Katz 2004).

While this first election has given a sense of the party response to the new law, there is much we do not yet know. We do not have a clear understanding about how federal campaign finance laws affected financing and strategies for nonfederal elections. Future research might explore data on nonfederal financing for the 2000 and 2004 state elections compiled by the Institute on Money in State Politics. Given the scope of the definition of federal election activity, it is possible that many state level races were affected, particularly in states where laws differed significantly from BCRA. By definition, federal election activity includes generic voter contacts that require spending with federal money. To what extent did state parties alter strategies to mobilize voters for state elections? Did they spend nonfederal money for this purpose, or was voter mobilization all rolled into one campaign funded with hard money?

Another outstanding question is the extent to which state parties continued the practice that had been growing before BCRA of farming out their field operations to consultants recommended by the national parties, particularly those based in Washington. Were the national parties still exercising direction over state parties as much as in previous elections? National parties continued to send hard money transfers to state parties in this election—not as much—but they may have used this money as leverage in getting state parties to hire consultants they preferred. It is also worth noting that the national committees appeared to run much of their campaign efforts directly from Washington. I estimate conservatively that the RNC and National Republican Congressional Committee (NRCC) spent about $172 million on voter mobilization and direct mail activities, while the Democratic National Committee (DNC) and Democratic Congressional Campaign Committee (DCCC) spent roughly $80 million. A great deal of this was direct mail, which was also intended for fundraising purposes as well.

Will the national committees continue to operate centrally from Washington or will more dollars flow toward state parties in 2006 and 2008? This is a particular concern for Democrats who still lag behind the Republicans in the size and sophistication of the state committees. In 2004, Republicans expanded on organizational models tested during the 2002 elections to recruit networks of volunteers who would mobilize their friends and neighbors. This model harkens back to the urban ward-based schemes of the party machines, though it is now designed for middle class voters in suburban communities. It will be interesting to see which strategy the Democrats pursue in 2006 and 2008 to counter the Republican organization in the states. In 2004, they pursued a dual strategy of deploying both state parties and 527 organizations to mobilize voters. They relied heavily on outside groups in battleground states as a way to use soft money because they feared being overwhelmed by Republicans under the hard money regime of BCRA. The dual strategy may have created more problems than it was worth for Democrats. The parties could not communicate under the coordination rules designated by BCRA. The regulatory fire wall that prevented Democratic state parties and partisan 527s from communicating may have muddied the Democratic message or made the GOTV operations less efficient than for Republicans (Carney 2004c).

From the Democratic perspective, the effects of BCRA on fundraising may be less problematic than its effects on putting together a coherent partisan operation. Will the Democrats continue to encourage the outside strategy of using 527s, or will they seek to build state parties? Soon after the election, pressure mounted from state party chairs to pick a leader at the DNC who is committed to helping build parties in the states (Nichols 2004). Howard Dean emerged as the first choice among many state party officials, in part, because he promised to use his successful fundraising experience to help invest in state and local party building. The intense lobbying by party officials in the states suggests that the national party did not invest its hard money in building up the state organizations in 2004.

One dilemma facing a party that wants to build organizations in the states—including third parties—is that it is difficult to raise money off-cycle for such investments. Creating the infrastructure for mobilizing voters takes enormous investments in time and money. Partisans need to begin this process well before the nominees are selected for the presidential contest. Will Republican and Democratic donors feel motivated to give money early to pursue these tasks?

Another question concerns the commitment of national committees to building parties in the states, even if they raise more hard money. National parties may have an incentive to build the party in future battleground states, but these long-term investments involve considerable short-term risks. Will they use precious hard money early in the process for organization building when it might make them lose an opportunity to inject money into a campaign later in the election cycle?

Raising hard money for party building will mean that the fundraising season might be less cyclical than previously. To have money early enough to make a difference in building organizational infrastructure, party fundraisers must seek donors well before the election season begins. Previous to the implementation of BCRA, the Democrats raised soft money during the off-season from wealthy donors like Haim Saban, the Power Rangers tycoon, who gave the national party funds to rebuild party headquarters in Washington and improve party technology. Under BCRA, they cannot repeat this strategy for rebuilding the state parties.

Party officials acknowledge that the hard money regime makes them think about ways of keeping donors involved in the off years. Jack Oliver, Finance Chair of the RNC, said during an election postmortem at the Campaign Finance Institute that "we have to think of ways to keep them engaged" (Oliver 2005). Thus, to raise funds in off-election years may require an ongoing campaign to stimulate the partisan base to give money. Likely, this will mean publicizing hot-button issues to make core partisan supporters receptive to party fundraising appeals, even when the election is more than a year away. Should this happen we can expect political parties to compete more effectively with a host of interest groups for ideologically interested donors. This dynamic, however, may contribute to the appearance of greater party polarization as party fundraisers seek to exploit ideological positions to raise additional funds early in the process.

NOTES

I would like to thank Bob Biersack and other staff at the Federal Election Commission for helping make these data available.

   1. The calculation is based on data provided by the Federal Election Commission. See figure 4.1.

   2. The Federal Election Commission allows state parties to pay for administration and overhead with fixed ratios of hard and soft money, based on the relative number of federal and state candidates on the state ballot.

3. The records for state level spending have recently been compiled by the Center for Public Integrity. These records became available too late for a thorough analysis in this chapter. Some of the aggregate financial figures, however, are reported later in this chapter.

4. In 2004, however, national committees had weaker incentives to send hard dollars—the only dollars they had—to state parties to fund advertisements. Instead, national committees spent these funds directly on advertising, either in coordination with the candidate or as independent expenditures. This explains, in part, why party spending surged among the national committees.

5. These estimates of spending on advertisements are based on the author's data, some of which are reported in Raymond J. La Raja, "State Parties and Soft Money: How Much Party Building?" (La Raja 2003a). See figures 4.3a and 4.3b.

6. This figure does not include other transfers from the Kerry presidential campaign committee, which totaled about $40 million according to the Federal Election Commission.

7. The administrative category does not reflect all spending on fundraising. The mobilization category includes direct mail, which is also an important tool for raising money.

8. For example, state party operatives (who asked to remain anonymous) explained how nonfederal funds for voter mobilization were moved into "target rich" state legislative races, which would also help the federal part of the ticket.

9. Telephone interview with Neil Reiff (Reiff 2004). National parties cannot work with state and local parties to raise and spend Levin funds. Moreover, Levin funded activity cannot reference a clearly identified candidate for federal office, and the activity may not be conducted through broadcasting, cable, or satellite communications.

II

INTEREST GROUPS AND ADVOCACY ORGANIZATIONS

5

BCRA and the 527 Groups

Stephen R. Weissman and Ruth Hassan

In the wake of the 2004 election, press commentary suggested that rising "527 groups" had undermined the 2002 Bipartisan Campaign Reform Act's ban on unlimited corporate, union, and individual contributions to political parties and candidates. According to the *National Journal*, backers of the new law who had "sought to tamp down dire warnings" that close to $500 million in banned soft money "would simply migrate from the parties to 527 organizations" were now "singing a different tune" (Carney 2004a). A *New York Times* editorial lamented, "No sooner had the [campaign finance reform] bill become law than party financiers found a loophole and created groups known as 527s, after the tax-code section that regulated them" (*New York Times* 2004c). The Federal Election Commission (FEC) had refused to subject 527s to contribution restrictions so long as their stirring campaign ads and voter mobilization programs steered clear of formal candidate endorsements such as "vote for" and "vote against." The result, reported the *Washington Post*, was a new pattern of soft money giving, with "corporate chieftains and companies such as Microsoft, Boeing, and General Electric" displaced as "key contributors" by "two dozen superwealthy and largely unknown men and women . . . each giving more than $1 million" (Grimaldi and Edsall 2004). Billionaire George Soros would top the list at $24 million.

While there is considerable truth in this emerging portrait, it is vastly incomplete and significantly distorted. Deeper analysis reveals that while 527 soft money was important in 2004, new 527 dollars did not replace most of the party soft money banned by BCRA. In addition, BCRA eradicated a significant sum of soft money collected by congressional "leaders" via 527 accounts. The simple image of Republican-created vs. Democratic-created 527s overlooks important political distinctions, particularly between groups that existed before BCRA and those that were constructed afterwards. It also understates the degree to which many of these partisan ties developed subsequent to the act of creation and became institutionalized.

Furthermore, the press's focus on about two dozen big 527 donors has distracted attention from broader 527 fundraising trends between 2002 and 2004 and what they portend in the future. These trends include a remarkable jump in trade union contributions, both stagnation and transformation in business giving, and, most important, a cross-sector increase in the willingness of donors to contribute at high levels. Analysis of the donors who provided the bulk of individual contributions in the last two election cycles reveals that they were mainly drawn from the ranks of individual soft money donors to parties. Yet it also shows that these ex-soft money donors gave far more to 527s in 2004 than they had previously given as soft money to parties. We conclude that while 2004 was the year in which small donors began to alter the financing of presidential campaigns, it was also one in which the unprecedented generosity of ex-party soft money donors demonstrated the potential for dramatic future expansion of 527 activities.

527S REPLACED SOME, BUT NOT THE MAJORITY, OF SOFT MONEY

In order to discover whether 527 money replaced traditional soft money in 2004, we had to determine how much the 527s received for federal elections in 2004 compared to 2002. In pursuing our research we were aware that some public discussion of 527 group finances had inflated the numbers by encompassing groups oriented to state elections—such as the Democratic and Republican Governors' Associations—and some had deflated the numbers by omitting labor union 527s with extensive federal activities.[1]

Limiting our analysis to 527s that were primarily or very substantially involved in federal elections, including those controlled by federal officeholders and candidates, we used an electronic database on 527 finances in the 2002 cycle provided by the Center for Public Integrity and electronic data on the 2004 cycle from the Internal Revenue Service 527 groups' website. To determine which groups were federal, we examined how they spent their money and described or presented their activities. The overwhelming majority of our eventual "federal" 527s were pretty thoroughly committed to federal races. Several others, mainly some of the labor union 527s, were heavily involved but also did substantial state and local work. We included a labor union 527 among our federal 527s only if we were able to clearly attribute *at least* a third of its total expenditures to specific federal elections. This is a conservative estimate because the IRS does not require that 527 expenditures for administration, personnel, media, and state party assistance be identified by specific election. Based on both the available data and statements by major union representatives, we are confident that a substantial majority of the $89 million reported spent by our eight union federal 527s in 2004 (as of December 12) went for federal elections.[2]

We restricted our analysis to federal 527s that reported at least $200,000 in donations in either the 2002 or 2004 election cycles, which includes almost all of the money that went into our federal 527s.[3] While it is possible that our data are incomplete because some 527s are not complying with federal financial reporting requirements, we found only one major instance in 2004. This was Moving America Forward, a political action committee (PAC) headed by Bill Richardson, the Governor of New Mexico and Chairman of the Democratic Convention. This group raised at least $2.9 million and, by its own account, was involved in some partisan voter mobilization efforts in federal as well as state and local contests in several presidential "battleground" states. It reported its finances only to the state of New Mexico (Armendariz 2004; Richardson 2004; Anderson 2004; Couch 2004). In a phone communication with the Campaign Finance Institute (CFI), Moving America Forward's counsel asserted that it was exempt from federal reporting under a provision of the law that, to the contrary, only excuses groups that are "solely" aiding the election of "any individual to any State or local public office . . . or political organization" (Public Law 107-276).[4]

Total Activity

After accounting for duplication due to intergroup transfers, we found that total contributions to federal 527s rose from $151 million in 2002 (including $37 million for soft money accounts of congressional "leadership PACs" later abolished by BCRA) to $424 million in 2004—an increase of $273 million. It is clear that there was a significant, post-BCRA increase in contributions to these non-party soft money vehicles. However, the national parties raised $496 million in soft money in the 2002 cycle; and state parties raised an estimated $95 million in soft money for federal elections in the same cycle.[5] This made a total of $591 million in soft money abolished by BCRA. But since the 527s raised only $273 million more in 2004 than in the last year of party and candidate soft money, this 527 money failed to replace $318 million of the $591 million.

- Pre-BCRA Party Soft Money   − $591 million
- Post-BCRA *Increase* in Federal 527 Soft Money   − $273 million
- Post-BCRA *Decrease* in Total Soft Money   − $318 million

But even this figure overestimates the 527s' importance in substituting for traditional soft money. National party soft money receipts had tripled between 1992 and 1996 and doubled from 2000–2004. And congressional leadership PAC soft money was also growing rapidly. There is little doubt that considerably more soft money than $591 million would have been collected for the 2004 elections in the absence of BCRA. This judgment is reinforced by the vast expansion of corporate and other soft money giving to party-connected "host committees" for the 2004 presidential nominating conventions (an increase from $56 million to $138 million since 2000), as well as the unanticipated high levels of donations to 527s by ex-soft money donors in 2004 that we explore below. In sum, BCRA made a great deal of difference in the amount of soft money available in 2004.

We should also be cautious about attributing all of the increase in 527 fund-raising from 2002 to 2004 to the post-BCRA environment. With the added cost of a presidential election in 2004, 527 groups might have increased their receipts over 2002 anyway. And some of the increased contributions may have also resulted from the unusual passion the presidential contest election inspired, which appears to have been associated with large increases in campaign giving generally.

All of the subsequent analysis of 527s in 2004 in this chapter is based on nearly final contributions and expenditures data made available by the IRS by December 12, 2004. The data cover $405 million of the $424 million raised during the full cycle and encompass all the relevant 527s except for the following, which reported raising approximately $5 million very late in the cycle: America Votes 2004, Colorado Conservative Voters, LCV II, Mainstream 2004, Reclaim Our Democracy, Republican National Lawyers, Save American Medicine, and The NEA Fund for Children and Public Education.

Tables 5.3 and 5.4 (see appendix) list federal 527s active in 2002 (with a separate subcategory for the soft money branches of leadership PACs) and 2004 along with their contributions and expenditures. The tables indicate which of the 527s were largely oriented to supporting Democrats or Republicans. After adjusting for transfers (mainly by the pro-Democratic Joint Victory Campaign in 2004, which served as the fundraising arm for America Coming Together and The Media Fund), the Democrats held major advantages in net contributions during both cycles ($106-$44 million in '02 and $321-$84 million in '04). The nearly four-to-one funding ratio in favor of the Democrats in 2004 is even higher than the three-to-one ratio that would have been obtained in '02 ($85-$29 million) without the now abolished leadership PACs.

"REPEATERS" AND "FIRST TIMERS" IN 2004

The 527 groups active in 2004 may be usefully divided into two categories. "Repeaters" (twenty-nine groups) were active in both the 2002 and 2004 cycles, while "First Timers" were active only in 2004 (fifty-one groups). See tables 5.5 and 5.6 in the appendix for details on these groups and their contributions.

These categories were also distinguished by their political characteristics. As the tables indicate, sponsors of twenty-two of the twenty-nine Repeaters groups also sponsored political action committees that contributed to candidates.[6] In their relationships to these entities as well as their political self-definitions, Repeaters generally represented relatively stable, more deeply rooted and longer term political interests. Some groups were associated with broad issue constituencies. Examples included the pro-free market Club for Growth, environmental organizations like the Sierra Club, and the labor unions. Other groups were anchored in issue-based party factions. Among these were EMILY's List, which supports Democratic pro-choice women candidates, and two centrist groups, the Republican Leadership Council and New Democratic Network (NDN).

In contrast, only seven of fifty-one First Timers in 2004 had associated PACs. (The largest First Timer, the pro-Democratic America Coming Together [ACT] had a PAC, but it was of slight importance. For most of the cycle, ACT expended just 2 percent of its funds through its "hard money" PAC account). First Timers mainly represented relatively transient or recently organized party or candidate interests. A prominent First Timer was Swift Boat Vets and POWs for Truth organized by veterans critical of Democratic presidential candidate John Kerry's Vietnam War performance. Other major groups included Citizens for a Strong Senate, established by former aides to Democratic Vice Presidential candidate John Edwards and active in several Senate races; The Media Fund, which was formed to promote the Democratic presidential candidate; the pro-Bush Progress for America, organized by former Bush campaign officials and consultants; and Americans for Jobs, an especially short-lived "drive-by" 527 that ran ads ambushing Democratic presidential aspirant Howard Dean shortly before the Iowa caucuses.

In 2004, as figure 5.1 illustrates, after adjusting for intergroup transfers, Repeaters raised $131 million (up from $96 million in 2002), but First Timers held sway with an imposing $274 million.

Figure 5.1 Federal 527s in 2004: Repeaters vs. First Timers

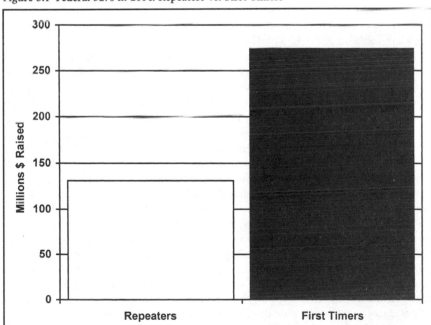

Among Repeaters, some groups did better in fundraising in 2004 and some did worse, as the percentage increases and decreases in table 5.5 show (see appendix). Large dollar increases were recorded by Service Employees International Union (SEIU), American Federation of State, County, and Municipal Employees (AFSCME), 21st Century Democrats, Club for Growth Inc., League of Conservation Voters, National Association of Realtors, National Federation of Republican Women, NDN, Progressive Majority, Planned Parenthood, and the Sierra Club. Groups showing large decreases included Communication Workers of America (CWA), College Republican National Committee, Republican Leadership Council, Republican Main Street Partnership, and the United Food and Commercial Workers Union (UFCW).

So while many observers have looked at the 2004 election through the prism of the biggest fundraisers—First Timer groups like America Coming Together and The Media Fund on the Democratic side and Swift Boat Vets, POWs for Truth, and Progress for America on the Republican one—it is important to remember that the Repeaters are also a very important part of the 527 picture.

PARTIES, PRESIDENTIAL CAMPAIGNS, AND THE NEW 527s

During the 2004 cycle, the two major parties, including their leading paid consultants and active notables, were involved, in varying degrees, in the creation, operation, or funding of several prominent 527 groups. The same was true of the Bush campaign and its associates. We reached this conclusion based on both press reports (which are cited in endnotes) and confidential interviews with knowledgeable individuals. The 527s in question included the largest fundraisers and spenders: America Coming Together and The Media Fund on the Democratic side and Progress for America on the Republican one. Other Democratic groups—America Votes and Grassroots Democrats—also benefited from party support. After accounting for transfers, the above groups raised a total of $186 million, or 46 percent of the $405 million in total 527 funds—but 67 percent of the $274 million in total First Timer funds.

Although parties and campaigns, and their close associates, helped foster major 527 groups, there is no available evidence that they engaged in illegal requests for soft money or illegal coordinated communications. On the contrary, the individuals involved in supporting the 527s appear to have been rather scrupulous in following the letter of the law and its regulations, which forbade parties, candidates, and their agents after November 6, 2002, from requesting or spending soft money in federal elections. After that date, the key supporters of 527s defined their roles publicly as independent of party and campaign structures, took steps to formally separate themselves (or, more precisely, parts of themselves) from close financial relationships with such structures, and seem to have refrained from coordinating their communications with the political campaigns. However, there is little doubt that *both before and after November 6, 2002,* the parties, the Bush campaign, and their close associates were at times complicit in, and actively facilitated, the rise of 527s. They acted through:

- permissiveness toward the activism of paid consultants with high standing and identification in both parties;
- the fundraising clout of a former president (Bill Clinton) who was closely linked to his party's national committee and presidential candidate; and
- various official winks and nods.

The area in which the parties and campaigns were most influential was fundraising.

Democrats

The Democratic effort began when Democratic National Committee (DNC) Chairman Terry McAuliffe established a Task Force on BCRA, which really got going when the law passed in 2002. Members included Harold Ickes, a paid adviser to McAuliffe, President Clinton's former Deputy Chief of Staff and a member of the DNC's Executive Committee; Minyon Moore, DNC Chief Operating Officer; Josh Wachs, DNC Chief of Staff; Joe Sandler, DNC counsel; Michael Whouley, a leading Democratic consultant; and former White House officials John Podesta and Doug Sosnik (Edsall 2002). Ickes thought the Democratic Party was far behind the Republicans in adopting technologies to attract hard rather than newly banned soft money. And he believed the Democratic 2004 presidential nominee would participate in the public primary financing system with its spending ceilings, leaving that candidate broke by spring. At the same time, President Bush would opt out of the public system and be flush with private contributions. The eventual outgrowth of the Task Force's deliberations was two 527 groups, The Media Fund and Grassroots Democrats. At a gathering of Democratic donors in October 2002, McAuliffe discussed Ickes' plans for The Media Fund. He also appealed for financial aid to a new organization to be established by Joe Carmichael, president of the DNC's Association of State Democratic Chairs (Stone 2002; Van Natta and Oppel 2002). This would meet the need for an organization outside the national party that could relate to state parties, give them guidance, and help them raise limited "Levin funds" and other soft money. Ickes would subsequently head up The Media Fund and help select the board and staff of Grassroots Democrats, led by Carmichael after resigning his DNC position.

The following month—with BCRA now in effect—Ickes attended a meeting at a Washington restaurant of pro-Democratic interest groups. It was convoked by Gina Glantz, Assistant to the President of the SEIU and former Campaign Manager for Bill Bradley's presidential campaign. Others in attendance included SEIU President Andrew Stern, former AFL-CIO Political Director Steve Rosenthal, EMILY's List President Ellen Malcolm (also on the DNC Executive Committee and a veteran of many "coordinated campaigns" with national and state Democratic committees), and Sierra Club Executive Director Carl Pope. The discussion concerned "taking on Bush" in the 2004 election where the Republicans seemed to enjoy a large financial advantage. Rosenthal and Stern discussed plans for a new, labor-backed organization that would emphasize ground operations (as opposed to TV and radio "air wars"). Participants also focused on the need to better coordinate interest group campaign operations (Cummings 2003). Ickes, who had obtained legal advice before attending this first post-BCRA meeting, was dropping the part of his portfolio with McAuliffe and the DNC that concerned campaign finance but continuing his consultancy on such matters as the party convention, nominating rules, and political advice. The consultancy would last until February 2004. (In 2002, The Ickes and Enright Group received $112,521 from the DNC through November 7. In 2003–2004, it received $123,860 from March 13, 2003, through February 18, 2004.)[7]

Ickes also attended a larger follow-up meeting in early May 2003, which discussed the establishment of America Votes to avoid duplication of effort by politically active groups. In reaction to a split between Rosenthal's Partnership for American Families and some of its previous labor backers, the group also contemplated creation of a new, broader-based voter mobilization group called America Coming Together (ACT) (Edsall 2003b).

As plans developed for ACT and America Votes, McAuliffe was "probably" kept informed by some participants and was formerly notified by Malcolm before the group was unveiled in August. By that time businessmen George Soros and Peter Lewis—armed with a brief from two consultants who had been recommended by ex-DNC BCRA Task Force Member John Podesta—had decided to pledge an initial $20 million to seed the new groups on the condition that ACT centralize its operations under Rosenthal and expand its planned ground-war activities from just a few to as many as seventeen "battleground" states. Malcolm and Ickes would soon lead a broad fundraising effort for both ACT and The Media Fund through still another 527 group called the Joint Victory Campaign (Cummings 2003; Mayer 2004; Stone and Barnes 2003).

Malcolm had "credibility" with certain cause-oriented donors because of her success as the leader of EMILY's List, which supported pro-choice Democratic women. Ickes' credibility flowed from his long Democratic political history and ties with Democratic Party leaders (he was the "political hack," joked one of his admirers). To engage potential donors, Malcolm and Ickes explained their well thought out campaign plans and their long-term goal of investing not just in an election but also in building a campaign infrastructure for the party. They felt they were giving the donors much more information than the party had and were therefore more accountable to them. They also assured many donors of their relationship to the party and the campaigns. Their message was, "We don't talk to the campaigns, are not connected with them, but they know and appreciate us and contributions are part of the public record and they are aware."

It quickly became clear that more political clout was needed with both major categories of potential donors: those, like Soros, seeking to realize "ideological" goals by getting rid of Bush and those interested in "access" to potential decision-makers. (This distinction should not be taken as absolute. Soros, for example, told reporter Jane Mayer, "I would be very happy to advise Kerry, if he's willing to listen to me, and to criticize him, if he isn't. I've been trying to exert some influence over our policies and I hope I'll get a better hearing under Kerry.") (Mayer 2004). It was decided to bring in former President Bill Clinton, who was extremely active in DNC fundraising and spoke "frequently" to Terry McAuliffe, whom he had selected as DNC chief. In other words, Clinton was not only the best-known Democrat but "a major force" in the DNC (VandeHei 2002b, 2003; Kaplan 2002). The goal was "to show the donors this was the real deal," to communicate, "I know them, you can trust them, this is the strategy." In October 2003—the same month in which he starred in party fundraisers in New York and Washington, DC (Theimer 2003; Lakely 2003)—the former president attended a dinner meeting of about fifteen people, mostly potential donors, at Soros's 5th Avenue New York City apartment. He told them that ACT met a critical need and that if ACT had existed in 2000 the Democrats would have won. As one of the 527 group leaders put it, "He koshered us. He gave the donors confidence, both ideological ones and the access ones." Clinton also encouraged about a dozen potential donors to The Media Fund at a meeting in Los Angeles in February 2004, a year in which he energetically raised money for both the DNC and Senator John Kerry's presidential campaign (Stone 2004a; Haberman 2004; Sweet 2004; China Daily 2004; The Frontrunner 2004). The leaders of ACT and The Media Fund were quite visible soliciting party donors and hobnobbing with the party and presidential campaign during the Democratic National Convention in Boston. They set themselves up on the second floor of the Four Seasons Hotel, down the hall from the DNC Finance Division which catered to large donors. Ickes, who was a delegate and member of the DNC Executive Committee, and Malcolm, who had resigned from the Committee when ACT was established, were also visible on the convention floor. Whatever their intentions, such conspicuous cohabitation undoubtedly burnished the groups' perceived identification with the party and presidential campaign (Rutenberg and Justice 2004a; Farhi 2004b).

Republicans

Republican efforts to foster independent groups developed more slowly. They centered at first on a 501(c)(4) advocacy group, Progress for America (PFA), which was doing grassroots work in favor of Bush administration policies. From the beginning this group was closely associated with the Bush administration, the RNC, and their consultants.

PFA was founded in 2001 by Tony Feather, Political Director of the 2000 Bush-Cheney campaign and partner in Feather, Larson, & Synhorst-DCI (FLS-DCI), a campaign consulting firm that worked for the RNC. On its website (www.fls-dci.com), the firm featured a tribute from Karl Rove, Bush's chief political adviser. From 2001 through 2003, PFA itself paid no salaries, benefits, or occupancy costs according to the group's Form 990 annual returns filed with the IRS. To avert a potential legal conflict between FLS-DCI's party and anticipated presidential campaign work and PFA's status as an independent political group, Feather relinquished his leadership of PFA as BCRA came into effect. He chose

Chris LaCivita, former Political Director of the National Republican Senatorial Committee, as the new president. During his service with PFA, LaCivita was a paid contractor with DCI Group, a public affairs and lobbying entity that shared a common partner with FLS-DCI—Tom Synhorst. Like Feather, Synhorst had extensive national Republican political experience, having served as an adviser to Bush-Cheney 2000 and in key roles in the floor operations of the 1996 and 2000 Republican conventions (Cillizza 2003b; Stone 2003).[8]

PFA's LaCivita spent much of 2003 wrestling with the problem of how to achieve the organization's goal of running pro-Republican federal political campaigns through a soft money 501(c)(4) group that was prohibited from having a primary mission of influencing elections. At one point he produced plans to spend about half of PFA's funds on campaign-oriented "issue advocacy" directed to the general public and half on express candidate advocacy directed to an enlarged group of "members." (The notion was that the IRS would not count "internal communications" as "political expenditures.") At PFA's October 2003 Issues Conference, an assemblage of political operatives, lobbyists, and donors was addressed by Ed Gillespie, RNC Chair, Ken Mehlman, Bush-Cheney 2004 Director; and Benjamin Ginsberg, counsel to both PFA and the presidential campaign (Drinkard 2004). The political operatives excused themselves when the question of donations came up.

When LaCivita departed PFA in the spring of 2004 to work on two Republican Senate campaigns, he was succeeded as president by DCI partner Brian McCabe. LaCivita would soon be better known as senior strategist for the anti-Kerry 527 group, Swift Boat Vets and POWs for Truth. The fledgling Swift Boat group had approached PFA for assistance, and the latter had recommended LaCivita. While handling the Swift Boat operation, LaCivita also returned briefly to PFA as a contractor.

By the late spring of 2004, FLS-DCI, the DCI Group, and PFA were all involved in the Bush campaign. FLS-DCI conducted message phone calls and telemarketing, respectively, for the Bush and RNC campaigns for which it was ultimately paid at least $19 million (Edsall and Grimaldi 2004).[9] DCI Group had a small contract for services at the Republican convention. And PFA had decided to organize a pro-Bush 527 in May 2004, following the FEC's decision not to regulate 527s. While each of these organizations was a separate unit with distinctive functions, they also had important relationships. The linchpin was FLS-DCI partner Tom Synhorst. He had established and was a partner in the DCI Group, which frequently used FLS-DCI as a vendor for phone work. Synhorst was also a "strategic adviser" and leading fundraiser for PFA both before and after it moved its campaign work from a 501(c)(4) "advocacy" group to a 527 political organization. Like Harold Ickes, Synhorst maintained that his personal 527 group work was in a separate "silo" from his firm's (FLS-DCI) work for the party and campaign. And like Ickes' efforts, Synhorst's activities were certainly visible to his firm's political clients, and his political relationships were presumably known to many potential 527 donors (Edsall 2004a; Stone 2004b; Getter 2004).[10]

As it sought funds, PFA confronted even more daunting obstacles than ACT and The Media Fund. Not only did the organization, like its Democratic counterparts, lack a long track record, but the Republican National Committee had called upon the FEC to limit the financing of 527s (Bolton 2004b). (President Bush would reiterate this position in reaction to the controversial Swift Boat group attack on Democratic nominee John Kerry (Bumiller and Zernike 2004). Moreover, the corporations that PFA initially looked toward as a main source of funds proved reluctant to contribute, often citing warnings from counsel about the uncertain legality of 527s (Cummings 2004a; Edsall 2004c). In response, PFA hired three "traditional Republican fundraisers." Ensconced at the Ritz-Carlton Hotel during the Republican convention in New York, it succeeded in enlisting both funds and fundraising assistance from two of President Bush's most ardent financiers: Alex Spanos and Dawn Arnall. Most important, it received the ultimate wink and nod from the Republican Party and the Bush campaign.

In a joint statement on May 13, 2004, RNC Chair Ed Gillespie and Bush-Cheney Campaign Chairman Marc Racicot declared that the FEC's inaction on 527s "has given the 'green light' to all non-federal '527s' to forge full steam ahead in their efforts to affect the outcome of this year's Federal elections, and, *in particular, the presidential race* [emphasis added]. . . . The 2004 elections will now be a free-for-all. Groups like the Leadership Forum, Progress for America, the Republican Governors' Association, GOPAC and others now know that they can legally engage in the same way Democrat leaning groups like ACT, The Media Fund, MoveOn, and Moving America Forward have been engaging" (Bush-Cheney Campaign and the Republican National Committee 2004). It should be noted that of the four pro-Republican groups named, the last two were not substantially engaged in federal elections, and the Leadership Forum was not involved in the presidential contest.

The phrasing was careful in avoiding words that the FEC might interpret as illegally "soliciting" and "directing" soft money, but PFA leaders considered the statement an official blessing that was central to their fundraising. As one key strategist commented, "If we weren't on the list, it would have been over. Our message had been we don't like 527s. Then the Republican Party and campaign said, 'Don't fight them anymore.' From there it was all up. We didn't have a Clinton to encourage donors like the Democrats had." PFA viewed its eventual donors as "ideological" supporters of the Bush administration rather than as seekers of special access.

In sum, the parties responded to BCRA in broadly similar ways. They permitted some of their leading political consultants, who were strongly identified with them, to serve their interests by generating new soft money pots. And party officials or politically active notables put the party imprimatur on selected 527 fundraising to reassure potential donors. The Democrats started early and were legally able to use the party apparatus to launch The Media Fund and Grassroots Democrats before BCRA fell into place. Then they forged relations with initiatives by interest groups and party factions. The Republicans got off the ground late, and party and campaign leaders were compelled to issue a careful official statement in order to overcome numerous obstacles. At the end of the day, though, each party committee and at least one presidential campaign were, to a significant degree, identified with a major 527 group (America Coming Together and Progress for America, respectively) that aspired to be active in future campaigns.

THE CHANGING MIX OF 527 DONORS

We analyzed contributions of $5,000 or more to our list of federal 527 groups. These accounted for all but $16,070,872 million of total receipts in 2002 and $15,134,945 million of total receipts in 2004. We discovered that there was a dramatic evolution in the three main categories of 527 donors from 2002 to 2004.[11] Labor union contributions increased from $55 million to $94 million, a major, but frequently overlooked, development. To put it another way, unions gave pro-Democratic 527s about four times as much as billionaire George Soros did. The major increase in labor donations to 527s signified that labor more than made up for the $36 million in soft money it gave (mainly through 527s) to national parties in the 2002 cycle.[12] On the other hand, business donations (meaning those not of individual businessmen but of corporations, trade associations, and individual incorporated entities like lawyers' and doctors' practices) declined from $32 million to $30 million (actually to $26 million if one omits a large contribution by the "Sustainable World Corporation," widely regarded as a nonfunctioning business representing Linda Pritzker, a member of one of the world's wealthiest families) (Wallison 2004). So business contributions to 527s in no way made up for the $216 million in soft money that business entities had given to national parties in the 2002 cycle.[13] The biggest change, though, came in donations by individuals, which rocketed from a mere $37 million to $256 million. Figure 5.2 illustrates all the changes.

Examining these three categories more closely, table 5.7 (see appendix) shows that the jump in union contributions between the two cycles was essentially the work of two large unions that were already giving to 527s: SEIU and AFSCME.

In 2002 a substantial part of labor's money ($21 million out of $55 million) went to labor 527s and was transferred to national and other Democratic Party Committees for federal elections. In 2004, labor's enlarged federal effort consisted mainly of labor 527s making cash transfers and furnishing in-kind assistance to new pro-Democratic 527s, particularly America Coming Together, Grassroots Democrats, The Media Fund, Moving America Forward, The Partnership for America's Families, and Voices for Working Families.

Within the business sector, there was more turbulence despite an overall stagnation in funds. Business donors who had given nearly $15 million of $21 million in business contributions to leadership PACs in 2002 vanished along with the soft money leadership PACs themselves in 2004. Also departing were businesses that had given almost $5 million to both federal organizations and leadership PACs. Making up for those losses, continuing business donors upped their giving from $12 million to $16 million, and more than $13 million more flowed in from new donors.

Contributions from certain categories of business plunged: communications,

Figure 5.2 Federal 527 Donors by Sector, 2002 and 2004 Election Cycles ($ *millions*)

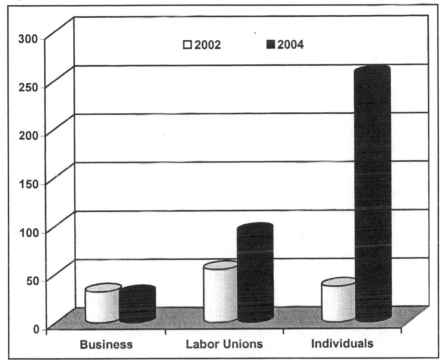

pharmaceutical, insurance, energy and transport corporations especially. Others ascended, including trial lawyers, private holding companies, realtors, and the U.S. Chamber of Commerce. The top recipient of business's donations continued to be the Repeater New Democratic Network. But in 2004 business turned away from previously favored Republican groups such as the Republican Leadership Coalition, Republican Leadership Council, and Republican Main Street Partnership, and toward the National Association of Realtors and newer pro-Republican groups like the November Fund and Progress for America.

Unlike both the business and labor sectors, new donors supplied the brunt of individual contributions in 2004 ($157 million). But continuing donors raised their giving as well: from $18 million to $99 million. Less significantly, donors who had provided $19 million in 2002 abandoned the 527 ship in 2004. There was once again a striking change in the recipients of donations. Of the ten top 527s benefiting from individual contributions in 2002, the first nine were Repeaters; but in 2004, only two of the first eight were Repeaters.

MORE DONORS GAVE AT HIGH LEVELS IN 2004

Probably the most remarkable development between the two election cycles was the increase in the size of top contributions in all three sectors.

Among labor unions the donor base remained relatively stable (rising from forty to forty-six unions). As we have seen, the two main givers (SEIU and AFSCME) were almost entirely responsible for the near doubling of union contributions between 2002 and 2004. As a result, their donations rose from 58 percent ($32 million) to 78 percent ($73 million) of total donations.

Although business giving was stagnant, and the number of businesses giving at least $5,000 fell dramatically (from 1,034 to 361), between 2002 and 2004 the average business contribution rose from $30,286 to $81,886. This was largely the result of increased giving by the top-most supporters. In 2002, it required seventy-eight businesses to generate 50 percent of the total money—in 2004 it took only seven donors.

But the most important change occurred among individuals. This was the sector that mainly powered the 2004 surge in giving to 527s. In 2002, there were 1,232 individuals who provided an average donation of $30,112. But in 2004, 1,887 donors produced an average contribution of $135,805—more than four times as high as 2002, with 50 percent more donors. The amount given by the typical donor didn't change very much: the *median* donation rose from $10,000 to $12,000. The *average* contribution went up dramatically because of the increased generosity of higher end givers in 2004. As table 5.1 indicates, this was overwhelmingly the result of two trends:

- multifold increases since 2002 in the number of donors who were willing to give $100,000 or more, which increased from 66 to 265; and
- the special 2004 role of twenty-four $2 million + donors who provided 56 percent of all individual contributions over $5,000.

What has often been forgotten is that while the top twenty-four donors provided $142 million, other individual large donors (especially $100,000 + ones) gave $114 million. The *general* willingness to give more at the high end was the basis of the expansion of individual giving from $37 million in 2002 to $256 million in 2004.

Table 5.1 Changing Patterns of Individual Giving to Federal 527s

Range of Donation	2002 Cycle			2004 Cycle		
	n	Amount	% of Total	n	Amount	% of Total
$2 Million and Over	0	$0	—	24	$142,497,241	56
$1 Million to $1,999,999	2	2,152,000	6	28	35,216,957	14
$500,000 to $999,999	8	6,132,190	17	25	16,380,500	6
$250,000 to $499,999	13	4,238,550	11	36	12,297,148	5
$100,000 to $249,000	43	5,872,372	16	152	20,360,946	8
$5,000 to $100,000	1,165	18,672,941	50	1,617	29,511,550	12
Total	1,231	37,068,053	100	1,882	256,264,342	100

THE LARGE DONORS GAVE MUCH MORE THAN
PREVIOUS SOFT MONEY DONATIONS

Who exactly were these generous individuals who, along with a few unions, pow-ered the overall boost in 527 finances from one cycle to the other? Do the data show that those who gave big money to 527s in 2002 and 2004 were mainly ex-party soft money donors? Yes. Does the scale of giving in 2004 indicate that such donors were mainly switching their soft money from one legalized vehicle to another? Not at all.

Table 5.2 provides a closer look at the 113 people who donated at least $250,000 to federal 527s in the '04 cycle. These donations accounted for $207 million of the $256 million in $5,000 and over contributions, that is, 81 percent of these donations.

As the table indicates, this group was replete with wealthy players in the pri-vate, corporate economy. (Several of the more modest descriptions under "Employer," though, fail to indicate the donor's economic base. For example, Alice Walton of "Rocking W. Ranch Inc." is a member of the family that owns 38 percent of Wal-Mart; Marian Ware of "Ware Family Office/Retired" is a member of the family that founded American Waterworks and ran it until 2003; Maconda O'Connor, "self/social worker" is the daughter of Houston business icon George Brown; and John Templeton is not only "Templeton Foundation/retired" but a world renowned financial investor who named and owned a major mutual fund.)

The two columns on the right side of the table show that 73 of the 113 large donors in 2004 (65 percent) had indeed been active in the former soft money system. Over the previous two cycles, 2000 and 2002, they had furnished a total of $50 million in soft money to national party committees. (In some instances, attributing to the individual the total soft money contributions of his or her company and those associated with it would have raised contribution levels, but not so much to have significantly changed the overall total.)[14] At the same time, eleven of these seventy-three individuals had given a little over $4 million to 527s in 2002. Yet in 2004 alone, as the table notes, the seventy-three former soft money donors provided $157 million to 527s—three times the combined amount they had given to parties in 2000 and 2002 and 527s in 2002. *Clearly what was happening was not only a shift in their soft money giving—from party to 527—but also a vast escalation in their total donations.*

It is also important to understand that these seventy-three ex-soft money donors, a dozen of whom had given the parties less than $100,000, comprised a relatively small percentage of individual soft money donors in the 2000 and 2002 cycles. According to www.fecinfo.com, there were 516 individuals or couples who gave at least $100,000 in soft money to the parties in 2000 and 319 who did the same in 2002.

It should also be noted, in view of the past predominance of corporate organi-zational party soft money, that only fourteen of the seventy-three large individual donors were specifically tied to the top 500 corporations that donated soft money in either 2000 or 2002.[15]

Table 5.2   Individuals' $250,000 + Contributions to Federal 527s in the 2004 Cycle and Their Recent National Party Soft Money Donations

			Party Soft Money 2000 & 2002	
Name	*Money to 527s*	*Employer*	*Dem*	*Rep*
Soros, George	24,000,000	Soros Fund Management	208,000	
Lewis, Peter	22,545,000	The Progressive Group	75,000	500
Bing, Stephen	13,902,682	Shangri-La Entertainment	7,385,000	
Sandler, Herb & Marion	13,007,959	Golden West Finance Group		
Perry, Bob	8,060,000	Perry Homes		140,000
Arnall, Dawn	5,000,000	Ameriquest Capital	250,000	1,000,000
Spanos, Alex	5,000,000	AG Spanos Companies		866,500
Waitt, Ted	5,000,000	Gateway	87,500	75,000
Pickens, Boone T.	4,600,000	PB Capital		145,000
Perenchio, Jerry/Living Trust	4,000,000	Chartwell Partners LLC		1,231,500
Rappaport, Andrew	3,858,400	August Capital	150,000	
Simmons, Harold	3,700,000	Contran Corp		21,700
Messinger, Alida	3,447,200	None	730,000	
Levy Hinte, Jeanne	3,425,000	Self/Writer		
Pritzker, Linda	3,365,000	Self/Investor		
Eychaner, Fred	3,075,000	Newsweb Corp	8,295,000	
Cullman, Lewis	2,651,000	Self/Philanthropist	6,000	
Walton, Alice	2,600,000	Rocking W Ranch Inc.		100,000
Glaser, Robert	2,229,000	Real Networks Inc.	90,000	
Lindner, Carl H.	2,225,000	American Financial Group	745,000	1,630,000
Varis, Agnes	2,006,000	AgVar Chemicals	808,000	
DeVos, Richard	2,000,000	Amway		425,000
Ragon, Terry	2,000,000	Intersystems		
van Andel, Jay	2,000,000	Alticor		100,000
McHale, Jonathan	1,800,000	Self/Investor		
Singer, Paul	1,785,000	Elliot Capital Advisors		570,500
Harris, John IV	1,660,700	None		
Hunting, John	1,627,000	None/Retired	25,000	
Mcclendon, Aubrey	1,625,000	Chesapeake Energy		
Field, Joseph	1,575,000	Entercom		
McNair, Robert	1,551,000	Palmetto Partners		50,000
Abraham, S. Daniel	1,320,000	Slim Fast Foods	2,543,000	
Rowling, Robert B.	1,250,000	TRT Holdings		
Mattso, Christine	1,200,000	Self/Homemaker	4,300	
Gund, Louise	1,155,000	Self/Philanthropist	1,028,000	
McCormack, Win	1,125,000	Tinhouse	20,000	
Lewis, Daniel	1,100,000	Retired		
Bing, Peter	1,089,257	Self		
Chambers, Anne Cox	1,082,000	Cox Enterprises/Philanthropist	225,000	
Gill, Tim	1,065,000	Gill Foundation	495,700	
Marcus, Bernard	1,050,000	Retired		804,500
Sillerman, Robert	1,050,000	The Sillerman Companies	990,000	
Jensen, G. J.	1,038,000	Housewife		75,000
Brunckhorst, Frank	1,025,000	Boars Head Provisions		
Buell, Susie Tompkins	1,020,000	Self/Retired	344,300	
Ortenberg, A&E Claiborne	1,017,000	Retired		
Rosenthal, Richard	1,007,000	Uptown Arts		

Aronson, Theodore	1,000,000	Aronson, Johnson, Oritz LP		
Carsey, Marcy	1,000,000	Self/Producer		
Clark, James	1,000,000	Self/Investor		
Earhart, Anne Getty	1,000,000	Self/Investor		
Ragon, Susan	1,000,000	Intersystems		
Bacon, Louis	950,000	Moore Capital Management		205,000
Ward, Tom	875,000	Chesapeake Energy		
Dyson, Robert	850,000	DysonKissnerMoran Corp	855,000	
Lewis, Jonathan	821,800	Progressive Insurance		
Huizenga, H. Wayne	820,000	Self/Investor		
Leeds, Gerald & Lilo	805,500	Retired	192,000	
Crow, Harlan	775,000	Crow Holdings		7,500
Lee, Barbara	770,000	Self/Philanthropist	232,000	
Ware, Marian	750,000	Ware Family Office/Retired		345,200
Stephens, Jackson	750,000	EOE Inc.		25,000
Sussman, S. Donald	720,000	Caremi Partners	1,545,000	100,000
Foos, Richard & Shari	662,500	Self/Psychotherapist	85,000	
O'Connor, Maconda	650,000	Self/Social worker		
Gilder, Richard	620,000	Gilder Gagnon Howe & Co. LLC		250,000
Childs, John	590,000	JW Childs Associates		750,000
Ware, Marilyn	550,000	Ware Family Office/Retired		186,800
Snyder, Harold	550,000	HBJ Investments	770,000	
Stephenson, James	550,000	Yancy Brothers Co.		10,000
Recanati, Michael	525,000	Maritime Overseas Corp	50,000	
Templeton, John	520,000	Templeton Foundation/Retired		585,900
McKay, Rob	520,000	McKay Investment Group	15,000	
Lindner, Robert	510,000	United Dairy Farmers		380,000
Colombel, Andrea	500,000	The Trace Foundation		
Hughes, B. Wayne Sr.	500,000	Public Storage Inc		956,200
Nicholas, Peter	500,000	Boston Scientific Corp		
Searle, Dan	500,000	Retired		
Troutt, Kenny	500,000	Mt. Vernon Investment Group		
Kieschnick, Michael	481,030	Working Assets	35,000	
Bass, Anne T.	480,000	Self/Investor		
Schwartz, Bernard	470,000	Loral Space & Comm Ltd	3,536,300	
Benter, William	463,750	ACUSIS LLC		
Bass, Robert	450,000	Keystone		
Corzine, Jon	450,000	US Senator	2,416,000	
Matthews, George	450,000	Retired		
Soros, Jonathan	439,000	Soros Management	50,000	
Burnett, Nancy	400,000	Sea Studios Foundation		
Orr, Susan	400,000	Telosa Software	145,000	
Bonderman, David	370,000	Texas Pacific Group	215,000	
Cofrin, Gladys	360,000	Self/Counselor	35,000	
Bridges, Rutt	350,000	Big Horn Center for Public Policy	30,000	
Maltz, David	332,050	Self/Developer		
Paulson, Wendy Judge	323,000	None/Volunteer NYC Teacher		
Manheimer, Virginia	316,295	Investor		
Day, Robert	300,000	Trust Co of the West		143,700
Entenza, Matthew	300,000	Attorney/Self		
Saunders, Thomas	300,000	Saunders Karp & Megrue		366,000
Schiffrin, Richard	300,000	Schiffrin Barroway LLP	20,000	
Daniels, George	298,503	Daniel Manufactoring Corp		

(continues)

Table 5.2   Continued

Name	Money to 527s	Employer	Party Soft Money 2000 & 2002 Dem	Party Soft Money 2000 & 2002 Rep
Gruener, Garrett	282,915	Alta Partners	75,300	
Bastian, Bruce	277,000	Self/Retired	310,000	
Hogan, Wayne	275,000	PathCanada	290,000	
Resnick, Stewart	275,000	Roll Intern Corp	125,000	
Lieberman, Leonard	263,000	Self/Consultant		
Doerr, John	260,000	Kleiner Perkins Caufield	475,000	
Gilmore, Elizabeth	260,000	Mertz Gilmore Foundation	20,000	
Buttenweiser, Peter	257,535	Buttenweiser & Associates	1,252,500	
Perry, Lisa	257,300	Philanthropist	775,200	
Kendrick, E. G. (Ken)	250,000	Datatel, Inc.		146,900
Powers, William	250,000	PIMCO		300
Schmidt, Wendy	250,000	Homemaker		
Stephens, Warren	250,000	*		
From All Donors (n = 113)			**(n = 46)**	**(n = 32)**
Total	206,990,376		38,054,100	11,693,700
Average Donation	1,831,773		827,263	365,428
Median Donation	820,000		220,000	166,850
From Soft Money Donors (n = 73)				
Total	157,299,562		49,747,800	
Average Donation	2,154,789		681,477	
Median Donation	775,000		208,000	

*No entry.

Table 5.8 (see appendix) profiles the sixty-six individuals who gave at least $100,000 to federal 527s in 2002. They accounted for more than $18 million of $37 million in contributions, that is, 50 percent of the total. Only twenty-three individuals gave at least $250,000 in 2002 (compared to 113 in 2004), and they provided only 34 percent of total individual donations (compared to 81 percent in 2004).

We expected that the forty-two soft money donors among the sixty-six individuals who contributed at least $100,000 to 527s in 2002 would have been less generous than their 2004 successors. After all, the party soft money system was still available to large donors in 2002. And that was the case. This smaller group of party donors had actually given the parties more soft money ($52 million rather than $50 million) over the 2000 and 2002 election cycles than the 2004 cadre. But they generated just $11 million for 527s in 2002—fourteen times less than the 2004 group did.

Without question, a segment of former party individual soft money donors have been the main funders of 527s. However post-BCRA *levels* of giving are not simply explained by the "hydraulic theory" that money, like water, inevitably finds its way around an obstacle. *Most* former individual soft money donors have not given large donations to 527s. But for those who did in 2004, one may say that a river of party soft money has turned into an ocean of 527 money.

THE FUTURE OF 527s

Despite the hard money fundraising success of both major parties in 2004, two of the leading First Timer 527s in 2004, ACT and PFA, indicated they planned to continue on in future federal elections (Cillizza 2004a; Justice 2004b; Cummings 2004b; VandeHei 2005). (ACT subsequently put their plans on hold.) And there are reasons to believe that 527s in general could play even larger roles in future elections than they did in 2004. First, the genie of huge contributions is out of the bottle, and it is unlikely to return, considering past trends in party soft money and convention host committee funding. Secondly, if the legal status of 527s and the relation of some of them to parties become institutionalized, or particular lobbying issues arise, some trade associations and corporations might be persuaded to overcome their current reluctance to provide soft money donations without direct political pressure from candidates. (During the 2000 cycle, a 527 representing the pharmaceutical industry, Citizens for Better Medicare, spent an estimated $65 million.) Thirdly, despite the presence of seventy-three individuals who had given parties soft money among the large 2004 527 contributors, the fundraising potential of ex-soft money donors has hardly been tapped. In 2000 alone, 214 individuals gave the parties at least $200,000 and 516 gave more than $100,000, according to www.fecinfo.com. Even if the passions that propelled campaign donors in 2004 subside somewhat in the nonpresidential year of 2006, they are likely to revive during the presidential contest of 2008.

However, developments in both the federal campaign finance and nonprofit legal regimes spawned the 527 phenomenon, and further changes in policy could influence its future. During the 1996 presidential campaign, a number of 501(c)(5) labor unions, 501(c)(6) trade associations, and 501(c)(4) advocacy groups made substantial expenditures unhampered by any contribution limits. Their entry in force was fostered by federal court decisions that seemed to liberate "issue advocacy" communications and partisan voter mobilization activities from campaign law restrictions (Common Cause 2000). It was also facilitated by the Internal Revenue Service's lack of clarity about which of these groups' activities were political and could therefore not be pursued as part of the organizations' primary missions (Hill 2001).

But after the election, a congressional investigation, the IRS's rejection of the Christian Coalition's longstanding application for 501(c)(4) status, and innovative proposals by nonprofit group tax lawyers helped make 527 groups the "loophole of choice" for unregulated contributions in the 2000 election. The 527s' advantages over other nonprofits included the ability to make elections their primary, even exclusive activity; absence of the 35 percent tax on the lesser of their political expenditures or investment income; and the exemption of their donations from a steep gift tax (Trister 2000). Despite new laws mandating public disclosure of 527 group finances (other nonprofits do not have to reveal their contributors), 527s have grown rapidly.

Proposals have been submitted to Congress and the FEC to restrict soft money contributions to 527 groups. If such a proposal were adopted, it is likely that efforts would be made to utilize the less efficient nonprofit vehicles that were so prominent in 1996. These kind of groups continue to be active in elections, with the 501(c)(6) U.S. Chamber of Commerce and Americans for Job Security and 501(c)(5) AFL-CIO leading recent examples. PFA's earlier efforts to develop ways to better utilize its 501(c)(4) structure for campaign purposes are also instructive. Much would depend on whether or not the FEC and IRS developed a common and coherent policy in determining when such groups had a major purpose of influencing elections.

With reformers raising the issue of 527 regulation with the FEC and Congress, a leading response to restrictive proposals is sure to be, "Where is the threat of corruption (or its appearance) that is the sole justification under current constitutional doctrine for limiting political speech?" After all, the 527s are not making contributions to candidates or parties; nor are they coordinating their spending with them. And many of the donors are promoting their ideologies rather than looking for individual favors. Aren't the 527 donors simply furthering independent political expression, and, in the words of one tax attorney, "allowing causes to have angels?" (Eilperin 2000).

However one might answer this question in the abstract, it will in fact be answered by Congress and the FEC in a real world context. It is this context that we have endeavored to portray as accurately as possible in this chapter. With our findings in mind, we might rephrase the question about potential corruption or its appearance in three parts:

- If 527 groups spend independently to support or oppose candidates in large enough amounts—and some of their donors give in the megamillions—is there a danger that candidates and parties will feel obligated? Will this sentiment permit 527 groups and donors, in the Supreme Court's words, to "exert undue influence on an officeholder's judgment" (or appear to do so)? (*McConnell v. Federal Election Commission* (540 U.S. 93 [2003]);
- If some organizations sponsoring 527 independent groups also sponsor PACs that channel contributions to candidates (as, for example, the Club for Growth and New Democratic Network do), is there a danger that the candidates and parties will look at 527 spending as simply another form of contribution? Will contributions to 527s thus foster, or appear to foster, "politicians too compliant with the wishes of large contributors"? (*McConnell v. Federal Election Commission*); and
- If individuals who are closely associated with party and campaign leaders establish, manage, and fundraise for certain 527 organizations, is there a danger that these 527s will become more or less identified with the parties, recreating the corruption threat of the former party soft money system?

There is nothing more hazardous in politics than predictions. But in the absence of policy change, we can expect that the 527 system will generally expand and become more complex. Repeater 527s, generally well rooted in interest group structures, will attempt to build on their recent growth. A few of the 2004 First Timers (notably PFA) are already beginning to seek ways of institutionalizing their successes in representing broad party interests. But the elections of 2006 and 2008 will probably again feature a host of new groups geared to shorter term candidate and party interests. The emerging 527 system may make campaigns somewhat more interesting but also more difficult to hold accountable. Finally, the preponderance of large donors is likely to raise—even more seriously than it does now—the question of what BCRA has really accomplished.

NOTES

1. The otherwise excellent listing of 527 groups active in federal races on the Center for Public Integrity website (see www.publicintegrity.org/527) omits all labor unions including those that were predominantly active in such races.

2. See, for example, the statements of Service Employees International Union representatives regarding the union's largely federal 2004 election activities in "A Union Chief's Bold New Tack," (Business Week Online 2004) and SEIU press release, "Anatomy of an Election Strategy" (Service Employees International Union 2004). Together, SEIU and its New York affiliate spent $51 million of the $89 million union federal 527 total in 2004.

3. Data from 2000, when the 527 phenomenon came into its own, is incomplete because public disclosure of 527 group finances was not established until the last six months of the cycle. According to the Center for Public Integrity, there were forty "federal-oriented" 527s that reported less than $200,000 in donations for the 2004 cycle; these groups collected only $2.5 million (see www.publicintegrity.org/527).

4. Adding subparagraph (3)(5)(i) to Section 527 of the Internal Revenue Code.

5. National party soft money contributions data are from www.fec.gov. Prof. Ray La Raja provided additional information on state party soft money spending for federal elections in the 2002 cycle based on his research in FEC databases. He also suggested the methodology we employ to calculate the state party-raised component in state party soft money spending through deducting national party transfers to state and local parties. For further information on this methodology, see Ray La Raja and Elizabeth Jarvis-Shean, "Assessing the Impact of a Ban on Soft Money" (La Raja and Jarvis-Shean 2001).

6. Information on PACs, which either shared expenses with their 527 soft money counterparts or were separately maintained by the same organizational sponsor, was obtained from Robert Biersack, Deputy Press Officer, Federal Election Commission, and from searches of committees on the FEC website (www.fec.gov).

7. See www.fecinfo.com (DNC expenditures, consultant fees, 2002); www.opensecrets.org/parties/expend.asp?cmte = DNC&cycle = 2004 (for 2004).

8. See also www.dcigroup.com.

9. See also www.opensecrets.org/parties/expend.asp?cmte = RNC&cycle = 2004.

10. DCI Group's Republican Party payments for the convention are listed at www.opensecrets.org.

11. In 2002 the additional "other" category comprised mainly party committees, but also 527s and their sponsors and Indian tribes. In 2004, with party soft money abolished, it consisted largely of 527s and to a much lesser extent, Indian tribes.

12. See discussion above on p. 3 of labor 527s' "federal" election spending, and www.fecinfo.com.

13. See www.fecinfo.com.

14. Most notably, Robert Rowling provided no soft money but those associated with the company he chaired (TRT Holdings) gave, in rounded numbers, $134,000; Aubrey McClendon and Tom Ward of Chesapeake Energy also gave no soft money while their firm provided $100,000. Peter Nicholas did not give, but his company gave $165,000. Among the soft money donors, George Soros provided $208,000 of Soros Fund Management's total of $743,000, Harlan Crow of Crow Holdings gave $7,500, but those associated with Crow Holdings provided a total of $335,000; Ted Waitt gave $162,500 while Gateway Inc. donated a total of $778,000; Harold Simmons of Contran Corp. gave $22,000, but his company provided $863,000, and Paul Singer of Elliot Capital Advisers gave $570,5000 while his firm provided $1.303 million.

15. Data on corporate giving of soft money from www.fecinfo.com.

APPENDIX

Table 5.3   **Federal 527 Organizations in the 2002 Election Cycle (>$200,000)**

527 Committee Name	Contributions	Expenditures
General—Democratic Oriented		
AFSCME Special Account	$ 19,575,709	$ 19,375,052
SEIU Political Education and Action Local Fund	7,674,610	5,505,063
IMPAC 2000	6,948,686	7,029,821
EMILY'S List	6,821,112	7,714,815
AFL-CIO COPE—Treasury Fund	5,533,588	5,732,568
Comm. Workers of America Non-Fed. Sep. Segregated Fund	4,511,305	6,970,539
1199 SEIU New York State Political Action Fund	4,298,508	4,536,751
New Democrat Network Non Federal	4,235,722	3,662,273
Laborers' Political League Education Fund	4,097,455	4,105,741
League of Conservation Voters, Inc.	3,524,000	1,694,248
Sierra Club Voter Education Fund	3,351,200	3,930,028
UFCW Active Ballot Club Education Fund	3,156,510	2,987,351
NEA Fund for Children & Public Education	2,556,846	2,430,841
SMWIA Political Education League	2,178,975	2,171,907
Campaign Money Watch	1,504,184	1,441,646
Mainstreet USA, Inc.	1,146,000	966,057
Working Families 2000	954,944	70,310
Campaign for Americas Future (Labor)	847,500	823,403
21st Century Democrats	772,908	856,329
Pro Choice Vote	654,300	642,911
Citizens for Michigan's Future	616,000	616,005
Voters for Choice Non Federal	541,935	607,716
Every Child Matters	515,857	384,198
Participation 2000 Inc.	509,650	173,541
Great Lakes '92 Fund, Inc.	494,690	592,850
Progressive Majority	295,765	118,782
Daschle Democrats, Inc.	244,489	229,921
Planned Parenthood Votes	228,642	1,010,869
Total (n – 28)	87,791,092	86,381,538
Net Total: After Transfers Among Groups	85,366,851	83,957,297
General—Republican Oriented		
College Republican National Committee, Inc.	$ 8,445,903	$ 10,650,711
Club for Growth, Inc.	4,215,967	4,905,651
Republican Leadership Coalition	3,915,342	4,132,661
Bush-Cheney 2000, Inc-Recount Fund	3,897,036	9,243,360
Republican Leadership Council (RLC)—State	2,237,025	2,861,762
Republican Main Street Partnership	1,802,548	1,880,577
The Leadership Forum	1,000,000	1,000,000
Wish List	864,800	1,046,375
Council for Better Government	721,354	707,980
National Federation of Republican Women	592,599	3,814,520
American Council of Life Insurers Non Federal PAC	520,952	489,600
National Association of Realtors 527 Fund	484,000	530,572

Table 5.3   Continued

527 Committee Name	Contributions	Expenditures
Republicans Abroad Non Federal	419,865	413,267
Republican Majority Issues Committee	267,555	311,374
Total (n = 14)	29,384,946	41,988,410
Net Total: After Transfers Among Groups	29,129,946	41,733,410
Leadership PACs—Democratic Oriented		
New American Optimists	$ 4,621,154	$ 4,617,824
DASHPAC Nonfederal Account	2,722,454	2,847,765
Searchlight Leadership Fund Non Federal	1,670,152	1,971,083
Lone Star Fund Non Federal Account	1,506,131	1,511,718
Effective Government Committee-Nonfederal Account	1,381,750	1,320,549
Citizen Soldier Fund—Nonfederal Account	1,353,400	1,365,460
National Leadership PAC Non Federal	1,051,266	1,126,257
Blue Dog Non Federal PAC	965,867	886,141
Glacier PAC Nonfederal	783,650	827,695
Congressional Black Caucus Political Action Committee	672,524	257,180
21st Century Leadership Fund	620,650	237,946
Mainstream America Political Action Committee	498,814	420,445
Committee for a Democratic Majority	455,704	536,434
Democratic Majority PAC	444,021	487,208
HillPAC-NY	356,100	351,043
Building Our Leadership Diversity PAC Non Federal	320,250	322,370
Leadership in the New Century PAC Non Federal	306,068	286,657
Florida 19 PAC	286,450	271,144
Committee for Leadership and Progress-NY	280,714	286,600
McAuliffe for Chair	266,378	308,902
DAKPAC Non Federal Account	231,759	242,515
Silver State 21st Century PAC Non Federal	222,423	223,548
Rhode Island Political Action Committee Non Federal	220,150	287,914
Bob Graham Leadership Forum	218,000	217,451
For Dems Non Federal	217,012	216,998
JFC Leadership Committee	210,900	95,750
Total (n = 26)	21,883,739	21,524,600
Net Total: After Transfers Among Groups	21,833,739	21,318,100
Leadership PACs—Republican Oriented		
Americans for a Republican Majority Non Federal Account	2,341,634	1,901,435
Rely On Your Beliefs Fund	1,716,776	1,719,831
KOMPAC State Victory Fund	1,134,595	1,088,088
New Majority Project PAC	1,026,900	1,098,198
Volunteer PAC Non Federal	955,785	953,254
Republican Majority Fund Non Federal Account	910,226	687,003
America's Foundation Non Federal Account	881,939	894,019
Congressman Tom Davis Virginia Victory Fund	837,349	856,477
Together for Our Majority Political Action Committee Non Federal	817,975	808,416
New Republican Majority Fund—State PAC	680,772	684,991
Campaign for America's Future (Utah)	549,373	338,073
Majority Leader's Fund	537,620	241,628

Battle Born State PAC	506,787	453,089
American Success PAC Non-Federal Account	462,528	332,881
Committee for a United Republican Team Non Federal	269,853	255,272
George Allen Committee	264,941	261,389
7th District Congressional Republican Committee	264,716	218,383
Friends of the Big Sky Non Federal Account	228,162	160,731
Washington Fund-State Account	201,910	207,317
GROWPAC Non Federal	201,147	210,873
Total (n = 20)	14,790,987	13,371,347
Net Total: After Transfers Among Groups	14,557,053	13,137,413
Federal 527s and Leadership PACs		
Total Democratic & Republican:	$153,850,755	$163,265,895
Net Total: After Transfers Among Groups	$150,731,079	$160,146,219

Table 5.4   Federal 527 Organizations in the 2004 Election Cycle (>$200,000)

527 Committee Name	Contributions	Expenditures
Democratic Oriented		
America Coming Together—Non Federal Account	$ 78,652,163	$ 76,270,931
Joint Victory Campaign 2004[a]	71,809,666	72,347,983
The Media Fund	59,394,183	54,429,053
SEIU Political Education & Action Fund	40,995,542	43,681,298
AFSCME Special Account	22,135,127	22,112,744
MoveOn.org Voter Fund	12,517,365	21,205,288
New Democrat Network Non Federal Account	12,221,608	12,194,451
Citizens For A Strong Senate	10,848,730	10,143,121
Sierra Club Voter Education Fund	8,727,127	6,147,176
EMILY's List Non Federal	7,684,046	7,983,328
1199 SEIU Non Federal Committee	7,477,295	7,445,101
Voices For Working Families	7,466,056	6,809,102
League of Conservation Voters Inc. 527	6,552,500	5,621,288
AFL-CIO COPE—Treasury Fund	6,336,464	6,332,448
Democratic Victory 2004	3,930,969	2,603,654
Laborers Political League Education Fund	3,665,284	3,486,802
The Partnership for America's Families	3,071,211	2,880,906
Grassroots Democrats	2,818,883	2,468,622
Stronger America Now	2,789,817	2,664,919
America Votes, Inc.	2,622,636	2,533,523
21st Century Democrats	2,542,116	1,255,859
SMWIA Political Ed League	2,164,830	2,051,382
Coalition to Defend the American Dream	1,935,844	1,609,000
CWA Non Federal Separate Segregated Fund	1,924,455	1,641,536
Music For America	1,667,820	1,507,324
Win Back Respect	1,382,227	1,083,184
Americans for Progress & Opportunity	1,306,092	1,305,667
Young Democrats of America	1,109,840	719,894
Environment2004, Inc.	1,107,080	1,117,370
Environmental Accountability Fund	1,084,807	965,107
American Family Voices Voters' Alliance, Inc.	1,060,000	1,108,628
Campaign Money Watch	1,022,842	993,921
Americans for Jobs	1,000,000	994,137
Democracy for America Non Federal	879,500	520,981
Planned Parenthood Votes	799,683	595,288
Revolutionary Women	789,640	827,417
Focus South Dakota, Inc.	687,450	619,767
Progressive Majority	659,300	766,104
PunkVoter, Inc.	636,161	1,020,593
Compare Decide Vote	600,000	538,294
The Real Economy Group	585,000	570,750
Campaign for America's Future—CC Fund	550,651	41,249
UFCW Active Ballot Club Education Fund	543,550	602,033
National Progress Fund	517,149	426,199
Environment2004 Action Fund	507,750	491,554

Organizing and Campaign Training Center	501,765	445,821
NJDC Victory Fund	484,461	421,782
Defenders of Wildlife Action Fund 527 Account	484,000	526,980
Arts PAC	464,753	189,211
Communities Voting Together	412,096	—
Bring Ohio Back	400,681	574,256
Click Back America	398,000	219,162
American Democracy Project	364,500	480,334
Clean Water Action Education Fund	343,300	231,796
! Si Se Puede ! Boston 2004, Inc.	331,000	239,182
Uniting People for Victory	284,000	228,194
Roofers Political Ed and Legislative Fund	232,432	263,152
Texans for Truth	225,495	486,929
National Democratic Ethnic Leadership Council	212,040	96,122
Total (n = 59)	403,918,982	397,137,897
Net Total: After Transfers Among Groups	321,185,549	314,404,464

Republican Oriented

Progress For America Voter Fund	$44,929,174	$35,437,204
Swift Boat Vets and POWs for Truth	17,068,390	22,424,420
Club for Growth	7,863,572	9,257,228
College Republican National Committee, Inc.	6,372,843	8,207,393
Club for Growth.net	4,115,037	3,927,530
National Association of Realtors 527 Fund	3,215,263	3,149,895
The November Fund	3,150,054	3,075,978
CA Republican National Convention Delegation 2004 Account	1,600,750	1,506,499
Republican Leadership Coalition, Inc.	1,456,876	1,439,110
National Federation of Republican Women	1,301,811	3,321,249
Americans United to Preserve Marriage	1,192,090	1,056,962
Americas PAC	1,081,700	1,056,666
Florida Leadership Council	878,500	729,366
Republican Leadership Council (RLC)	753,303	772,625
The Leadership Forum	696,973	501,255
Softer Voices	676,100	764,436
Wish List Non Federal	585,197	703,997
Main Street Individual Fund	471,600	253,612
Republicans Abroad Non Federal	444,057	501,717
Council For Better Government	294,000	297,000
Concern for Better Government	236,000	187,100
Total (n = 21)	98,383,290	98,571,242
Net Total: After Transfers Among Groups	83,922,290	84,110,242

Republican and Democratic Oriented Committees

Total (n = 80)	$502,302,272	$495,709,139
Net Total: After Transfers Among Groups	$405,107,839	$398,514,706

[a] Joint Victory Campaign 2004, a fundraising conduit for other 527s, represents $70,879,391 of the $97,194,433 in total transfers.

Table 5.5   Repeaters: Federal 527 Organizations Active in Both the 2002 and 2004 Cycles (>$200,000)

Committee Name	Associated PAC	2002 Contributions	2004 Contributions	% Δ
1199 SEIU New York State Political Action Fund	X	$ 4,298,508	$ 7,477,295	74
21st Century Democrats	X	772,908	2,542,116	229
AFL-CIO COPE—Treasury Fund	X	5,533,588	6,336,464	15
AFSCME Special Account	X	19,575,709	22,135,127	13
Campaign for Americas Future (Labor)	X	847,500	550,651	− 35
Campaign Money Watch (Reform Voter Project)		1,504,184	1,022,842	− 32
Club for Growth Inc.	X	4,215,967	7,863,572	87
College Republican National Committee, Inc.		8,445,903	6,372,843	− 25
Communications Workers of America Non Fed. Separate Segregated Fund	X	4,511,305	1,924,455	− 57
Council for Better Government		721,354	294,000	− 59
EMILY's List	X	6,821,112	7,684,046	13
Laborers' Political League—Education Fund	X	4,097,455	3,665,284	− 11
League of Conservation Voters, Inc.	X	3,524,000	6,552,500	86
Mainstreet USA, Inc. (American Family Voices Voters Alliance)		1,146,000	1,060,000	− 8
National Association of Realtors 527 Fund	X	484,000	3,215,263	564
National Federation of Republican Women	X	592,599	1,301,811	120
New Democrat Network Non Federal	X	4,235,722	12,221,608	189
Planned Parenthood Votes	X	228,642	799,683	250
Progressive Majority	X	295,765	659,300	123
Republican Leadership Coalition		3,915,342	1,456,876	− 63
Republican Leadership Council (RLC)—State	X	2,237,025	753,303	− 66
Republican Main Street Partnership (Main Street Individual)	X	1,802,548	471,600	− 74
Republicans Abroad Non Federal		419,865	444,057	6
SEIU Political Education and Action Local Fund	X	7,674,610	40,995,542	434
Sierra Club Voter Education Fund	X	3,351,200	8,727,127	160
SMWIA Political Education League	X	2,178,975	2,164,830	− 1
The Leadership Forum		1,000,000	696,973	− 30
WISH List	X	864,800	585,197	− 32
UFCW Active Ballot Club Education Fund	X	3,156,510	543,550	− 83
Total (n = 29)		$98,453,097	$150,517,915	53
Net Total: After Transfers Among Groups		$95,952,004	$131,174,015	37

Table 5.6   First Timers: Federal 527 Organizations Active Only in the 2004 Cycle (>$200,000)

Committee Name	Associated PAC	Contributions
America Coming Together Nonfederal Account	X	$78,652,163
Joint Victory Campaign 2004	X	71,809,666
Media Fund		59,394,183
Progress For America Voter Fund		44,929,174
Swift Boat Vets and POWs for Truth		17,068,390
MoveOn.org Voter Fund	X	12,517,365
Citizens For A Strong Senate		10,848,730
Voices For Working Families		7,466,056
Club for Growth.net		4,115,037
Democratic Victory 2004	X	3,930,969
The November Fund		3,150,054
The Partnership for America's Families		3,071,211
Grassroots Democrats		2,818,883
Stronger America Now		2,789,817
America Votes, Inc.		2,622,636
Coalition to Defend the American Dream		1,935,844
Music for America		1,667,820
CA Republican National Convention Delegation 2004 Account		1,600,750
Win Back Respect		1,382,227
Americans for Progress & Opportunity		1,306,092
Americans United to Preserve Marriage		1,192,090
Young Democrats of America		1,109,840
Environment2004, Inc.		1,107,080
Environmental Accountability Fund		1,084,807
Americas PAC		1,081,700
Americans for Jobs		1,000,000
Democracy for America Non Federal	X	879,500
Florida Leadership Council		878,500
Revolutionary Women		789,640
Focus South Dakota, Inc.		687,450
Softer Voices		676,100
PunkVoter, Inc.		636,161
Compare Decide Vote		600,000
The Real Economy Group		585,000
National Progress Fund		517,149
Environment2004 Action Fund		507,750
Organizing and Campaign Training Center		501,765
NJDC Victory Fund		484,461
Defenders of Wildlife Action Fund 527 Account	X	471,600
Arts PAC	X	464,753
Communities Voting Together		412,096
Bring Ohio Back		400,681
Click Back America		398,000

(continues)

Table 5.6   Continued

Committee Name	Associated PAC	Contributions
American Democracy Project		364,500
Clean Water Action Education Fund		343,300
! Si Se Puede ! Boston 2004, Inc.		331,000
Uniting People for Victory		284,000
Concern for Better Government		236,000
Roofers Political Education and Legislative Fund		232,432
Texans for Truth		225,495
National Democratic Ethnic Leadership Council		212,040
Total (n = 51)		$351,771,957
Net Total: After Transfers Among Groups		$273,925,859

Table 5.7   Labor Union Donations to Federal 527s in the 2002 and 2004 Cycles (>$5,000)

Donor	2002 Contributions	2004 Contributions	%Δ
AFGE	$ 25,000	$ 145,000	480
AFL-CIO	5,803,532	6,941,559	20
AFSCME	19,807,709	22,550,324	14
American Federation Of Teachers	71,000	1,815,000	2,456
American Postal Workers Union	100,000	500,000	400
Communications Workers Of America	4,244,242	2,407,038	−43
IBEW	134,500	1,087,750	709
IBPAT	15,000	375,000	2,400
Ironworkers International	21,000	45,000	114
LIUNA	3,741,387	3,070,428	−18
International Association Of Machinists	610,000	105,000	−83
National Education Association	2,477,000	207,500	−92
SEIU	12,085,613	50,636,054	319
SMWIA	2,131,200	1,990,000	−7
United Auto Workers	275,000	1,145,000	316
UFCW	3,203,510	869,050	−73
UNITE	55,000	275,000	400
United Steel Workers	135,000	210,000	56
IAFF	5,000	10,000	100
Total (n = 19)	$54,940,693	$94,384,703	72

Table 5.8   Individuals' $100,000+ Contributions to Federal 527s in the 2002 Cycle and Their Recent National Party Soft Money Donations

Name	Money to 527s	Employer	Party Soft Money 2000 & 2002	
			DEM	REP
Messinger, Alida	$ 1,088,000 *		$ 730,000	
Kirsch, Steven	1,064,000	Proper Software Corp	3,904,000	
Bing, Stephen	999,089	Shangri-La Entertainment	7,385,000	
Hunting, John/Living Trust	949,000	Self/Retired	25,000	
Harris, Jay	849,000 *			
Hiatt, Arnold	814,000	Stride Rite Foundation		
Searle, Dan	730,000	Kinship Corporation		
Harris, John	716,000 *			
Fonda, Jane	638,100	Self/Seymour 1989 Trust		
Gund, Louise	527,000	Self	1,028,000	
Perry, Bob	480,000	Perry Homes/Self		140,000
Distler, Stephen	470,000	EM Warburg Pincus & Co.		136,600
Stephens, Jackson	368,500	EOE Inc.		25,000
Corzine, Jon	354,500	US Government	2,416,000	
Buttenwieser, Peter	327,500	Peter Buttenwieser & Assoc.	1,252,500	
Wagenfeld, Sandra	306,000	Aviatech Inc.		
O'Connor, Maconda	300,000	Self		
Brooks, Paula J.	299,050	Self/Royal Wolff Ventures		276,500
Crow, Harlan	280,000	Crow Family Holdings		7,500
Paulson, Wendy	278,000 *			
Gilder, Richard	275,000	Gilder Gagnono Howe & Co.		250,000
Cofrin, Gladys	250,000	Self	35,000	
Levine, S. Robert	250,000	Armstrong Investments Corp.		
Williams, John	235,000	Self		
Lecompte, Janet	205,729	Self		
Malcolm, Ellen	200,000	EMILY's List	1,000	
Burnett, Jason	200,000	AEI/Brookings		
Motley, Ronald	200,000	Ness Motley		
Perenchio, Jerry	199,000	Chartwell Partners LLC		1,231,500
Turner, Tab	189,000	Turner & Assoc.	15,000	
Chambers, Merle	185,000	Leith Ventures	489,000	
Hull, Blair	170,000	Hull Group/Retired/Philathropist	25,000	
Cofrin, Mary Ann	165,000	Self	130,000	
Greenwood, Amalia	162,044	Retired		750
Eychaner, Fred	160,000	Newsweb Corp.	8,295,000	
Schwartz, Bernard	158,000	Loral Space & Communications	3,536,300	
Hume, William	154,000	Basic American Inc.		100,000
O'Quinn, John	150,000	O'Quinn & Laminack	2,615,000	
Trumpower, Mike	150,000	Retired		
Palevsky, Max	150,000 *			
Powers, John	145,000	Self		
Reuss, Margaret M.	141,450 *			
Rooney, J. Patrick	132,000	Woodland Group		17,500
Hindery, Leo	130,000	YES Network	1,440,200	
Devos, Richard	120,000	Amway		425,000

Pacey, O. E.	115,966 Retired		
Saban, Haim	115,000 Saban Entertainment/Self	12,655,000	
Guerrera, Domenic	113,882 Retired		1,500
Orr, Susan	109,701 TRAC	145,000	
Cumming, Ian	105,000 Self/Lacadia National Corp.	985,000	
Hoffman, Shepard	105,000 Self/Stanley Mandel & Iola	5,000	
Corzine, Joanne	105,000 Self		3,000
Shaw, Gregory	101,000 Microsoft	92,000	
Manheimer, Virginia	100,300 Self		
Donahoe, Eileen	100,200 Self		
Byrd, Wade	100,000 Self	46,000	
Leeds, Gerald & Lilo	100,000 Institute for Student Achievement	192,000	
Baron, Frederick	100,000 Self	345,000	
Alameel, David	100,000 Aflan Group	100,000	
Eisenberg, Lewis	100,000 Granite Capital Corp.	215,900	
Gilchrist, Berg	100,000 *		
Hyde, Joseph	100,000 *		
Mars, Jacqueline	100,000 *		
Patterson, Cary	100,000 Nix Petterson & Roach LLP	905,500	
Reaud, Wayne	100,000 Reaud Morgan & Quinn	605,000	
Sandler, Steven	100,000 Self		

From All Donors (n = 66)		(N = 29)	(N = 13)
Total	$18,485,011	$49,400,500	$2,827,750
Average Donation	$280,076	$1,703,466	$217,519
Median Donation	$163,522	$489,000	$136,600

From Soft Money Donors (n = 42)			
Total	$11,460,266	$52,288,250	
Average Donation	$272,863	$1,243,530	
Median Donation	$161,022	$203,950	

*No entry.

6

Interest Groups and Advocacy Organizations After BCRA

Robert G. Boatright, Michael J. Malbin, Mark J. Rozell,
and Clyde Wilcox

Before the Bipartisan Campaign Reform Act (BCRA) passed, much of the public rhetoric about it had to do with the role of special interests in politics. Logically, therefore, most people expected the law to have a significant impact on interest groups. But there was little agreement about what those effects would likely be. In this chapter, we examine the 2004 elections for early evidence. The focus will be on organizations that participated in elections before BCRA passed, as opposed to new participants who joined the fray afterwards.

Predictions during the pre-BCRA dispute tended to fall between two polar positions. For the sake of simplicity let us call them the naïve and the cynical. The naïve view was that prohibiting soft money and regulating electioneering would mean that much of the money formerly spent on these items would disappear from the federal election arena. The cynical view liked to use what we and others have described as the "hydraulic" metaphor about money in politics—a metaphor that presents political money as a water-like substance that inevitably will seep around a law's prohibitions until it can find a way once again to flow freely. In contrast with both of these perspectives, we have argued that the way an organization adapts to new election laws will vary both with the organization and with the times. The adaptations will depend internally on an organization's goals and resources and externally on a number of contextual considerations besides the law, including both political considerations, such as competitiveness, and less political ones, such as the changing economics and technology of communications (Boatright et al. 2003). This chapter will use the 2004 elections to test these perspectives by asking the following questions.

- *Soft money:* BCRA prohibited the national political parties (and state or local parties engaged in federal election activity) from raising soft money. We ask:
  - Did the people and organizations that contributed significant amounts of soft money in 2000 and 2002 find new federal election outlets for their contributions or spending in 2004?
  - If the answer is not uniform, was there a systematic difference between those who participated financially in 2004 and those who did not?
- *Electioneering:* BCRA prohibits corporations and labor unions from paying (directly or indirectly) for candidate-specific broadcast advertising within sixty days of a general election or thirty days of a primary. We ask:
  - Amount and timing: Did the new rules result in interest groups' buying less candidate-specific broadcast advertising or shifting the timing of this advertising? Did specific organizations that had previously purchased political broadcast advertisements continue to do so?
  - Alternative activities: Did some organizations shift away from advertising and toward voter mobilization and other forms of nonbroadcast activity? If so, are there systematic differences between those that shifted and those that did not? Where there has been a shift, was BCRA the reason?

To preview our answers:

- *The soft money prohibition did have a significant effect in 2004 on the former soft money donors of 2000 and 2002.*
  - The vast majority of former soft money donors did *not* increase either their hard money contributions to candidates and parties or their contributions to independent committees organized under section 527 of the tax code. Among business givers (who made up the bulk of soft money donors), a few gave a lot more money, but most cut down. Large publicly traded corporations, which were a major source of soft money in 2000 and 2002, were far less likely to participate in 2004. Labor unions and a few individual megadonors increased their giving.
- *The electioneering rules had marginal effects on interest group advertising in 2004.*
  - *Number and timing of ads*—Even though corporate and labor treasury money can no longer pay for ads within the sixty-day window, there were almost as many electioneering ads within the window in 2004 as in 2000. There was a decline in the *percentage* of total ads broadcast within the sixty days, but this was because of a major increase in ads before the sixty-day window. The total number of ads surprised some who had supported BCRA in the expectation that it would reduce electioneering. But it was not so surprising to those who saw the literal text of the law as only affecting certain funding sources for broadcast advertising within a specific time period. Some of these latter supporters had predicted that advocacy organizations would continue to play a robust political role.
  - *Organizations that shifted*—Most 2004 electioneering ads were sponsored

by new, presidency-focused 527 committees. The picture looks different for ongoing organizations. Many of these shifted resources *away* from television ads to voter mobilization. But because the shift in emphasis predates BCRA, it cannot be attributed to the new law.

SOFT MONEY DONORS

According to the Federal Election Commission, the six major national Democratic and Republican party committees raised a combined total of $495 million of soft money in 1999–2000 and $496 million in 2001–2002 (see chapter 2, table 2.1). Itemized soft money contributions to Democratic and Republican committees came to $436 million in 1999–2000 and $446 million in 2001–2002, excluding transfers among party committees.

- In 1999–2000, 48 percent of these itemized soft money contributions came from corporations, 39 percent from individuals, 7 percent from labor organizations, 5 percent from trade associations, and 1 percent from other sources.
- In 2001–2002, 42 percent came from corporations, 36 percent from individuals, 8 percent from labor, 6 percent from trade associations, 7 percent from candidates' committees or politicians' PACs, and 1 percent from other sources.

Thus, corporations were financially the most important set of donors affected by BCRA's ban on soft money. In addition, most of the individual donors were corporate executives whose contributions are grouped by some analysts together with those of their employers. While we have significant reservations about treating an individual employee's contributions as if they reflect the same concerns as an employer's, we nevertheless find the grouping useful because of the question we are trying to answer. After BCRA became law, several observers predicted that corporations that used to donate soft money to the parties from their corporate treasuries might (1) step up their efforts to persuade employees to contribute hard money to candidates either directly or through the companies' PACs or (2) redirect some corporate contributions or large individual contributions from business owners and other corporate executives to 527 committees. The only way to know whether this occurred is to establish a baseline that includes individual as well as corporate contributions. Some also predicted an increase in corporate contributions to nonprofit issue advocacy organizations (organized under section 501(c)(4) of the tax code) or to trade associations (organized under section 501(c)(6)). However, a lack of disclosure makes it impossible for us to analyze support for these organizations here.

Our analysis began with data supplied by the Center for Responsive Politics (CRP) on all entities whose organizational or individual contributions collectively equaled at least $100,000 in soft money given to the major national party committees in *either* 2000 or 2002. We included contributions from an organization's treasury as well as all contributions from individuals employed by the organization. We then further limited the list to corporations, trade associations, and labor organizations that gave $100,000 or more soft money in *both* 2000 and 2002 *and* that gave (through organizational or individual contributions) some hard money or 527 contributions in 2004. We used these criteria because organizations that gave at least $100,000 in soft money in both of the earlier elections and were also active in 2004 should be the ones most likely to compensate for the soft money ban by increasing other activities. Thus, the selection criteria were biased in favor of finding substitution and compensation.

The combined criteria produced a database of 429 organizations accounting for 43 percent of the political parties' total soft money receipts in 2000 and 49 percent in 2002. CRP collected and separately accounted for all individual and PAC contributions from people associated with these 429 organizations for all three election cycles. This allowed us to compare their activity in 2000 and 2002 (when the organizations or those connected with them gave soft money) to 2004 (when they did not). The goal was to see whether hard money contributions rose significantly in 2004.

For these same organizations (and individuals associated with the organizations), we also compared Internal Revenue Service records of 527 contributions in 2003–2004 to similar data for 2001–2002. The Center for Public Integrity (the Campaign Finance Institute) supplied the 527 data for 2002; CFI analyzed the IRS data for 2003–2004. We did not analyze 527 data for 1999–2000 because 527 disclosure did not begin until the second half of 2000, and even then, the information about individuals only sporadically included employers. Disclosed receipts for federally active 527s in 2000 (as defined in chapter 5) totaled $74.7 million. We cannot say what fraction of this came from individuals or organizations that meet our criteria. In 2002, just about half of the contributions to federally active 527s came from the organizations in our study and individuals associated with them, so it is reasonable to assume a similar percentage (equaling $37 million) as a rough estimate of potential contributions to 527 committees by those organizations during the disclosed portion of 2000. In the detailed analysis, we sought to determine whether the soft money donors of 1999–2002 increased their 527 giving from 2001–2002 to 2003–2004.

The results are presented in table 6.1. To economize on space, we should forewarn the reader that the "organizational giving" line in each set of organizations presents two different kinds of giving. Organizational giving under the "soft money" and "527" columns refers to contributions directly from the organization. The organizational line in the hard money column refers to political action committee (PAC) contributions, which are hard-money contributions given to the PAC by individuals.

At first glance, the table seems to support the idea that that the former donors of political party soft money would increase other forms of election giving.

- In the 2000 election cycle, hard money plus soft money from these organizations and associated individuals totaled *$402 million*, not counting 527

Table 6.1 Hard Money, Soft Money, and 527 Contributions, 2000–2004, from Donors Who Made Soft Money Donations of at Least $100K in Both 2000 and 2002

Type	n	2000			2002				2004		
		Soft	Hard	Total	Soft	Hard	527	Total	Hard	527	Total
Corp.	370										
Indiv		60,182,320	60,388,335	120,570,655	77,378,153	36,591,466	3,767,055	117,736,674	89,941,111	62,968,270	152,909,381
Orga[a]		113,174,126	68,337,225	181,511,351	115,147,262	73,908,073	12,608,255	201,663,590	84,542,929	6,148,700	90,691,629
Trade	40										
Indiv		695,217	759,275	1,454,492	199,304	612,134	0	811,438	1,300,200	590,000	1,890,200
Orga[a]		11,672,197	21,378,932	33,051,129	16,593,793	22,950,722	3,072,401	42,616,916	26,353,810	3,995,263	30,349,073
Labor	19										
Indiv		900	421,481	422,381	0	232,626	0	232,626	527,986	0	527,986
Orga[a]		28,618,950	36,660,620	65,279,570	35,084,595	37,461,389	54,764,193	127,310,177	35,405,405	91,974,665	127,380,070
Total	429	214,343,710	187,945,868	402,289,578	244,403,107	171,756,410	74,211,904	490,371,421	238,071,441	165,676,898	403,748,339

Sources: CFI analysis of data from Center for Responsive Politics, Center for Public Integrity, Federal Election Commission, and Internal Revenue Service. See accompanying text.

Note: All organizations that gave (or whose employees gave) at least $100,000 to parties in 2000 and 2002 and were active in 2004 are included in this summary. Soft money could have been given directly by organization treasuries, or by employees, or both.

[a] The line for organizations represents different things in the hard money, soft money, and 527 columns. For soft money and 527 contributions, this is money from the organization's treasury. For hard money, we use this line to report PAC receipts, which are given to a PAC in limited amounts, generally by individuals.

money. Including an estimate for 527-giving, the total rises to about *$439 million.*

- In 2002, hard money, plus soft money, plus 527 money from these organizations (and associated individuals) totaled *$490 million.*
- In 2004, hard money and 527 money totaled *$404 million.*

Thus, the total amount of electoral money from these organizations dropped by only $35 million from 2000 to 2004 (including estimated 527-giving in the 2000 total). Because these organizations were responsible for more than $200 million in soft money in 1999–2000, one therefore would be tempted to say that the soft money had "come back."

But the situation looks different when examined more closely. It is misleading to compare the gross totals from one year to another if we are looking for adaptation by former soft money donors. One reason is that hard money would naturally have increased from one cycle to the next without any effort from the soft money donors. A second reason is that the combined totals mask very substantial, systematic variations among donors.

First, consider the increase in hard money. The bulk of the soft money in 2000 and 2002, as well as most of the 2004 increases in hard money and 527-giving, all appear in the "corporate" section of table 6.1.[1] Within the "hard money" category, corporate PAC money increased, but at a rate no more rapid than for PACs in previous election cycles (Federal Election Commission 2005a). The same can be said of individual contributions from corporate employees. These increased by $30 million from one presidential year (2000) to the next. In percentage terms, this is roughly equivalent to the general increase among all donors in the record fundraising year of 2004, so it would be hard to argue that the increase for this particular group of donors was mainly the result of their employers' inability to give soft money. The donors were more likely to have been moved by the same considerations that caused millions of new donors to give during a highly polarized and intense election.

What about the large increase in 527 contributions from former soft money donors? To help explain this increase, we ran the information in table 6.1 again for corporations only, because corporations represent the bulk of soft money donors. This time, however, we divided the corporations into publicly traded versus privately held ones, with publicly traded corporations further broken down by their financial size. The financial size (or market capitalization) categories employ cutoff points used by standard financial research sources, collapsed into three groups. (The 527 data are presented for 2002 and 2004 only, because the 2000 disclosures generally did not include employers.)

Table 6.2 shows that in 2000 and 2002, *large corporations* (with a market valuation of $10 billion or more) contributed almost three-quarters of all the soft money given to the parties by publicly traded corporations in our database. More than 80 percent of this money came from corporate treasuries and not from corporate-related individual contributions. Individual hard money contributions from people employed by these large corporations did increase by almost 40 per-

Table 6.2 Corporate Soft Money Donor's Financial Activity by Type and Size of Firm for Firms Giving More Than $100K in Soft Money in Both 2000 and 2002

	n	2000 Soft	2000 Hard	2002 Soft	2002 Hard	2002 527s	2004 Hard	2004 527s
Publicly Traded Corporations								
Market Capitalization Value:								
Large (>$10 billion)	108							
Individual		10.3	31.0	9.0	17.1	0.9	43.0	1.4
Org.[a]		64.8	45.4	66.8	49.3	7.6	56.9	1.6
Total		79.5	76.4	75.8	66.4	8.5	99.9	2.9
Medium ($2–10B)	54							
Individual		6.5	5.4	5.0	3.2	0.2	7.5	3.0
Org.[a]		14.2	7.1	14.7	8.6	1.6	9.7	0.4
Total		26.2	12.5	19.7	11.8	1.8	17.3	3.4
Small (< $2B)	28							
Individual		4.8	3.1	4.1	1.7	0.1	3.0	10.4
Org.[a]		7.0	2.2	5.8	2.6	0.5	2.4	1.1
Total		18.6	5.3	9.9	4.3	0.6	5.4	11.6
All Public	190							
Individual		21.6	39.6	18.0	22.0	1.2	53.6	14.8
Org.[a]		85.9	54.7	87.3	60.5	9.7	69.1	3.2
Total		107.5	94.2	105.3	82.5	10.9	122.6	17.9
Privately Held Corporations	180							
Individual		38.6	20.8	59.3	14.5	2.6	36.3	48.2
Org.[a]		27.3	13.7	27.9	13.4	2.9	15.5	3.0
Total		65.9	34.5	87.2	28.0	5.5	51.8	51.2
All Corporations	370							
Individual		60.2	60.4	77.4	3.8	36.6	89.9	63.0
Org.[a]		113.2	68.3	115.1	12.6	73.9	84.5	6.1
Total		173.4	128.7	192.5	16.4	110.5	174.5	69.1

Sources: CFI analysis of data from Center for Responsive Politics, Center for Public Integrity, Federal Election Commission, and Internal Revenue Service. See accompanying text.

Note: All corporations that gave (or whose employees gave) at least $100,000 to parties in 2000 and 2002 and were active in 2004 are included in this summary.

[a] The line for organizations represents different things in the hard money, soft money, and 527 columns. For soft money and 527 contributions, this is money from the organization's treasury. For hard money, we use this line to report PAC receipts, which are given to a PAC in limited amounts, generally by individuals.

cent from one presidential year (2000) to the next (2004). However, 527-giving by these largest corporations and the individuals associated with them actually *declined* by almost two-thirds from 2002 to 2004.

Midsized corporations ($2 billion–$10 million market capitalization) also reduced their 527-giving from corporate treasuries between 2002 and 2004. But individuals associated with these midsized corporations gave *seventeen times* more 527 money in 2004 than in 2002. Individuals associated with *smaller corporations* (market values of $2 billion or less) gave *almost 100 times more* to 527s in 2004. Moreover, individuals associated with *privately held firms* increased their 527 giving by nineteen times over their 2002 level. The patterns are stark. Corporations tended not to give much treasury money to 527 committees. Individuals (generally the owners or top managers) from smaller corporations were far more likely than individuals from larger ones to give to 527 committees.

But even these findings seriously overgeneralize what happened in 2004. Individuals associated with corporations gave $97 million more to 527 committees in 2004 than in 2002. But it turns out that ten individuals in our corporate-related list gave $1 million or more to 527 committees during the 2004 cycle. These ten megadonors alone accounted for $52 million in 527 contributions in 2004. This is two-thirds of all 527-giving (individual and organizational) by all of the corporations in our study. Furthermore, four of those ten individuals account for more than 80 percent of the 527 contributions from all individuals associated with the 190 publicly held corporations in our database.[2] The other six donors were responsible for more than 80 percent of the 527 money contributed by individuals associated with 180 privately held corporations.[3] Virtually all of the money from this $1 million-plus group went to the major 527 committees involved in the presidential election (America Coming Together, The Media Fund, Move On, Progress for America, and Swift Boat Vets).[4] But these same ten people—who gave a total of only $321,865 to 527 committees in 2002—were responsible for only $2 million in soft money in 2000 and $5 million in 2002. In other words, if we want to use terms like "replacement" money, we would be saying that the $2 million or $5 million that these people or their businesses gave in soft money before BCRA had been "replaced" by $52 million in individual contributions to 527s. Clearly, this is not mere replacement; something more is going on than water finding its level.

It would be worthwhile to compare this top group of ten megadonors to the rest of the former soft money donors. These ten donors and their corporations represent 3 percent of the corporations; they gave less than 4 percent of the corporate soft money in our database. The remaining 361 (98 percent) of the corporations gave 96 percent of the soft money in 2000 and 2002: in 2004, 237 of our 361 remaining corporations gave nothing at all to the 527 committees; the other 124 corporations gave a combined total of only $16 million in corporate or individual money—less than one-third of the amount given by the ten individual megadonors.

This finding underscores the importance of defining one's questions precisely. If you look solely at the total number of dollars, it appears that a fair amount of the soft money coming from the donors in our database was "replaced" in 2004. But the answer is different if you want to know about BCRA's effect on the typical soft money donor. Corporate donors represented more than 85 percent of the organizational donors in our database who gave $100,000 or more in soft money in both 2000 and 2002. Excluding the extraordinary contributions from the big ten donors to the 527 committees, it turns out that the remaining 98 percent of the corporations—who in turn represent 84 percent of all of the major organizational soft money donors—spent a lot less money on federal elections in 2004 than they had spent in the recent past.

The findings are consistent with our general theoretical framework for the relationship between an organization's goals, resources, and electoral activities. Many large corporations give contributions not so much to affect election outcomes as to develop and maintain a relationship with an officeholder. About 85 percent of corporate PAC money in any election year generally goes to incumbents (Ornstein, Mann, and Malbin 2002). For many large corporations, soft money decisions were meant to serve the same institutionally cautious goals as PAC contributions. When large corporations used institutional (corporate treasury) money to give soft money, they typically were responding to requests from officeholders, party officials, or their agents. Without the request, the donation would not have occurred. Most of the top executives in large corporations saw soft money contributions as business decisions, not as expressions of a personal political agenda.

Therefore it follows that the considerations that stimulated soft money giving do not automatically transfer to 527 committees. For one thing, officeholders do not ask for the contributions to 527s, so the potential reward is no longer so direct. At the same time, 527 advertising also carries substantial risks for business donors. Most corporations are reluctant either to spend their own money in an identifiable way or to give visibly to another nonparty organization that purchases advertising in a closely contested race because publicly engaging in controversial electoral activities is bound to annoy a significant percentage of the people who hear the message. Unlike corporate "feel good" community advertising or focused noncandidate issue advertising, a polarizing political message has a potential downside for business, alienating current and potential customers. For most large publicly held corporations, these combined considerations— along with the legally uncertain footing of 527s during much of 2004—seem to have fed a political caution consistent with past behavior. In contrast, the donors associated with smaller businesses give individual contributions or contributions from the treasuries of privately held corporations that they own. While they may have to weigh business considerations similar to those of the larger corporations, these executives are much freer, and more able financially, to pursue a personal political agenda.

The net effect of the abolition of soft money, therefore, was not to reduce the role of all individuals who had earned their wealth in a business but to substantially displace the role of large, publicly owned corporations. To be sure, money from these larger corporations does show up in contributions to the national political party conventions. (The two 2004 convention host committees raised $139 million in private contributions, much of it from former soft money donors. The 2000 committees raised a total of $56 million privately; see Weissman and Hassan 2004.) Between host committees, presidential inaugural committees, 501(c)(6) trade associations, and 501(c)(4) issue organizations, the largest corporations may well find new, undisclosed ways to participate in the future. But it does appear as if BCRA reduced their role in 2004.

ELECTIONEERING

BCRA's second major set of provisions—Title II in the law—regulated electioneering. Under the law, corporations and labors unions cannot pay for or contribute to a fund that directly or indirectly pays for electioneering. Electioneering is defined as a broadcast radio or television commercial that names a candidate and (1) that is aired within sixty days of a general election or thirty days of a primary (the "window") and (2) that is broadcast to a potential audience of at least 50,000 people within the relevant election constituency. In addition, any organization that spends more than $10,000 per year on electioneering must disclose any donor of $1,000 or more. We were interested in (1) whether prohibiting corporate and labor funding for ads within the window influenced the frequency, timing, or sponsorship of those interest group advertisements that did appear in 2004 and (2) whether the decisions by some interest groups to emphasize non-broadcast activities could be attributed to BCRA.

A. Number and Timing of Interest Group Ads

To review BCRA's possible effects on political advertising by interest groups, we considered the number, timing, and sources of advertisements in the 2000, 2002, and 2004 election cycles that mentioned a federal candidate. For several elections, the Wisconsin Advertising Project from the University of Wisconsin has been capturing the placement information (including station identification and time of placement), along with storyboards and images, for every political advertisement broadcast in covered media markets. In the database, a new record is generated every time an advertisement runs. For 2000 the data, supplied by the Campaign Media Analysis Group (CMAG), covered the nation's seventy-five largest media markets, which included more than 80 percent of the country's population. For 2002, CMAG data included one hundred markets. In 2004, the project's data came from the Nielsen Company and included all 210 of the country's media markets. Since each record contains the station identification as well as the media market or city, we were able to compare advertising in the same seventy-five markets for all three elections. For a more complete picture, the following table also presents information about 2004 advertising in all 210 markets nationwide. For each year, we present the number of ads by all interest group advertisers for the full year, followed by the number within the sixty-day pregeneral election period defined in BCRA.

As table 6.3 shows, the number of candidate-specific interest group advertisements in the top seventy-five media markets almost doubled between 2000 and 2004. There were almost as many ads (80 percent) within the sixty-day window in 2004 as in 2000. Late advertising was down in proportional terms not because

Table 6.3 Number of Candidate-Specific Broadcast Television Spots Purchased by Nonparty Organizations, 2000–2004

	2000			2002			2004			
Org.	Top 75 Markets	Top 75 w/in 60 Days	Org.	Top 75 Markets	Top 75 w/in 60 Days	Org.	Top 75 Markets	Top 75 w/in 60 Days	(210 Markets)	(210 Markets) 60 Days
Labor										
AFL-CIO	17,050	9,779	AFL-CIO	4,244	2,945	AFL-CIO	5,642	0	(10,962)	(0)
NEA	511	511	NEA	194	194	Comm. Qual. Educ. (NEA)	3,783	63	(5,238)	(63)
Am. Family Voices	447	0	Others	405	397	UAW	1,754	1,754	(2,664)	(2,664)
Others	59	0				SEIU	1,206	979	(2,213)	(1,731)
						AFSCME	430	0	(2,111)	(0)
						Others	833	580	(1,314)	(1,314)
Subtotal	18,067	10,290		4,843	3,536		13,648	3,629	(24,502)	(5,772)
Liberal										
Planned Parenthood	5,916	5,916	Sierra Club	1,611	1,078	Media Fund	40,430	5,000	(74,915)	(9,442)
EMILY's List	3,514	3,445	Emily's List	896	0	MoveOn	24,257	3,944	(43,143)	(7,314)
Handgun Control	2,867	2,443	LCV	830	830	New Democrat Network	5,755	5,546	(10,609)	(10,196)
Sierra Club	2,245	1,715	Ref. Voter Proj.	665	419	Ctzns For Strong Senate	3,830	3,830	(6,136)	(6,136)
LCV	1,705	1,705	NARAL	386	386	LCV	3,182	2,861	(3,425)	(3,035)
Cmpgn Prog. Fut.	1,262	979				EMILY's Lst	2,399	851	(3,955)	(851)
NAACP	468	468				Stronger Amer. Now	742	742	(1,289)	(1,289)
Others	692	98	Others	478	478	Others	2,217	2,094	(3,143)	(2,820)
Subtotal	18,669	16,769		4,866	3,191		82,812	24,868	(146,615)	(41,083)

Business

Citzns Better Medicare	10,876	10,753	United Seniors Ass.	10,915	9,055	Am. for Job Security	2,290	133	(134)	(5,279)
Amer. for Job Security	6,069	5,007	Amer. Job Security	1,615	1,615	United Seniors Ass.	1,470	6	(6)	(2,291)
Chamber of Comm.	7,574	7,574	Amer. Med. Assoc.	915	725	Nat. Assoc. Realtors	922	922	(922)	(1,701)
Business Roundtable	4,884	4,571	Nat. Assoc. Realtors	200	200	Amer. Med. Assoc.	442	442	(1,109)	(1,109)
Amer. Med. Assoc.	577	543	Others	400	131	Others	297	191	(455)	(734)
Others	857	497								
Subtotal	30,837	28,945	Subtotal	14,045	11,725	Subtotal	5,421	1,694	(2,626)	(11,114)

Conservative

U.S. Term Limits	978	37	Club for Growth	1,574	817	Progress for America	8,960	7,433	(19,498)	(23,354)
Am. Limited Terms	535	195				Swift Boat Vets	5,077	4,078	(6,836)	(8,690)
NRA	395	358				Club for Growth	4,760	1,602	(2,934)	(8,151)
Others	39	39				Am. United to Preserve Marriage	549	549	(705)	(705)
						NRA	538	484	(1,029)	(1,083)
						Others	1,015	688	(1,130)	(1,827)
Subtotal	1,947	629	Subtotal	1,574	817	Subtotal	20,899	14,834	(32,132)	(43,810)
Total	68,470	56,633		25,328	19,270		122,782	45,025	(81,613)	(226,041)

there was less of it, but because there was almost seven times more interest group advertising before sixty days in 2004 than in 2000. Of course, it is likely that without BCRA some of the earlier advertising in 2004 would have run within the sixty-day window.

Under BCRA, advertising within the sixty-day window must rely exclusively on contributions from individuals. This produced a shift among advertisers. Two-thirds of the ads within sixty days in 2000 were paid for either by the AFL-CIO or by business-funded organizations. In 2004, the relatively small amount of late advertising by business and labor was funded by political action committees (American Medical Association, National Association of Realtors, United Auto Workers, and Service Employees International Union). The major late advertisers were issue and ideological groups of the following descriptions, all of which purchased their ads with money from individual contributions: (1) new 527 committees (The Media Fund, New Democrat Network, Citizens for a Strong Senate, and Americans United to Preserve Marriage); (2) organizations that set up (or always had) segregated accounts or PACs funded only by individuals (Club for Growth, MoveOn, EMILY's List, and the NRA); and (3) one organization (League of Conservation Voters) whose political fund had always depended solely on individual contributions.

In 2004, interest group advertising before the sixty-day window was dominated by four organizations, all of which concentrated their ads on supporting John Kerry or opposing George Bush after the primary contest effectively was over. These were The Media Fund, MoveOn, the AFL-CIO, and Communities for Quality Education, which was funded by the National Education Association (NEA). President Bush's campaign discouraged supporters from using 527s until later in the campaign season (see chapter 5). Most races below the presidential level were still in a primary rather than general election mode.

Sectors

Looking within sectors: labor's advertising was down a bit but diversified; business ads were down substantially; liberal and conservative issue and ideological groups were both up but with a significant shift among players.

LABOR
By 2000, the AFL-CIO had already scaled back from its television advertising of 1996 (Boatright et al. 2003), but its 17,050 spots in 2000 still outnumbered any other interest group's for that year(see table 6.3). The AFL-CIO cut back its advertising further in 2002 and then leveled off for 2004 when it shifted all of its spending before the sixty-day window. The number of labor ads in 2004 was down 25 percent from 2000, but more players were involved. The AFL-CIO's drop after 2000 was almost matched by 2004 increases from the NEA, Service Employees' International Union (SEIU), and UAW. Some of these labor organizations also contributed to The Media Fund, a pro-Democratic 527 committee described in chapter 5.

BUSINESS

Business organizations reduced their candidate-specific advertising significantly from 2000 to 2004. Business groups bought more television spots than labor in 2000, with 30,837 candidate-specific business spots aired in the top seventy-five media markets, compared to labor's 18,067. Nearly one of every six business ads that year was in support of George W. Bush for President, with most of those ads purchased by an organization called Citizens for Better Medicare.[5] In 2002, business ads dropped by more than half, to 14,045 spots. The United Seniors Association alone accounted for more than three-quarters of the business ads total, with Americans for Job Security responsible for an additional 11 percent.[6] In 2004, business ads declined again to 5,421 spots, which was less than one fifth of the 2000 number. Instead of business ads outnumbering labor ads three to one (as they did in 2002), labor ran more than two and a half times as many ads as business in 2004.

It is worth noting what kinds of business organizations have participated in electioneering. We noted earlier that many corporations had an incentive to give soft money (to respond to party leaders) and but felt an equally strong incentive to avoid becoming identified with candidate-specific issue ads (because candidate advertising can alienate potential customers or clients). Therefore, business ads in 2000 were not the products of individual corporations but of peak associations (Chamber of Commerce and Business Roundtable) or other organizations whose donors could legally remain hidden (Citizens for Better Medicare before the enactment of 527 disclosure legislation, Americans for Job Security, and United Seniors Association). After BCRA, less business money was forthcoming, and most of the ads shifted to a period before the window, when disclosure by non-527 groups is not required.

ISSUE AND IDEOLOGICAL GROUPS

The major increase in candidate-specific advertising in 2004 came from among the organizations that table 6.3 collects under the headings for "liberal" and "conservative" groups. These include at least three different kinds of entities: ongoing specialized issue groups, ongoing organizations with broad agendas, and newer 527 organizations formed after BCRA. Issue groups and ideological organizations face very different incentives from those of business groups when deciding on campaign strategy. For these groups, giving soft money to a party meant losing control over resources. Issue groups might want to work with party leaders, but they also need to build support for themselves. Communicating directly with the public about politics does indeed use resources to influence the outcome of an election, but it can also help the organization shape the policy agenda, build a constituency, and strengthen its reputation for action.

Nonetheless, the data show a decided shift among TV advertisers away from established issue groups and toward the new 527 committees. Planned Parenthood, Handgun Control, Sierra Club, NAACP, NARAL Pro-Choice America, and the two pro-term limit groups were significant broadcast advertisers in 2000 or 2002 but not in 2004. Conversely, most of the major advertisers in 2004—

The Media Fund, MoveOn, New Democrat Network, Citizens for a Strong Senate, Progress for America, Swift Boat Vets, and Americans United to Save Marriage—were either brand new for 2004 or not significant advertisers in the past. One reason might simply have to do with money: even if an organization finds television useful, the medium is expensive. Several of the ongoing issue groups that bought television ads in 2000 (including Planned Parenthood, NARAL Pro-Choice America, Handgun Control, and the NAACP) were the beneficiaries of large contributions that helped underwrite their election activities. Without special contributions, those advertising campaigns could not have taken place. But the new emphasis in 2004 cannot be explained only by a shortage of money for TV. Ongoing organizations had other reasons for shifting, as we shall see.

B. Shifts in Activities: Coalitions and Mobilization

Our second set of questions about the impact of BCRA's electioneering provisions concern whether ongoing organizations that existed before BCRA shifted toward nonelectioneering activities, and whether BCRA was the reason for this shift. For answers, we had to move beyond the kind of hard data we had been using. Because we were probing strategic reasoning as well as raw activity levels, we interviewed a diverse set of organizational leaders over the course of three election cycles. (This was part of a larger study to document their thoughts as they reviewed and changed their election strategies.) For convenience, we summarize the relevant 2004 material under four headings—labor, liberal, business, and conservative groups.

Labor

The appropriate context for understanding labor's 2004 election strategy has to begin with 1996, the first election after John Sweeney became president of the AFL-CIO and the first after Republicans gained a majority in both chambers of Congress. The AFL-CIO's $36 million political campaign in 1996 was a political watershed for the labor movement. Approximately $25 million of this money was directed not only at labor members and their families but also at the general public through television and radio advertisements. These ads criticized vulnerable Republican House members for their positions on education, health care, and other issues. During 1998 and 2000, however, the AFL-CIO reduced its spending on broadcast advertising and chose to concentrate instead on direct contacts with its members. By 2000, the AFL-CIO reportedly was spending $46 million on its election-related activities (Lawrence 2000).

The labor federation spent an estimated $21 million on broadcast advertising during the full 1999–2000 cycle (Annenberg Public Policy Center 2001). While the methodologics used by those who reported the 1996 and 2000 numbers were not consistent, it does appear that spending on television advertising dropped somewhat over the four years while nonbroadcast spending doubled. In a Campaign Finance Institute forum, the AFL-CIO's political director Steven Rosenthal said that the federation's studies of its own activities showed that face-to-face communication was far more effective than television for achieving labor's political goals (Malbin et al. 2002). The labor federation developed a network of more than one thousand paid staff members, as well as many volunteers, who registered and made direct contact with voters, most of whom were labor union members and their families (Biersack and Holt 2004).

Meanwhile, during the same years in which labor organizations were increasing their internal mobilization activities, they were also increasing their activity in coalitions with nonlabor groups that advocated women's issues, civil rights, or the environment (Gerber 1999). These coalition efforts increased dramatically in 2004. With labor union membership down to 13.9 million people (or 12.9 percent of the voting age population) and with many of the Republican Party's gains coming in Sunbelt states that have a low union presence, labor strategists felt they simply had to reach out beyond their own members. When he announced that he was leaving the AFL-CIO in 2002, Rosenthal said: "We've gotten very good at mobilizing union members to participate in elections and electing more pro-worker candidates, but we still have to improve dramatically on how we can create an environment so workers can organize" (Greenhouse 2002).

The vehicles that many labor, liberal, and Democratic Party activists chose for coalition building after 2002 were new 527 committees. The initial effort essentially was a turnout-oriented labor 527, the Partnership for America's Families (Partnership), which had its first reported receipts and expenditures in April 2003. The board included leaders of the Service Employees' International Union (SEIU), the Hotel Employees and Restaurant Employees International Union (HERE), the United Food and Commercial Workers (UFCW), and the American Federation of State, County, and Municipal Employees (AFSCME). Soon after its formation, however, the organization became embroiled in a visible internal dispute that led several union leaders (including the head of AFSCME) to resign from the board. Sweeney eventually stepped in and brokered a compromise, but the effects lingered.

In August 2003, Ellen Malcolm of EMILY's List announced the formation of a new organization, America Coming Together (ACT). From the beginning, ACT's leadership included leaders from both labor and nonlabor organizations. In fact, the original November 2002 meeting that spurred the 527 movement among pro-Democratic organizations included Malcolm, Rosenthal, SEIU President Andrew Stern, longtime Democratic activist Harold Ickes (who later became president of The Media Fund and then ACT), and Carl Pope, executive director of the Sierra Club (see chapter 5). Rosenthal was ACT's executive director and brought most of the Partnership's staff with him. ACT received relatively few direct contributions of money from labor unions: $4 million from SEIU, $1 million from the Teamsters Union, and $600,000 from the International Brotherhood of Electrical Workers (IBEW). However, if one includes in-kind contributions that SEIU claims to have made to support ACT's mobilization effort (see below), labor's combined cash and in-kind contributions may have accounted for more than a quarter of ACT's spending. The AFL-CIO itself was not directly involved in ACT, nor was it a major financial contributor. Nevertheless, ACT's strategy was a natural extension of the AFL-CIO's canvassing strategy of the previous several elections.

The AFL-CIO reportedly spent $45 million on mobilizing its own members in 2004, largely following a more sophisticated version of its personal contacting strategy of 2000 and 2002 (Williams 2004). The federation reported that it had 5,000 members doing paid political work, a three- to fivefold increase from 2000, and that it had 200,000 members doing volunteer work (Williams 2004). The AFL-CIO's 527 committee also grew from $5.5 million in 2002 to $6.3 million in 2004. Its 527 contributions in 2004 went to Voices for American Families, The Media Fund, Moving America Forward, and the Partnership for America's Families. In general, most labor unions seem to have spent most of their federally oriented 527 money for externally oriented activities—soft money contributions in 2000 and 2002 and independent 527 organizations in 2004. Internal mobilization of labor union members and their families was generally funded directly from union treasury funds.

Other unions also increased their own spending. The most significant of these were the SEIU and AFSCME. Although a postelection accounting is not available, Andrew Stern, president of the SEIU, estimated in an interview before the election that his union would spend about $65 million on electoral politics in 2004. This was to have included about $40 million to cover the salaries of SEIU members who took leaves to work either within or alongside ACT to mobilize voters in battleground states. This money appears to have come from the SEIU's 527 committee, which increased its spending massively, from $12 million in 2002 to $55 million in 2004. Stern also estimated before the election that the SEIU would spend $20 million to mobilize its own members and their families nationally and about $5 million on state and local elections (Business Week Online 2004).

AFSCME's 527 committee grew from $19.6 million in 2002 to $22.1 million in 2004. While it is not possible to estimate precisely how much of this money was spent on federal versus state and local elections, union officials acknowledged at least 40 percent was clearly federal. Among other things, AFSCME's funds helped support external mobilization activities by Voices for Working Families, Moving America Forward, and Partnership for America's Families, as well as television advertising by The Media Fund. We do not know the scale of AFSCME's internal mobilization efforts. In other labor 527 committee spending in 2003–2004, the IBEW reported spending $9.4 million; HERE, $4 million; the National Education Association (NEA), $3.9 million; and the Sheet Metal Workers, $2.1 million. Other, smaller unions sometimes had the good fortune to have their members concentrated in battleground states, so these groups could do mobilization work without having to send members elsewhere. The United Mine Workers (UMW), for instance, has large contingents in two states (West Virginia and New Mexico) that were considered toss-ups in the election (Williams 2004). Labor unions were also active in several Senate and House elections, but the bulk of their efforts were in the presidential race.

Although labor's mobilization efforts increased, the overall results of the 2004 election were disappointing for unions. The percentage of union members who supported the Democratic presidential ticket was comparable to 2000: one exit poll showed that two-thirds of union members voted for Kerry (Strope 2004). But the percentage of voters who were union members was down from 18 percent in 2000 to 14 percent in 2004, and the percentage of voters from union households was down from 27 percent in 2000 to 24 percent. (The 2004 percentages are from Strope (2004); the 2000 figures are from the authors' interviews with labor union officials.) It is hard to know how to read these figures. It may simply be that, in an election where mobilization is so important to both parties, labor's efforts become less of a factor in comparative terms even if in absolute terms they are no less effective than before.

Liberal

Liberal advocacy organizations also increased their emphasis on voter mobilization activities between 2000 and 2004. As mentioned previously, the high level of television advertising by some of these ongoing groups in 2000 stemmed partly from one-time contributions designed to influence a presidential election. Without those contributions (and without the presidential election), advertising naturally fell in 2002. While new organizations, such as MoveOn and The Media Fund, more than picked up the advertising slack, the older groups' emphasis on voter mobilization also reflected conscious learning and self-study.

Perhaps the most influential and formal of these studies was conducted for the National Association for the Advancement of Colored People's National Voter Fund. The NAACP-NVF commissioned Donald Green and Alan Gerber to analyze the effectiveness of its registration efforts. Political scientists from Yale, Green and Gerber had been working to perfect experimental design techniques for studying voter turnout (Green and Gerber 2004). Many of the liberal interest groups were swayed by the authors' conclusions that face-to-face, personal contact was superior to other mobilization methods. In 2004, several other organizations sought to employ their experimental method. Several groups targeting young voters, including 21st Century Democrats and the Public Interest Research Group's (PIRG's) New Voter Project, consulted with Green and Gerber about evaluating their efforts. But for the most part, group evaluations of their own activities are less scientific. Research results tend to blend with the shared interpretations of group leaders (be they allies or opponents), politicians, journalists, or other political analysts. A bandwagon effect developed. As more groups touted their "ground war" efforts, others felt inclined to pursue similar efforts.

But the really new element in 2004, not present in 2002, was the specific attention the groups paid to *coordinating* their efforts. This effort at coordination within the electoral arena in 2004 bore a strong resemblance to what many of these and other organizations had already been doing in a legislative lobbying context. In recent decades, interest groups of all kinds have increasingly come to use coalitions for lobbying on specific issues. In the best systematic study of these coalitions to date, Kevin Hula found them to be more structured than issue networks or *ad hoc* alliances. They have "core members" and "tag-alongs" and are designed to solve problems of information sharing and coordination (Hula 1999). The coalitions in Hula's study had typically conducted both "inside" lobbying campaigns and high profile media campaigns. It was an easy step for organizations to apply what they had learned from grassroots lobbying to the electoral arena.

In their evaluations of the 2000 election, several advocacy groups discovered that their efforts had been weakened because they had not known what other groups were doing. In studies of union members in battleground districts in 2000 and 2002, participants saved and dated political mail they received and also noted television advertisements, phone calls, and personal contacts. These studies demonstrated that many allied groups sent their mailings or ran advertisements at the same time, thus preventing each group's message from being received clearly (Richards 2003). In some cases, approaches that had been rejected by one group after focus group testing were used by other, like-minded groups. Some organization leaders we interviewed told us that, after hearing these evaluations, they felt they could be more effective if they shared more of their information before acting.

America Votes was founded in July 2003 by some of the same groups that came together behind ACT precisely to make it easier for liberal and labor organizations to coordinate their growing mobilization efforts in the electoral arena. By 2004, the coalition comprised thirty-one labor unions and liberal issue groups, including both well-established groups and some of the larger new 527 organizations. Because of its founding date, America Votes has been described in the press as being a consequence of BCRA (John Harwood 2004). BCRA's ban on soft money may well have fueled the urgency these organizations' supporters felt, which in turned helped open the wallets of donors for this election. Nevertheless, the roots of this effort go back several years.

Most group leaders agree that *something like* America Votes would have been formed even without BCRA, but America Votes was able to increase its reach by synchronizing its efforts with several of the newer 527s that were a more direct outcome of BCRA. Apart from $500,000 in seed money from individuals, America Votes was funded through $50,000 contributions from four labor unions (AFL-CIO, AFT, SEIU, and AFSCME) and several liberal groups (ACT, The Media Fund, NARAL Pro-Choice America, the Human Rights Campaign (HRC), EMILY's List, the Sierra Club, MoveOn.org, and LCV), $100,000 from the NEA, $60,000 from the Trial Lawyers' Association, and smaller contributions from Planned Parenthood, People for the American Way, the Brady Campaign, and others. ACT, mentioned earlier, was formed from a coalition of preexisting groups. (For more on ACT, see chapter 5.)

America Votes was active in seventeen states in 2004. Member groups shared polling, targeting, and candidate training sessions. They divided states into geographic regions for voter contacting, and they coordinated their rapid response efforts. America Votes also sought to integrate groups dedicated to mobilizing younger voters—such as 21st Century Democrats and ClickBackAmerica (the component of MoveOn.org dedicated to younger voters)—with traditional, older interest groups. Part of the long-term goal of this effort was to expand the voter files of these groups and fill in information on younger voters for all of these organizations.

By sharing information about these matters, the participating groups hoped to improve each other's messages, ensure that groups were clear about the timing of each group's efforts, and compare notes on what approaches or strategies were working best. There is some evidence that this worked. Groups that did not have the resources to canvass an entire neighborhood or city on their own would divide the area with other groups, or groups with a particular expertise or interest in one part of the country could ensure that other groups were aware of this interest. For example, we were told in an interview that Planned Parenthood concentrated a substantial percentage of its resources in 2004 on unmarried female voters in Oregon; other groups developed similarly narrow targets.

Beyond coordination, the major component of this election's change in group activities was its emphasis on volunteers and activists. Many organizations, such as the Human Rights Campaign and NARAL Pro-Choice America, set up their own training academies. Others, such as the League of Conservation Voters, sought to develop stronger ties with their state and local affiliates in order to take advantage of the skills of local activists. This enabled groups to ensure that volunteers were adequately trained and that they stayed "on message." Several newly formed organizations, including Wellstone Action and Democratic GAIN, also trained volunteers. Wellstone Action, formed by members of the campaign staff of the late senator, conducted workshops for aspiring campaign activists in more than twenty cities. The group trained people from America Coming Together, America Votes, and several of the organizations targeting younger voters.

Finally, other groups emphasized candidate recruitment. Progressive Majority collaborated with Democracy for America, the organization formed by Howard Dean following his withdrawal from the Democratic primaries, to support state legislative candidates in several states. In addition to raising money for these candidates, Progressive Majority developed candidate-training materials on virtually every aspect of campaigning, as well as on ways to frame progressive ideas in a campaign. This recruitment effort grew out of a long-standing perception among Democratic activists that the party had neglected to build its local foundations for national politics. There was also a conscious attempt to emulate the infrastructure of training organizations, advocacy groups, and think tanks that they believed had abetted the Republican gains of the 1990s.

In short, liberal advocacy organizations had begun before BCRA to develop the distinctive operational methods they employed in 2004, but the 2004 election cycle deepened the effort substantially. The general shift toward voter mobilization was well established before BCRA. This was fueled by several non-BCRA elements of the political context. First, the narrowing of competition and close division of party control meant that high political stakes were focused on identifiable states and districts. Second, it is expensive to reach and persuade new supporters through broadcast advertising in a saturated market. Third, in a race in which voters make up their minds early, it becomes more efficient to mobilize one's supporters than to persuade undecided voters. Finally, because the battle for the presidency in 2004 was closer than the battle for control of the House or Senate, the groups were more willing to focus on that one election.

But even though the groups had chosen their paths before BCRA, BCRA certainly fueled the intensity of their efforts. The absence of party soft money, combined with their intense animus against George W. Bush, gave the groups a powerful reason to work together toward what they saw as a common goal. Hence the groups were willing to focus on a coordinated attempt to boost turnout, rather than spend their energies trying to make their own issues and voices heard over the din. It remains to be seen whether such coordination will continue in the 2006 elections or in a future presidential election that might not be so heavily dominated by issues that do not fit into the various groups' issue niches.

Business

Although business organizations have a long history of lobbying Congress, their participation in elections until recent years centered only on giving money. According to many business group leaders, businesses typically worked to mobilize voters only as a reaction to other groups' activities or to particular legislative actions. This changed in the mid-1990s for two reasons, both related to the shift in majority control of Congress to the Republican Party. First, organized labor increased its election-related activity in 1996. Seeing the Democrats' defeat in 1994 as partly the result of low turnout among Democratic voters, including labor voters, organized labor launched its already mentioned 1996 efforts to reverse those results. Hence, business countermobilization can be seen in part as an example of organizational imitation and learning. The second reason business shifted its activities was that the GOP's majority was precarious. The narrowness of control fueled the intense electoral concerns of congressional leaders, which in turn heightened the desire of leaders of peak business associations to be effective politically and to be seen as being effective.

Whatever the precise sequence, business groups responded strongly to the change in the interest group environment (labor mobilization) and to the shift of institutional power within Congress. The Coalition: Americans Working for Real Change was formed during the 1996 election in direct response to the AFL-CIO's 1996 electioneering activities. It was the precursor of many other business coalitions that have been active in the past four election cycles. However, the early efforts seemed to concentrate on issue advertising. In 1998 and 2000, according to many in the business community, labor successfully outmobilized business. Organizational leaders thought that business groups' strategies of televised issue advocacy ads and soft money contributions were not adequate to counter labor's efforts.

As a result, for business as well as for other organizations, the shift away from TV began before BCRA. This was evident by 2002. And as with labor, the shift away from persuading the general public through television was accompanied by a shift toward putting more emphasis on other means of communication. After reaching many of the same conclusions as labor leaders about the difficulty of reaching voters through broadcasting, organizations such as the Business-Industry Political Action Committee (BIPAC), the Chamber of Commerce, and the National Federation of Independent Businesses (NFIB) sought to expand their grassroots efforts and to use the Internet to relay political information to employees. To some extent, the business leaders seemed to want to use the Internet the way labor was using face-to-face contact. It is also worth noting that this was essentially an *internal* effort, an attempt to reach employees, just as labor was trying to reach union members and families. So far, it has not been an effort like those of the liberal 527 committees to mobilize voters more generally.

One significant business mobilization effort has been BIPAC's Prosperity Project. The Project consists of web-based descriptions of candidates' views and votes on issues of concern to businesses. BIPAC provides the information, derived from its database, but the information and the site's overall appearance are customized for each participating business. The Prosperity Project also provides information about online voter registration, absentee ballots, and early voting. The Project was piloted in 2000 among several large corporations, including Halliburton, Proctor and Gamble, and Exxon-Mobil. By 2002, it had grown from 50 companies to 184 companies, and by 2004, BIPAC was claiming that it had delivered 30 million political messages, 812,000 voter registration forms, and 789,000 early voting forms. Although the Project had also been expanded to include thirty-one state-level projects in 2002, it was more focused in 2004, covering thirteen states. BIPAC reduced its Project costs by seeking a partner in each of these states, generally a state Chamber of Commerce or Association of Manufacturers.

The success of the Prosperity Project ultimately depends not only on BIPAC but also on how businesses themselves promote the project. In our interviews with corporate PAC directors, all agreed that the project could be successful if companies worked hard to steer employees to it, but in many cases companies are reluctant to do this. Several of the more political groups, however, have not only encouraged employees to use it but have supplemented it with their own materials. For instance, the Associated Builders and Contractors also provides a series of "Toolbox Talks," sample political speeches that employers can give that help workers make voting decisions, without straying from the law regarding such communications. And although corporate PACs are legally prohibited from collecting employees' individual contributions and bundling them together to exceed the PAC contribution limit, some groups have sought to establish parallel programs. The Associated Builders and Contractors included on its website a flash video describing what it viewed as the most important races in the country. The National Association of Realtors has instituted a "direct giver" program in which it solicits pledges from members to give to particular campaigns, and then requests that members notify the organization when they have made their contributions. This is not quite bundling, but just one step short. Over $400,000 was pledged for this program in 2004.

It is difficult to evaluate the success of business groups' new mobilization ventures conclusively. However, it is possible to assess one specific aspect. Shortly after BCRA became law, some predicted that business would attempt to mobilize corporate employees to contribute more money to their companies' PACs (Hitt and Hamburger 2002; VandeHei 2002a). This seems not to have happened. Corporate PACs gave about 14 percent more to congressional candidates running in 2004 than in 2002. Contributions from trade/member/health PACs increased by 9 percent. While these increases are significant, they should *not* be attributed to BCRA because business PAC giving had also shown comparable spurts in the previous two presidential election years (Ornstein, Mann, and Malbin 2002).

Conservative

While the opposition of liberal advocacy organizations to President Bush gave them a unifying motivation for coalitional activities, there is less of a unifying thread to the changes in the electoral activities of conservative advocacy groups over the past three election cycles. In part, this is because there are far fewer large, ongoing advocacy groups on the right than there are on the left. More importantly, it was the Republican Party that led the general mobilization efforts for its ticket, whereas interest groups largely filled that role for the Democrats (see chapter 2). In effect, the party has absorbed much of the conservative movement of the 1980s and 1990s. Social conservatives, and gay marriage opponents in particular, were said to have been a major element of the Bush victory in several states, and it was reported that the Bush campaign sought to encourage voter mobilization by evangelical churches. Still, groups such as the Christian Coalition, the National Right to Life Committee, and other staples of the conservative movement in years past were not particularly visible in 2004, replaced by newer and more dispersed organizations. The only nonbusiness interest groups on the right that have maintained a visible electioneering presence or have been major campaign contributors in all of the past three election cycles have been the Club for Growth and the National Rifle Association. These organizations are quite different from each other, but because their donor bases and resources differ from those of the groups discussed above, we shall offer a few words about each.

Club for Growth

The Club for Growth is perhaps the foremost contemporary example of an entrepreneurial interest group, one developed by a small coterie of people seeking to fill a gap in the interests represented by groups. Far from seeking coalitions with other groups, Steven Moore, the Club's president through 2004, spoke openly of seeking to establish a "market niche." The group has described itself as the "moral compass of the Republican Party," backing long-shot conservative challengers and open-seat candidates, often to the dismay of GOP leaders. Originally formed in 1999 as a bundling group, the Club bundled and spent over $9 million in the 2002 cycle, making it one of the largest organized interests on the right. The group had 6,800 members going into the 2002 election. While this number is not trivial, it also is not large enough to make it worthwhile to consider internal voter mobilization as a serious campaign strategy.

While much of the growth in the group's resources has probably been the result of either successful promotion by Moore or the successes of the group's candidates, BCRA has also played a role. Executive Director David Keating contends that the limit on contributions to the parties and the increase in individual hard money contribution limits have helped bundling organizations. Yet the group has expanded well beyond bundling over the past two election cycles. The Club has increased its advertising, creating separate PACs and 527s to permit advertising throughout the cycle while remaining consistent with BCRA's electioneering restrictions. The Club's future may be a bit cloudy: after what was reported in the press as a "power struggle," Moore resigned from the Club in early 2005 to start the Free Enterprise Fund. The successor president is former Rep. Patrick Toomey, whom the Club had supported in an unsuccessful 2004 Senate primary race against Arlen Specter (Gerstein 2005). Despite any questions about the Club's future, it is clear that the electioneering ban did *not* lead to a shift in the Club's activities, since the Club in its various legal forms purchased and placed three times as many ads in the top seventy-five markets in 2004 as in 2002, including double the number inside the sixty-day window (see table 6.3).

NATIONAL RIFLE ASSOCIATION
In several ways, the National Rifle Association is similar organizationally to advocacy groups on the left, only larger. The NRA claims 3.8 million members, who run the gamut from dedicated political activists to individuals who join primarily because of material benefits the group provides to hunters and marksmen. The organization was one of the most outspoken plaintiffs in the *McConnell* case, and it has devoted a substantial amount of its resources to testing the limits of BCRA. In 2004, the group introduced its own radio station on the Sirius Satellite Radio Network. Because of BCRA's "media exception" provision, the radio station could broadcast news from the NRA's point of view without running afoul of the electioneering provision. But NRA Executive Vice President Wayne La-Pierre argued that the radio station was in large part symbolic, declaring, "Someone needs to show the court and the politicians how absurd their speech gag on the American public is" (Associated Press 2004). Most of the NRA's more influential political activity was, however, done through the mail or through the Internet.

Despite the NRA's high-profile challenge to BCRA and its subsequent testing of the law, it was not in a position to spend as much on politics in 2004 as it spent in 2000. In his *McConnell* district court deposition, LaPierre said that the NRA spent "millions more than we had on hand" to defeat Gore (LaPierre 2002). The NRA scaled back its spending substantially in 2002. By late 2003, internal opponents of LaPierre were claiming that the group's membership had declined, and it was running a deficit of $100 million—a result of its activities in the BCRA case and in contesting lawsuits against gun manufacturers (Strom 2003). Nevertheless, the NRA's hard money activity through its PAC (which paid for its candidate commercials) has not changed dramatically. Receipts for the

NRA Political Victory Fund were $6.6 million in 1996, $7.8 million in 1998, $17.9 million in 2000, $10.5 million in 2002, and $12.8 million in 2004. In short, the electioneering ban has not had a significant direct impact on the NRA.

CHRISTIAN CONSERVATIVES
The electioneering provisions also had little effect on Christian conservative (or other "movement" conservative) organizations because these groups generally did not use broadcast advertising. Because many observers after the 2004 election wrote about the importance of the "moral values vote," some have sought to understand what precipitated the successful mobilization of Christian Right voters. In interviews with a number of religious conservative leaders, few mentioned the older and more familiar Christian Coalition, National Right to Life Committee, or Eagle Forum when asked to name the most important religious conservative groups in 2004. Instead, the names that came up were rarely mentioned in the media: Alliance for Marriage, Redeem the Vote, Americans of Faith, Priests for Life, iVoteValues.com, Conservative Victory Fund, Let Freedom Ring, and also the better-recognized National Association of Evangelicals. Our knowledge of their expenditures is limited because most of these organizations do not disclose their finances under federal election law.

One example of a largely ignored organization was Let Freedom Ring, Inc., headed by Colin Hanna, a former Chester County, Pennsylvania, commissioner. Hanna had earlier refused to remove a plaque of the Ten Commandments from a courthouse wall, setting off a lawsuit in which he ultimately prevailed. In 2004 Hanna organized Let Freedom Ring as a 501(c)(4) nonprofit advocacy organization which received a $1 million grant from John M. Templeton, Jr. Let Freedom Ring concentrated much of its church outreach and grassroots mobilization in the key electoral states of Pennsylvania and Ohio. It conducted a series of ten meetings with 1,700 pastors in those states to inform them of their legal rights in campaigns. It also underwrote the costs for distributing 300,000 voters' guides in those states (including one by Focus on the Family), and it distributed (nationally to 12,000 churches) copies of a documentary entitled "Inner Strength." The documentary emphasized the faith factor in the politics and policies of President Bush and of Senators Rick Santorum and Zell Miller. One-fourth of the documentaries were distributed to churches in Ohio alone. The group also funded voter registration drives and electoral advertising campaigns in key states.

Let Freedom Ring was just one of a number of religious conservative groups playing a role in 2004. Although the Republican Party and the Bush campaign were directly active in mobilizing evangelical conservatives and religious Catholics—taking on most of the voter mobilization work that was being done for the Democrats by the new 527 committees—the role of the new 501(c)(3), 501(c)(4), and 527 groups should not be ignored. Turnout among evangelical conservatives in particular was significantly lower in 2000 than it had been in 1996, and that fact deeply worried the Bush reelection campaign. In 2004, with some conservatives sounding alarms about the continued decline of the Christian

Coalition, a number of smaller grassroots groups moved into the role of mobilizing the Christian Right. The success of the GOP campaigns as well as of the initiatives opposing gay marriage is likely to embolden these groups to remain active, as well as to encourage new ones to form. However, this activity has all taken place among organizations whose activities are not clearly understood (in part because they are not disclosed) and on a plane that is independent of BCRA.

CONCLUSION

The Bipartisan Campaign Reform Act had a significant effect in 2004 on some interest groups' political contributions but less of an effect on their direct communications with voters. The ban on party soft money reduced the amount given or spent by large public corporations and individuals associated with them. These individuals did increase their hard money giving, but at a rate no greater than all other individual givers in an intensely polarized electoral climate. The new 527 committees did make up quantitatively for a significant fraction of the lost soft money, but the mix of players was different, with a handful of megadonors replacing the large corporations.

The electioneering ban had a smaller impact. The number of broadcast ads increased, with adjustments made by the sponsoring organizations to meet legal requirements: ads within sixty days of the election were funded by individuals rather than by corporate or labor union treasury money, while earlier ads were open to funding from all sources. It is possible, of course, that without BCRA, corporations and labor unions would have provided the money for even more advertising inside the sixty-day window. So perhaps the quantitative effects ought to be judged against a plausible hypothetical and not just against past elections. In any case, it is noteworthy that most of the electioneering ads in 2004 were bought by the newer 527 groups, funded mostly by contributions from individuals.

Longer-established advocacy organizations have shifted their emphasis away from advertising and toward voter mobilization. This was especially true for labor and liberal organizations but also to some extent for business. Conservative organizations in our study either have increased their electioneering since BCRA (Club for Growth), have stayed the same (NRA), or never did much electioneering before BCRA (conservative Christian groups). At most, the quantitative and qualitative effects of BCRA's electioneering rules in 2004 were subtle.

We cannot yet know whether the changes of 2004 will last. For example, organizations that cooperated with each other in 2004, sublimating their specific issue identities to help reelect or defeat a sitting president, could choose to differentiate themselves in another political environment—one that is less partisan, less dominated by a few issues, or less focused on a single race. The former soft money donors that sat on the sidelines in 2004 could come back if some of the 527s become functionally identified with the parties, and the donors come to see these contributions as a way to curry favor with party leaders. Or, if the 527s do not take on this identity (and/or if contributions to the 527s are regulated by new legislation), then some businesses might choose to underwrite nonprofit 501(c) issue organizations or trade associations that could expand their election-related activity, as long as that activity does not fall within BCRA's definition of electioneering. Whether this happens will depend in part on which of two incentives dominates for the potential donors. If they strongly wish to participate but are deterred by publicity, some corporations *might* choose the 501(c) path. But many would not. Organizations previously pulled only reluctantly into the system could continue to stay home, leaving politics to be funded to a greater degree by individuals—whether they give limited hard money contributions to the candidates and parties or unlimited soft money donations to the 527s. Whatever the outcome, we can be sure the results will be too complex to be explained by water-filled metaphors about political hydraulics.

NOTES

1. There was also a significant uptick in 527 activity by labor organizations between 2002 and 2004. Since labor's 527 activity in 2002 includes the money labor 527s gave to the parties, the increase of $37 million in labor's 527 activity in 2004 represents a real increase and not a transfer of soft money to the 527s.

2. Ted Waitt, Gateway Corp. ($5 million); Harold Simmons, Contran Corp. ($3.5 million); Carl Lindner, American Financial Group ($2.225 million); Ann Cox Chambers, Cox Enterprises ($1.132 million).

3. George Soros ($24.5 million); Alex Spanos ($5 million); Dawn Arnall ($5 million); Agnes Varis ($2.06 million); Richard DeVos ($2 million); Paul Singer ($1.785 million).

4. The donors in the previous two notes appear in the tables in chapter 5, but not all of the 527 donors in chapter 5 appear here.

5. Citizens for Better Medicare (CBM) was a coalition of business and health groups formed by the Pharmaceutical Manufacturers Association of America and supported by organizations including the U.S. Chamber of Commerce, National Association of Manufacturers, among others (Campaign Finance Institute Task Force on Disclosure 2001). It formed in 1999 and purchased candidate-specific ads only during the 2000 cycle. At least one of CBM's supporting organizations appeared to have transferred its financial support to the United Seniors Association in the 2001–2002 election (see the next endnote).

6. Because United Seniors is registered with the Internal Revenue Service as a nonprofit 501(c) organization, it does not have to disclose the identity of its donors. However, research by the Public Citizen shows that most of the group's 2002 funds probably came from the Pharmaceutical Research and Manufacturers of America (Public Citizen's Congress Watch 2002, 2004). Americans for Job Security (AJS) is a 501(c)(6) trade association originally supported by contributions from the American Insurance Association and American Forest and Paper Association (Campaign Finance Institute Task Force on Disclosure 2001). As a trade association, AJS does not have to disclose its current donors.

III

AIR WARS AND GROUND WARS

7

Much More of the Same: Television Advertising Pre- and Post-BCRA

Michael M. Franz, Joel Rivlin, and Kenneth Goldstein

Before the passage of the Bipartisan Campaign Reform Act (BCRA), television advertising was the main way candidates for office communicated with voters. Before the passage of BCRA, political advertising was carefully targeted and focused on markets and states with competitive contests. Before the passage of BCRA, parties and interest groups were major players in the campaign air war, often airing more advertisements than the campaigns of the candidates they were supporting. Before passage of BCRA, potential voters were often confused about who exactly was paying for the ads that they were seeing. Before passage of BCRA, political professionals believed that negative advertising was a particularly effective way to define an opponent—especially a less well-known one. Before passage of BCRA, there was a division of labor with parties and interest groups much more likely to produce and air ads attacking a candidate they opposed than the candidates themselves. And finally, in each and every election in the twenty years before passage of BCRA, commentators, pundits, and the public would complain that the campaign we were currently in was the most negative and nasty in history.

After BCRA was passed, signed into law by President Bush and upheld by the Supreme Court, many experts predicted that the shape and volume of television advertising would look drastically different in a post-BCRA world. Pundits tended to agree that BCRA might solve what former Senator Tom Daschle of South Dakota once called the "crack cocaine" problem of politics (Daschle 1998).[1]

- Political scientist James Gibson, for example, predicted, "I think there's going to be tremendously less advertising as a result of this" (Branch-Brioso 2003).

- Kathleen Hall Jamieson, director of the University of Pennsylvania's Annenberg Public Policy Center, said advertising "accuracy will go up a bit, and their advocacy," or negativism, "will go down a bit" (Memmott 2004).
- Meredith McGehee, president of the Alliance for Better Campaigns, asserted that one "result is that you have a less negative tone. If you go negative, it is viewed as potentially damaging to your candidacy" (Christensen 2004).
- Senator John McCain said, "It will take $500 million out of American political campaigns to start with. . . . It will force the parties back to the traditional kinds of grassroots politics and organizing that characterized campaigns before the soft money explosion began in the late 80s" (Abrams 2002).
- Senator Maria Cantwell released a statement saying, "This bill is about slowing the ad war. It is about calling sham issue ads what they really are. It is about slowing political advertising and making sure the flow of negative ads by outside interest groups does not continue to permeate the airwave" (Cantwell 2002).

In short, according to the experts, with the passage of BCRA, the era of big and negative television advertising was supposed to be over. Well, at the risk of giving away our punch line too soon, it is clear that many of these predictions were drastically off the mark. Put simply, television advertising before the passage of BCRA looked a lot like advertising after the passage of BCRA. What we saw in 2004 was more of the same—indeed *much* more of the same. To be sure, there were some differences, but the same fundamental factors that determined the targeting and tone of advertising in previous years determined the targeting and tone of political advertising in 2004.

In writing about the 2000 campaign, two of us argued that the volume and tone of political advertising in a particular media market was driven by the competitiveness of races in that market (and the competitiveness of a given state in the presidential election); that advertising emanated from a number of different sponsors, namely candidates, interest groups of all shapes and sizes, and political parties; that political advertising in a given race or region was usually balanced between Democratic and Republican sponsors; and that the tone of advertisements—a crucial characteristic of political advertising that has important implications for the types of messages that voters receive—varied across sponsors, race competitiveness, and time (Freedman, Franz, and Goldstein 2004). Truth be told, we can say virtually the same thing with 2004 in hindsight. In other words, in the first paragraph to this chapter, we could replace the words "before BCRA" with the words "after BCRA" and still have an empirically accurate introductory paragraph.

When all was said and aired in 2004, more than three million political spots had been broadcast in the nation's 210 media markets for candidates up and down the ballot.[2] More than $600 million was spent on television advertising in the presidential contests alone, more than in any presidential campaign in history (Seeyle 2004). In all, the presidential candidates and their party and interest group allies broadcast over a million ads in the 2004 election, well more than twice the number aired four years earlier. Furthermore, even a casual observer of advertising would have concluded that this campaign was not particularly positive; even with the new requirement that candidates appear in and "stand by" their ads, negativity was the norm as the charges and accusations flew.

The chapter is organized as follows. We begin with a quick review of the major provisions within BCRA that applied to television advertising. We then evaluate the lessons learned from the 2004 campaign using data from the University of Wisconsin Advertising Project that tracked, monitored, and coded all political ads aired in all the nation's 210 media markets.

We make four major points: first, the most important independent variable in almost every major model of political advertising remains the competitiveness of the race, and this is true despite changes prescribed by BCRA; second, the "stand by your ad" provision had negligible effects on the tone of advertising; third, interest groups and soft money continued to play a major role, albeit in different forms (adapting to BCRA provisions); and finally, some of the big stories from the 2004 campaign were not to a great degree the consequence of BCRA but of other factors.

BCRA AND POLITICAL ADVERTISING

BCRA contained two major directives concerning television advertising. The first provision concerned how parties and interest groups paid for television ads, as well as what constituted—and how we termed—a regulated public communication. Before BCRA, and particularly in the elections of 1996 2002, party and interest group campaign finance lawyers relied on the "magic word" test in determining how they could pay for television advertisements. As the law was constituted by the late 1990s, so long as parties and interest groups avoided using "magic words" in their public communications, the ad could be funded with soft money, which were funds raised by interest groups and parties for the purpose of electioneering in nonfederal races and for genuine political and nonelectoral speech.

The Supreme Court first elucidated the "magic words" distinction in 1976 in *Buckley v. Valeo* (424 U.S. 1 [1976]). In its famous footnote 52, Court justices speculated as to what words or phrases were clearly ones that set an election ad apart from an issue ad. The justices settled on eight such words and phrases— "vote for," "elect," "support," "cast your ballot for," "Smith for Congress," "vote against," "defeat," and "reject." By the late 1990s, the standard had become set: if "magic words" were mentioned in a television ad for a federal race, it was classified as "express advocacy," which meant it must be paid for with hard money funds. Omitting "magic words" allowed the ad to be classified as "issue advocacy"—or genuine political speech—putting that communication outside the reach of election law regulators.

Critics asserted that the Court never truly intended the "magic word" distinction (mentioned only in a footnote of the *Buckley* ruling) to become the bright line test between issue and express advocacy. After all, the simple avoidance of magic words allowed parties and interest groups to spend millions on advertisements that mentioned federal candidates—and advocated or opposed those candidates—but went unregulated by the Federal Election Commission (certainly a loophole one could drive a truck through). Also relevant for reformers was the observation that candidates (who, by definition, can raise and spend only hard money and so had no incentive to avoid using the magic words) only used magic words in a small proportion of their ads (11.4 percent in the 2000 election, for example).

As such, reformers passed BCRA with the hopes of changing the stakes. First, by all but eliminating party soft money, reformers hoped to force party officials to raise, and contributors to spend, only hard money dollars. They made that task a bit easier by raising the hard money maximum on contributions from $1,000 to $2,000 on contributions to federal candidates and from $20,000 to $25,000 on contributions to federal parties.[3] With the elimination of party soft money came the near disappearance of unregulated and party-sponsored issue ads that mentioned federal candidates.[4]

Second, BCRA changed the boundary between issue and express advocacy. The new legislation established a subtle but important difference between express advocacy advertisements and a new category called "electioneering communications." Post-BCRA, express advocacy refers to the same advertisements aired in the pre-BCRA era—hard money ads that contain magic words. As before, only candidates, parties, and political committees can sponsor and air express advocacy ads.

Despite this, any ads that mention federal candidates but avoid magic words—those that went completely unregulated in years past—were termed electioneering communications. The law prohibits interest groups from airing electioneering communications within sixty days of a general election (and thirty days of a primary) unless the spot was paid for with regulated hard money.

These changes created two potential "loopholes" that leave some electioneering communications unregulated. First, any ad that mentions or pictures a federal candidate but airs outside the sixty-day window is under the same rules as before BCRA, meaning it can be funded with soft money. As such, groups not registered with the FEC are and were in 2004 permitted to air these ads outside the two month window. Second, even with the sixty-day provision, interest groups funded only by soft money contributions from individuals (such as the enormous contributions of George Soros) used such funds to air ads that are unregulated (again, so long as they avoid magic words).

The second major provision relevant to television advertising required every candidate-sponsored ad to include a full-screen view or "clearly identifiable photographic image" of the candidate with the candidate's voice claiming responsibility for the content of the ad. Rarely noted by pundits during the course of congressional debate, this provision became one of the most recognized—and joked about—changes in the content of television ads, as John Trever's cartoon makes clear (Walsh 2004).

Figure 7.1

© *John Trever, Albuquerque Journal, 11/4/2004*

Reformers had long advocated the "stand by your ad" provision, which placed a burden on advertisers to devote four or five seconds of a thirty-second spot to the disclaimer (Rutenberg 2003). Proponents assumed that candidates would be less likely to engage in negative attacks if they were required to appear in and take responsibility for the content of an ad. The "stand by your ad" provision was added by Representative David Price (D-NC), who modeled the requirement on a similar regulation in North Carolina law. Price explained in a press release:

> The American people are sick of the relentlessly negative tone of campaigns, particularly in presidential races. "Stand By Your Ad" isn't just about restoring civility to campaigns. It's also about restoring people's faith in our political process (Price 2004).

Many pundits predicted that the "stand by your ad" provision meant that advertising would be more positive in tone in 2004. Furthermore, it was assumed that the provision would make it easier for citizens to determine who was airing which ads.

Our analysis will be able to clearly test these expectations, to see if BCRA was able to reduce the volume of advertising and whether the "stand by your ad" provision had any impact on the tone of television advertising. In many senses, then, the 2004 campaign is a natural experiment of the effects of BCRA.

ABOUT THE UNIVERSITY OF WISCONSIN
ADVERTISING PROJECT

The University of Wisconsin Advertising Project collects and analyzes information concerning political advertising, ranging from issue advocacy and ballot measures to electoral contests for offices ranging from coroners and sheriffs' races to the presidency. The project uses targeting and content data supplied by TNS Media Intelligence/Campaign Media Analysis Group (TNSMI/CMAG) and Nielsen Monitor-Plus. Both TNSMI/CMAG and Nielsen Monitor-Plus electronically monitor advertising by tracking the output of television stations across the nation. The systems work by differentiating the unique digital fingerprint of each different ad. A unique code is given to each new ad detected, which is then downloaded, and each subsequent airing in any of the markets being tracked is then logged.[5] This log includes data of the market, station, date, time, estimated cost, and even the programming that the spot aired on. In addition, Nielsen Monitor-Plus is able to give information on the audience levels and demographics watching each spot. University of Wisconsin Advertising Project staff then view each ad and code them according to over eighty questions, regarding who the ad is for, who pays for the spot, as well as content questions such as the tone or issues mentioned in the spot. These data, going back through multiple election cycles, are the basis of the analysis below.

THE LESSONS OF 2004

The Wisconsin Advertising Project tracked the airing of over three million political ads in all of the nation's 210 markets throughout the 2004 campaign. Comparing only markets that we tracked in both 2000 and 2004 (top seventy-five markets) we estimate that nearly twice as much money was spent on television advertising in the presidential general election race alone.

All told, we make four major points about advertising in 2004, which we highlight below.

- First, regardless of what one is trying to explain (volume of ads, targeting, or tone), the most important causal variable remains the same—competitiveness.
- Second, the "stand by your ad" provision resulted in a noticeable change to the look of ads, but it may have had only marginal effect on their content.
- Third, parties and PACs adapted with hard money, but the sixty-day provision forced some groups to air ads earlier in the campaign.
- Fourth, differences between the 2004 and 2000 air wars had less to do with BCRA than with other factors. This is true for some of the major stories and controversies of 2004—that is, Swift Boat's ads and early barrages of advertising.

COMPETITIVENESS

Advertising volumes within a locale vary due to the *competitiveness* of the races being run within media markets, not whether offices are up for election.[6] This means the volume and nature of the advertising citizens are exposed to during an election year differs greatly across the United States, even in a year when voters in all 210 markets are able to cast a presidential ballot.

In looking at this most recent campaign, we find ads focused primarily in places where there was a race to be run. Indeed campaign advertising—and campaign activity in general—was extremely narrowly targeted in 2004. The extent of this targeting is worth spelling out. Only ninety-four media markets (out of 210 nationwide) located in only twenty-one states received *any* advertising at all during the 2004 presidential campaign. More than half of all Americans—57 percent of the electorate—did not see a single ad broadcast in their home media market. And during the final month of the campaign, 87 percent of all presidential ads were concentrated in just forty-four media markets in a shrinking number of battleground states, home to only 27 percent of the electorate. Presidential television advertisers effectively excluded almost three quarters of the electorate in the closing period of the campaign.

For citizens living in competitive, battleground states like Ohio, Florida, Wisconsin, and Nevada, the campaign was ubiquitous. The candidates made frequent visits, and campaign ads were ever present. In contrast, save for a small proportion of spots on national cable, citizens living in four of the largest states in the country—California, New York, Texas, and Illinois—were exposed to no television advertising in the presidential race.

In the last week of the campaign, voters living in Racine, Wisconsin, were targeted with 2,224 presidential spots and 599 spots from Russ Feingold's semicompetitive Senate reelection bid. In comparison, thirty miles south, in Waukegan, Illinois, there were no presidential spots (in fact none at all in 2004), and only 261 spots in the uncompetitive Senate race between Barack Obama and Alan Keyes.

It is of particular note that six of the nation's top ten media markets (New York, Los Angeles, Chicago, San Francisco, Dallas, and Atlanta) were not targeted at all during the 2004 presidential campaign. There was some advertising on national cable networks such as CNN, FNC, and ESPN, but this spending comprised a small proportion of the campaigns' ad budgets and did not come close to matching the volume of broadcast advertising in competitive markets. Voters in these markets—most of the voters voting in the presidential election—simply were not exposed to presidential ads because their states were not seen as competitive.

This trend is consistent with advertising patterns we have tracked in previous years. In 2000, for example, in San Antonio, only 531 election ads were aired during the entire year. Similarly, Wichita, Oklahoma City, and Baltimore were each home to fewer than 2,000 broadcast political spots during the course of the entire 2000 campaign. What do these markets have in common? They were all in states that were clearly safe for either Bush or Gore, and they were all devoid of competitive Senate races.

In contrast, other markets drew saturation levels of advertising for months before Election Day because they were in competitive presidential states or had competitive contests for other offices, or in some "perfect storm cases" they had both. In 2000, such perfect storm markets included Detroit (32,456 spots aired) and St. Louis (30,554). In Michigan it was Spencer Abraham versus Debbie Stabenow and in Missouri, John Ashcroft faced Mel Carnahan and then his widow, Jean.

In 2004, markets such as Tampa Bay saw 38,361 spots aired for federal candidates as Betty Castor competed with Mel Martinez to replace Bob Graham as senator of one of the most intense presidential battlegrounds. Viewers in Denver saw 32,519 federal election spots, as beer magnate Pete Coors battled Attorney General Ken Salazar for Ben Nighthorse Campbell's Senate seat in a state that became a battleground state later in the presidential contest. Competitiveness is the primary factor in dictating the volume of advertising being seen in any particular locale.

Historically, competitiveness has also been the primary factor driving the tone of advertising. This leads to our next point about the possible effects of BCRA, and in particular the "stand by your ad" provision on the nature of advertising in the 2004 elections.

STAND BY YOUR AD

As shown above, many pundits predicted that the "stand by your ad" provision meant that advertising would be more positive in tone. Furthermore, it was assumed that the provision would make it easier for citizens to determine who was airing which ads.

The University of Wisconsin Advertising Project found that in 2004 over one in three (36 percent) ads aired in federal races were purely negative (only talking about the opposing candidate). One in four (25 percent) were contrast advertisements (ads that both attack an opponent and talk about one's own candidacy) and 39 percent were positive. These proportions are similar to what we found in 2000 where 28 percent of ads aired were negative, 26 percent were contrast, and 45 percent were positive, with the presidential race causing much of the slight decrease in positive airings in 2004.

As shown in table 7.1, advertising in Senate and House races was slightly more positive in 2004 than in 2000. Comparing the tone of congressional candidates in 2000 and 2004 we see little change, with 58 percent of ads paid for by congressional candidates in 2000 being positive, a number that increased only to 60 percent of ads in 2004. The more positive tone of 2004 congressional campaigns, in comparison to 2000, was largely because parties and interest groups (whose ads have tended to be more negative) were less likely to engage in congressional contests in 2004 than they had in previous years (see figure 7.2). This change is dif-

Table 7.1   Tone of Ads by Sponsor and Race, 2000–2004

Office	Sponsor	% Positive 2000	% Positive 2002	% Positive 2004
Presidential				
	Candidate or Coordinated	64.8	N/A	43.6
	Party	37.2	N/A	8.6
	Interest Group	0.0	N/A	7.5
	Overall	46.2	N/A	31.5
U.S. Senate				
	Candidate or Coordinated	61.8	67.8	62.8
	Party	10.2	25.3	10.4
	Interest Group	47.5	43.5	31.6
	Overall	48.3	52.2	54.8
U.S. House				
	Candidate or Coordinated	57.8	65.3	57.5
	Party	15.8	30.1	13.4
	Interest Group	28.9	82.8	74.4
	Overall	42.7	57.5	47.8

Figure 7.2   Proportion of Senate and House Ads Paid for by Candidates, Parties, and Interest Groups, 2000–2004

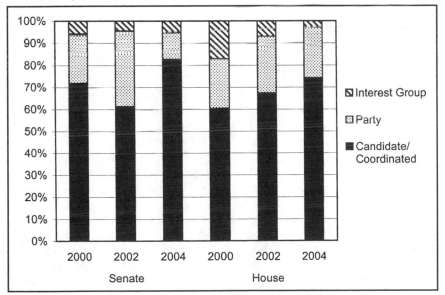

ficult to link to the "stand by your ad" provision. Without a presidential contest on the top of the ballot, we may very likely see groups reengage in Congressional races in 2006 and the tone return to its pre-BCRA levels.

Looking at just those ads aired in House elections in 2002 and 2004, there is a decrease in the proportion of positive spots aired, and House and Senate candidates (who are mandated to "stand by their ads") were less positive than in 2002. This finding is in part related to advertising before the first anniversary of the 9/11 attacks, where ads were more positive in tone (before returning, by Election Day, to comparable tone levels as in 2000). Nevertheless, the fact that federal candidates, forced to "stand by their ads," aired either exactly the same or less positive ads than in the two previous cycles (in which they were not forced to "stand by their ads") should be persuasive evidence of the inability of this provision to discourage candidates from going negative.

Some may argue that monitoring the volume of negative ads doesn't measure a change in the "nastiness" of ads. Such nastiness is extremely hard to measure, but consider just three examples.

- In the first district of Oregon, Goli Ameri ran an ad with the words "Wu used a pillow to muffle her screams" emblazoned across the screen in a spot against the incumbent, David Wu.
- In the open seat race for the U.S. Senate in Oklahoma, Brad Carson had an ad which included the phrase "As a doctor, Tom Coburn sterilized an underage girl without her consent" against his opponent, who was the ultimate winner.
- And in the open seat Senate race in Florida, the victorious Mel Martinez used an ad to accuse his opponent Betty Castor of allowing "a terrorist cell to poison her university."

In each case the candidate is seen taking credit for the commercials. In an election cycle that saw candidates both "standing by ads" *and* accusing opponents of attempted rape, unauthorized sterilizations, and turning a blind eye to terrorism, the election clearly was not free of nastiness.

So what *does* drive the tone of advertising? The simple answer is competitiveness. Where there is competition, there is negativity, and where there is no serious opponent to berate or when the opponent is too powerful to be defeated, there is not.

This assertion follows from both our own historical analysis and the political science literature on the tone of advertising. Strong candidates, secure in their victory, have no need to risk backlash effects of mentioning opponents (or risk giving them the oxygen of publicity). Those candidates running in unwinnable races are often not running to win, but for other reasons (Canon 1993). All of these, with the possible exception of the discussion of issues, appear consistent with such underdogs running campaigns that are more positive. If victory were not attainable, the risk of backlashes of going negative could do damage to their party and their personal or professional reputations and could be seen as taking away some of the "joy of running for office."

Competitive races, with candidates running to win, and where the benefits of negative campaigns outweigh the potential risks, are typically more negative (while less competitive races are more positive). There is little that BCRA did do to change this fundamental maxim, as table 7.2 clearly shows. Indeed, the differences in tone between competitive and noncompetitive races are far greater than the differences in tone between 2004 and previous years—a pattern which suggests a relatively weak effect of the "stand by your ad" provision.

Some anecdotal evidence and internal conversations with campaign staffers, on both sides, suggest that the "stand by your ad" provision also did little to make sponsorship more clear. Citizens already assumed that any ad aired on behalf of a candidate or against an opposing candidate was paid for by the favored candidate. Thus, candidates taking responsibility for an ad did little to add to information about those particular ads. The corollary was that viewers assumed that 527 ads were paid for by candidates. With no "stand by your ad" provision for MoveOn.org or Progress for America Voter Fund, the most controversial ads of the campaign often remained cloaked in mystery.

PARTIES AND GROUPS

In terms of the volume of advertising, the Bush campaign had a significant advantage over the Kerry campaign in most media markets. Thus, if we only looked at those ads made and paid for by the candidates' campaign committees, we would conclude that the Bush campaign won the battle to dominate the airwaves, broadcasting more spots in more places. Yet, when Kerry-supporting groups—such as The Media Fund and MoveOn, as well as the DNC, labor unions and other allies—are added to the mix, we see that combined Democratic spending vastly outpaced combined Republican spending.

As figure 7.3 shows, throughout the campaign, but especially, in March and April and again in August, the Kerry campaign was likely to rely much more on interest group allies and independent party efforts to fund its television advertising barrages. This outside group spending in support of Kerry (or attacking Bush) was most noticeable in the period in which Kerry was short of money immediately after his primary victories in which the Bush campaign had a huge hard money advantage. When the Kerry campaign made public its intention to come off the air after the Democratic convention in order to save general election funds in August, the DNC's independent expenditures accounted for over two-thirds (67 percent) of the spots supporting Kerry or attacking Bush.

In contrast, outside groups paid for only a tiny portion of spots promoting Bush or attacking Kerry throughout the general election campaign, as shown in figure 7.4. In addition, the Bush campaign was first (in September) to take advantage of a loophole in BCRA that allowed candidates to *share* the costs of ads with their parties. The campaigns deemed that the loophole allowed such

Table 7.2 Tone of Ads by Office and Competitiveness, 2000–2004

Office	Tone	2000		2002		2004	
		Competitive	Noncompetitive	Competitive	Noncompetitive	Competitive	Noncompetitive
U.S. Senate							
	Attack	31%	21%	34%	15%	27%	13%
	Contrast	34	18	18	12	27	18
	Promote	35	61	48	73	46	69
U.S. House							
	Attack	45	21	31	19	44	17
	Contrast	23	18	20	12	23	20
	Promote	32	61	49	69	33	63

Figure 7.3   Proportion of Advertising on Behalf of Kerry, by Sponsor, by Month

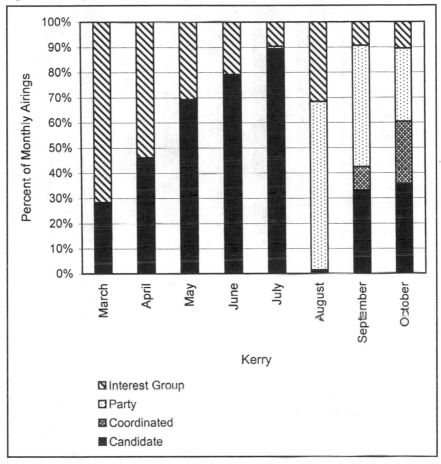

coordinated expenditures to occur so long as the ads did not solely advocate the election of the presidential candidate. This meant that ads using phrases such as "John Kerry and liberals in Congress want to . . ." or "under George Bush and right-wing Republican . . ." appeared. These spots contained the disclaimers "Approved by John Kerry and paid for by the Democratic National Committee and authorized by Kerry-Edwards 2004 Inc.," and "Paid for by Bush-Cheney '04 Inc. and the Republican National Committee and approved by President Bush." In addition, the candidates abided by the "stand by your ad" provisions and orally approved of each spot, which is the reason why these spots are included with candidate airings in our above analysis of tone.

Perhaps one of the most controversial aspects of BCRA was the limits placed on interest group activity within the last sixty days of the general election. These limits were expected to reduce the volume of ads aired by outside groups overall and, in particular, toward the end of the campaign.

Figure 7.4   Proportion of Advertising on Behalf of Bush, by Sponsor, by Month

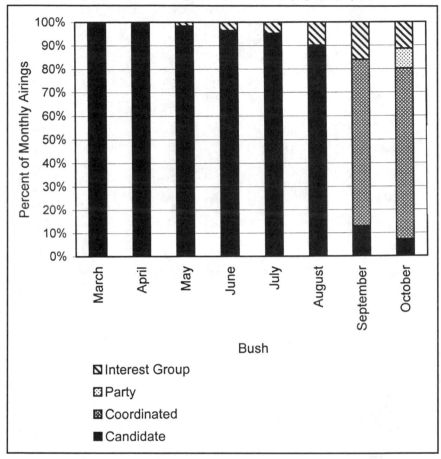

Bush

🞖 Interest Group
🞖 Party
🞖 Coordinated
■ Candidate

For 2000 and 2004 (in the seventy-five markets we tracked in both years), we compared the number of groups on the air as well as the number of spots aired by interest groups before and after the final sixty days of the campaign. These results are shown in table 7.3. Most importantly, the table shows that interest groups nearly doubled the number of ads they aired in federal races, from 77,687 in 2000 to 142,898 in 2004. The macro story from these numbers is that BCRA did little to stem the intensity of interest group electioneering on television.

The distinctions between 2000 and 2004 become starker when looking at ad frequency before and after the sixty-day period. In 2000, groups aired over three times as many spots *after* the sixty-day period (compared to before that period). In stark contrast, in 2004 groups aired twice the number of ads *before* the sixty-day period. This change does not signal less group advertising; quite the opposite—almost six times as many interest group spots aired in federal races before

Table 7.3 The Effect of the "60-Day Window" on Interest Group Ads in the Top 75 Markets

	Before 60 Days of the General Election						Within 60 Days of the General Election					
	# of Groups Airing Spots		# of Group Airings		% of Ads That Were Group		# of Groups Airing Spots		# of Group Airings		% of Ads That Were Group	
Office	2000	2004	2000	2004	2000	2004	2000	2004	2000	2004	2000	2004
Federal	27	43	17,064	97,554	6.7	20.2	36	57	60,623	45,344	12.4	7.8
President	11	28	3,652	88,759	2.6	24.1	15	47	20,198	35,531	16.4	13.0
Senate	11	9	3,584	5,259	5.1	7.1	18	10	9,999	7,342	5.9	4.7
House	12	9	9,828	3,536	22.5	8.8	21	8	30,411	2,471	15.6	1.6

Note: Interest groups that aired ads under different names are counted as one group, even if the ads were paid with different "types" of money (i.e., hard or soft funds). Therefore, ads with the tagline, "MoveOn.org," "MoveOn Voter Fund," or "MoveOn PAC" are counted as one—rather than three—interest group(s).

the last sixty days of the election in 2004 as in the comparable period in 2000. This is a trend explained in part by the early Democratic group presidential spending discussed above. All told, there was some shifting of ads from the post-sixty-day period to pre-sixty-day period (a BCRA effect), but the huge onslaught of ads over the summer was also from new groups (i.e., MoveOn.org and Swift Boat Veterans, which did not air ads in 2004) and their desire to buttress Kerry or Bush over the summer (a political effect).

Furthermore, the number of interest group ads on behalf of Senate and House candidates decreased in the sixty-day period, with the largest drop occurring in House races (from 30,411 ads in the final months of 2000 to only 2,471 in 2004). Even this result can be explained in part by interest groups' shift up the ticket. Despite interest groups comprising a smaller percentage of all presidential ads aired within the sixty-day window (16.4 percent in 2000 compared to 13 percent in 2004), the sheer number of interest group presidential ads in this period went up in 2004 (from 20,198 in 2000 to 35,531 in 2004), a trend explained by the increase in candidate and coordinated ads between 2000 and 2004. At the same time, the number of interest groups sponsoring ads in the presidential race went up compared to 2000, both before and after the sixty-day period (from eleven to twenty-eight in the pre-sixty-day period and from fifteen to forty-seven within the sixty-day time frame).

All told, interest groups shifted resources away from Senate and House races and toward the presidential race, most notably before the sixty-day period starting in early September. Thus, after BCRA we do not see fewer advertisements or voices. We see more interest group voices (probably the result of soft money diverting from parties to 527s) and earlier advertising in the presidential race.

In order to assess whether interest groups have truly abandoned sixty-day advertising in House and Senate races, we need to wait until 2006. Certainly some initial evidence points to a BCRA effect in these lower ticket races. The biggest interest group spenders on general election House ads in 2000 were the pharmaceutical group Citizens for Better Medicare (CBM) and the labor group AFL-CIO, which together accounted for over half (54 percent) of the advertising done by interest groups in House races. Neither of these groups, which in 2000 used soft money to air their ads, aired any spots in House races in 2004, which may somewhat account for the huge decrease in group advertising in House races with the advent of BCRA. In the future, groups such as CBM and the AFL-CIO may switch to hard money efforts to fund advertising in House races, but we will not know this until at least 2006.

SWIFT BOAT AND THE EARLY START

For almost the entire month of August, the nation was embroiled in a debate over John Kerry's military record. To be sure, Kerry himself laid the groundwork for this national conversation, by making his Vietnam War experience the centerpiece of the Democratic National Convention at the end of July. But the debate was sparked by a series of ads sponsored by Swift Boat Veterans for Truth, a 527 organization.

The group's first and most notorious ad aired only 739 times in only seven, relatively small media markets (Charleston, Dayton, Green Bay, La Crosse, Toledo, Wassau, and Youngstown). It featured the allegations of several Vietnam veterans who, among other things, accused Kerry of lying to obtain his Purple Heart and Bronze Star and betraying his country in his 1971 U.S. Senate testimony. Although it appears that only one of the men featured in the ad had ever served as a crewmate of Kerry, the ad's charges made national headlines for several days running and provided fodder for talk radio and Sunday morning newsmaker programs for several weeks, during which the Kerry campaign seemed to keep a low profile. News organizations began to poke holes in the evidence presented by the Swift Boat Veterans group, but in doing so, they kept the story alive for several weeks and, in order to debunk them, ended up repeating the group's accusations.

As the coverage of the Swift Boat ads demonstrates, on rare occasion an ad will capture the attention of the news media, and it will be repeated over and over on television broadcasts. The result is that more Americans may actually see the ad during a news broadcast than during its paid presentation. Before the Swift Boat Veterans launched their ads, the classic examples of this phenomenon were Lyndon Johnson's "Daisy Girl" ad in 1964 (with its images of a young girl picking daisy petals and the mushroom cloud of a nuclear blast), and the "Willie Horton" spot attacking Democratic candidate Michael Dukakis in 1988 (featuring the famous "mug shot" of Horton, alleged to have aroused racially laden fears about crime (Mendelberg 2001; West 2001).

These spots, like the Swift Boat Veterans ads of 2004, were broadcast only a handful of times but achieved notoriety through extensive free media coverage. Such ads likely have an impact on viewers—and on the course of the campaign—far beyond what their broadcast numbers would suggest. The Swift Boat ads' impact on the campaign had little to do with BCRA, especially airing as it did, well before the last sixty days of the election.

Another story of the 2004 campaign was the comparatively early start to the presidential general election. The first flight of advertisements in the general election came only days after John Kerry clinched enough delegates to secure his party's nomination. The ads, paid for by the Bush campaign, were first aired on March 4th, eight months before Election Day. To be sure, we have seen early starts to presidential election advertising campaigns before. Bill Clinton broadcast his first ads in his 1996 reelection campaign in June of 1995, seventeen months before the general election and ten months before his opponent was known. Still, the ads that Clinton aired in 1995 and 1996 were part of relatively small buys that aired for a week or two at a time.

As is shown in figure 7.5, both sides in the 2004 presidential campaign went up in March with levels of advertising seen before only in the last weeks of the campaign. Indeed, with only short lulls and respites, the campaigns kept this barrage up for the duration of the campaign. In fact, St. Patrick's Day seems to have

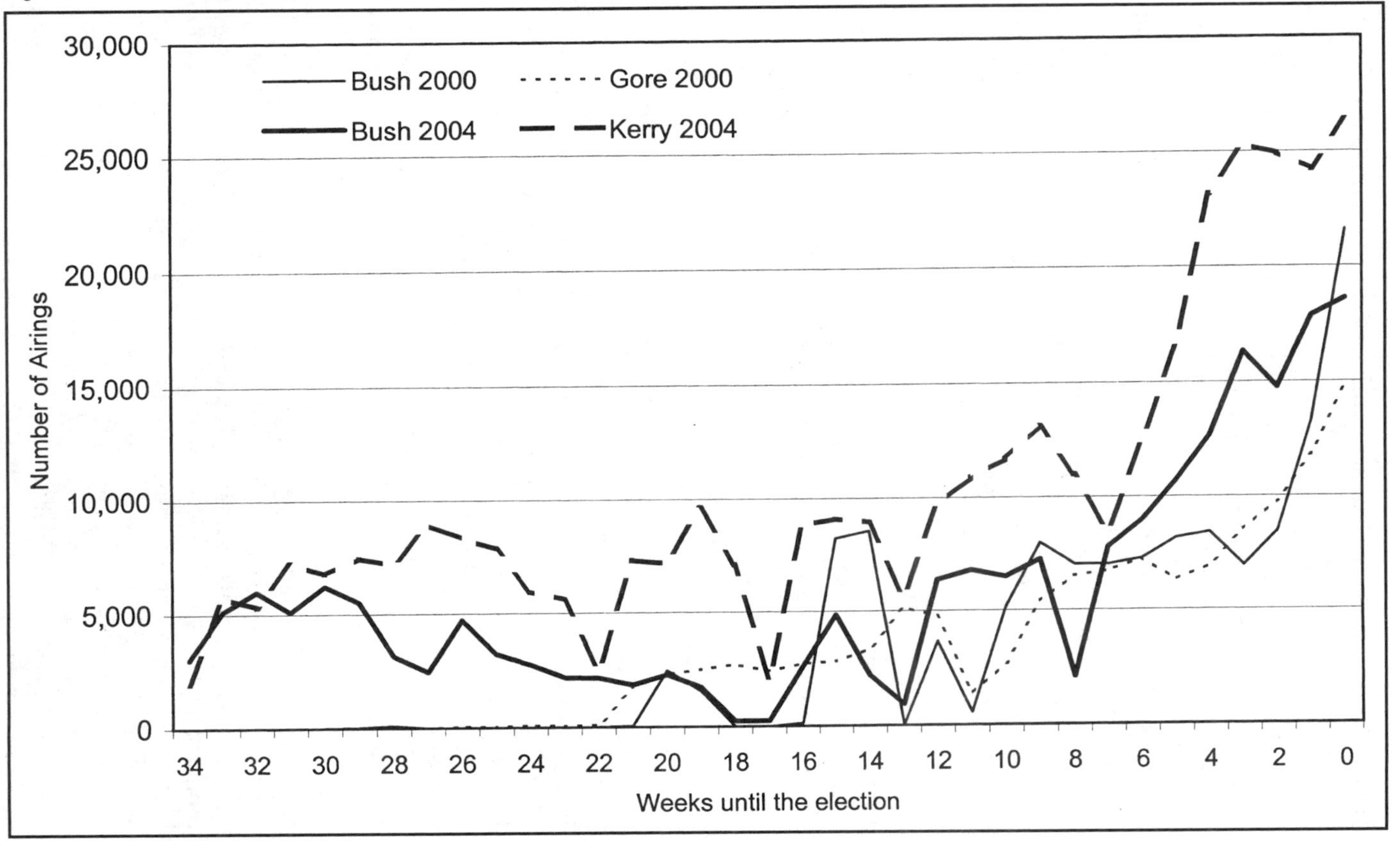

Figure 7.5 Advertising in Top 75 Media Markets over Time by Candidates, Parties, and Interest Groups, 2000–2004

replaced Labor Day as the unofficial start of the general election campaign. By Labor Day 2004, more than 600,000 presidential spots had already aired in 94 of the nation's 210 media markets. And, again, the most notorious ad of the election cycle—the first spot produced by Swift Boat Veterans for Truth—was broadcast in mid-August.

One major reason for this early onslaught of advertising was the ability of both campaigns, aided in part by BCRA's increase of the hard money donation limits from individuals, to not take matching funds (and the regulations associated with them) for the primary election. This allowed both sides (once the Kerry campaign had refilled its "primary" war chest after sealing the nomination in early March), to spend huge amounts of this primary money in the months before they officially received their parties' nominations at the conventions—much of which was spent (by both sides) in attempts to define John Kerry. In addition, as is noted above, outside groups and parties, particularly on the Democratic side, invested huge amounts on early advertising.

CONCLUSION

Advertising in post-BCRA America is largely the same as in pre-BCRA America. Advertising campaigns remain focused on competitive contests (and competitive states in the presidential election); the volume of advertising has not shown any noticeable decrease; parties and interest groups remain on the air, and even with the demands of candidates to "stand by their ads," the tone of the spots remains as negative as ever.

Many of those viewing the huge increase in campaign activity beyond the airwaves, such as the voter mobilization efforts by the Bush campaign and Democratic groups such as Americans Coming Together, suggested that this was an indicator of the demise, or at least the decline of television as the principal medium of campaigns. The year 2004, however showed that advertising is not a zero-sum game. More mobilization does not automatically mean less television advertising; 2004 saw record levels of both get-out-the-vote activities *and* record sums spent on television advertising by candidates and interest groups. Not only did the money flow in new directions when confronted by the obstacles of campaign finance reform, but also campaigners were able to take advantage of new fundraising techniques and aspects of BCRA, such as the increased contribution limits, to increase the volume of money flowing down the electoral stream.

Our analysis does not mean that BCRA did not have any impact on campaigns or political fundraising or that the law failed to meet all the aims of its authors. Instead, we show that some key expectations regarding changes in the volume and tone of advertising were shown to be unwarranted expectations when tested in the 2004 elections. Those seeking to decrease the volume of advertising or make the tone of campaigns more positive must therefore look for options beyond BCRA in its current form.

NOTES

1. During debate on a previous iteration of campaign finance reform, Daschle argued, "Negative advertising is the crack cocaine of politics. We're hooked on it because it works. We're hooked on it because we win elections using it. There's no accountability, no reporting. It's publicly not tied to any candidates."

2. These data were provided by Nielsen Monitor-Plus, which tracks political television advertising in all 210 media markets across the nation, to the University of Wisconsin Advertising Project.

3. Also important to note is that these hard money maximums—*for individuals*—are now indexed to inflation. Contributions from PACs to parties and candidates were not changed, however, nor were they indexed to inflation. PACs can still only contribute $5,000 maximum to candidates for each election.

4. For many, such a change in the law was supposed to favor Republicans, who are historically more adept at raising hard money contributions than Democrats. As the 2004 election made clear, however, the soft money change did not disadvantage the DNC in its hard money efforts.

5. Nielsen Monitor-Plus tracks all 210 U.S. media markets, and TNSMI/CMAG tracks the largest 100 media markets.

6. Some residents of uncompetitive states may be exposed to "spillover" advertising as media markets do not respect state boundaries. This means that in 2004, residents of southern New Jersey were inundated with presidential spots intended for Pennsylvania residents also residing in the Philadelphia media market. Those living in northern New Jersey, living within the New York media market, would not have seen any presidential spots.

7. Interest groups that aired ads under different names are counted as one group, even if the ads were paid for by different "types" of money (i.e., hard or soft funds). Therefore, ads with the tagline, "MoveOn.org," "MoveOn Voter Fund," or "MoveOn PAC" are counted as one—rather than three—interest group(s).

8

Stepping Out of the Shadows?
Ground-War Activity in 2004

David B. Magleby and Kelly D. Patterson

Commentators normally focus their attention on campaign money spent on television. The year 2004 was not completely different in this regard as the impact of television advertising by groups on both the left and the right often dominated national coverage. However, competitive federal elections in 2004 also received attention because of the massive effort that political parties, candidates, and interest groups devoted to the ground war. The parties and their allied groups set contact and registration goals that awed even the most jaded reporters. Competitive congressional races and presidential battleground states witnessed a concentration of effort on voter registration and mobilization; personal contact by campaigns at the workplace, church, or other setting; and targeted communications via telephone, mail, and email on an unprecedented scale. The rediscovery of these more personal and targeted communications actually began during the 1997–1998 election cycle and continued to expand through the midterm elections of 2002. Passage of BCRA that same year helped reinforce the emphasis on the ground war in 2004 because of the act's electioneering advocacy provisions, which apply to broadcast communications but not to the ground war. In this chapter we examine the broad contour of the ground war in 2004 and assess the impact of BCRA on these activities.

With the advent of television and the growth in dominance of media consultants, grassroots politics and more targeted voter communications became less frequently used. Television, according to one book, "eventually became the prime source of political and electoral information for many Americans" (Dulio, Nelson, and Thurber 2000). As a result television also became the prime medium of communication for candidates, parties, and interest groups. The same authors go on to say that "As candidate-centered elections became a political reality, candidates and their teams of consultants gravitated toward television as a means for disseminating their message" (Dulio, Nelson, and Thurber 2000). As candidates increasingly turned to television and radio advertising, the parties and interest groups followed suit. This use of television grew as parties and interest groups turned to soft money and to issue advocacy to get out messages that often supported the electoral ambitions of the candidates (Magleby 2000b).

The shift to a greater reliance on personal contact, workplace communications, targeted mail, and phone banks has been gradual but took a significant step forward in 1998 with a shift in strategy by the AFL-CIO. In the 1996 cycle, the AFL-CIO expended a total of $35 million, the majority of which the organization allocated toward television and radio. But it also allocated $15 million for field operations (Birnbaum 1996). In 1998, however, the union's core political activity was directly threatened by ballot initiatives that would require annual renewal of political contributions by union members to their unions. The measures were named by their advocates as "paycheck protection." As the unions fought back, they rediscovered the importance and effectiveness of personal contact followed by persuasion mail and reminder phone calls (Magleby and Patterson 2000).

The unions successfully defeated paycheck protection and have since expanded their ground-war operation into candidate races. The architect of labor's ground operation, Steve Rosenthal, has tried to "bring a personal dynamic back into politics" (Lawrence 2000). The dynamic relies on personalizing the contact and providing additional information that demonstrates why the union believes the election should be important to the individual. In the 2002 election cycle, Rosenthal illustrated the power of personalizing each contact. He stated that "there was a situation in Cleveland at one point, where I was doing phone calls with some union members. The guy in the cubicle next to me leaned over and said, 'If you're calling operating engineers, don't say you're calling from the union, say you're calling on behalf of the union.' I said, 'Why?' and he said, 'We all know each other.' I said, 'How many members are there in your union?' He said, 'About 2,200.' I said, 'And you all know each other?' He said, 'Pretty much.' I listened to his next two or three calls and it was, 'Hi, Mr. Smith, this is Joe Dugan, I work with your sons Tommy and Mike . . .' Each call he would personalize it like that. It was so much more valuable than most of the other contacts that campaigns make. We see that all the time" (Rosenthal 2003).

Other interest groups on the left have also developed extensive and sophisticated ground-war strategies including mail, phone banks, and personal contact. Some even deploy staff during the final weeks of the campaign to work side-by-side with party staff in the competitive House and Senate contests. Increasingly these groups see the effectiveness of ground-war efforts and will spend funds for those efforts even when total funding is limited. In 2002 groups such as the National Education Association, the Democratic Governor's Association, and various other groups pooled their resources to create a unified field operation to register and contact voters in the Arkansas Senate race. They viewed these efforts as more important than television or other forms of advertising (Barth and Parry

2003). In some ways these collaborations helped to set the stage for the tremendous coordination in 2004 among progressive groups under the umbrella of America Votes.

Coming out of the 2000 election, Karl Rove and the Republicans had "labor envy." There was widespread speculation among the Republicans that the Democrats in general and labor in particular had bested them at the mobilization game. In response, the Republicans and their allied groups began to fine-tune their ground-war operation. A party official confirmed this dynamic when he said that "[t]he early rumblings of an increased emphasis on ground-war tactics by Republicans in 2002 came as an outgrowth of the voter mobilization efforts in the 2000 George W. Bush campaign by Karl Rove and Kenneth Mehlman, and some consternation within the Republican Party in the aftermath that they did not do better in the closing days of the campaign" (Dyke 2003).

As we briefly document in this chapter, the Republicans and their allies, including the business community, the NRA, and conservative churches, have created their own large-scale and effective ground-war operation. It includes use of the Internet, mail, phone, personal contact, and is not limited to currently registered voters. Rather, it also seeks to register voters and help them vote early by absentee ballot or in person. While television advertising remains the most visible and expensive component of most election operations, currently few candidates for federal office feel comfortable waging a campaign without extensive and effective ground-war operations. In this chapter we outline how BCRA has accelerated the trend toward ground-war activities. We also examine some of the developments in ground-war operations and their reliance on increasingly sophisticated methods of identifying and targeting voters. We compare several Senate and House races to assess the growth and changes in these operations over the last two election cycles. Finally, we conclude with a discussion of the future of ground-war activities and how the participants in campaigns may further refine their efforts to reach voters through means other than television or radio.

BCRA AND ITS EFFECTS ON GROUND-WAR
STRATEGY IN 2004

While not written with this as its purpose, BCRA had the effect of accelerating the shift toward a greater reliance on personal voter contact, registration, mobilization, direct mail, internal communications within businesses or unions, telephone contacting, and email. As noted, these ground-war activities had already been receiving added emphasis before BCRA. In our 2002 study, we found that "[p]olitical parties and allied interest groups waged expanded ground-war campaigns in 2002. In the 1998 and 2000 elections, interest groups produced more direct mail, print and radio advertisements, and phone banks than did the political parties; the parties focused more on television advertisements. However, in

2002, while maintaining their presence on television, the parties also expanded their ground-war efforts to exceed those of the interest groups" (Monson 2004).

BCRA ostensibly created incentives for the shift to ground-war activity by not including these activities in the definition of electioneering communications. Electioneering communications were defined by the act as broadcast, cable, or satellite communication by a "person" (including an organization) not previously covered by the law (i.e., not a candidate, party, or PAC) that referred to a clearly identifiable candidate, publicly distributed within thirty days of a primary election or sixty days before a general election, and targeted to the relevant electorate. Corporate or union treasury money could not be used to fund this type of communication, just as it could not for previously covered activity. But *non-broadcast* activity by these other persons—like voter registration, direct mail, and phone banks—*could* be funded by corporate and union treasury funds. These funds had been a major source of party soft money through 2002 but had long been banned from covered election expenditures. The fact that these funds were prohibited from use in broadcast during the critical weeks just before an election but could be spent on direct voter contact and mobilization provided the groups with an incentive to invest even more heavily in their ground-war operations. Little corporate money in fact did migrate to 527 organizations in 2003–2004 (*New York Times* 2004c). Unions, however, contributed substantial amounts to these groups in the 2004 election cycle.

BCRA may have helped accelerate more expansive internal communications with employees or members in corporations, unions, and other organizations. These efforts even included well-developed websites with downloadable voter registration forms, absentee ballot request forms, and information on early voting such as Business and Industry Political Action Committee's (BIPAC) *Prosperity Project* website and the Chamber of Commerce's *Vote for Business* website.[1] Internal communications could be paid for with treasury funds that again could not be used to pay for broadcast electioneering communications. Various groups availed themselves of the opportunity to mobilize voters through internal communications. The NEA had nine staff in Ohio and sent direct mail to members. All of the 135,000 members in Ohio received at least two pieces of mail. They also received email and phone calls all in an effort to mobilize them to vote for Senator Kerry (Friel 2004). Labor's new group, Working America, added people to the rolls of "member" for communication purposes (Podhorzer, Goodman, and Boundy 2004).

BCRA's limiting what groups and individuals could do in terms of expenditure and required disclosure caused groups and individuals to view the unrestricted ground war as an opportunity to try and influence the outcome of the election. For example, not only must 527 organizations not use corporate or union treasury funds to fund broadcast electioneering ads within the window, anyone who makes an electioneering communication costing over $10,000 must also file disclosure within twenty-four hours of the public distribution of the communication to the FEC. This disclosure must include a list of all contributors. This cumbersome reporting system can be completely skirted by groups not otherwise covered by campaign law through ground-war activities.

It is important to underscore that BCRA was not the sole cause of the greater emphasis on the ground war. The unexpected surge in hard money donated to candidates and parties also encouraged the growth of this effort. The willingness of individuals and groups to invest in the 527 and 501(c) organizations that, in turn, also wanted to emphasize the ground operations, only amplified the increase that occurred in previous elections.

THE COMPETITIVE ENVIRONMENT
OF THE 2004 ELECTION

The 2004 elections were presidency centered, with voters on both sides feeling strongly about the outcome of the election. In many ways the 2004 election began in the immediate aftermath of the 2000 presidential election with the contested ballots in Florida and the very narrow margins in New Hampshire (Bush 50.67), Wisconsin (Gore 50.12), Iowa (Gore 50.16), Oregon (Gore 50.24), and New Mexico (Gore 50.03). While the election was ultimately resolved in 2000 by the U.S. Supreme Court in *Bush v. Gore* (531 U.S. 98 [2000]), the bitter taste of defeat lingered for many Democrat leaning interest groups and elites.

With control of both the House and the Senate up for grabs in the 2000 and 2002 election cycles, interest groups and parties had a plethora of races from which to choose during those cycles. However, pundits believed that the Democrats had only a slim chance to gain a Senate majority and virtually no chance to take control of the House in 2004 (Cook 2004). This was the second election cycle following redistricting, and as a general rule, House elections become less competitive as the decade progresses. Incumbents learn how to hold on to their districts, and campaign funds flow to them (Jacobson 2001). Even with a second round of redistricting in Texas that secured the defeat of four Democrats, the number of competitive House races reached historic lows (Walter 2004). Early on in the cycle, some Senate races looked like they might be quite competitive, but many of them took place in conservative states where Republicans possessed a clear advantage. Consequently, interest groups and parties believed they had fewer competitive House and Senate races from which to choose.

Interest groups did not seem to be put at a loss in 2004 by the fact that there were so few competitive congressional races. Their focus centered squarely on the presidential race. It is important to underscore the point that elections have become a team sport with not only the candidate campaigns but parallel efforts mounted by political parties and interest groups. There is widespread evidence of the centrality of the presidential contest and an almost conscientious neglect of congressional elections in the 2004 election cycle. Groups such as the League of Conservation Voters (LCV), which long emphasized congressional elections even in presidential election years, concentrated most of their 2004 effort on the presidential contest. The LCV was not alone: it belongs to America Votes, a coalition of organizations supporting John Kerry that is described below. In the presidential contest, American Votes and its best-funded component, America Coming Together (ACT), did a great deal of voter registration and mobilization in an effort to defeat George W. Bush. This outside effort paralleled an expanded Democratic party operation. DNC general election manager Michael Whouley stated that the "[t]he Democratic National Committee and the Kerry-Edwards campaign will have 250,000 volunteers on the ground on Election Day, compared to 90,000 four years ago for Democratic nominee Al Gore. . . ." (Roth and Frank 2004).

While the Democrats relied on outside groups such as ACT and the America Votes coalition to enhance their ground operation, the Republicans mounted their ground operation largely from the RNC through the 72-Hour Task Force. It was clear that while the Republicans had won the White House in 2000, they emerged from that campaign with something to prove in 2004. Their agenda was not only to win the 2004 popular vote but also to transform the GOP grassroots operation.

The emphasis on the presidential election was exacerbated by the fact that there were few competitive congressional races in the presidential battleground states. With only Florida and Colorado as exceptions, the competitive U.S. Senate races in 2004 were not in presidential battleground states. Rather most of the highly contested U.S. Senate races were in Bush strongholds like Alaska, Oklahoma, North and South Carolina, and South Dakota. Competitive U.S. House races in 2004 were again few in number and often not in states where the presidential ground war made much difference. When forced to choose between the congressional races and the presidential race, most interest groups opted for the presidential.

DISTRIBUTION OF GROUND-WAR ACTIVITY IN 2004

We will examine developments and strategic applications of four different ground-war tools: voter registration and mobilization, direct mail, telephone calls, and internal communications and the Internet. All four elements were used by candidates, parties, and interest groups in 2004. Some received more emphasis by one side or player than another.

Voter Registration and Mobilization

Both parties and allied groups were aware of the research of Donald P. Green and Alan S. Gerber of Yale University who found that "as a rule of thumb, one additional vote is produced for every fourteen people who are successfully contacted by canvassers" (Green and Gerber 2004). In many respects the approaches taken by the RNC's 72-Hour Task Force and on the Democratic side by America Coming Together were remarkably similar. Target populations received a personal visit, follow-up mail, and phone calls, with a final mobilization push before the early voting, absentee voting, or election-day voting opportunities.

The target populations in both cases were systematically drawn from large databases or voter files that had been merged with other information, including, in the case of the Republicans, up to one hundred variables on consumer and other patterns of behavior.

Voters whose past behavior or profile suggested they were good prospects for registration and/or mobilization were targeted. In this sense the effort did not constitute a door-to-door effort but rather a household and person-specific effort. Both sides used census and other information to identify precincts and areas where their registration and activation efforts would bear the most fruit.

Personal contact and encouragement to register were also part of both sides' efforts with allied groups. These groups included churches, unions, employees, members of organizations like the NRA, Sierra Club, National Right to Life, Planned Parenthood, and American Association of Retired People (AARP).

Several groups became involved in a coordinated effort to mobilize voters on the Democratic side, all operating under the umbrella of America Votes. Participants in America Votes included over thirty independent organizations listed in appendix A. This coalition is noteworthy for its high level of cooperation and coordination. Groups that normally compete in the same policy domain like the LCV and Sierra Club worked closely together in America Votes. The same was true of the pro-choice advocacy organizations and other groups involved. One incentive for participation in America Votes was the large data file the group constructed on voters. Participation in the coalition meant the group had access to this file. Frequent America Votes meetings facilitated cooperation and minimized duplication of effort. In Florida, for example, the LCV conducted its voter canvass and registration efforts in Orlando while the Sierra Club concentrated on Tampa, and EMILY's List focused on Palm Beach and Broward Counties.

Direct Mail

Campaigns have long communicated with voters through the mail. Recent elections have seen much greater use of the mail in competitive races, even more selective targeting of the mail to particular voters, and combining the mail with face-to-face and telephone conversations as a reinforcement tool. Mail, which traditionally went out in the final days and weeks of the campaign, has been used earlier in the election cycle. Moreover, individual voters and households are now more likely to receive multiple pieces of mail dispersed over the campaign, with a final get-out-the-vote piece arriving on the eve of the election. While groups vary the order of personal contact, mail, phone contact, and email communications, consultants describe the combination as a "sandwich" referring to mail between two personal contacts.

To cut through the clutter of the large volume of mail in competitive races, consultants design their mail to stand out. The size, color, and look of the mail is intended to be attention getting. We know from our past research that voters pay close attention to the source of the mail, giving more attention to mail from individuals or groups they know and trust (Magleby and Monson 2004). The NRA, for example, has a bright orange postcard, which it mails to its membership and sportsmen's groups on the eve of the election reminding people to vote. Some candidates have mimicked the NRA and produced their own orange postcards for the same purpose.

In 2004, party committees, candidates, and interest groups made extensive use of direct mail, often more than they had in any previous election. ACT, for example, had at least eighty unique mailers, the DNC at least eighty pieces, the AFL-CIO had sixty-four, and the U.S. Chamber of Commerce had sixty-one. State parties often did their own mailers in addition to the national party committees. The Ohio Democratic Party did fifty-two mailers while the Ohio Republicans did twenty-five. The Republican National Committee (RNC) distributed fifty-six unique pieces of mail in Ohio, while the DNC produced twenty-six unique pieces of mail for Ohio. The difference between the two parties reflects a more centralized approach by the Republicans, while the Democrats left more responsibility for mail to the state parties.

The mail in 2004 emphasized a wide range of themes and issues and was targeted to particular voters based on data collected on the voters at their doorstep, over the telephone, or based on a demographic profile. Groups often relied on their members to personalize these approaches. The NEA had teachers in non-battleground states write postcards to swing voters to convince them to vote. ACT used handwritten letters from the canvassers as a way to break through the clutter of mail that arrives during the final weeks of the election.

Telephone Calls

The telephone remains an important means of communicating with voters and was used extensively in 2004. As noted, it was often part of an integrated communications strategy including personal contact, mail, and email. The conventional wisdom is that live phone calls are more effective than recorded messages. These calls are often followed-up with mail on the themes and messages identified by the voter as important. The calls are also useful in canvassing voters for their candidate preferences and likelihood of voting.

Campaigns by parties, candidates, and groups still use recorded calls in part because they are relatively cheap. The use of celebrities in these recorded calls helps generate interest and attention. In 2004 NARAL Pro-Choice America used Cynthia Nixon from *Sex in the City* while the Bush/Cheney campaign had messages from President George W. Bush, First Lady Laura Bush, Barbara Bush, President George H. W. Bush, and Arnold Schwarzenegger.

The telephone was used by candidates, parties, and groups as part of their get-out-the-vote (GOTV) efforts on Election Day and in states with early voting then as well. In some battleground states households received as many as eleven calls in one day.[2] Raul Damas, National Grassroots Director at the RNC, reported that during the last weeks before the campaign, the headquarters of the Republican party in Washington became one big phone bank operation. They used every phone in the building and added more as the election drew near to "call out the vote." They utilized the voter vault list of registered voters to make phone calls. Damas also recounted his experience in South Florida on Election Day, where voters were contacted via phone in GOTV efforts. "Most voters," Damas said, "had either voted, been contacted, or were on their way to vote. People knew it was Election Day" (Damas 2004).

Internal Communications and the Internet

Candidates, party committees, and interest groups also used the Internet on a large scale to provide information to members or subscribers, to help mobilize people for rallies and events, to show ads, and to provide voter registration, early voting, and voting place location information. Leaders in this effort include the BIPAC and the United States Chamber of Commerce. These websites provided information in easily downloadable format for businesses to create their own election scorecards of candidate issue positions and to facilitate people registering and voting. Another organization with an aggressive Internet effort is MoveOn.org. This organization, created in response to the Clinton impeachment trial in 1998, used the Internet as a means of communicating with voters in new ways. It created ads specifically for the web in addition to the typical television ads. MoveOn.org also sponsored an ad contest, allowing voters to sum up the Bush presidency in sixty seconds. Using the Internet to unite voters on the ground, MoveOn.org was able to inspire voters to hold bake sales, attend concerts, and host house parties, all in the name of defeating the president. Groups like the AFL-CIO, ACT, and EMILY's List also had ambitious web-based resources in 2004.

The political parties and candidates also made greater use of the Internet than in any previous cycle. The large number of financial donations through the web was a significant development in the 2004 cycle. Candidates on all sides utilized Meetup. Meetup is a website designed to help people with similar interests meet in person. John Kerry supporters in Salt Lake City, Utah, who joined Meetup were able to get together each Thursday at 7:00 p.m. Candidates had links to Meetup on their websites to give supporters the opportunity to meet each other. The campaigns also gave people the opportunity to volunteer over the Internet, setting up various levels of commitment, from signing up for a weekly email update to being deployed to a swing state for two weeks before the election. The campaigns electronically offered those who were interested an opportunity to participate.

GROUND-WAR ACTIVITY IN
BATTLEGROUND STATES/RACES

One consequence of relatively few competitive contests is that party and interest group resources are targeted toward only a small subset of all federal elections. Voters in an intensely fought federal election are not only more likely to see more television and radio advertising but also more personal contact, mail, and phone calls than voters in noncompetitive environments. In some states or districts, both sides turn to ground-war tactics because of scarcity of broadcast time or highly inflated costs of that time. Stephen Moore, president of the Club for Growth, noted that his organization could not afford to advertise on the air in the Denver market because of the overlapping and competitive House, Senate, and presidential races in the area (Moore 2004). Even party committees couldn't compete as prohibitive costs forced the National Republican Senatorial Committee (NRSC) to leave the Denver market alone, letting Peter Coors fend for himself on the air (Davis 2004).

During the 2004 election season, we conducted a three-wave panel survey of registered voters to examine the extent to which voters in battlegrounds were exposed to more campaign communications than voters in noncompetitive environments.[3] Table 8.1 summarizes the different levels of voter exposure to campaign communication for these environments. We organize the table into three columns. The column labeled "Battleground" contains the percentage of voters in battleground states who received a particular form of campaign communication. The "Nonbattleground" column displays the percentages for voters in nonbattleground states.

Parties and interest groups made a significant effort to contact individuals and to persuade them to vote early when possible. The difference between voters in battleground and nonbattleground states who reported being contacted about early voting reflects their efforts. Approximately 28 percent of the individuals in battleground states said they had been contacted while only 7 percent in nonbattleground states reported such contact. As we described earlier, the parties and groups placed a great deal of emphasis on this kind of mobilization because they considered early votes to be "votes in the bank." Voters in battleground states were also more likely to vote early or to vote absentee. These differences once again reflect the intensity of the ground war and its attendant mobilization activities in the battleground states.

Not surprisingly, voters in battleground states also experience more intense campaigns. Voters in the battleground states reported receiving more letters or mail, face-to-face contact with campaigns, and phone calls. The only categories without major differences between battleground and nonbattleground states were email contact and solicitation for donations. It makes sense that a relatively costless enterprise such as emails would be sent out more broadly than a mailer. It also makes sense that the parties, interest groups, and the campaigns would solicit funds nationally rather than limit themselves to battleground states.

Overall the patterns in the data suggest that voters experience campaigns dif-

Table 8.1   The Greater Intensity of Ground-War Activity in Battleground States/Races

Intensity of Campaign	Battleground[a]	Nonbattleground
Voted	89.1	86.1
Voted early	8.4	7.7
Voted absentee	15.7*	11.6
Contacted about voting early[b]	28.0**	7.2
Received letter/mail from campaign	72.4**	48.5
Mean # letter/mail[c]	2.0**	1.2
Median # letter/mail[c]	1.0	0.0
Received a request to donate money	23.8	21.1
Had face-to-face contact with campaign	21.4**	12.1
Received phone call from campaign	69.4**	50.4
Mean # phone calls[c]	1.9**	0.9
Median # phone calls[c]	1.0	0.0
Received email from campaign	15.2	12.9
Heard radio ad from campaign	68.0**	58.8
Saw TV ad from campaign	94.3**	88.8
N	576	829

*$p < .05$
**$p < .001$

Source: The 2004 Election Panel Study, BYU Center for the Study of Elections and Democracy and UW-Madison Wisconsin Advertising Project. Electronic resources from the EPS website (http://csp.polisci.wisc.edu/BYU_UW/). Madison, WI: University of Wisconsin, Wisconsin Advertising Project [producer and distributor], 2004, Wave 3.

Note: In most cases, two-sample proportions tests were used to determine if there were statistically significant differences between battleground and nonbattleground states/races. In the cases of "Mean # letter/mail" and "Mean # phone calls," two-sample t-tests were used.

[a] Battleground states/races were: AR, AZ, CO, FL, IA, LA, ME, MI, MN, MO, NH, NM, NV, OH, OR, PA, WA, WI, and WV. These states/races were classified as battleground based on June 2004 reports from the Cook Political Report, ABC News, and the *Washington Post*.

[b] Only respondents who voted early or by absentee ballot were asked this question; therefore, its *N* is 124 for battleground and 138 for nonbattleground.

[c] Per day during the last week of the campaign.

ferently depending on where they live. Voters in battleground states can expect a great deal of attention from candidates, parties, and interest groups. This survey does not ask individuals to differentiate between the sources of the communications they receive—only whether or not they experience a particular form of communication. However, it is clear that the attention focused on these states produces a different political recollection from the voters than those who live in less competitive states.

ASSESSING THE GROUND WAR
ACROSS ELECTION CYCLES

Prior to the passage of BCRA, observers developed a particular body of knowledge about noncandidate campaign activity. The national parties participated by making both independent and coordinated expenditures, registering and mobilizing voters, and cooperating with state political parties, especially to spend the large amounts of soft money they were able to raise and spend. As we discussed above, the parties targeted most of this activity toward the competitive races. Such targeting makes sense. They primarily desire to win elections, thereby maximizing the number of seats they hold. Interest groups generally seek to influence public policy and will participate in campaigns as a means to elect individuals who share their policy preferences or to gain access to elected individuals. Even before the passage of BCRA, interest groups faced slightly different regulatory hurdles than did political parties. Groups—except for PACs sponsoring "independent expenditures" within FECA—were constrained by law from coordinating with campaigns and from explicitly saying things like "vote for" or vote against" a candidate in their communications. The "express advocacy" line was not a barrier to electioneering before BCRA, as groups found ways to communicate an electioneering message without using these words (Magleby 2000a). Like parties however, interest groups normally allocated their resources to those races where they had the best opportunity to win seats. Our current research, described here, seeks to find out whether these allocation patterns continue to hold in a post-BCRA world.[4]

To help assess how parties and interest groups may have altered their ground-war strategy in response to BCRA, we need to examine their allocation decisions over time. As part of the study of outside money in congressional campaigns, the Center for the Study of Elections and Democracy (CSED) at Brigham Young University has monitored the ground activities of parties and interest groups in congressional campaigns since 1998.[5] There are a few cases in which the Center has collected data in the same House district in different election cycles. It has also monitored Senate races in states over two consecutive election cycles. These cases, some in which the candidates are the same from one cycle to the next, make it possible to assess the strategies of the parties and the groups in an electoral jurisdiction that changes very little from one election to the next. Nevertheless, it is not a definitive test of the way in which BCRA may affect the decisions made by the groups and the parties. A group that participated in one election cycle may choose not to participate in a subsequent race for reasons unrelated to changes in campaign finance law. However, through elite interviews and measurement of the volume of activity (e.g., number of calls, pieces of mail) we can establish the extent to which these political actors responded to various incentives built into the new campaign finance law.

The parties and the groups targeted several races in 2004 that they had also targeted in 2002. In the Utah Second Congressional district, Representative Jim Matheson, a Democrat, faced a rematch with Republican John Swallow. The Utah State Legislature drew the district favorably for a Republican. Representative Matheson won a narrow victory in 2002 although the parties and interest groups devoted little to the race until the very end. In 2004 the National Republican Congressional Committee (NRCC) spent a great deal more in the district than it did in 2002. The NRCC spent a total of $987,829.98 on independent expenditures in this race.[6] It spent some of its funds on controversial mailers that did little to burnish Swallow's image. By looking at this race in 2002 and in 2004, it will be possible to ascertain how groups and parties perceive the new campaign environment in which they work. Both Arizona-1 and New Mexico-1 also found their way back on to the competitive list. Representative Renzi won by less than 4 percentage points in 2002 and did not carry a majority of the sprawling district. Representative Wilson in New Mexico faced a rematch in 2004 with Richard Romero. These cases are particularly important because they allow us to hold the candidates and the competitiveness of the district constant.

National observers also picked the South Dakota at-large race to be highly competitive. In 2002 former governor Bill Janklow won the open seat in a competitive contest with Stephanie Herseth. Outside groups and the parties paid close attention to the race, but the conservative leanings of the state ultimately gave the nod to Janklow. The district became competitive again when Janklow gave up his seat after being convicted of vehicular manslaughter, and Herseth replaced him by winning the special election in June 2004. Herseth faced a stiff challenge in the general election from Larry Diedrich. Consequently, South Dakota had three consecutive House races that the outside interests strenuously contested. In both the Utah and South Dakota cases, Democrats held on to seats in Republican-leaning districts.

Uniquely enough, South Dakota also experienced two consecutive Senate races where the parties and the interest groups invested a great deal of time and money. The 2002 Senate race between Tim Johnson and John Thune attracted national attention. The parties and groups spent heavily in this race because control of the Senate was at stake. In 2004, the contest between Johnson and Senator Daschle reignited the passion but for different reasons. Republicans wanted to rid the Senate of the person they believed was responsible for obstructing their agenda. Democrats wanted to return their leader to power.

By examining the ground-war activity in these races across different cycles, it should be possible to determine the extent to which both parties and interest groups have adapted to a campaign environment in which they both have significant incentives to target and mobilize voters on the ground. Nobody believed that overall spending on broadcast media would become less important. However, we certainly expect to see increased or at least stable levels of nonbroadcast activity across the different election cycles. The increased or relatively constant levels of participation from groups and parties would suggest that they believe in the effectiveness of ground-war operations and see them as part of an ongoing effort to win elections.

We approach these data, though, with a bit of caution. While having two consecutive cycles to compare ground-war activity provides some evidence of the commitments of campaign participants to this form of participation, there are intervening factors that may influence the actual allocations. For example, with so much emphasis placed on the presidential campaign by the parties and the interest groups, there may be more efforts at ground-war mobilization made by fewer participants. As we have already stated, most of the groups believed that there were fewer competitive opportunities in the 2004 congressional races. Many of the groups also decided to devote their resources to the presidential campaign. Consequently, even stable levels of ground-war activity by noncandidate groups in House and Senate races would indicate the importance of these efforts, especially during an election cycle dominated by presidential politics.

Participation, as gauged by the number of party entities participating, has dropped slightly from the 2002 to the 2004 elections in the competitive races for which we have collected data in both cycles. On average in 2002, approximately six party committees participated in competitive Senate or House races. This number drops to just over four in the 2004 election cycle. The lower number for 2004 perhaps reflects changes brought about by BCRA. In 2002 the state party committees could participate more easily because of the availability of soft money. With the ban on soft money, the congressional campaign committees assumed much of the responsibility for participating in the congressional races. The national committees are not participating in congressional races, most likely because all of their resources are focused on the presidential race. As stated though, the National Republican Congressional Committee (NRCC) and Democratic Congressional Campaign Committee (DCCC) are still active. Even though the state parties are still involved, they are not doing nearly as many mailers likely due to the soft money ban, leaving the candidates to do more of their own mailers.

Interest groups continue to participate in competitive congressional races at about the same rate. In 2002 an average of 20.5 interest groups, partisan and nonpartisan, generated at least some form of ground-war activity. The number increases only slightly to 21.7 in 2004. The South Dakota Senate races in both cycles attracted the most attention. A total of thirty-four groups in 2002 and thirty-nine groups in 2004 lavished attention on South Dakota voters. Overall, the data do not provide a clear answer. The number of party entities participating in the ground war has dropped in the last two years. The BCRA soft money ban may help explain that decline. On the other hand, the number of interest groups participating in these elections has increased slightly. We also know that much of the interest group activity in 2004 was directed at the presidential race, and the data we are comparing here is only to congressional elections. This fact means that the conclusions should be approached with some caution.

The number of noncandidate entities tells only part of the story. A smaller number of groups can pour additional resources into races thereby keeping activity high across two different cycles. With the smaller number of party entities in 2004 than in 2002, we might expect a decrease in the amount of ground-war activity from the parties. The average amount of ground war from the parties in a competitive race was 58.5 ads or contacts in 2002 and almost 34.3 in 2004. The 2002 South Dakota Senate race accounts for much of that difference. The Johnson/Thune race produced 131 unique communications from the political parties. By contrast, the Daschle/Thune race generated only fifty-two unique communications from the party. Even without the 2002 race in the average, there is still a substantial difference between the amount of party activity in the 2002

Table 8.2 Party Participation in Ground-War Activity

Race	Year	Party	Email	Mail	Person	Phone	Party Subtotal	Total Ads	# of Party Org	Total # of Org in Race
South Dakota										
At-Large	2002	D	2	24	1	4	31	45	2	5
		R	—	13	1	—	14		3	
	2004	D	1	—	—	1	2	37	2	4
		R	9	18	1	7	35		2	
Senate	2002	D	4	43	1	5	53	131	3	6
		R	—	73	2	3	78		3	
	2004	D	1	6	—	—	7	52	2	4
		R	18	21	1	5	45		2	
Utah										
District 2	2002	D	—	3	1	1	5	24	2	5
		R	—	19	—	—	19		3	
	2004	D	—	4	—	—	4	20	1	3
		R	—	14	—	2	16		2	
Arizona										
District 1	2002	D	—	7	—	2	9	36	3	7
		R	—	25	—	2	27		4	
	2004	D	—	13	—	1	14	33	2	5
		R	—	18	—	1	19		3	

(continues)

Table 8.2 Continued

Race	Year	Party	Email	Mail	Person	Phone	Party Subtotal	Total Ads	# of Party Org	Total # of Org in Race
Colorado										
District 7	2002	D	—	10	2	2	14	50	2	8
		R	—	30	4	2	36		6	
	2004	D	—	4	—	—	4	28	3	5
		R	—	24	—	—	24		2	
New Mexico										
District 1	2002	D	—	29	—	6	35	65	2	5
		R	—	27	1	2	30		3	
	2004	D	—	13	—	—	13	36	3	5
		R	—	23	—	—	23		2	
Average	2002	D	3.0	19.3	1.3	3.3	24.5	58.5	2.3	6.0
		R	0.0	31.2	2.0	2.3	34.0		3.7	
	2004	D	1.0	6.8	0.0	1.0	7.3	34.3	2.2	4.3
		R	13.5	19.0	1.0	3.8	27.0		2.2	

and 2004 cycles. Interest groups took a slightly different path than the political parties. Interest groups distributed an average of 28.3 unique pieces in 2002. In 2004 the average increased to 35.5. Parties therefore tended to put fewer pieces into the races in 2004 than they did in 2002. Interest groups, however, picked up some of the slack and actually increased their activity from 2002.

We can only draw a few tentative conclusions from a comparison of these congressional races. First, parties did not appear to participate as much in 2004 as they did in 2002. Perhaps the decline in activity has more to do with the way in which the parties chose to participate in 2004. With the increased amount of hard money available to them, they may have decided to put more effort into the air war. Second, the parties may not have sensed as much need to support the ground war. Many of the races in the final analysis were not as competitive as they had been in 2002. Parties understand how difficult it is to unseat an incumbent. Also many of the races in our sample were rematches. As the races unfolded it became clear that many of them would not be as competitive as they had been in 2002. Finally, the interest groups maintained levels of activity in these races but perhaps not as much as might have been expected given the competitiveness of some of the congressional races at the beginning of the cycle. Many of the groups that traditionally participated in congressional races made an explicit decision to devote their resources to the presidential campaign. Therefore, even though BCRA provides incentives for the groups to become active in ground activity, their levels in 2004 did not meet what might have been expected in some of the most competitive congressional races.

CONCLUSION: WHERE DOES THE GROUND WAR GO FROM HERE?

Even though the ground war in congressional elections may not have been as large as predicted, the overall ground war in 2004 received unprecedented amounts of attention. This attention took the form of funds from parties and interest groups and coverage from the media. Parties and groups poured most of their efforts into a few battleground states in the presidential election contest. The sheer size and scope of the ground war in the battleground states intrigued the media. Major media outlets began reporting on the voter mobilization plans of America Coming Together soon after the *New York Times* highlighted the organization on August 8, 2003 (Janofsky 2003). Steady coverage continued through Election Day, when the *Washington Post* reported on the "sophisticated techniques" and "old-fashioned shoe leather" tactics occurring in seven battleground states (Balz and Edsall 2004). In the aftermath of the election, political operatives now debate the effectiveness of the ground war and what could possibly account for the election results in several of the battleground states.

It is clear though that a larger and more sophisticated ground-war strategy may be in the offing. The parties and interest groups availed themselves of incredibly sophisticated methods for finding and targeting voters. Many of the

Table 8.3   Interest Group Ground-War Activity

Race	Year	Party[a]	Email	Mail	Person	Phone	Group Subtotal	Total Ads	# of Group Org	Total # of Org in Race
South Dakota										
At-Large	2002	D	—	10	—	3	13	26	5	16
		R	—	13	—	—	13		9	
		NP	—	—	—	—	0		2	
	2004	D	5	9	—	8	22	36	9	18
		R	—	7	—	1	8		6	
		NP	5	1	—	—	6		3	
Senate	2002	D	—	20	2	1	23	45	14	34
		R	—	20	—	2	22		16	
		NP	—	—	—	—	0		4	
	2004	D	6	11	—	5	22	69	10	39
		R	—	35	2	5	42		26	
		NP	5	—	—	—	5		3	
Utah										
District 2	2002	D	—	10	—	5	15	23	5	15
		R	—	4	—	2	6		7	
		NP	—	2	—	—	2		3	
	2004	D	—	3	—	—	3	10	1	5
		R	—	7	—	—	7		4	
		NP	—	—	—	—	0		0	

Arizona										
District 1	2002	D	—	8	—	8	16	26	7	14
		R	—	10	—	—	10		7	
		NP	—	—	—	—	0		0	
	2004	D	—	14	—	8	22	50	13	29
		R	—	25	1	1	27		15	
		NP	—	1	—	—	1		1	
District 7	2002	D	2	6	1	2	11	28	8	23
		R	—	10	2	2	14		11	
		NP	—	3	—	—	3		4	
	2004	D	—	5	—	—	5	20	4	15
		R	—	11	1	—	12		6	
		NP	—	2	—	1	3		2	
New Mexico										
District 1	2002	D	—	12	—	2	14	22	9	21
		R	—	8	—	—	8		12	
		NP	—	—	—	—	0		0	
	2004	D	—	8	—	3	11	28	12	24
		R	—	12	1	1	14		10	
		NP	—	3	—	—	3		2	
Average										
	2002	D	2.0	11.0	1.5	3.5	15.3	28.3	8.0	20.5
		R	0.0	10.8	2.0	2.0	12.2		10.3	
		NP	0.0	2.5	0.0	0.0	0.8		2.2	
	2004	D	5.5	8.3	0.0	5.3	14.2	35.5	6.0	21.7
		R	0.0	16.2	1.3	3.0	18.3		10.5	
		NP	5.0	1.8	0.0	1.0	3.0		2.0	

[a] D stands for Democratic leaning, R stands for Republican leaning, and NP stands for nonpartisan.

methods used to contact voters had been developed and tested in previous congressional elections. With the stakes of the presidential election so high, the parties and interest groups invested huge sums of money to create and maintain detailed voter files that made microtargeting a reality. Just as lessons learned in 2000 and 2002 set the stage for 2004, the lessons learned in 2004 will shape the ground war in future cycles. These lessons will be integrated with changes in election law. For example, competitive states with early voting and liberal absentee voting rules can expect even more attention from parties and interest groups. Also the various "treatments" voters saw in the battleground states will probably be exported to competitive congressional races in the next cycle. The ground war has become an increasingly important part of campaign activity. And more and more people are beginning to notice it.

NOTES

We gratefully acknowledge the financial support for this project provided by the Pew Charitable Trusts, the Smith Richardson Foundation, the Joyce Foundation, and the Carnegie Corporation of New York. Quin Monson, our coinvestigator on this project and the 2002 project, provided helpful comments and suggestions on this chapter. Stephanie Curtis, Kristina Gale, Betsey Gimbel, and Richard Hawkins have been our research associates on the 2004 project and deserve a grateful acknowledgment as well. Data reported in this chapter are drawn from a three-wave panel study conducted in collaboration between the Center for the Study of Elections and Democracy at Brigham Young University and the Wisconsin Advertising Project at the University of Wisconsin, Madison. Professors Kenneth Goldstein and Charles H. Franklin collaborated with us on the survey.

    1. See www.bipac.org and www.voteforbusiness.com.
    2. A cousin of the FEC press officer, Robert Biersack, received eleven phone calls in one afternoon (Biersack 2004).
    3. See appendix B.
    4. This research does not seek to answer whether or not interest groups allocate resources in noncompetitive races. Research by Magleby and Monson shows rather convincingly that groups do not engage in much activity outside of competitive races. What this particular piece of research seeks to show is the ways in which parties and groups participate in competitive races. For example, what strategies do they pursue when mobilizing voters and how much effort do they devote to the ground war?
    5. See appendix B.
    6. See www.fec.gov.

APPENDIX A

The thirty-two members comprising the America Votes coalition are as follows: ACORN, AFL-CIO, AFSCME, America Coming Together (ACT), American Federation of Teachers, Association of Trial Lawyers of America, Brady Campaign to Prevent Gun Violence United With the Million Mom March, Clean Water Action, Defenders of Wildlife Action Fund, Democracy for America, EMILY's List, Environment2004, The Human Rights Campaign, League of Conservation Voters, The Media Fund, MoveOn.org Voter Fund, Moving America Forward,

Music for America, NAACP National Voter Fund, NARAL Pro-Choice America, National Education Association, National Jewish Democratic Council, National Treasury Employees Union, Partnership for America's Families, Planned Parenthood Action Fund, SEIU, Sierra Club, USAction, Voices for Working Families, Young Voter Alliance, and 21st Century Democrats.

APPENDIX B

The Brigham Young University/University of Wisconsin Panel Survey interviewed 2,782 registered voters in the forty-eight contiguous states plus the District of Columbia with oversamples in Ohio and Florida. The interviews were conducted from June 24 through July 3. Second and third interviews of the same individuals took place between September 12 and 20 and November 3 and 16, respectively. Because a "panel survey" involves the same people being interviewed at more than one point in time, it is possible to measure changes in their opinions in response to the campaign. Polls that conduct only a single interview make measurement of the impact of the campaign on changes in opinion quite difficult.

The survey was designed to oversample the most competitive states to give more precise estimates of political opinions there, while still accurately representing nonbattleground states and the national population as a whole. Those states considered battleground states in this study were Arkansas, Arizona, Colorado, Florida, Iowa, Louisiana, Maine, Michigan, Minnesota, Missouri, New Hampshire, New Mexico, Nevada, Ohio, Oregon, Pennsylvania, Washington, Wisconsin, and West Virginia.

IV

CANDIDATES AND ELECTIONS

9

The First Congressional Elections After BCRA

Gary C. Jacobson

The 2004 elections were the first to take place under the revisions in campaign finance rules embodied in the Bipartisan Campaign Reform Act of 2002 (BCRA). What effects, if any, did it have on the financing of the House and Senate campaigns? Broadly speaking, the answer is "very little." Although BCRA may have rechanneled some campaign funds, made it a bit easier to raise funds from individuals, and induced some marginal changes in some campaign finance practices, there is little to suggest that BCRA had any substantive effect on the cost, conduct, extent, competitiveness, or results of the 2004 congressional campaigns. This is not surprising; the characterization of BCRA as "the most far-reaching and controversial attempt to restructure the national political process in a generation" is accurate only because is has no competitor (Ortiz 2004). At most, BCRA returned congressional campaign finance practices to where they had been a decade earlier.

BCRA was intended mainly to close the "soft money" loophole in party fundraising and to rein in advocacy groups that had been spending unlimited and unreported sums on independent campaigns under the guise of "voter education," or "issue advocacy," but the act also contained provisions that had a more direct effect on congressional campaign finance. It raised the individual contribution limit to $2,000 per candidate per campaign (primary and general election campaigns are treated separately), doubling the limit that had been in place since 1974. This provision made up for slightly more than half the erosion in real dollars of the original limit ($1,000 in 2004 is equivalent to about $258 in 1974). BCRA also provided even higher contribution limits for donors contributing to candidates who were running against self-financed millionaires. (For a summary of BCRA, see appendix 1.) None of these changes was entirely inconsequential, but the flow of campaign funds is so thoroughly dominated by the strategic considerations that shape congressional campaign finance that their substantive effects were swamped by other, far more fundamental considerations.

Resources are not unlimited, and therefore most contributors—individuals and organizations alike—deploy funds where they have the greatest chance of affecting the outcome or currying favor with the winner. No one wants to waste money on hopeless candidacies. Consequently, money is raised most readily by incumbents (most of whom are sure winners), candidates for open congressional seats (which typically produce more competitive races), and challengers facing incumbents who for one reason or another appear vulnerable (Jacobson 2004). Incumbents in trouble usually attract the most money (and other assistance), as the partisan incentive to invest in races where the outcome is in doubt and money might actually matter combines with the incumbents' usual advantage in tapping contributors. The distribution of campaign funds in any given election year is thus strongly shaped by the configuration of competitive House and Senate races. In 2004, that configuration featured a dearth of competitive House races, reducing the need for contributors to make allocational trade-offs and leaving plenty of money for the proportionally more numerous tight Senate contests.

THE CONTEXT OF HOUSE ELECTIONS IN 2004

Competitive House races were remarkably few in 2004, with both long and short-term circumstances contributing to the dearth. By the measure of district-level presidential voting, the number of House seats held by the "wrong" party (Democrats in Republican-leaning districts, Republicans in Democratic-leaning districts) and the number of competitive districts both shrank by about half between 1992 and 2002 (from eighty-one to forty in the first category, and from seventy-two to thirty-eight in the second. The remaining seats classified as "safe" by this measure thus grew from 281 to 356 (Jacobson 2003). This was partly a consequence of Republican gains in 1994, which occurred mainly in districts the party should have been winning all along, but it was also partly a consequence of redistricting after the 2000 census. In addition to the successful Republican gerrymanders in Florida, Michigan, Ohio, Pennsylvania, and Texas that enhanced the party's already notable structural advantage in House elections,[1] redistricting reduced the overall number of competitive House seats by strengthening marginal incumbents. Of the twenty-five districts Republicans won in 2000 with less than 55 percent of the major-party vote, eighteen were made more Republican by increasing the proportion of voters who had favored George W. Bush in 2000; of the nineteen similarly marginal Democratic districts, fifteen were given an increased share of constituents who had voted for Al Gore. Thus three quarters of the marginal districts in the country were made safer through redistricting, half of them by more than 2 percentage points (in the 2000 presidential vote share). Partly as a result, only four of the 382 incumbents seeking reelection in 2002 were defeated by challengers. (Four more lost to other incumbents in face-offs forced by redistricting.)

The scarcity of seats where local partisanship or missteps by the incumbent gave the out party hope in 2004 was compounded by the absence of a national surge toward either party. Conditions traditionally thought to influence national electoral tides—namely, the state of the economy and the public's evaluation of the president's performance—were effectively neutral once the new post-9/11 consideration, terrorism, was added to the mix. The economy's performance during the entire Bush administration was mediocre by historical standards, but growth accelerated in the year leading up to the election and the economy's earlier weakness could be blamed, in part, on the damage done to markets by the attacks of 9/11. President Bush's job approval ratings in national polls also fell into a politically neutral range. Although declining from the record-high Bush enjoyed during the immediate post-9/11 rally, they generally remained above 50 percent until early 2004 and stayed close to this mark through the election. The relatively low performance ratings Americans gave the president on the economy were offset by notably higher performance ratings on his handling of terrorism, leaving the president's overall approval rating at a level that offered neither party's congressional candidates a discernible advantage (Jacobson 2005).

More important, the *composition* of Bush's overall approval ratings promised neither party's congressional candidates any help. Bush enjoyed overwhelming support from Republicans, achieving the highest job approval ratings within his own party of any president in the more than fifty years pollsters have been asking the question. But his approval ratings among Democratic identifiers fell steeply after the post-9/11 rally and by 2004 had fallen to the lowest level ever recorded among the rival party's identifiers—as low as 8 percent in one September 2004 Gallup Poll (Jacobson 2005). These partisan differences in approval of Bush were echoed in voters' responses to virtually all of the polling questions regarding which party would handle various policy issues better, as well as about the state of the economy and the overall direction of the country (Jacobson 2005; CBS News Poll 2003). In such a highly polarized atmosphere, neither party could anticipate attracting many partisan defectors on Election Day, further dampening prospects for taking House seats from the other side. Thus, approaching elections of 2004, with no clear partisan tide in sight, neither party saw much opportunity to take many seats from the other, and the consequence was the lowest level of competition for House seats ever observed.

The scarcity of competition is evident in figure 9.1, which displays the percentage of competitive seats as defined by *Congressional Quarterly* in the October of each election from 1982 to 2004.[2] Notice that in the 1980s and 1990s, elections that followed redistricting (1982, 1992) featured a relatively high number of competitive races, reflecting the opportunities and uncertainties created by the reshuffle of district lines. Competition then tended to diminish during the rest of the decade as parties and candidates learned from experience where challenges were likely to be futile and gave up trying. The redistricting after the 2000 census did not have this effect; instead, it reduced the number of competitive races. By

Figure 9.1   Competitive House Elections, 1982–2004

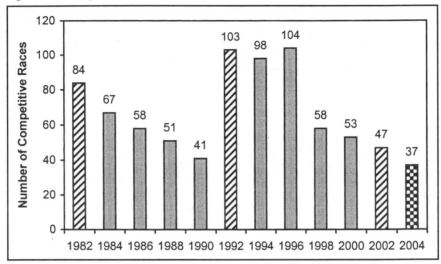

Note: Competitive races are those classified by *Congressional Quarterly* as "toss-ups" or "leans Democratic (Republican)"; uncompetitive races are those classified as "safe" or "Democrat (Republican) favored."

2004, the number of such races had fallen to the lowest in the period, thirty-seven, amounting to less than 9 percent of all House seats.

In a departure from past elections, even open House seats contests were relatively quiet in 2004. Only eleven of the thirty-five were classified as competitive by *Congressional Quarterly*. (In 2000 and 2002, more than half of the open seats were rated competitive.) One reason is that only nine of these seats were in the "wrong" party's hands according to the district's 2000 presidential vote; in twenty-one open districts, the 2000 presidential vote for the candidate of the party already holding the seat exceeded 55 percent.

CAMPAIGN MONEY IN THE HOUSE ELECTIONS

The dearth of competitive House races had its predictable effect on campaign finance. As they have done for years, incumbents continued to raise and spend large sums even when feebly opposed or even unopposed (Jacobson 2004).[3] Their average level of spending continued its long upward trend (figure 9.2). Contests for open seats were also generously funded on average, but only because very high levels of spending in the hottest contests offset uncompetitive levels of spending by the weaker of the two candidates in the rest (amounting to about half these contests). The challengers' average expenditures were essentially flat, as they had been since 1996, but this is not surprising in light of the small number of competitive races. If analysis is confined to potentially competitive districts (defined here as those won by the incumbent with less than 60 percent of the

Figure 9.2   Campaign Spending in Contested House Elections, 1980–2004

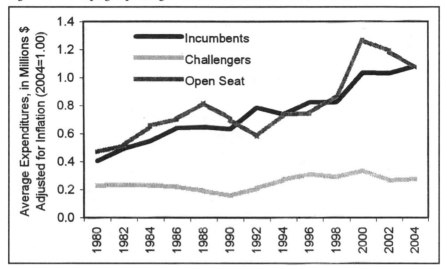

Source: Federal Election Commission.

vote in 2002),[4] funding was comparable to that for challengers in 2000 and 2002, averaging more than $823,000 (figure 9.3). Average spending by incumbents increased in these contests (as well as overall), so the financial gap between officeholders and their opponents continued to widen, as it has for more than two decades. The number of challengers spending at least $1 million on the campaign was second highest on record in 2004 (figure 9.4). Promising House challengers were neither starved for funds—no challenger who got at least 45 percent of the vote spent less than $700,728, and all but two spent more than $1 million—nor provided with greater sums than would be expected from the patterns established in previous election years.

BCRA, then, did nothing to disrupt the system of mutually reinforcing decisions and expectations that link candidates and contributors with each other and with perceived electoral prospects. As usual, the better the electoral odds, the more likely races were to attract high-quality challengers, and the more money was contributed to their campaigns (Jacobson and Kernell 1983). For example, 39 percent of challengers in districts won by the incumbent with less than 60 percent of the vote in 2002 had previously held elective public office, compared to 14 percent of the challengers in less promising districts. The challengers with elective office experience raised on average about $623,000, more than three times as much as the average for the rest ($198,000). Thus high-quality candidates continued to attract campaign money, and the availability of campaign money continued to attract high-quality candidates. Only the shortage of plausible opportunities to take an incumbent's seat depressed challengers' overall finances in 2004.

Figure 9.3   Campaign Spending in Competitive Races, 1972–2004

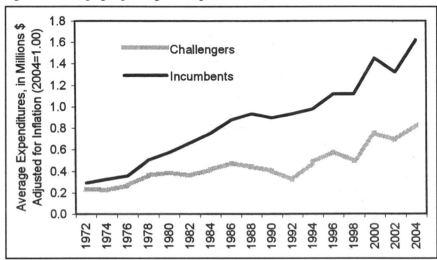

Note: Competitive House races are defined as those in which the incumbent received less than 60 percent of the major party vote in the previous election.

Figure 9.4 $1 Million House Challenges, 1972–2004

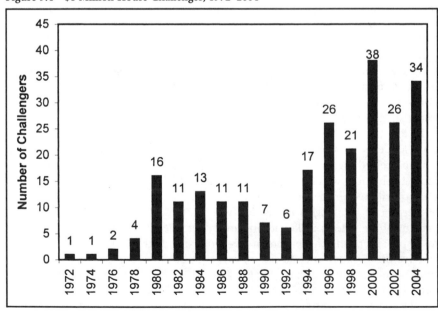

Note: Entries are based on spending data adjusted for inflation.

In none of the comparisons in figures 9.2 to 9.4 do the 2004 data stand out in any way from the long-term trends. BCRA may, however, have modestly altered the source of campaign dollars. By doubling the old ceiling on individual contributions to $2,000 per candidate per campaign while leaving the PAC limit untouched at $5,000, BCRA increased the potential payoff from soliciting money from individuals. As figure 9.5 indicates, the proportion of contributions to House candidates coming from individuals was higher in 2004 than in any of the previous eight elections. Yet the trend has been upward for some time, and the increase in individual donations might also be a product of the rapid expansion of Internet fundraising in 2004.

More compelling evidence that BCRA's higher individual contribution limit altered the fundraising mix lies in the doubling between 2002 and 2004 of the share of campaign receipts coming from individual contributions in excess of $1,000 (from 6.5 percent to 14.2 percent). The increase in funds from this category accounts for 8.4 percent of total 2004 receipts and fully 67.6 percent of the growth in receipts over 2002. As table 9.1 indicates, these changes generally affected candidates to about the same degree regardless of party or incumbency status, although Republican challengers apparently picked up a little more from such donations than other types of House candidates. These figures do not vary much by the competitiveness of the race, although successful challengers and candidates in the two Texas districts pitting incumbents against one another got a somewhat larger proportion of such funds (17.9 percent and 21.2 percent, respectively). So far, then, BCRA's raising of the individual contribution limit has probably put a little more money in candidates' hands without significantly altering its distribution across types of candidates.

In the end, the expectation that 2004 was not a year in which either party could take many seats from the other was amply fulfilled. Only seven House

Figure 9.5   Sources of House Campaign Contributions, 1988–2004

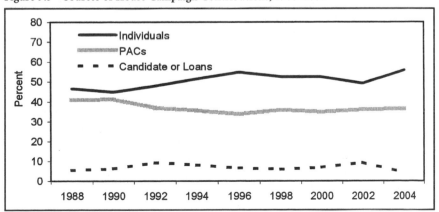

Note: Data for 2004 are through the November 22 reporting period; other years are through December 31.
Source: Federal Election Commission.

Table 9.1 Individual Contributions to 2004 House Candidates in Excess of the Old Limit ($1K) as a Percentage of Total Net Receipts

	N	Average Per Candidate in Excess of $1K From $1K+ Donors	Average New Dollars in Excess of $1K from $1K+ Donors	Average Total Net Receipts	Above $1K as Percent of Total Net Receipts	New Dollars Above $1K as Percent of Total Net Receipts
All	728	122,699	72,600	861,866	14.2	8.4
Dem	364	109,152	63,970	777,138	14.0	8.2
Rep	364	135,828	80,371	946,898	14.3	8.5
Incumbent	401	157,893	95,393	1,133,092	13.9	8.4
Dem	190	148,091	92,861	1,047,562	14.1	8.9
Rep	210	168,197	99,157	1,211,890	13.9	8.2
Challenger	262	50,346	30,510	352,451	14.3	8.7
Dem	143	40,795	21,132	347,321	11.7	6.1
Rep	119	60,831	39,867	358,616	17.0	11.1
Open Seat	65	194,111	122,887	1,241,943	15.6	9.9
Dem	31	181,103	117,798	1,102,401	16.4	10.7
Rep	34	205,972	125,641	1,369,172	15.0	9.2

Sources: Center for Responsive Politics (for amounts received per donor), Federal Election Commission, and Campaign Finance Institute.

Note: New money from above-$1,000 donors is defined as money in 2004 minus money in 2002 from above-$1,000 donors.

members lost their seats in the general election; of these, four were Democratic victims of a 2003 Texas Republican gerrymander; two lost to challengers, and two lost to other incumbents. (Two additional Texas Democrats were defeated in the primary but replaced in the House by other Democrats.) All of the successful challengers were very well funded, none spending less than $1.5 million. The House election results thus reflected the same political fundamentals that shaped campaign finance activities in 2004—activities which, as always, contributed in turn to the realization of those fundamentals on election day.

THE SENATE

The Senate seats up for election in 2004 offered a much higher proportion of potentially competitive races, and campaign funds flowed accordingly. With few exceptions, Senate seats are rarely as securely in one party's hands as are most House seats. Senate incumbents lose about three times as frequently as House incumbents; over the past twenty years, thirty-nine states have chosen senators from both parties. Competition in 2004 also reflected the particular partisan configuration of Senate seats at stake and patterns of voluntary retirement. Ten of the nineteen seats defended by the Democrats were in states won by Bush in 2000, including five open seats, all in the South. Only three of the fifteen Republican-held seats were in states won by Gore, including only one of the three Republican open seats, so most of the battles were for the Democrats' turf. In the end, Republicans won all of the Democrats' southern seats and Republican John Thune defeated Democratic minority leader Tom Daschle in South Dakota; Democrats took two of the three open Republican seats, giving the Republicans a net gain of three Senate seats.

CAMPAIGN MONEY IN THE SENATE ELECTIONS

As always, campaign finances reflected the competitive situation in the 2004 Senate races. Total spending in Senate contests was second only to the all-time high set in 2000, when the total was inflated by the $61 million Jon Corzine invested in his successful campaign to represent New Jersey in the Senate and a very expensive contest for New York's open Senate seat ($82 million spent in total). Trends in Senate campaign spending broken down by incumbency status appear in figure 9.6. Comparisons of Senate spending across time are tricky because of the huge differences in states' populations and variations in the sets of states and incumbents from one year to another. Hence, although the data for 2004 in figure 9.6 suggests that challengers were shortchanged in 2004, on a per-voter basis, they were not (table 9.2). Per-voter spending was on average substantially higher for all three categories of Senate candidates in 2004 than it had been in contests for the same set of seats in 1998.

Although most incumbents were spared serious challenges, at least ten faced

Figure 9.6   Campaign Spending in Contested Senate Elections, 1980–2004

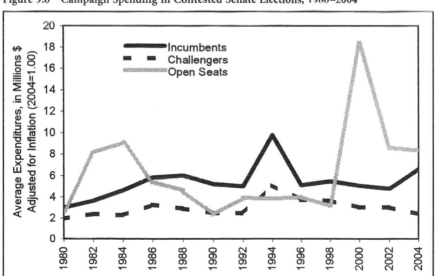

Source: Federal Election Commission.

experienced, reasonably well-financed opponents, and eight ended up winning less than 60 percent of the vote. The finances of the three closest of these contests, in which the incumbent won less than 55 percent of the vote, are listed in table 9.3. The South Dakota race was in a financial class by itself, with more than $34 million spent campaigning in a state with fewer than 570,000 voting-age citizens. The more than $60 per voter spent by Daschle and Thune is by far the most on record and more than five times as much as was spent the last time Daschle sought reelection (and nearly three times as much as was spent by the candidates in the 2002 South Dakota race between Thune and incumbent Democrat Tim Johnson, itself an astonishingly expensive contest) (Bart and Meador 2004). Remarkable sums were also spent in Alaska, where the popular former governor Tony Knowles challenged Republican incumbent Lisa Murkowski, who had been appointed to the Senate by her father when he vacated the seat to become governor in December 2002. The $24 per voter spent in this race was more than nine times as much as had been spent six years earlier. Although per-voter spending always tends to be higher the smaller a state's population—economies of scale have a strong effect on Senate campaign spending patterns—these sums still far exceed the norm. Much of this money came from out of state, eloquent testimony to the nationalization of the battle to control the Senate.

Both the Alaska and South Dakota races were widely expected to be tight; the third close contest involving an incumbent, in Kentucky, was not, and the campaign spending patterns were thus rather different. Challenger Daniel Mongiardo was given little chance until the incumbent, Republican Jim Bunning, began behaving erratically during the campaign. Some late money flowed into Mongiardo's campaign, and he eventually received help from his party, but he still wound up spending 30 percent less in real terms than had Bunning's 1998 opponent. Bunning's spending was also on the low side for a seriously threatened incumbent. This was the one 2004 race where a timely infusion of additional money might have altered the outcome.

The intense competition for the open Senate seats, whose fate was expected to determine control of the Senate, is reflected in campaign finance data in table 9.3. In six of these contests, both candidates were generously financed, in every case but one at much higher levels than their predecessors in 1998. The data also reflect the fact that the principal contenders were the kind of first-tier candidates who are usually the best fundraisers, including eight current or former members of the House, three statewide officeholders, two former cabinet secretaries, and

Table 9.2 Senate Spending Per Voting-Age Resident, 1998–2004

Year	Incumbents	Challengers	Open Seats
1998	$1.92	$0.64	$1.05
2000	2.68	1.21	2.98
2002	2.81	1.47	2.11
2004	3.51	1.87	1.71

Note: Spending is adjusted for inflation (2004 = 1.00).

Table 9.3　Senate Campaign Spending in Selected Races, 2004

	Vote	Expenditures	$ Per Voter	Total $ Per Voter	Total $ Per Voter, 1998	Change from 1998
Competitive Challenges						
Alaska						
Lisa Murkowski (R)	51.6%	5,429,904	11.80			
Tony Knowles (D)	48.4%	5,767,707	12.54	24.34	2.58	843%
Kentucky						
Jim Bunning (R)	50.7%	6,075,399	1.94			
Daniel Mongiardo (D)	49.3%	3,104,981	0.99	2.93	2.96	0%
South Dakota						
Tom Daschle (D)	49.4%	19,975,170	35.11			
John Thune (R)	50.6%	14,660,147	25.76	60.87	11.47	431%
Competitive Open Seats						
Colorado						
Ken Salazar (D)	52.4%	9,886,551	2.91			
Peter Coors (R)	47.6%	7,328,620	2.31	5.22	1.80	190%
Florida						
Betty Castor (D)	49.4%	11,384,224	0.87			
Mel Martinez (R)	50.6%	12,451,863	0.95	1.82	0.68	168%
Louisiana						
Chris John (D)	29.3%	4,868,185	1.47			
David Vitter (R)	51.0%	7,206,714	2.17	3.64	1.55	135%
North Carolina						
Erskine Bowles (D)	47.7%	13,357,851	2.11			
Richard Burr (R)	52.3%	12,853,110	2.03	4.14	3.70	12%
Oklahoma						
Brad Carson (D)	43.9%	6,256,444	2.38			
Tom Coburn (R)	56.1%	5,013,817	1.90	4.28	1.16	269%
South Carolina						
Inez Tannenbaum (D)	45.1%	6,156,183	1.97			
James DeMint (R)	54.9%	9,036,086	2.89	4.86	2.95	65%
Other Open Seats						
Georgia						
Denise Majette (D)	40.9%	2,470,272	0.39			
John Isakson (R)	59.1%	8,007,578	1.25	1.64	2.54	−35%
Illinois						
Barack Obama (D)	72.1%	14,244,768	1.51			
Alan Keyes (R)	27.9%	2,545,325	0.27	1.78	2.93	−39%

Note: Incumbents in italic.

the heir to the Coors name and beer fortune. The principal exception was in Illinois, where the Republican primary winner, Jack Ryan, withdrew after embarrassing revelations about his first marriage and was replaced by Alan Keyes, a Maryland resident most noted for treating campaigns as an opportunity to indulge in socially conservative oratory. Keyes was crushed by charismatic Illinois State Senator Barack Obama, who thus became the only African American in the Senate. Georgia Democrat Denise Majette's attempt to make it two was underfunded and fell far short. In these two more lopsided contests, overall spending was substantially lower than it had been in the same states in 1998.

Clearly, BCRA did nothing to inhibit the flow of funds to competitive Senate candidates in 2004. As with House campaigns, BCRA's higher ceiling on individual contributions may have made a difference; the proportion of money supplied by individuals was significantly ($p < .05$) higher than it had been at the comparable point in the previous seven elections (figure 9.7). But this could also be a consequence of the unusually small share of funds provided by the candidates themselves in 2004.

Did campaign money have anything to do with the Republican Senate gains in 2004? Republicans won most of the Senate seats thought to be in play, but with the possible exception of Kentucky, which became competitive only late in the campaign, no losing Democrat could plausibly blame defeat on a shortage of funds. But by generously funding Thune's challenge to Daschle, Murkowski's defense against Knowles, and all of the Republicans seeking open Democratic seats in the South, Republicans positioned themselves to cash in on the extraordinary degree of partisan polarization generated by the presidential race. Reflecting the stark partisan differences in assessments of Bush and his administration, presidential voters were unusually loyal to party in 2004 (Jones 2004).[5] The political atmosphere surrounding the presidential contest was not conducive to parti-

Figure 9.7   Sources of Senate Campaign Contributions, 1988–2004

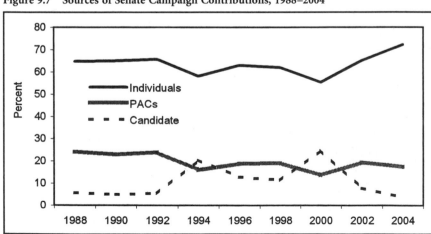

Source: Federal Election Commission.

san defection and ticket-splitting at the Senate level, especially where incumbency was not a factor. Thus seven of the eight open seats went to the party that won the state in the 2000 and 2004 presidential elections (Colorado is the exception). All of the Democratic candidates for the open seats in the South except Majette ran ahead of Kerry, to be sure, but not by enough to win. Daschle and Knowles ran more than ten points ahead of Kerry but still lost. In all, ten of the eleven races listed in table 9.3 were won by the party that also took the state's electoral votes. With both sides having more than adequate funding for a full-scale campaign in most of these contests, the results ended up reflecting the states' underlying partisan divisions, this, of course, to the Republicans' great good fortune.[6]

OUTSIDE MONEY, NEGATIVE CAMPAIGNS, AND MILLIONAIRE CANDIDATES

As in other recent congressional elections, plenty of action took place outside of the candidates' campaigns. The activities of party committees and outside groups are documented in several other chapters in this book, so I will mention them only briefly here. The Hill campaign committees overcame some, but not all, of the loss of resources occasioned by the ban on soft money by raising more hard money than ever. The House committees (figure 9.8) were more successful in this regard than the Senate committees (figure 9.9). The limited number of potentially competitive races in 2004 assured, however, that there was plenty of money to spend where it might conceivably make a difference.

The Hill committees coped with the ban on spending soft money by putting the hard money to work, exploiting the independent spending option to an unprecedented extent (figures 9.10 and 9.11). As we saw in chapter 3, their efforts focused heavily on the handful of close House and Senate races, and the sums invested were impressive.

The principal effect seems to have been to increase the already grossly lopsided distribution of campaign resources. For example, the Gini index, which measures distributions on a scale of 0.0 (complete equality) to 1.0 (complete inequality—one recipient gets everything), applied to the 2004 House challengers, rises from .76 to .80 when independent party spending is added to the House candidate's total. The Gini index for independent party spending alone was .96; more than 99 percent of these funds went to help challengers who were already among the top 10 percent of spenders. Independent party spending in support of incumbents was almost as skewed, with a Gini coefficient of .96 (compared to .33 for candidate spending); 92 percent went to incumbents who spent at least $1.5 million on their own. Among candidates for open seats, independent party spending was distributed about the same as candidate spending (a little over 80 percent of both went for the top half of open-seat spenders), which had the effect of increasing the concentration of resources in these races as well; the Gini coefficient rises

Figure 9.8   Hard and Soft Money Spent by House Campaign Committees, 1992–2004

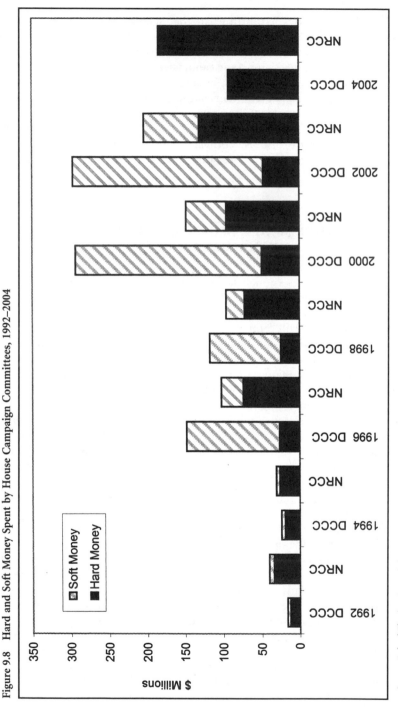

Source: Federal Election Commission.

Figure 9.9   Hard and Soft Money Spent by Senate Campaign Committees, 1992–2004

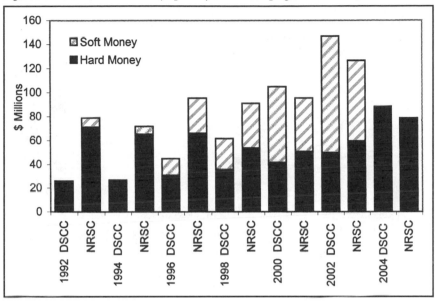

Source: Federal Election Commission.

Figure 9.10   House Campaign Committee Spending, 1992–2004

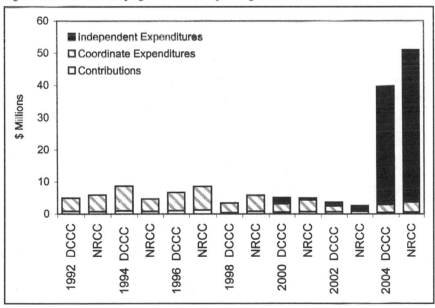

Source: Federal Election Commission.

Figure 9.11   Senate Campaign Committee Spending, 1994–2004

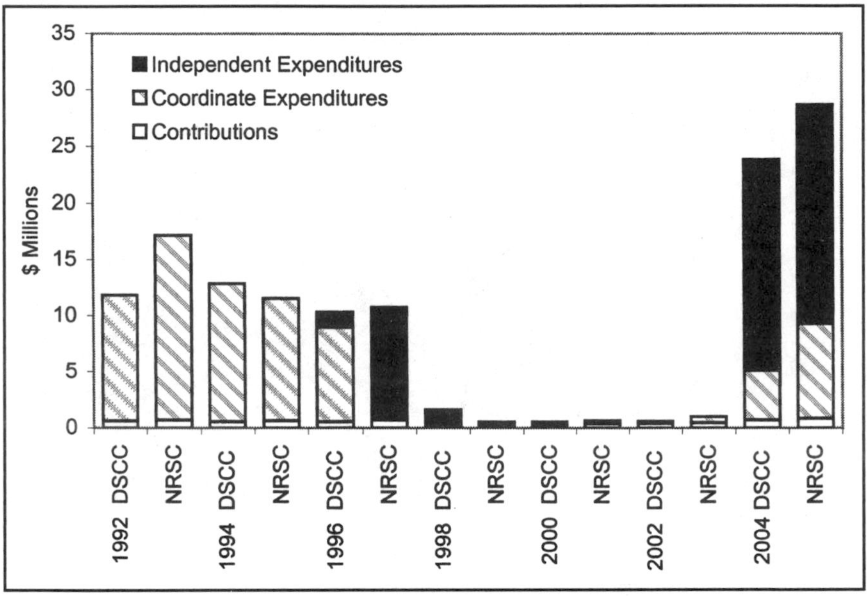

Source: Federal Election Commission.

from .50 to .76 when independent party spending is added to the total for open seat candidates.

Although it is clear that independent party expenditures magnified the degree to which resources were concentrated in the most competitive races, their effect on election results is more doubtful. When independent expenditures by the respective parties are included as variables in a regression equation estimating the House vote as a function of district partisanship, incumbency, and the candidates' spending levels, their coefficients are statistically insignificant, and they add nothing to the explanatory power of the equation. This remains true if separate equations are run for incumbent-held and open House seats. Perhaps the parties effectively offset one another; the correlation between independent expenditures by the two parties was .89 in House races. For this and other reasons, a fuller understanding of the effects of independent party spending will require more sophisticated statistical analysis as well as additional financial information (for example, on spending by 527 groups).

On the Senate side, party independent spending was also statistically unrelated to the vote (with other pertinent variables controlled). In most cases it added 5 to 25 percent to the favored candidate's total resources, but only in races where the candidate was already amply funded. The possible exception is Oklahoma, where the $2.3 million spent by the Republican Party on Tom Coburn's behalf erased Democrat Brad Carson's spending advantage.

In addition to the formal party committees' increased use of independent expenditures, the informal party comprised of the Members (acting through their leadership political action committees and principal campaign committees) increased their giving to other candidates as well as to the parties (see chapter 3). Since the ban on soft money thus seems to have induced the parties to expand their financial bases, BCRA's intentions were fulfilled in 2004 without the least inhibiting the parties' participation in congressional campaigns. Whether the parties' income and participation will remain as strong when political passions are running lower, we do not yet know.

Outside groups—mainly 527 committees—also invested heavily in some of the competitive House and Senate races, in some cases contributing, along with the party committees, to a level of saturation campaigning difficult to imagine unless one lived in a targeted state or district. As long as highly polarized parties continue to fight for control of the House and Senate, inspiring individuals, parties, and other groups to put their money where their political passions lie, BCRA will not stand in their way.

Political passions inspire harsh negative attacks on candidates. One component of BCRA was intended to inhibit negative campaigning by requiring candidates to "stand by" their ads. Broadcast ads are now required to include a "clearly identifiable" image of the candidate and statement by the candidate that he or she has approved the communication. The idea was to discourage mudslinging by forcing candidates to take direct personal responsibility for it. There is no evidence that this provision reduced negative personal attacks in 2004 (see chapter 7), but it may have sharpened the division of labor in which candidates take the high road while allied organizations do the dirty work. The Republican Hill committees' allocation of independent expenditures in 2004 (overwhelmingly against Democrats rather than for Republicans) may be a case in point.

Finally, although BCRA adjusted its contribution limits to accommodate the incumbent's nightmare of facing a multimillionaire opponent unconstrained by campaign finance laws, the track record of self-financed candidates in 2004 suggests that these fears were, at least in this election, wildly overblown. Only one of the twenty-two House and Senate candidates who spent more than $1 million of their own money won (Michael McCaul, a Texas Republican who won an open seat without an opponent in the general election); two thirds of them did not even win the primary and thus a place on the general election ballot (Center for Responsive Politics 2004). Whether BCRA contributed to their sorry track record is unclear at this time; the specific effects of this provision are discussed more fully in chapter 10.

CONCLUSION

BCRA's effects on congressional campaign finances have so far been marginal. At most, it has returned campaign funding practices to where they were a decade earlier. This is not surprising because BCRA's reforms targeted activities (soft money, campaigning under the guise of "issue advocacy") that were until recently peripheral to congressional campaigns and, in any case, could be replaced rather easily (e.g., by the 527s or by raising more hard money). Doubling the limit on individual contributions seems to have made raising money a little easier, but in inflation-adjusted terms, the new ceiling merely reinstitutes the status quo circa 1982. More important, BCRA did nothing to alter the strategic considerations that dominate decisions to contribute and spend campaign money, the consequences of which were on full display in 2004. Nor could any currently feasible legislation make much difference in this regard, at least without the Court's abandonment of *Buckley* or a Constitutional amendment allowing spending limits. The realities are that modern campaigns are expensive because communicating with voters is expensive; limits on campaign spending are unconstitutional unless accepted voluntarily in return for public funds; financing congressional campaigns with tax dollars has no effective constituency; and campaigns must therefore depend on private sources of money. And with the sharply polarized electorate and the intense partisan struggle for control of Congress, there is no shortage of private sources willing to supply what is needed.

Ordinary Americans, assaulted with annoying political ads, believe that too much money is spent on campaigns and typically support spending as well as contribution limits by wide margins. But the real problem is that in most congressional races, particularly for House seats, one side lacks the wherewithal to get its story out to the voters. It most cases this is of little practical consequence (no amount of campaigning by the losing side would change the outcome), but there are usually at least a few contests where the result might have been different if both candidates were adequately funded (only the Kentucky Senate race fits this category in 2004).

Because challengers have virtually no chance of winning without having a lot of money to spend, any reform that makes it harder to raise money threatens to reduce competition. BCRA has not, by the evidence of 2004, made it any harder to mobilize campaign resources, so in this regard at least, its designers have obeyed the dictum, "first, do no harm." Whether BCRA can actually make elections more competitive, at least at the House level, is more doubtful because competition depends so heavily on the partisan makeup of constituencies and the strategic decisions of candidates and contributors, variables totally beyond BCRA's influence.

NOTES

1. Republicans enjoy a structural advantage because their voters are distributed more efficiently than are Democratic voters. Consider: Al Gore won the national popular vote in 2000 by 540,000 of the 105 million votes cast. Yet the distribution of these votes across the 2000 House districts yielded 228 where Bush outpolled Gore, but only 207 where Gore outpolled Bush. After the Republican gerrymanders, there were 240 districts in which Bush outpolled Gore but only 195 with Gore outpolled Bush.

2. *Congressional Quarterly* classifies seats as safe Republican, Republican favored, leaning Republican, no clear favorite, leaning Democratic, Democrat favored, or safe Democratic. These classifications are usually quite accurate; in 2004, all of the seats classified as safe or favored went to the party

so designated; only three of the thirty classified as leaning to a party were won by the other party. For figure 9.1, I count seats classified as leaning to a party or toss-up as competitive. For 2004, the data are from the *New York Times* (*New York Times* 2004a); for earlier years, they are from the October election previews in the *CQ Weekly Report*.

3. The average unopposed House incumbent had reported spending more than $600,000.

4. I employ this definition of *potential* competitiveness for figure 9.3 rather than *Congressional Quarterly's* classification (figure 9.1) or the actual election results because both of these alternatives are in part the *result* (rather than the cause) of challengers' funds. Using the lagged district vote provides a cleaner measure of the effect of (anticipated) competitiveness on fundraising.

5. According to Gallup, Bush's support among Republicans rose from 92 to 95 percent between his first and second election, while his support among Democrats dropped from 10 to 7 percent.

6. In all, twenty-seven of the thirty-four Senate contests were won by the party whose presidential candidate won the state's electoral votes, tying 1964 for the highest level of congruence in president-Senate election results in the past half century. When the 2004 winners are added to the continuing Senate membership, fully 75 percent of Senators now represent states where their party's candidate won the most recent presidential election, the highest proportion in at least fifty years.

10

Self-Financed Candidates and the "Millionaires' Amendment"

Jennifer A. Steen

At all levels of American government, many candidates provide substantial amounts of personal money to their own campaigns. This practice, known as self-financing, dates to the beginning of the Republic, when "politics . . . was a gentleman's pursuit and candidates paid their own expenses" (Mutch 1988); however, in the twenty-first century self-financing candidates are often seen less as gentlemen and more as a scourge of democracy.[1] Nonetheless, wealthy candidates' right to personally finance their campaigns is guaranteed by the Supreme Court's decision in *Buckley v. Valeo* (424 U.S. 1 [1976]), which invalidated limits on self-financing enacted by the Federal Election Campaign Act (FECA) Amendments of 1974 (Public Law 93-443). The *per curiam* opinion held that FECA's "ceiling on personal expenditures by candidates on their own behalf . . . imposes a substantial restraint on the ability of persons to engage in protected First Amendment expression."

Twenty-six years later, Congress devised a creative way to undermine the advantage to self-financing without running afoul of the First Amendment and *Buckley*. A provision of the Bipartisan Campaign Reform Act (BCRA) known as the Millionaires' Amendment (Public Law 107-155, sections 304 and 319) attacks the "rich candidate problem" (as *Washington Post* editorial writers once dubbed it) on two fronts, making it easier for self-financers' opponents to raise money and harder for self-financers to recoup campaign-invested personal funds after an election. The law establishes "trigger" amounts of self-financing; if those amounts are exceeded, a self-financer's opponent (or opponents) can raise three or six times the normal limit from an individual donor, depending on the circumstances. In some cases, self-financing also enables unlimited coordinated expenditures by the opposing party. The Millionaires' Amendment also prohibits self-financers from repaying more than $250,000 in campaign self-loans after the date of an election. These provisions were intended to render self-financers' opponents more competitive without restricting wealthy candidates' ability to self-finance political expression.

This chapter evaluates the impact of the Millionaires' Amendment on congressional elections in 2004, the first cycle under BCRA. I begin with a brief discussion of the goals and concerns articulated in the legislative debate, which establishes the yardstick against which the Millionaires'-Amendment's effect is gauged. I then present figures compiled from the Federal Election Commission's (FEC) repository of campaign finance records, describing self-financing activity and the response thereto. The discussion uses specific terms to refer to different kinds of activity. *Personal expenditures* and *self-financing* are amounts of contributions and loans from a candidate to his or her own campaign committee. These amounts are not reduced by the amount of loan repayments. *Opposition personal funds* is an amount calculated from a formula devised by the FEC which offsets an opponent's personal expenditures by a candidate's own self-financing and any fundraising advantage he or she enjoys. A candidate's personal expenditures can exceed the Millionaires'-Amendment threshold without triggering increased contribution limits if the *opposition personal funds* amount is below the threshold. *Excess contributions* refer to the amount of contributions from individuals exceeding the regular limit of $2,000. For example, an individual contribution of $3,000 reflects an excess contribution of $1,000.

There is no way to know exactly how the Millionaires' Amendment changed the course of the 2004 elections given the number of strategic decisions that were likely affected and our uncertainty about how any one of them would have been decided under the pre-BCRA rules. Still, the analysis strongly suggests that the Millionaires' Amendment had a limited impact on the political landscape in 2004. This finding is consistent with the author's earlier "what if?" simulation of the 2000 elections under BCRA (Steen 2003).

THE BENCHMARK: GOALS OF THE MILLIONAIRES' AMENDMENT

The legislative record suggests that the Millionaires' Amendment was justified by the same fundamental goal that animated self-financing caps originally included in the 1974 FECA amendments: equality among candidates. During a 1971 hearing, Senator John Pastore (D-RI) warned that without limits on personal spending "only the wealthy or those who are able to obtain large contributions from limited sources will be able to seek elective office. Neither situation is desirable and both are inimicable [sic] to the American system" (U.S. Senate 1971). His colleague, Senator Frank Ross (D-UT) agreed. "I think nothing is more important than to make running for political office available to any citizen of this

country and to do away with the advantage given those who have great wealth"
(U.S. Senate 1971 1971).

Sixteen years after FECA and fifteen years before BCRA, the Millionaires'
Amendment was conceived by Senator Pete Domenici (R-NM) who echoed his
predecessors' concern for political equality when he cautioned from the Senate
floor, "Unless we are careful, Mr. President, the congressional marketplace will
become a Gucci boutique. I am convinced that any reform package must address
this obvious inequity . . . [I]n a democracy we must not allow individuals who
control vast wealth to enter the election booth with a big, sometimes unassail-
able, advantage" (*Congressional Record* 1987b). Speaking in support of Domenici's proposal, Senator Dennis DeConcini (R-AZ) warned, "We are making
elective office only available to a certain class of citizen" (*Congressional Record*
1987a). This theme was picked up again as members debated BCRA, which
included a variant of Domenici's fourteen-year-old proposal. Representative
Shelley Moore Capito (R-WV) called the Millionaire's Amendment "a way to
correct what I believe is one of the most glaring inequities in the current system"
(*Congressional Record* 2002a). (Capito's view may have been influenced by experience—in 2000 her Democratic opponent self-financed $5.6 million in his pri-
mary and general election campaigns; in the 2002 rematch she was anticipating
when she uttered these words he self-financed nearly $8 million.) Representative
Tom Davis argued that the Millionaires' Amendment "evens the playing field for
candidates who are challenging millionaires or who are challenged by millionaires" (*Congressional Record* 2002b).

While proponents touting the Millionaires' Amendment expected an equaliz-

---

Table 10.1 Key Provisions of the Millionaires' Amendment

- Defines *opposition personal funds* as the difference between a candidate's personal spending
  and his or her opponent's personal spending, offset by any fundraising advantage the
  candidate enjoys over the self-financing opponent.
- Establishes "threshold amounts" of personal spending in House and Senate races. Threshold
  amounts are $350,000 for House campaigns; for Senate campaigns threshold amounts vary
  with the states' voting-age population.
- Increases limits on contributions from individuals to candidates whose *opposition personal
  funds* exceed threshold amounts. Limits are tripled for House candidates; for Senate
  candidates limits may increase by a factor of three or six, depending on the opposition
  personal funds amount and the state threshold.
- Removes limits on party coordinated expenditures for House candidates whose *opposition
  personal funds* exceed threshold; removes limits on party coordinated expenditures for some
  Senate candidates, depending on the opposition personal funds amount and the state
  threshold.
- Caps amount of excess contributions and party expenditures at 100% (House) or 110%
  (Senate) of *opposition personal funds* amount.
- Restricts the amount of candidate self-loans that can be repaid after an election.

Source: Federal Election Commission *Record*, vol. 29, no. 2, February 2003.

ing effect, some observers believed it was a self-serving ploy by congressional incumbents to maintain their traditional advantages. The president of Common Cause railed against the Millionaires' Amendment; "It is disappointing but not entirely surprising to see that the Senate's first move out of the gate on the campaign finance debate is to put forward an amendment dealing with their own self-interests rather than the public interest. [This] amendment . . . reveals the preoccupation that incumbents have with preserving their advantage over challengers" (Harshbarger 2001). Some senators saw the provision in similar terms. As Senator Carl Levin (D-MI) noted in floor debate, "In the effort to level the playing field in one area, we are making the playing field less level in another area" (*Congressional Record* 2001). Senator Chris Dodd (D-CT) noted the extreme irony in "the idea that somehow we [incumbents] are sort of impoverished candidates." Dodd reminded his colleagues,

[W]e are talking about incumbents who have treasuries of significant amounts and the power of the office which allows us to be in the press every day, if we want. We can send franked mail to our constituents at no cost to us. . . . We do radio and television shows. We can go back to our States with subsidized airfares. . . . I find it somewhat ironic that we are here deeply worried about the capital that can be raised and the candidate who is going to spend a million dollars of his own money to level the playing field (*Congressional Record* 2001).

Perhaps in response to this line of criticism, the version of the Millionaires' Amendment eventually enacted included a provision to discount a candidate's self-financing advantage by his fundraising disadvantage (if such a disadvantage existed). Still, the anticipated effect of the Millionaires' Amendment was thus twofold but oddly self-contradictory: to put candidates on equal footing financially but also to preserve incumbents' traditional advantage over self-financed challengers. After describing the 2004 congressional elections we will consider whether reality meshed with the forecasts.

SELF-FINANCING IN THE 2004
CONGRESSIONAL ELECTIONS

Candidate Loans

One provision of the Millionaires' Amendment limits the amount of campaign self-loans that can be repaid after an election. This restriction is intended to deter self-financing by making it a riskier strategy. Prior to BCRA, rich candidates could lend money to their campaigns secure in the knowledge that if they won, it would not be difficult to raise money from contributors and recoup some (or all) of their self-investment.[2] This is probably why most self-financing prior to BCRA took the form of personal loans instead of contributions. From 1984 through 2002, House and Senate candidates loaned a total of $729 million to their campaigns. They only contributed one-sixth as much, $124 million. This lending strategy paid off for some of these candidates, as those elected to Congress were able to recoup a total of 30 percent of their initial self-loans by repaying themselves in subsequent election cycles.[3] Members elected in 1990 recouped the largest percentage of self-loans, 63 percent, of any entering class.

Under the Millionaires' Amendment, candidates' loan repayments are strictly limited. Each candidate can recoup a maximum of $250,000 by repaying self-loans with contributions received after the date of an election. Furthermore, candidates have only twenty days after an election in which they can repay amounts exceeding $250,000 using contributions received on or before Election Day. These provisions were intended to make self-financing less attractive as a campaign-funding tactic than it was before BCRA.

One cannot judge the effectiveness of this provision with certainty because it is impossible to determine how much money 2004-cycle candidates would have lent their campaigns in the absence of the Millionaires' Amendment. Still, it is worth noting that self-lending declined from 2002, the last cycle before BCRA took effect, to 2004. Fewer candidates loaned their campaigns more than $250,000 (sixty-eight in 2004, compared to seventy-five in 2002) and the total amount of self-loans declined (from $101 million in 2002 to $83 million in 2004). However, it appears that many candidates simply substituted self-contributions for self-loans, as the total amount of self-contributions increased from $10 million in 2002 to $43 million in 2004.[4] In other words, the total amount of personal funding increased from $111 million in 2002 to $126 million in 2004. It thus appears that the Millionaires' Amendment's loan-repayment restriction was effective at deterring candidates from funding their campaigns with generous self-loans but did not reduce overall levels of personal spending.

Still, *overall* levels of personal spending may not be the best measure of whether the loan-repayment restriction "worked," as it was specifically intended to discourage candidates from lending large amounts to their campaigns. It is possible for overall self-financing to increase from one cycle to the next because of a single extreme self-financer, while at the same time fewer candidates self-financed generously. Indeed, this appears to have been the case in 2004. Fewer candidates exceeded the Millionaires'-Amendment thresholds (forty-eight in 2004, compared to fifty-seven in 2002),[5] but one of them—Illinois Senate candidate Blair Hull, who lost the Democratic primary—invested nearly $30 million in his own campaign. Hull's personal expenditure exceeded all other candidates' in 2002 and 2004 by more than $20 million and accounts for the entire increase in total personal expenditures from 2002 to 2004.

Exceeding the Threshold and Tripping Increased Contribution Limits

The Millionaires' Amendment establishes "threshold amounts" of self-financing for each election, and candidates who exceed those thresholds trigger two forms of assistance for their opponents, increased limits on contributions from individuals and, in some cases, lifted caps on coordinated party spending.

The threshold amount for all House elections is $350,000; for Senate elections the threshold varies by state according to the voting-age population.

In the 2004 congressional elections, forty-three candidates self-financed more than the "threshold amounts" in thirty-nine distinct contests.[6] Two or more self-financers faced each other in seven contests, and five self-financers exceeded the threshold in both a primary and a general election. This represents a decrease from fifty-seven candidates in the 2002 cycle whose personal expenditures exceeded the thresholds subsequently enacted. Of course we cannot know whether more candidates would have self-financed in 2004 had the Millionaires' Amendment not existed, although at least one rich candidate (Pete Coors, beer magnate and Republican Senate nominee in Colorado) openly acknowledged that he was consciously avoiding the trigger amount in his state (Tankersley 2004).

Many of these candidates did not trip the Millionaires' Amendment because the law's definition of *opposition personal funds* follows a formula that accounts for a candidate's own self-financing and fundraising. For example, Democrat Charlie Broomfield self-financed $400,000 in Missouri's Sixth Congressional District, $50,000 more than the Millionaires'-Amendment threshold for House campaigns. Broomfield did not exceed $350,000 in personal spending until after the primary, so none of his Democratic opponents were eligible to raise money under increased limits. In the general election Broomfield faced Republican incumbent Rep. Sam Graves, whose fundraising advantage over Broomfield as of December 31, 2003, was $519,030, enough to offset—and even to exceed—Broomfield's advantage in personal funds. Graves was thus bound by the regular contribution limit of $2,000 per person per election.

Incumbent Protection?

Table 10.2 lists the top self-financer in each of the nineteen general election contests in which one candidate exceeded the Millionaires-Amendment self-financing threshold, along with the self-financer's opponent. Notably, there were ten contests in which the Millionaires' Amendment was not triggered despite at least one candidate exceeding the Millionaires'-Amendment threshold for personal spending. Eight of those were challenges to incumbents whose off-year fundraising offset self-financing in calculating the "opposition personal funds amount." Five other incumbents were eligible for increased individual-contribution limits, but only one, Steve LaTourette (R-OH), appears to have taken advantage of this. LaTourette's challenger, twenty-six-year-old heiress Capri Cafaro, invested $1.7 million in her campaign, enabling LaTourette to raise $134,950 in excess of the regular $2,000-per-person limit after Cafaro triggered the Millionaires' Amendment on September 3.[7]

One might be tempted to conclude that the Millionaires' Amendment is not, as some critics charged, an incumbent-protection racket after all, since only a single incumbent used it to raise additional funds, and even that one congressman benefited but marginally. The Millionaires' Amendment conceivably could

Table 10.2   General Election Candidates Whose Personal Expenditures Exceeded Millionaires'-Amendment Thresholds

Election	Biggest Personal Spender	Total Personal Expenditures	Opposing Candidate	Eligible for Increased Limit
Senate				
CO	Peter Coors	$952,000	Ken Salazar	Y
CT	Jack C. Orchulli	1,332,775	Christopher J. Dodd[a]	N
KY	Daniel Mongiardo	707,521	Jim Bunning[a]	N
MD	E. J. Pipkin	1,099,000	Barbara Mikulski[a]	N
NC	Erskine Bowles	1,547,012	Richard Burr	N
WI	Tim J. Michels	1,755,000	Russell D. Feingold[a]	N
House				
GA-6	Thomas E. Price	499,000	None	N
IN-9	Michael E. Sodrel	515,244	Baron P. Hill[a]	N
MO-5	Jeanne L. Patterson	1,534,000	Emanuel Cleaver II	Y
MO-6	Charles Broomfield	400,000	Samuel B. Graves[a]	N
NV-03	Tom Gallagher	977,002	Jon C. Porter[a]	Y
NY-26	John R. Davis Jr.	1,257,280	Thomas M. Reynolds[a]	Y
OH-14	Capri Cafaro	1,766,258	Steven C. Latourette[a]	Y
OR-5	Jim D. Zupancic	395,531	Darlene Hooley[a]	N
PA-15	Joseph E. Driscoll	518,611	Charles W. Dent	N
PA-17	George Scott Paterno	353,000	Tim Holden[a]	N
TX-9	Alexander Green	360,999	Arlette M. Molina	Y
TX-10	Michael McCaul	1,972,000	Lorenzo Sadun	Y
VA-10	James Socas[b]	499,000	Frank Wolf[a]	Y

Source: Compiled by the author from the Federal Election Commission's electronic files oth04.zip and byrept04.zip

[a] Incumbent candidates.

[b] Socas reportedly loaned his campaign $150,000 on October 26, 2004 (Barakat 2004), although Socas failed to notify the FEC and his opponent of the last-minute loan, and it does not appear in his post-general FEC filing.

have deterred challengers from self-financing quite enough to trip increased fundraising, although this does not appear to have happened. Self-financing challengers either exceeded the thresholds by a large margin or stayed well beneath them. There is not one challenger who self-financed as much as possible without triggering increased fundraising eligibility for an incumbent opponent. However, the Millionaires' Amendment may have helped incumbents indirectly by deterring potential self-financers from running. After steadily increasing over ten previous election cycles, the number of incumbent-challengers whose personal expenditures exceeded BCRA's thresholds dropped from seventeen in 2002 to thirteen in 2004.

Fundraising Under Increased Limits

Ninety-three candidates were eligible to raise money under increased contribution limits, eighty-five in primaries and eight in general elections. Thirty-seven of them—including three incumbents—did not report a single contribution from an individual exceeding $2,000. Together the fifty-six candidates who did raise excess contributions had 9,824 contributors who gave at least $2,000, nearly one-third of whom (3,187) took advantage of the relaxed limits of the Millionaires' Amendment and contributed additional amounts. About one-tenth (1,084) contributed $6,000, the maximum allowed in most Millionaires'-Amendment races. Self-financing Senate primary candidates in Florida, Illinois, South Carolina, and Wisconsin tripped the second Millionaires'-Amendment trigger, which allows contributions of up to $12,000. Only 209 donors contributed $12,000, and most of them supported either Dan Hynes (who had eighty-six $12,000 contributors) or Barack Obama (who had fifty-nine $12,000 contributors) in the Illinois Democratic primary. All other eligible candidates reported fourteen or fewer $12,000 contributors each.

There was significant variation in the degree to which self-financers' opponents were able to take advantage of the Millionaires' Amendment. Candidates' receipts attributable to Millionaires'-Amendment contributions ranged from zero dollars to the $2.3 million reported by Dan Hynes. (The reader is reminded that $2.3 million is the sum of all contributions above the regular $2,000 limit *after* subtracting $2,000 from each.) Hynes was closely followed by his Democratic opponent, Barack Obama, who reported $1.9 million in excess contributions. The median total of excess contributions was $3,248; the median of nonzero total excess contributions was $31,505. Table 10.3 lists the candidates whose excess contributions summed to $20,000 or more.

Variations in Millionaires'-Amendment fundraising related to a number of factors, the most significant of which appears to be the length of time in which the increased individual-contribution limits were in effect. Consider for example two candidates who raised similar amounts (nearly $2.6 million) of non-Millionaires'-Amendment funds, both of them Senate candidates who lost their primaries. In Illinois, Democrat Dan Hynes raised more than $2.3 million in contributions in excess of $2,000 for his primary campaign, while former Representative Bill McCollum from Florida, a Republican, only raised $481,709 in excess of the regular limits for his primary. The marked difference between these two men's Millionaires'-Amendment fundraising hauls is in part a function of timing. Blair Hull triggered the Millionaires' Amendment in Illinois on February 14, 2003, more than a year before the Senate primary, giving his Democratic opponents plenty of time to court above-$2000 donors. In contrast, when Doug Gallagher triggered the Millionaires' Amendment in Florida on June 15, 2004, McCollum only had 77 days in which to resolicit his maxed-out contributors. Indeed, among all candidates in Millionaires'-Amendment elections, the earlier the Millionaires' Amendment was triggered, the more they were able to raise in excess contributions. This trend is illustrated by figure 10.1, which plots excess contributions against the Millionaires'-Amendment "window," or the time between when the Millionaires'-Amendment threshold amount was exceeded and the date of the election. (Excess contributions are expressed as a percentage of all contributions of $200 or more to take account of variations in candidates' fundraising ability not directly related to the Millionaires' Amendment. The Ordinary Least Squares regression line is drawn through the points in figure 10.1 to illustrate the general relationship between excess contributions and the win-

Table 10.3   Candidates Whose Excess Contributions Totaled $20,000 or More

Candidate	Number of Contributors Exceeding $2,000	Total Amount of Contributions Exceeding $2,000	Total Receipts 2003–2004
General Election			
Emanuel Cleaver II (D-MO-5)	56	$22,500	$1,570,424
*Steven C. LaTourette (R-OH-14)**	179	134,950	2,033,084
Senate Primaries			
Mel Martinez (R-FL)	857	812,370	9,281,294
Larry Klayman (R-FL)	79	52,580	3,089,084
Bill McCollum (R-FL)	528	481,709	4,524,324
Johnnie B. Byrd (R-FL)	642	185,925	2,775,847
Joyce W. Washington (D-IL)	47	35,906	881,965
Barack Obama (D-IL)	632	1,869,067	15,059,431
Daniel W. Hynes (D-IL)	674	2,316,884	6,735,396
Maria Pappas (D-IL)	87	293,400	1,094,719
Gery J. Chico (D-IL)	434	953,686	3,168,865
Andrew J. McKenna (R-IL)	424	438,900	4,438,199
Steven J. Rauschenberger (R-IL)	86	178,561	989,733
John L. Borling (R-IL)	37	48,250	337,861
Bob Anthony (R-OK)	92	58,250	836,594
Thomas A. Coburn (R-OK)	145	45,950	3,058,987
Mark Struthers McBride (R-SC)	32	93,091	256,705
Charles M. Condon (R-SC)	277	266,596	1,555,674
James W. DeMint (R-SC)	344	260,800	8,988,160
David M. Beasley (R-SC)	290	596,025	2,778,001
Robert T. Welch (R-WI)	125	149,519	1,266,077
Tim J. Michels (R-WI)	162	169,891	4,014,283
House Primaries			
Daniel E. Lungren (R-CA-3)	111	64,250	1,416,395
Thomas E. Price (R-GA-6)	172	96,950	2,521,338
Charles C. Clay (R-GA-6)	76	40,200	1,284,647
John Schwarz (R-MI-7)	27	24,477	874,670
Bradley L. Smith (R-MI-7)	65	59,475	702,880
Clark Bisbee (R-MI-7)	47	27,105	521,109
Vernon L. Robinson (R-NC-5)	90	74,425	2,809,770
James R. Helvey III (R-NC-5)	245	117,675	1,456,683
Sanford D. Lyons (R-NC-10)	80	57,500	798,104

Source: Compiled by the author from the Federal Election Commission's electronic files *webl04.zip, indiv04.zip,* and *oth04.zip.*

Note: Candidates who won the relevant election are indicated by *italics.* Incumbent members of Congress are indicated by *.

dow of opportunity.) On average, candidates raised $1,607 in excess contributions per day between the date the Millionaires'-Amendment threshold was exceeded and the date of the election. Senate candidate Mel Martinez, an eventual primary and general election winner, posted the top average excess-fundraising rate of $10,550 per day after Doug Gallagher exceeded the threshold in Florida's Republican primary.

Of course, the length of time the Millionaires'-Amendment window was open was to some extent under the millionaires' own control. Some candidates exceeded the trigger at the last minute, limiting their opponents' ability to raise money. For example, through October 25, 2004, Democrat James Socas loaned and contributed $349,000 to his campaign in Virginia's Tenth District, just $1,000 less than the threshold amount for House races. On October 26 Socas loaned his campaign an additional $150,000 (Barakat 2004). Anticipating Socas's move, the campaign manager for his opponent (U.S. Rep. Frank Wolf) commented, "This has been their whole strategy during the campaign—wait until the end of the campaign and spend his own money" (Bonaiuto and Keisman 2004). No other self-financer tripped the Millionaires' Amendment less than three weeks before the general election. Furthermore, eleventh-hour personal-spending sprees were common in general elections before BCRA. In my analysis of self-financing in 1992–2000 I reported on "extreme" self-financers' tendency toward "impulse spending" in the final days of general elections (Steen 2006),

Figure 10.1 Excess Contributions (as a Percent of Total Itemized Contributions), by Number of Days in Millionaires'-Amendment Window

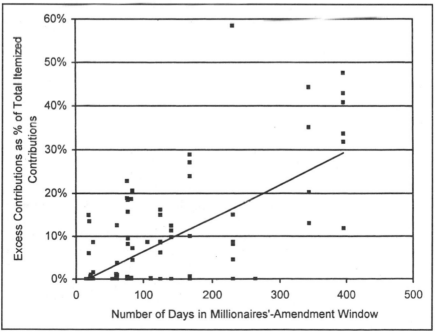

and the self-financing class of 2004 was no more prone to late self-financing than their predecessors. (In the Socas-Wolf contest, the Millionaires' Amendment was moot because Socas failed to report his last-minute loan to the Federal Election Commission; a complaint is currently pending.)

Prior to BCRA, big spenders tended to front-load primary election self-financing (Steen 2006). The new regulatory context gives self-financers incentives to hold onto their wallets as long as possible, but candidates in 2004 still tended to make personal expenditures early in the primary election. No candidate tripped the Millionaires' Amendment less than two weeks before a primary, and only six did so with less than one month remaining in the primary campaign.

Another source of variation in candidates' Millionaires'-Amendment fundraising is the individual nature of each candidate's contributor base. Candidates who relied on large numbers of small donors benefited from the Millionaires' Amendment less than candidates who relied on big givers. In South Carolina's Republican Senate primary, U.S. Representative Jim DeMint and former Governor David Beasley were both eligible for higher contribution limits thanks to self-financer Thomas Ravenal, a developer. DeMint's contributor base emphasized small donations, with a median itemized contribution of $850 and total unitemized contributions of $311,193; Beasley enjoyed support from bigger donors, with a median itemized contribution of $1,000 and total unitemized contributions of only $50,492.[8] Beasley was thus able to raise considerably more under the Millionaires' Amendment than DeMint—$596,025 compared to $260,800—although DeMint's total haul from individual contributors was larger. Beasley's fundraising is especially impressive since he entered the primary a full year after DeMint and six months after Ravenal exceeded the Millionaires'-Amendment threshold for South Carolina. Beasley raised twice as much as DeMint in excess contributions in half the time.

Under the Millionaires' Amendment the maximum amount that can be raised in excess contributions is 100 percent (in House races) or 110 percent (in Senate campaigns) of the *opposition personal funds* amount. This limit was purely theoretical in 2004 as no candidate came within striking distance of it. Former Governor Beasley came closest, raising excess contributions totaling 19.5 percent of his opposition personal funds.

Increased Contribution Limits: The Big Picture

In the vast majority of elections, Millionaires'-Amendment fundraising did not substantially shift the balance among candidates. Among all of the primary and general election opponents to candidates who exceeded self-financing thresholds, only thirteen raised more than 10 percent of their total campaign funds from Millionaires'-Amendment contributions. Furthermore, twelve of those thirteen candidates lost in the primary, none to the big-spending self-financer. In other words, the Millionaires' Amendment helped only a few candidates, and even most of those candidates had bigger worries than the self-financer in their race.

A notable exception is Barack Obama, who defeated self-financer Blair Hull and several other candidates in the Democratic primary for senator from Illinois. Obama raised $4.6 million in itemized individual contributions for his primary campaign, with nearly $1 million coming under the increased limits of the Millionaires' Amendment. Still, it is not at all clear that the Millionaires' Amendment was decisive in Illinois. Blair Hull's campaign self-destructed amid charges that he had physically and verbally abused his former wife, which undermined his efforts at least as much as if not more than Obama's extra fundraising. Furthermore, Obama's main rival was state Comptroller Dan Hynes, who raised even more money under the Millionaires' Amendment ($1.2 million) than Obama did.

A similar situation was found in Florida's Republican Senate primary, in which software-company founder Doug Gallagher self-financed $6.6 million. Mel Martinez, who resigned as secretary of the U.S. Department of Housing and Urban Development to run, raised $812,370 of his $4.4 million from individual primary contributors thanks to the Millionaires' Amendment. However, Martinez easily defeated Gallagher, facing tougher opposition from former congressman Bill McCollum.

Party Coordinated Expenditures

In House races and some Senate races, tripping the Millionaires' Amendment results not only in higher limits for increased individual-contributions limits but also in increased limits on coordinated expenditures by political parties. (Parties can spend only until their excess spending and excess individual contributions to the candidate reach the opposition personal funds amount.) This potential boost to self-financers' opponents went unused in 2004, as no political party organization exceeded the normal expenditure limit. In Senate elections no self-financer spent enough to unleash party spending; only five candidates did so in House races, but all five were grossly uncompetitive. In three contests the self-financer was handily defeated, suggesting that extra party spending was unnecessary. The other two were in districts where the self-financers' respective parties were dominant, and the self-financers prevailed by large margins (more than forty-five points), suggesting that party spending would have been wasted. Indeed, the only candidate supported by party spending in these five races was incumbent Steve LaTourette, who enjoyed all of a $114 expenditure on his behalf.

CONSEQUENCES

As the preceding analysis has illustrated, the Millionaires' Amendment does not seem to have had an obvious impact on congressional elections. Few candidates benefited significantly from increased individual contribution limits, and no candidate enjoyed unfettered party spending. The modest effect on fundraising was perhaps joined by a subtle reshaping of self-financers' behavior, as 2004 saw a drop-off in the number of extreme self-financers running for Congress. In politics perception is often more important than reality, and the perception that the Millionaires' Amendment would negate self-financers' monetary advantage may have caused some wealthy aspirants to scale back their personal investments or even to forgo campaigns entirely.

Advocates of financial equality on the campaign trail may be disappointed by the limited results of the Millionaires' Amendment, but they may take solace in knowing that it did not give extra help to incumbents, as some feared it would. The total number of threshold-exceeding self-financers who ran against incumbents decreased slightly, from seventeen to thirteen, but there is no indication that the Millionaires' Amendment deterred legions of self-financers from challenging incumbents. Nor should we worry that the Millionaires' Amendment undermines the only advantage challengers can ever hope to enjoy over incumbents: Steve LaTourette was the only incumbent who enjoyed increased fundraising under the Millionaires' Amendment in 2004.

NOTES

1. Many examples of public criticism of self-financing can be found in Steen (2006), especially chapter one.

2. Unlike pre-BCRA self-loans, self-contributions could not (and still cannot) be refunded to the candidate. The Federal Election Commission has suggested that a refund of a candidate's self-contributions would constitute a "conver[sion of] excess campaign funds to the personal use of the candidate," prohibited under the Federal Election Campaign Act (Federal Election Commission 1998).

3. This figure excludes Senator Jon Corzine, whose $60 million in self-loans during the 2000 election cycle account for about one-twelfth of *all* self-loans made from 1984 through 2002. If Corzine is included, the subsequent election repayment rate falls to 21 percent. However, some of these members took loan repayments during the cycle in which they were first elected. If these repayments are added to amounts repaid in subsequent cycles, the repayment rate rises to 29 percent (with Corzine) or 42 percent (without Corzine).

4. Even if one disregards Illinois Senate candidate Blair Hull, who contributed nearly $30 million to his unsuccessful primary campaign in 2004, self-contributions more than doubled from 2002 to 2004.

5. These numbers were calculated using the electronic files *WEBL04.DAT* and *WEBL02.DAT* posted by the Federal Election Commission on its ftp site. For each House and Senate candidate these files list the total amounts of loans and contributions from the candidate's personal funds for the entire cycle. In some cases, these total amounts do not exactly match the totals reported in electronic files itemizing individual transactions, which are the basis for the analysis in this chapter. Thus the total number of threshold-exceeding candidates in 2004 is reported as forty-three instead of forty-eight in the next section. I examined the actual reports (FEC Form 3) for the five candidates who constitute the difference and was unable to ascertain whether they did or did not actually exceed the Millionaires'-Amendment thresholds because of ambiguities or inconsistencies in the reports. I decided to report two different numbers of threshold-exceeding candidates because most of the analysis required data aggregated from individual transactions, but in comparing election cycles it seemed prudent to use comparable data (i.e., *WEBL04* and *WEBL02*).

6. These numbers were calculated by adding up the amounts of individual self-loan and self-contribution transactions reported in the electronic files *indiv04.zip* and *oth04.zip* posted by the Federal Election Commission on its ftp site. The version of these files used for this chapter were updated

on December 6 and December 12, respectively, and thus do not include any self-financing activity reported after those dates. Please see the appendix for more detail about the data used herein.

7. Cafaro's personal expenditures had exceeded $350,000 on June 30, but LaTourette's fundraising in 2003 required her to self-finance an additional $188,137 before LaTourette's opposition personal funds amount exceeded $350,000. LaTourette's Millionaires'-Amendment fundraising constituted a scant one-fifteenth of his total receipts in the 2004 cycle. LaTourette might have found company in Rep. Frank Wolf (R-VA), who claimed (and indeed appears) to have become eligible for Millionaires'-Amendment fundraising when his opponent, James Socas, brought his cumulative self-financing to $499,000 on October 26, 2004. However, Socas notified neither the FEC nor Wolf of his personal expenditure, prompting Wolf to file a complaint with the FEC. The complaint is still pending at this writing, and Wolf was not able to raise excess contributions.

8. Candidates are only required to itemize contributions from donors who give more than $200. Median itemized contributions were calculated based on all contributions reported for the primary or runoff election in the FEC file *indiv04.zip*, and I attempted to consolidate multiple contributions from single individuals (see the appendix for consolidation methodology). Unitemized contributions were tallied by Brendan Glavin of the Campaign Finance Institute from the summary page of FEC Form 3 in reports filed through June 2.

APPENDIX

Calculating individual contributions: I identified individuals who contributed $2,000 or more to a single candidate using the electronic file *indiv04.zip* posted by the Federal Election Commission on its ftp site. The version of the files used for this chapter was updated on December 6, 2004, and thus does not include any contributions reported after that date. The file includes one record for each separate contribution of $200 or more. To calculate the total amount of an individual's contributions in a particular election I combined all contributions made by individuals with identical or nearly identical names. First I parsed the field labeled "ITEM-NAME" to separate surnames, first names, middle names, prefixes, and suffixes. Contributors with the same first name and surname were presumed to be one person unless they had different middle names, initials, or suffixes. Thus "ABBESS, LEONARD L JR" and "ABBESS, LEONARD JR" are coded as the same person, but "ADAMS, ALFRED B III" and "ADAMS, ALFRED G JR" are not.

Calculating personal expenditures: Personal expenditures were calculated using the electronic files *indiv04.zip*, which lists contributions, and *oth04.zip*, which lists loans. The versions of these files used for this chapter were updated on December 6 and December 12, respectively, and thus do not include any self-financing activity reported after those dates. I selected all entries labeled as contributions or loans from the candidate. I also selected all entries that were not so labeled but for which the contributor name matched the candidate's name. I then sorted the entries by transaction date and calculated the cumulative personal expenditure per date.

Calculating opposition personal fund: To calculate a candidate's opposition personal funds one must use the amount of non-self-financed receipts reported by the candidate himself and his self-financing opponent in the June 30, 2003, or December 31, 2003 reports. These amounts were extracted from the file *byrpt04.zip*.

I will provide the Stata do-files I created to calculate these amounts to anyone who requests them.

11

A Public Funding System in Jeopardy: Lessons from the Presidential Nomination Contest of 2004

Michael J. Malbin

The Bipartisan Campaign Reform Act (BCRA) did little directly to change the presidential campaign finance system in place since 1974. However, BCRA did increase the maximum individual contribution from $1,000 to $2,000. Because the new law increased the value of large contributions, while being silent about the public matching fund formula that is supposed to increase worth of small ones, the general expectation was that BCRA, through a back door, had affected the presidential system substantially.

Since George W. Bush had rejected public financing for the 2000 primaries—raising a record number of $1,000 contributions in the process—it was widely predicted that Bush in 2004 would reject public funding again and persuade his former $1,000 donors to increase their contributions (Wilcox et al. 2003). This in turn would put severe strains on any Democrat who stayed in the system. The general expectation therefore was that one or more Democrats would also be likely to opt out of the system (Campaign Finance Institute Task Force on Financing Presidential Nominations 2003). As it happened, Bush, John Kerry, and Howard Dean all did opt out of public funding, with Bush and Kerry eventually raising and spending more than five times as much as they would have been allowed to spend had they accepted matching funds. However, Bush's money did not come from simply the same old donors. Most of his, and Kerry's, donors were new.

The major policy question about presidential finance to emerge from 2004 was whether the public matching fund system still served a useful purpose. With three leading candidates opting out, the general opinion among political professionals has been that no serious candidate in the future can afford to accept public funding unless the system is changed. Indeed, by the end of the 2004 primary season, there were clear rumblings—particularly from the Kerry campaign—that the general election system was also in trouble. Despite the system's flaws, however, it is clear that without some kind of public funding system, Sen. Kerry would have faced no serious competition at all after Howard Dean lost the Iowa caucuses. None of the other challengers would have been competitive without matching funds, just as Kerry himself could not have challenged Dean without public funding if he were not wealthy. With the system's viability so clearly at risk, it is important to consider what this might mean for future elections.

INTERSECTING RULES

Recent problems with the presidential funding system trace back to a simple historical fact: the public funding system came into being at a time when the modern presidential primary system was also new. Since then, the primary system has changed markedly, but there has been no corresponding change either in the way the public funding system supports candidates or in the unrealistic restraints it tries to put on their spending.

The first presidential primaries were held in 1904, but what made the primaries the dominant mode of selection were the delegate selection reforms the Democratic Party put into effect for 1972. In 1968, 38 percent of the Democratic Party's convention delegates and 34 percent of the Republican delegates were from states that held primaries. By 1972, the percentages had gone up to 61 percent for the Democrats and 53 percent for the Republican. In 1976, 73 percent of the Democratic and 68 percent of the Republican delegates came from primary states (Wayne, 2000:12).

The first election under the new delegate selection rules, 1972, coincidentally was also the election during which burglars hired by the Committee for the Reelection of the President (CRP) broke into the Watergate offices of the Democratic National Committee. Richard M. Nixon resigned the presidency under pressure in 1974 after the White House's attempt to cover up CRP's role came unraveled. CRP's fundraising practices also led to the Federal Election Campaign Act amendments of 1974 (FECA) (Public Law 93-443). The 1974 law contained important new disclosure requirements and contribution limits, but the most innovative sections probably were the presidential public funding provisions. For the general election, the law provided a flat grant of $20 million to major party candidates (with a proportional formula for minor parties), adjusted every four years for inflation. In 2004, the adjusted amount came to $75 million. In return, candidates who accepted public funds for the general election had to agree not to spend more than the flat grant.

For the primaries, the 1974 law created a mixed private-public system combined with a spending limit for participating candidates. The system provides $1 in public matching funds for up to $250 per contributor per candidate. This formula has not changed since 1974. The basic spending limit for participating candidates was $10 million in the original law and about $37 million in 2004. With additional funds permitted for fundraising, legal, accounting, and compliance costs, the total 2004 spending limit was about $49 million. Participating candidates are also expected to follow state-by-state spending limits, which have come to be enforced loosely. Under the rules as written, state limits varied in 2004 from a low of $746,000 for the smallest states (including New Hampshire) and $1.3 million for Iowa, up to a maximum of $15.6 million for California.

While the public funding system has always had critics, it served its intended purposes for a while. But then it became outdated. The campaign finance provisions of 1974 were designed to fit elections of the 1970s. In 1976, a relatively unknown governor of Georgia, Jimmy Carter, used public funds to win the Iowa caucuses on January 19 and the New Hampshire primary on February 26 against more established candidates. Carter then used his success to raise money for the next set of contests. Primaries were sequenced at what now seems a leisurely pace, with the full contest lasting more than three months, well into June. On the Republican side, the former governor of California, Ronald Reagan, took on a sitting president and came within a hair's breadth of winning. As with Carter's, the Reagan campaign depended on small contributions and matching funds to remain solvent. Ford's victory was in doubt until the GOP convention in August. As we shall see below, Carter and Reagan were only the first two of a series of serious competitors who would not have been viable without public funds.

Compare the timing of the 1976 primaries with the timing of more recent contests. Since 1988, states have been "frontloading" the delegate selection process by moving their primary dates earlier (Mayer and Busch 2004). Bob Dole clinched the 1996 Republican nomination by March 17—months earlier than Carter or Ford. George W. Bush's and Al Gore's 2000 victories were settled a week before Dole's in 1996. In 2004, the calendar moved up another week. Almost 60 percent of the Democratic convention delegates were chosen by the "Super Tuesday" primaries of March 2, when John Edwards, Sen. Kerry's last serious opponent, dropped out of the race.

Compressing the calendar has had major consequences for election finance. Candidates who wanted to win in 2004 had to be prepared to run a national campaign early, rather than a series of state campaigns, so they had little time to raise money between one primary and the next. After the Iowa caucuses of January 19 and New Hampshire's primary on January 27 came six additional primaries on February 3, including ones in Arizona, South Carolina, and Missouri. Michigan's caucuses were four days later, on February 7. After only four primaries during the rest of February, surviving candidates then had to prepare for "Super Tuesday" on March 2—nine primaries, including California, New York, and Ohio. Florida and Texas would come the following week (March 9) followed by Illinois on March 16.

This schedule left candidates with few campaigning options. Personal campaigning after Iowa and New Hampshire was out of the question. Free news coverage could not be counted on to fill in the gap. The topics covered by the news would be out of the candidate's control and would probably focus on "horse race" stories or the day's latest allegation rather than the candidates' policies or qualifications. For a candidate to get his own message across, advertising was essential. And while the Internet may hold promise for disseminating messages cheaply in the future, expensive television advertising was still the vehicle of choice for reaching large numbers of people quickly.

These calendar-driven realities led directly to the pressures that caused three candidates to reject public funding in 2004. For the thirty years since the public funding system came into being, successful participating candidates have typically spent almost the full spending limit by the time they wrapped up the nomination, whenever that was. Spending up to the limit is not new, but frontloading the calendars means that spending becomes frontloaded too. The successful and runner-up candidates of 1996 and 2000 had spent almost up to the limit for the full election cycle by March (Campaign Finance Institute Task Force on Financing Presidential Nominations 2003).

Given the accelerated spending and the difficulties of raising new money quickly, the candidates of 2004 were well advised, if they could, to have enough money by the end of December to carry them well into February (Mayer and Busch 2003). Indeed, the conventional wisdom among journalists was that the candidate with the most money at the end of the odd-numbered year would win. The conventional wisdom was overstated, of course: Bill Bradley did not lose to Al Gore in 2000 because he had slightly less money. Both candidates had enough, and the race was decided on other grounds. But the general idea was right. Candidates have to raise a lot of money early to make it through this timetable. Typical estimates bandied about in early 2003 suggested that a strong underdog would raise at least $15 million in the off year, while the front-runner probably would raise at least $25 million. To translate these numbers into daily activities, a person who raises $15 million in one calendar year must raise an average of $41,000 a day for 365 days; to raise $25 million in a year means raising $68,000 a day. With this amount of money needed so early, the primary calendar helps stack the race in favor of front-runners with well-oiled fundraising capabilities.

The pressure to spend early means that candidates who survive the early contests will run up against the spending limit later in the season. Candidates who are not the front-running favorites of large donors typically need help from public funding. To get public money, they agree to a spending limit. The system is voluntary, but the money and the limits are linked. That is not a major problem as long as everyone abides by the same limit, but lately that has not been so. In 1996, billionaire Steve Forbes became the first serious presidential challenger to announce he would step outside the public funding system to finance his own campaign. He spent $42.6 million, mostly his own money, in a year when the spending ceiling was $37.7 million. Bob Dole beat Forbes but spent the full limit to do so. When the incumbent President Clinton launched negative advertising against Dole in the spring, the GOP winner could not respond. In 2000, George W. Bush, knowing Forbes would be running again, referred specifically to 1996 when he announced that he would not take public funding. "I'm mindful of what happened in 1996 and I'm not going to let it happen to me," Bush said (Glover 1999). Bush's principal opponent, John McCain, did take public funds. Without them, he never would have made it as far as he did. McCain dropped out of the race after losing seven of the eleven Super Tuesday primaries. (He won four of the five New England states and lost California, Georgia, Maine, Maryland, Missouri, New York, and Ohio.) But McCain would have found it almost impossible to continue even if he had done better. To reach Super Tuesday, he had spent up to his limit, and he would have had to run in the coming month against someone who did not face the same constraint. The spending limit that drove Bush out of the system in the beginning thus became a trap for his opponent at the end.

Once Bush and Vice President Gore had effectively won their nominations in March 2000, each could turn his attention to the general election. With no spending limit, Bush could conceivably have emulated the 1996 Clinton by running advertising at a time when Gore, having reached his limit, was out of money. But between 1996 and 2000, the parties had perfected using "soft money" for candidate-specific "issue advertising" that did not count against the party contribution limits or the candidate's spending limit. By spending about $15 million in soft money during the "bridge period" between Super Tuesday and the convention, the Democratic National Committee was able to keep pro-Gore advertising on the air. Soft money was, in effect, the party's safety net for the bridge period in 2000. But that safety net would not be available in 2004 because the Bipartisan Campaign Reform Act of 2002 (BCRA) had outlawed national party soft money. The concern about being trapped by Bush thus helped fuel Dean's and Kerry's decisions to reject public funding in 2004, just as a similar fear about being trapped had influenced Bush four years before.

THE POLITICAL CONTEXT IN 2004: "IT'S ALL ABOUT BUSH"

For almost all of the other political players in 2004, President's Bush's demonstrated fundraising prowess dominated the campaign finance picture. Democratic candidates had to measure their campaigns against the knowledge that if they got through the primaries, they would be up against Bush for five months before they would get public funds for the general election. The Democratic National Committee shared the same fear, as did the most significant donors to the new, liberal 527 organizations.

Networks and Goals

The President's performance in 2000 had given all of these players good reason to worry. Since 1976, no candidate before 2000 had raised substantially more than the spending limit. Bush raised more than double the limit. Beginning with fundraising networks from his father's presidential campaigns and his own as Governor of Texas (Green and Bigelow 2002), Bush had $96 million in net receipts in 2000, shattering all previous records. At the heart of this success were the "Pioneers"—people who agreed to solicit and raise at least $100,000 to elect Bush as President. Five hundred fifty people signed up to become Pioneers, 241 of whom were identified by the campaign as having reached the $100,000 goal (Texans for Public Justice 2004). These 241 people alone accounted for a minimum of $24.1 million. (They undoubtedly raised more, but the campaign did not publicly identify how much money each raised.) According to John C. Green and Nathan S. Bigelow, the success was based on "accountability and competition":

> Each Pioneer has his or her own personal account code with the Bush campaign, so that each person could get credit for the money he or she raised. The Bush campaign carefully monitored the incoming contributions, bestowing praise and status to the Pioneers who met the $100,000 pledge. This system of monitoring and rewards created strong incentives among the Pioneers that tapped into the competitive drive of business executives, lawyers, and politicians (Green and Bigelow 2002).

But the Pioneers were far from the whole story. The Bush campaign had 60,116 donors who gave the legal maximum of $1,000, most of whom gave that amount in a single check. This money from $1,000 donors—more than double Gore's take from all individual donors in whatever amount—represented 65 percent of Bush's contributions from individuals. The sheer size of the donor list also meant that more than half of Bush's $1,000 contributions probably came from outside the Pioneer network.

No one expected Bush's 2004 fundraising to stop there. After BCRA raised the contribution limits from $1,000 to $2,000, estimates of Bush's 2004 fundraising capabilities immediately skyrocketed. If Bush could convert most of his $1,000 donors into $2,000 donors, the reasoning went, he would start with a fundraising base of $120 million in addition to the $35 million he raised from other donors in 2000. As an incumbent President running without primary opponents, and no spending limit, the President clearly was in a position to raise more than he had in 2000. The minimum estimate, therefore, was that the President would raise at least $150 million. The campaign itself talked about $175 million and then $200 million. These goals frightened potential opponents but turned out to be modest.

Fast Start

Because of the war with Iraq, which began in March 2003, the Bush-Cheney '04 Committee did not file organizational papers with the Federal Election Commission until May 16. Beginning with an initial cash transfer of $671,000 left over from 2000, the campaign did not hold its first fundraising event until mid-June. In a remarkable two weeks between June 17 and June 30, the President appeared at seven fundraising events (in Washington, DC, California, New York City, and Florida) that raised $16.45 million; Vice President Dick Cheney appeared at four events, raising $2.8 million; and First Lady Laura Bush appeared at two, raising an additional $1.3 million (Public Citizen 2003). By June 30, the committee reported more than $35 million in receipts, about $1 million a day since it began fundraising! The next reporting period began as the previous one ended, with President Bush attending fundraising events in Dallas on July 18 and Houston on July 19 that pulled in $7 million between them. In the quarter from July 1 through September 30, Bush-Cheney '04 raised $50.1 million, followed by fourth quarter fundraising of $47.5 million. By the end of 2003, the Bush campaign committee had raised $132.7 million, compared to $139.6 million raised during 2003 by the ten Democratic challengers combined. That averaged more than $600,000 a day since the committee had registered with the FEC on May 16. To put this amount of fundraising in perspective, it is the equivalent of more than a dozen $2,000 contributions every hour for twenty-four hours a day, seven days a week. After spending $33.6 million in 2003, President Bush began 2004 with $99.1 million cash on hand.

One reason for this fundraising success was the same networking idea that proved so successful four years before. But there were new wrinkles this time. Instead of having only a single recognition level for Pioneers who raised at least $100,000, the campaign added $200,000 Rangers, as well as a group of about ninety-five Mavericks, who were fundraisers under 40 years old who brought in at least $50,000. (Some of the Mavericks were also Pioneers or Rangers.) By the time of the Republican convention in August 2004, 221 Rangers and 327 Pioneers had raised a minimum of $76.9 million. This was a substantial expansion over the networks of 2000. Of the 241 people who were Pioneers in 2000, only a little more than a half (123) repeated as either Pioneers or Rangers in 2004. The remaining 425 Pioneers and Rangers of 2004 had not been Pioneers in 2000 (Texans for Public Justice 2004; Edsall, Cohen, and Grimaldi 2004; Justice 2005).

Turnover among Donors

The campaign had an even higher turnover among donors than among fundraisers. Based on past survey research and on interviews with fundraising professionals, we at the Campaign Finance Institute had expected to find when we analyzed campaign donor records that most people who gave money to President Bush in 2000 would do so again in 2004. This did not happen. There was more turnover among donors than we had been led to expect, not only for Bush but for all candidates. In fact, the numbers are so striking that it would be valuable to do further research to see why the results are so inconsistent with past findings that described donors to federal elections as a small and relatively static pool of repeat contributors. For example, 50 percent of all congressional donors and 46 percent of presidential donors have said in recent surveys that they contribute in most elections (Brown, Powell and Wilcox 1995; Francia et al. 2003; Wilcox et al. 2003).

These past impressions of a small and habitual donor pool have been based on survey research; the CFI findings are based on the first systemic review of *all* presidential donors in the Federal Election Commission's records. CFI found that only 30 percent of the 93,865 people who gave more than $200 to President Bush in 2000 (the threshold amount for disclosure) gave again in 2004. Even more surprisingly, only 31 percent of the 61,116 who gave the maximum contribution of $1,000 gave in *any* disclosed amount ($200 +) in 2004. In other words, more than two-thirds of President Bush's 2000 donors did not give again in 2004. Moreover, this was *not* peculiar to the Bush campaign. Our instinct tells us that Bush donors should have been more loyal than other donors over these two elections, since he was the only candidate to have run in both cycles. This turns out to be correct. Only 25 percent of Al Gore's $200 + donors, and 21 percent of Bill Bradley's, gave more than $200 to any presidential candidate in 2004. *Thus, there appears to be much more churning in the system—much more moving in and out— than we had previously thought.* As a result, the campaign had to find many new donors for 2004—and it did. Eventually, 150,722 people gave more than $200 to Bush-Cheney '04, according to the Campaign Finance Institute's analysis of FEC reports. Almost four out of every five (118,807 donors or 78.8 percent) were people who had *not* given to the campaign in 2000.

Large and Small Donors

While President Bush, like John Kerry, eventually raised unprecedented amounts in unitemized contributions below $200—a subject to which we shall return later—the bulk of the President's *itemized* contributions came from people who gave the highest permissible amount. The number of people who gave the maximum $2,000 to the President in 2004 was slightly higher than the number who gave the then-maximum $1,000 in 2000 (61,229 versus 61,116). These $2,000 donors represent 41 percent of the total number of itemized donors (donors who gave more than $200) in 2004. The number of donors who gave $1,000 or more in 2004 (including the $2,000 donors) numbered 89,697, or 60 percent of the itemized donors.

As a percentage of *money*, the role of the $2,000 donor was even more impressive. For subsequent tables in this chapter, we analyze *contributions* made in 2000 and 2004 rather than *contributors* because the merged data for contributors (showing the cumulative amount given by donors who give more than once to a candidate) are not yet available for 2004. Contributions of $2,000 ($112.5 million) accounted for 44 percent of President Bush's total money from individuals in 2003–2004, *including* the money from small donors. Contributions of $1,000 or more ($147.0 million) accounted for 57 percent. Because of the influx of donors who gave in small amounts ($200 or less), the percentage of money coming from large donors is down slightly from four years earlier, when Bush's $61.6 million in $1,000 contributions accounted for 65 percent of his receipts from individuals, eight percentage points higher than in 2004. (See table 11.1 for a

Table 11.1 Presidential Fundraising from Individual Contributions, 2000 and 2004 ($ millions; through September of election year)

Candidate	Total Net Receipts[a]	Total Public Dollars	Total Indiv. Contrib.	$1,000 & Up Contrib.	$1,000 & Up as % Total Indiv.	$2,000 & Up Contrib.[b]	($2,000 & Up Contrib. as % of Total Indiv.[b])	$200–999 Contrib.	$200–999 as % of Total Indiv.	Less Than $200 Contrib.	Less Than $200 as % of Total Indiv.
2004											
Wesley Clark	$28.4	$7.6	$17.3	$8.5	49%	$5.3	(31%)	$3.4	20%	$5.4	31%
Howard Dean	51.1	0.0	51.1	9.7	19%	3.9	(8%)	11.1	22%	30.6	60%
John Edwards	31.7	6.6	21.6	15.4	71%	10.4	(48%)	3.5	16%	3.0	14%
Richard Gephardt	21.2	4.1	14.3	10.2	72%	6.4	(45%)	2.3	16%	1.8	13%
Bob Graham	5.0	0.0	4.4	3.2	73%	2.2	(50%)	0.9	19%	0.4	9%
John Kerry	234.6	0.0	215.5	94.2	44%	52.4	(24%)	43.1	20%	79.6	37%
Dennis Kucinich	12.4	3.0	7.9	0.9	11%	0.4	(5%)	1.5	19%	5.5	70%
Joe Lieberman	18.5	4.3	14.0	10.5	75%	6.2	(44%)	2.5	17%	1.2	9 %
Carol Moseley Braun	0.6	0.0	0.5	0.3	51%	0.1	(27%)	0.1	27%	0.1	24%
Al Sharpton	0.7	0.0	0.5	0.3	64%	0.2	(45%)	0.1	24%	0.1	13%
All Democrats	404.2	25.6	347.2	153.3	44%	87.7	(25%)	68.6	20%	127.7	37%
George W. Bush	269.6	0.0	257.4	148.7	58%	113.3	(44%)	31.6	12%	78.7	31%
All Republicans	269.6	0.0	257.4	148.7	58%	113.3	(44%)	31.6	12%	78.7	31%
Total	673.8	25.6	604.6	301.9	50%	201.0	(33%)	100.2	17%	206.4	34%

(continues)

Table 11.1 Continued

Candidate	Total Net Receipts[a]	Total Public Dollars	Total Indiv. Contrib.	$1,000 & Up Contrib.	$1,000 & Up as % Total Indiv.	$2,000 & Up Contrib.[b]	($2,000 & Up Contrib. as % of Total Indiv.[b])	$200–999 Contrib.	$200–999 as % of Total Indiv.	Less Than $200 Contrib.	Less Than $200 as % of Total Indiv.
2000											
Bill Bradley	49.0	12.5	29.2	18.8	65%	N/A	N/A	6.9	23%	3.8	13%
Al Gore	49.4	15.5	33.9	21.3	63%	N/A	N/A	6.3	18%	6.8	20%
All Democrats	98.4	28.0	63.1	40.2	64%	N/A	N/A	13.3	21%	10.6	17%
Gary Bauer	16.8	4.9	7.6	1.1	15%	N/A	N/A	2.0	26%	4.6	60%
George W. Bush	95.6	0.0	92.3	61.7	67%	N/A	N/A	17.5	19%	14.8	16%
Elizabeth Dole	5.1	0.0	5.0	3.1	61%	N/A	N/A	1.1	21%	0.9	19%
Steve Forbes	47.9	0.0	5.5	1.7	31%	N/A	N/A	1.0	17%	3.0	53%
Allen Keyes	4.8	4.2	8.0	0.4	5%	N/A	N/A	1.2	16%	6.4	80%
John McCain	56.3	14.5	28.1	9.7	34%	N/A	N/A	7.5	26%	11.5	41%
Dan Quayle	7.8	2.1	4.1	1.7	41%	N/A	N/A	0.7	16%	1.8	45%
All Republicans	234.3	25.7	150.7	79.4	53%	N/A	N/A	31.0	20%	43.1	29%
Total	332.7	53.7	213.8	119.6	55%	N/A	N/A	44.2	20%	53.7	25%

Notes: These numbers reflect net year-end totals for Bush and Kerry that have been netted to avoid double counting of receipts. The widely reported amounts of $249 million for Kerry and $274 million for Bush are gross total receipts. Percentages may not add to 100 due to rounding.
[a] Includes matching funds, PAC contributions, loans and other funds, but not contribution refunds and offsets.
[b] All $2,000 and up contributions are included in $1,000 and up contributions.

summary of all candidates' receipts, as well as the amount from small and large contributions, for the full electoral cycles in 2000 and 2004.)

As important as large-dollar contributions were for the President over the full sweep of his 2003–2004 campaign, they were even more important for him—and for most of his opponents—in the year before voting. As of December 31, 2003, Bush-Cheney had raised a total of $132.7 million, $129.5 million of which came from individuals. Almost four-fifths of these early individual contributions (79 percent) were for $1,000 or more. By the end of December, these $1,000 or more contributions already came to almost as much ($101.9 million) as the total amount that Bush had raised from all sources for the full cycle of 1999–2000 ($105 million). And almost two-thirds of the individual contributions in calendar year 2003 (64 percent) came from $2,000 contributions. While, as we shall see, the proportional importance of large contributions was not unusual for candidates' early fundraising in 2003–2004, the sheer amount of money being raised from major donors was unprecedented.

Bush Sets the Context

These were the numbers that Democrats were seeing during the closing months of 2003, when they had to decide whether they would accept at most $15–$18 million in matching funds in return for committing themselves to a $50 million spending limit. Because the government normally distributes its checks shortly after the first of the year, candidates have to decide by December, at the latest, whether they wish to participate. Candidates who had no serious prospect of raising $50 million had an easy choice: take the public funds and do not worry about a spending limit that was beyond reach. But for candidates who might reach that level—Howard Dean and John Kerry—President Bush was setting the framework within which they would choose.

THE DEMOCRATS' MONEY PRIMARY: THE INSIDERS SEEK BIG DONORS

In February 2003, the *Atlanta Journal and Constitution* wrote a financial "horse race" story about the Democratic presidential candidates whose framework reflected the thoughts of many political professionals:

> The first race in the 2004 Democratic presidential campaign is for cash. . . . In every campaign since 1980, the candidate who raised the most money by the start of the election year went on to win the nomination. So the cash primary, lasting from now [early 2003] until the first voting in Iowa and New Hampshire next January, is a race to raise as much money as possible (Shepard 2003a).

The article declared John Kerry to be the front-runner of the first stage in what some political scientists have called the "invisible primary" (Hadley 1976; Buell

1996), because Kerry was in a position to transfer $2.9 million in leftover Senate funds to his presidential campaign. Rep. Dick Gephardt of Missouri was declared to be in a strong second place because he could transfer $2.6 million, followed by Sen. John Edwards ($2 million) and Sen. Joseph Lieberman ($696,942) (Shepard 2003. See also Nagourney 2003).[1] Howard Dean, the former Governor of Vermont, barely registered in these early press accounts.

Kerry's status as the press's putative front-runner did not last long. The Massachusetts Senator raised $7 million in the first quarter of 2003. That was a big number, but the bragging rights went to John Edwards, who raised $7.4 million. More than half of Edwards's first quarter money came from his fellow trial lawyers (Edsall and Cohen 2003). But like Kerry's so-called lead at the beginning of the year, Edwards's financial lead did not last (see table 11.2).

After fast starts, both Edwards's and Kerry's fundraising fell off markedly while Lieberman's went up and down, and Gephardt's stayed steady. Like many of their predecessors in past elections, these four "insider" candidates were depending on large contributions from a small number of donors. By the year's end, many of the party's loyal donors were waiting to see which candidate would have the political strength to move forward. Meanwhile, the "outsider" candidates, Wesley Clark and especially Howard Dean, were causing some to begin questioning their old fundraising assumptions.

LARGE AND SMALL DONOR FUNDRAISING

The dependence of the four insider candidates on major donors was not new. One of the original goals of the public matching fund system was to heighten the importance of small donors. Ronald Reagan and Jimmy Carter did raise much of their money in small contributions. But the system had almost relentlessly been steering candidates toward major donors at least since 1988 or 1992 (Cam-

Table 11.2 Major Candidates' Receipts in 2003 ($ *millions*)

Candidates	Jan.– Mar.	Apr.– Jun.	July– Sept.	Oct.– Dec.	Cumulative 2003 Receipts	% of all 2003 Individual Contrib. in Amounts of: $1,000+	<$200
Clark	—	—	3.4	10.3	13.8	53	28
Dean	2.6	7.6	14.8	16.0	41.3	22	56
Edwards	7.4	4.5	2.6	1.9	16.4	80	7
Gephardt	3.5	3.9	3.8	3.0	16.6	72	12
Kerry	7.0	5.9	4.0	5.2[a]	23.5	73	13
Lieberman	3.0	5.3	3.6	2.2	13.9	74	8
Bush	—	35.1	50.1	47.5	132.7	79	15

Source: Campaign Finance Institute, derived from FEC data.
[a] Kerry's receipts for the fourth quarter included $2.9 million in personal loans to his campaign.

paign Finance Institute Task Force on Financing Presidential Nominations 2003).

According to research conducted by the Campaign Finance Institute for CFI's Task Force on Presidential Nomination Financing, approximately 774,000 people contributed money to a presidential candidate in the 2000 election. About 100,000 gave to more than one candidate, so that CFI found about 834,000 donor-candidate pairings—combining all contributions from the same donor to the same candidate into one record. Of these 834,000:

- An estimated 569,000 donors gave in amounts that cumulated to $100 or less to any one candidate (averaging an estimated $52 per contributor).
- Another estimated 101,000 donors gave $101 to $250.
- Some 52,245 donors gave $251 to $999.
- Some 112,365 donors gave $1,000.

Thus, about 68 percent of the donors gave $100 or less and 13 percent of the donors gave $1,000 (CFI 2003:105) But most of the money came from the small group of top-dollar donors. The four candidates responsible for most of the fundraising in 2000 raised more than 60 percent of their money from $1,000 donors (Gore 63 percent, Bradley 66 percent, Bush 72 percent, and McCain 45 percent) (CFI 2003:31).

Fundraising is driven toward large contributions because of some simple facts. It takes twenty $50 contributions to equal one $1,000 contribution without matching funds. For a publicly funded candidate with a one-for-one match on the first $250, it still takes 12.5 $50 contributions ($50 becomes $100 with a one-for-one match) to equal one $1,000 contribution (which was worth $1,250 after a match). BCRA doubled the contribution limit but did nothing to change the public funding formula. Under the new system, therefore, a $50 contribution, matched, is still worth $100, but a maximum contribution—now $2,000—is worth $2,250, or 22.5 times as much as the small donor's $50.

In the first stages of a campaign, candidates often must ask for large contributions personally. But when you divide the number of minutes per day into the amount of money its takes for a candidate to run a presidential campaign, there is no way to raise enough solely through personal contacts. The candidate needs a "force multiplier." Democratic candidates have traditionally relied on organized interest groups to help them reach out, but candidates of both parties also raise much of their money for the primaries by relying on politically active intermediaries who host events for them in major fundraising centers (New York, Los Angeles, and Washington for both parties, along with Dallas and Houston for Republicans). George W. Bush's major innovation, as noted, was to take networking to new levels in 2000 and 2004 with his Rangers and Pioneers. The question is whether there are any feasible alternatives to high-donor networking for presidential candidates who have to run in expensive, frontloaded primaries.

One alternative might be to reach out to small donors, but the arithmetic in past years has been problematic. People who give $50 do not part with their money any more easily (maybe even less so) than people who give $1,000. Donors respond to appeals; they are more likely to accept those appeals if they know something about the person who is asking for money. For small donors, however, the appeal must be made even more indirectly than it is within donor networks. The more distant or indirect the appeal, the more broadly will the candidate have to be known among the general public for the appeal to draw a response. This is why most appeals to small donors presuppose a campaign that has already caught fire or a candidate who is well-known before the campaign or a well-known endorser. Small donor appeals cannot be the first step: the question is whether they can be the basis for the steps that come next.

Before now, the modern presidential candidates who have been most successful at raising money in small amounts have been Ronald Reagan, Jesse Jackson, Pat Robertson, Pat Buchanan, and Gary Bauer. All were able to make distinctive appeals. Most of the appeals were issue-based or ideological. In almost all cases, the initial "prospecting" appeals to small donors had to be made by using direct mail, although repeat donors could be reached over the telephone. The kicker is that with direct mail, it could easily cost $1 to raise $1 from new donors. Matching funds would double the yield, but this would still leave the cost at 50 cents to raise a dollar. The process could become more profitable after repeat solicitations to previous supporters yield higher rates of return, but that would come later in the game, after some success. Prospecting for low-dollar contributions, therefore, is a high-risk, low-benefit investment for most candidates, especially during the early phases of a campaign season. Because fundraising for large contributions costs much less per dollar raised, a candidate has to find even more small donors than the original arithmetic suggests to equal the net value of a large one. Instead of taking forty $50 contributions to equal one $2,000 contribution (or 22.5 of the smaller contributions if the candidate takes matching funds), it could take at least half again as many of the $50 contributions to equal the larger one's net value, after fundraising costs have been deducted.

In the fundraising logic that prevailed through 2000, less than one-quarter of one percent of the population gave any money to a presidential candidate. Even though most donors had midrange incomes and gave less than $100, there were fewer than 800,000 donors for the entire 2000 presidential election, and the candidates' funding was dominated by only 112,000 mostly well-to-do people who gave $1,000 each. The funding balance would be shifted radically if even one percent of the voting-age population were to contribute to presidential candidates during the primaries. But it is hard to see how candidates would ever have the resources or the incentive to make this happen, as long as the *costs* and *benefits* of raising small versus large contributions remained as they were.

HOWARD DEAN TESTS THE LOGIC

A CFI task force report on presidential funding recommended an increase in the *benefits* from small contributions. The report recommended changing the matching fund formula: instead of dollar-for-dollar matching for the first $250 from each contributor, the CFI task force recommended a three-for-one match for the first $100 (Campaign Finance Institute Task Force on Financing Presidential Nominations 2003). Former Vermont Governor Howard Dean's 2004 presidential campaign tackled the same problem from the opposite direction. Because his candidacy had to function within the system as it was, he could not alter the benefits. In fact, Dean eventually went so far as to reduce the financial benefits that he would get from each small contribution when he decided not to accept matching funds. He was able to do this by radically altering the *cost* side of the equation—scrapping direct mail and raising his money through the Internet. Instead of spending a dollar for every dollar raised, the Internet holds out the possibility of spending less than a nickel.

In 2000, Senator John McCain had already shown other politicians that a candidate could raise a lot of money quickly over the Internet, when he raised $2 million that way in the four days after winning the New Hampshire Republican presidential primary. The McCain campaign reportedly raised a total $6.4 million over the Internet in all (Cornfield 2004). However, according to people we interviewed from McCain's campaign staff, many of his Internet donors after New Hampshire were repeat donors who were solicited over the telephone and then steered to the campaign's website to make a contribution. The question the Dean campaign set out to answer in 2004 was whether Internet participation could become a more significant part of a campaign's basic strategy. Without support from major donors, the Dean campaign had no other choice.

Howard Dean began his outsider's long-shot campaign for the presidency by traveling often, on a low budget, to the early primary and caucus states. The issues he emphasized early in his campaign made it hard to pinpoint him along a left-to-right scale: he was for balancing the budget, against new gun control laws, and against the unfunded mandates in President Bush's education program; but he was also for strong environmental regulation, civil unions for gay couples, and universal health insurance.

The Dean campaign then received a major boost from a shift in the national policy agenda. On September 4, 2002, President Bush announced that he would seek congressional approval to use force against Iraq. On October 10, the House voted 296–133 to authorize the use of force (H.J. Res 114). Republicans voted 215–6 to support the resolution; Democrats divided, with eighty-one supporting the resolution and 126 opposing it. (One independent also opposed the resolution.) Rep. Gephardt was one of the leaders among Democrats gathering support for the resolution. The Senate endorsed the resolution the next day by a vote of 77–23, with Republicans voting 48–1 in favor, Democrats split 29–21, and one Independent opposed. Sen. Lieberman was an early and strong supporter of the resolution; Senators Kerry and Edwards also voted for it. Two Democrats running for the presidency voted no—Sen. Bob Graham of Florida and Rep. Dennis Kucinich of Ohio—but Graham withdrew from the race in October 2003, and Kucinich faced formidable obstacles to rising to the top tier of challengers. This put Dean into position to take advantage of a near vacuum.

Over the next several months, Dean became the party's leading antiwar candidate. His fiery rhetoric and the clarity of his positions began to gather a larger audience. The breakthrough among national political activists may have come at the two-day winter 2003 meeting of the Democrat National Committee in Washington, DC, at which all of the presidential candidates were invited to speak. Dean's speech openly criticized the Democratic Members of Congress who, he said, had compromised too much with the Bush Administration:

> What I want to know is why in the world the Democratic Party leadership is supporting the President's unilateral attack on Iraq. . . . What I want to know is why are Democratic Party leaders supporting tax cuts. . . . What I want to know is why we're fighting in Congress about the Patient's Bill of Rights when the Democratic Party ought to be standing up for health care for every single American. . . . I'm Howard Dean, and I'm here to represent the Democratic wing of the Democratic Party. (Trippi, 2004)

Even if they were not prepared to endorse his campaign, Dean's message resonated strongly with party professionals. The *Atlanta Journal and Constitution* quoted former Atlanta Mayor Maynard Jackson as saying that Dean "stole the show." Donna Brazile, the Gore-Lieberman campaign manager in 2000, said of the physician and former governor, "He's got the medicine to cure my depression" (Shepard 2003b).

Soon, the intensity of feeling about the war began translating into financial support. Dean's $2.6 million in receipts during the first quarter of 2003 put him fifth among Democrats but was surprisingly close to Lieberman's $3 million and Gephardt's $3.5 million. The support tapped into what reporter Thomas B. Edsall described as "the new Democratic elite: affluent, well-educated professionals." The top zip codes in donors' addresses were from Beverly Hills, Pacific Palisades, and Palo Alto in California and Cambridge, Massachusetts. While some of these zip codes may not be unusual for a Democratic candidate, the occupational profile was: Dean had many more professors, writers, and artists and fewer chief executive officers as donors than did the other Democrats (Edsall 2003a).

Only about $600,000 of Dean's first quarter's totals came over the Internet, with about two-thirds of that coming during the quarter's last week (Trippi 2004). There was a story behind that $400,000. By early 2003, Joe Trippi had signed on as Dean's campaign manager. Trippi was a veteran political consultant who also had acted as a consultant for the past several years for several technology firms, including Wave System and Progeny, a Linux platform company. "On my very first day in the Dean campaign headquarters, that January," Trippi wrote later, "I offered up the closest thing I had to a strategy: 'We need to put up a link to this Web site, Meetup.com'" (Trippi 2004). Meetup.com is a website that helps arrange meetings in public places among like-minded people on self-defined subjects, ranging from food tastes to Wicca. After an initial test quickly garnered 2,700 Dean supporters, the campaign paid Meetup.com a fee of $2,500 to continue organizing—"not a bad initial investment for a site that would eventually boast 190,000 Dean members" (Trippi 2004). This website was primarily a tool for identifying supporters, showing them there were others who thought as they did and organizing them (or helping them organize themselves) at personal meetings. At the end of the first quarter of 2003 there were 22,000 supporters, energized in part by Dean's appearance at "Meetups" in March.

The key to the campaign's use of the Internet was to get beyond seeing the medium either as a passive website-billboard or as another form of direct mail fundraising. Instead, the Dean campaign used the Internet—especially email networks and blogs (weblogs, primarily used as open-ended message boards)—to stimulate interwoven activities that would expand the support base and organize volunteers, as well as raise money. Zephyr Teachout, Director of Internet Organizing for the Dean campaign, described this strategy at a CFI event on February 27, 2004:

> The core of all major-donor fundraising is the same as low-donor fundraising, and low-donor fundraising online, which is that it is about relationships. . . . In a relationship you don't come and ask for money every day. . . . If I come to you every day and say, here's what's going on, come join me at this event, here's how I feel today, here's what's happened, and then on the tenth day I say I really need five bucks to get to the train station, you're a lot more likely to do that. . . . The other part of that personal relationship is the relationship that happens between people— there's the central one-to-many relationship [with the candidate at the center] and there's also the many-to-many relationships (Campaign Finance Institute, 2004b).

The $400,000 the Dean campaign raised over the Internet in the last week of March was stimulated by just such a peer-to-peer communication. Someone in the network, not organized at the top by the campaign, sent a message that others distributed through emails and blogs (Trippi 2004). It was an early indication of what was to follow.

The success during March led the campaign to redouble its Internet efforts during the second quarter. This built toward a late-June crescendo, when Gov. Dean formally "announced" his candidacy. According to Trippi, the campaign had raised $3.2 million during the quarter, as of June 22, when Dean appeared on the Sunday morning television interview show, *Meet the Press*. Over the next week, the campaign raised an additional $2.8 million, $2 million of which came over the Internet. The campaign was using the picture of a baseball bat on its home page, with a rising line to track incoming contributions. Feeding into the sense of momentum, 317,639 participants voted in an online "primary" conducted by the liberal MoveOn.org, which issued a press release on June 27 saying that Dean had come in first with 44 percent of the votes (MoveOn.org 2003). Two days before the end of the reporting period, Trippi upped the fundraising goal from $4.5 million to $6.5 million and made the goal public. By midnight, June 30, the supporters had raised $7.6 million during the quarter, $828,000 of which came in during the last twenty-four hours (Trippi 2004). This made Dean far and away the strongest Democratic fundraiser during the second quarter. And the vast majority of his donations, unlike those of his Democratic opponents, came from small donors.[2]

THE REST OF 2003 AND THE DECISION
TO REJECT PUBLIC FUNDING

Dean's Internet fundraising accelerated during the rest of 2003, at a time when most of his opponents were finding it difficult to raise money (see table 11.2). After starting the race as a dark horse, Dean came to be seen as the front-runner, months before the first primary. *Time* and *Newsweek* both ran full cover stories on Dean in their issues dated August 11. On August 15, the Associated Press reported that Dean was reconsidering whether to accept public funding and spending limits because of his campaign's fundraising success (Fournier 2003). The campaign raised $14.8 million between July 1 and September 30, more than three times as much as Kerry, whose $4 million was the next highest amount among Democrats for the quarter.

On November 8, Dean announced that he would in fact opt out of the matching fund system. He wrote to his supporters that living within the spending limit would give the incumbent President Bush a $170 million spending advantage. However, one suspects that Dean's decision was not only about Bush. By opting out of the limits, Dean was also freeing himself from state-by-state spending limits in Iowa, where research by the Wisconsin Advertising Project has shown that early advertising substantially exceeded the state spending limits. (See the remarks by Kenneth Goldstein at Campaign Finance Institute 2004b.)

Once Dean announced his decision, two other candidates said they would consider following him. One was retired General Wesley Clark. Clark was a late entrant into the race, announcing his candidacy on September 17. His brief run, which had the backing of many of former President Clinton's supporters, had some earmarks of a "Stop Dean" campaign. Many Democrats who desperately wanted to defeat President Bush were afraid that Dean could not do it. With the other Democratic campaigns apparently not doing well, many began to look at Clark. The Clark campaign was run in a highly professional manner, with an Internet operation described by some computer sophisticates as second only to Dean's. The $10.3 million that Clark raised in the fourth quarter of 2003 (following $3.4 million during September) was the third strongest fundraising quarter for any Democrat that year, behind only Dean's third and fourth quarter receipts. Despite the strong showing, Clark decided he could not afford to turn his back on public funds.

The other candidate affected by Dean's announcement was John Kerry. Kerry had already told reporters in September, "If Howard Dean decides to go live outside of it, I'm not going to wait an instant. . . . I'm not going to disarm" (Kranish 2003). On November 13, five days after Dean, Kerry announced that he would follow the Vermonter out of the system. The decision had all the same advantages that it had for Dean, with one important addition. Accepting public funds not only forces a candidate to live within spending limits but prohibits him from giving or lending more than $50,000 to his own campaign. On December 18, Kerry lent his campaign $850,000 and said he would mortgage his house to lend the campaign more. By the end of December, he had lent the campaign $2.9 million; another $3.5 million followed in January. The loans kept the campaign afloat at a time when his other fundraising had hit a dry hole. Opting out of the system therefore let Kerry remain active in the campaign long enough to become the acceptable alternative to Dean among Democrats in Iowa and New Hampshire.

SPEND-DOWN TIME: IOWA AND NEW HAMPSHIRE THROUGH SUPER TUESDAY

By year's end, the candidates seemed ready to spend whatever money they had in order to win early. By then, most were cash poor and thoroughly dependent on the infusion of public money they were to receive early in January. The major exception among the cash poor was Kerry, who by the end of January was to lend his campaign about twice the amount he would have received from the Treasury.

Because of the primary schedule, the candidates in 2004 spent more money, more quickly than ever. At a February CFI event, the University of Wisconsin's Kenneth Goldstein estimated that the candidates spent $11.5 million to purchase airtime in Iowa and another $14 million for New Hampshire. Overall in the early states, Goldstein said that Dean spent $11 million, Clark $10.5 million, Kerry $8.5 million, Edwards $6.5 million, Gephardt $5 million, and Lieberman $4.5 million (Campaign Finance Institute 2004b). On other occasions, Goldstein has also said that the methodology by which these estimates were produced probably underestimates the real cost. For all of the candidates except Dean, advertising through the New Hampshire primary cost a substantial portion of the previous full year's receipts.

Table 11.3   Spending, Cash, Debts, and Public Funds, Year-End 2003 ($ *millions*)

Candidates	Cumulative Spending[a]	Cash on Hand[a]	Debts[a]	Matching Funds Certified Jan. 2
Clark	10.4	3.4	0.4	3.7
Dean	31.7	9.6	1.2	0
Edwards	16.1	0.3	0.6	3.4
Gephardt	15.0	1.6	1.1	3.1
Kerry	23.7	1.6	3.8	0
Lieberman	13.3	0.6	0.3	3.6

Sources: Candidate disclosure reports filed with FEC; FEC, "FEC Approves Matching Funds For 2004 Presidential Candidates." Press Release, 30 December 2003.

[a] As of December 31, 2003.

In addition to the candidates' spending, at least two organizations ran attack ads criticizing Dean: the conservative Club for Growth and a 527 committee created for the occasion called Americans for Jobs, Healthcare and Progressive Values. Because the latter committee stopped advertising more than thirty days before the caucuses, when BCRA's electioneering provision would have kicked in, the 527 did not have to disclose its supporters until after the primary. Some of its organizers had previously worked for Dick Gephardt, but the Gephardt campaign said that it had no involvement with the organization.

As is well known, the Dean campaign collapsed on January 19 in Iowa, where he finished a distant third with only 18 percent support from the caucus participants. Gephardt finished fourth with 11 percent and dropped out of the race. With Clark and Lieberman passing up Iowa to concentrate on New Hampshire, voters who were looking for an alternative to Dean shifted to Kerry (who won Iowa with 38 percent) and Edwards (who came in a strong second with 32 percent). Both had been far behind Dean in public opinion polls in the weeks leading up to the caucuses.

Kerry had also been behind Dean in New Hampshire polls but defeated him in that state's January 27 primary with 39 percent of the vote to Dean's 26 percent. Clark came in third (13 percent) with Edwards a close fourth (12 percent) and Lieberman fifth (9 percent). Seven states held primaries a week after New Hampshire, on February 3. Kerry won five convincingly (Arizona, Delaware, Missouri, New Mexico, and North Dakota). Clark defeated Edwards by less than a percentage point in Oklahoma: each received 30 percent of the vote to Kerry's 27 percent. Edwards won South Carolina with 45 percent to Kerry's 30 percent. Lieberman withdrew from the contest after failing to place higher than fourth anywhere.

By the time this round of primaries was over, most of the candidates had spent almost all they had raised. The public funds distributed in early January accounted for almost three-fifths of Edwards's spending during the month. It seems obvious that without that money, he would not have been in a position to come in second in Iowa. Public funds also accounted for 85 percent of Gephardt's January spending and 90 percent of Lieberman's. The following table shows the top candidates' cumulative spending, cash on hand, and debts as of January 31.

By early February, political realities were affecting fundraising. Gephardt and Lieberman were out of the race. Edwards and Kerry had been given a modest boost by the February 3 results. The next week, Edwards came in second to Kerry in Tennessee (41 percent to 26 percent) and Virginia (52 percent to 27 percent), with Clark finishing a close third in Tennessee (23 percent) and a distant third in Virginia (9 percent). Clark withdrew from the race on February 11.

Meanwhile, the Dean campaign was struggling politically, shifting campaign managers the day after losing the New Hampshire primary. Nevertheless, after coming in second to Kerry in Michigan (Feb. 7), Washington (Feb. 7), and Maine (Feb. 8), Dean was able to persuade his base of small donors to come through for a last stand in the Wisconsin primary on February 17. After finishing

Table 11.4   Spending, Cash, Debts, and Public Funds, January 2004 (*$ millions*)

	Public Money Received January	Individual Contributions Received in January	Spending in January	Cash on Hand Jan. 31	Debts Jan. 31	Additional Matching Funds Certified Jan. 30
Clark	3.7	2.5	11.9	0.4	3.4	1.4
Dean	0	6.1	10.9	5.0	2.8	0
Edwards	3.4	2.1	5.9	0.5	0.4	0.3
Gephardt	3.1	0.6	3.6	1.8	0.9	0.6
Kerry	0	4.1	7.1	2.1	7.2	0
Lieberman	3.6	0.4	4.0	0.7	0.5	0.4

Sources: Candidate disclosure reports filed with FEC; FEC, "FEC Approves Matching Funds For 2004 Presidential Candidates." Press Release, 30 January 2004.

third, with only 18 percent of the vote to Kerry's 40 percent and Edwards's 34 percent, Dean dropped out of the race on February 18.

After Kerry won three more primaries on February 24 (Hawaii, Idaho, and Utah), the March 2 Super Tuesday primaries were decisive. By this time the race was down to two serious candidates (Kerry and Edwards) and two who had never been competitive (Kucinich, who did come in second in Hawaii, and the Rev. Al Sharpton). Kerry won nine of the ten primaries held on Super Tuesday. Edwards won none. The narrowest margin was in Georgia, where Kerry beat Edwards, 47 percent to 41 percent. The next smallest was in Ohio, where Kerry had three votes for every two votes for Edwards. In seven states (California, Connecticut, Maryland, Massachusetts, Minnesota, New York, and Rhode Island), Kerry outpolled Edwards by at least two to one. Dean won his home state of Vermont. Edwards withdrew from the race the next day, March 3.

An important point about the financial implications of frontloading emerges when comparing January's spending (table 11.4) to February's (table 11.5). February's spending had to pay for that month's seven primaries (excluding the

Table 11.5   Spending, Cash, Debts, and Public Funds, February 2004 (*$ millions*)

	Public Money Received February	Individual Contributions Received in February	Spending in February	Cash on Hand Feb. 29	Debts Feb. 29	Additional Matching Funds Certified Feb. 29
Clark	1.4	1.1	2.1	0.8	3.5	1.8
Dean	0	3.5	6.3	2.8	1.7	0
Edwards	0.3	3.8	6.1	1.3	2.3	0.9
Kerry	0	7.9	8.3	2.4	7.7	0

Sources: Candidate disclosure reports filed with FEC; FEC, "FEC Approves Matching Funds For 2004 Presidential Candidates." Press Release, 1 March 2004.

seven held February 3, some of the spending for which was reported in January). The February reports also covered most of the campaigning in the ten Super Tuesday states. Despite the number of states (twenty-four) holding primaries or caucuses between February 3 and March 2, the total amount spent by the leading candidates in January and February was roughly the same. In addition, we know that most of the candidates' activities and advertising in the final quarter of 2003 focused on Iowa and New Hampshire. Clearly, the spending per voter was *much* lower in the later (and larger) states. Indeed, the candidates spent less in all states during the month than a competitive Senate candidate typically would spend during the final month of a campaign in only *one* of the larger states.

It is also worth noting the contributions to candidates during February. Because Edwards withdrew on March 3, the February financial reports mark the end of the contested phase of the process. Kerry's $7.9 million in contributions from individuals during February was by far his best fundraising month during the campaign to date. We stress this point because the amount, which seemed large at the time, was about to look smaller.

By the end of February, Kerry had spent a cumulative total of $39.1 million. This was about $10 million more than Edwards, but $10 million less than Dean, and less than the spending ceiling if Kerry had taken matching funds. The candidates who came in second and third in the fundraising race—one in the matching fund system and the other not—came in first and second among the voters. The campaign was about to enter a new phase.

SUPER TUESDAY THROUGH THE CONVENTIONS

On March 4, two days after Super Tuesday, Bush-Cheney '04 began airing television advertisements. The first ads praised the President's leadership. Within days, the campaign was criticizing Sen. Kerry's record. During the month of March alone, the Bush-Cheney campaign spent $49.6 million—as much as the full two-year spending limit for a publicly funded candidate, doubling the amount it had spent during the entire campaign cycle until then. An estimated $40 million of this went for television advertising.

Sen. Kerry spent "only" $14.5 million in March. That was much more than his campaign had spent in January ($7 million) or February ($9 million) but was not up to the incumbent's level. However, Kerry was helped by other Democratic candidates and by independent groups. In the months before Super Tuesday, all the Democrats took on the President in most of their advertising. In a March 25 press release, Ken Goldstein's Wisconsin Advertising Project described the cumulative Bush and Democratic candidates' advertising as being nearly equal (Wisconsin Advertising Project 2004). Pro-Democratic 527 groups spent approximately $222 million from March through July, which was about ten times as much as pro-Republican groups spent during the same time period. The spending by 527 groups fully made up for Kerry's shortage in the weeks after

Super Tuesday (Campaign Finance Institute Task Force on Financing Presidential Nominations 2005).

Kerry's financial shortage did not last long. From the Democratic Unity fundraising dinner of March 25 until the convention in late-July, the presumed nominee raised money at a pace that no other candidate, except Bush, had ever matched. The Kerry campaign learned from others, imitating their successes. For major contributors, Kerry learned from Bush. His 266 Vice-Chairs (responsible for raising $100,000 each) and 298 Cochairs ($50,000 each) were successfully patterned after the President's 221 Rangers ($200,000) and 425 Pioneers ($100,000) (Public Citizen 2004). The vice-chairs and cochairs raised at least $41.3 million for Kerry. While that did not equal the minimum of $76.9 million raised by Bush's Rangers and Pioneers, $41.3 million is nothing to sneeze at.

For small donors, Kerry learned from Dean. The process began slowly. Josh Ross, the Kerry campaign staff person in charge of the effort, was not hired until late November 2003. At the end of 2003, Kerry had raised only $2.5 million (13 percent of his individual contributions) in amounts less than $200. At the end of March the under-$200 total was still only $6 million. The takeoff began almost immediately after Super Tuesday. From March through August, Kerry raised $57 million in contributions of $200 or less out of a six-month total of $207 million. Over the full cycle, Kerry raised $79 million in small contributions, amounting to 31 percent of his individual contributions (Campaign Finance Institute 2004a). Ross said that the campaign had raised $82 million over the Internet. (Also reminiscent of Dean, JohnKerry.com boasted 750,000 volunteers and an email list of 2.5 million, with 130,000 Kerry supporters on Meetup.com.) (Justice 2004c; Samuel 2004).

By the time the year was over, the Kerry campaign had $235 million in net receipts, all but $41 million of it after Super Tuesday. The campaign was so successful financially that those running it "exhaustively debated" whether to reject public funding for the general election (Edsall and VandeHei 2004; Rutenberg and Justice 2004b). The issue came up because the campaign strategists were concerned about the sequencing of the two conventions. With the Republican convention more than a month after the Democrats convention, Kerry would have to make his decision about public funds before he could be sure what Bush would decide. Some feared President Bush might reject public money after Kerry had taken it. If that happened, Kerry would have been trapped by the spending limit while Bush would be free of it. In the end, Kerry did take the grant. In future years, however, other candidates will surely consider the option again.

Bush-Cheney '04 raised a net total of $270 million, but the campaign moved at a different pace from the challenger's. By spring, the campaign stopped holding major fundraising events, steering major donors toward contributing to the party instead. In the six months from March through August, the campaign raised $102 million, which was a significant amount, but less than half of Kerry's total over the same period. Small donor fundraising did pick up over these months, with Bush's $51 million slightly below Kerry's $57 million. For the full election cycle, Bush raised $78 million in small contributions to Kerry's $79 million. However, Bush relied less than Kerry on Internet fundraising. While the Bush campaign claimed more volunteers recruited online (1.2 million to Kerry's 750,000) and a larger email list (6 million to 2.5 million), its online fundraising brought in only $13 million (Samuel 2004). Most of the remaining $65 million in small contributions apparently came through the mail.

At the end of the process, the two candidates had raised nearly a half billion dollars, almost evenly divided between them. As skimpy as the resources were for Democrats during the competitive weeks of January and February—when the candidates had to worry whether they could afford to buy advertising—these two winners had more than enough to be heard. Whatever else would decide this election, neither of these general election candidates would suffer from a lack of money.

CONCLUSIONS AND POLICY IMPLICATIONS

George W. Bush and John Kerry did well for themselves by opting out of the public matching fund system. In contrast, at least four of the 2004 candidates— John Edwards, Wesley Clark, Richard Gephardt, and Joseph Lieberman— depended on public funds to keep their campaigns viable long enough for the voters make their decisions in Iowa and New Hampshire. One of them, Edwards, did well enough in the primaries to be asked to run for the Vice Presidency on Kerry's ticket. This made Edwards only the most recent example in a twenty-eight-year series.

The following list shows a few of the significant underdog candidates since 1976—including three future presidents—who were just about out of money, running against well-funded opponents, when an infusion of public funds made it possible for their campaigns to remain viable. The list first appeared in *So the Voters May Choose*, the 2005 report of the Campaign Finance Institute's Task Force on Financing Presidential Nominations.[3]

- *Ronald Reagan (1976)* had only $43,497 cash on hand at the end of January 1976. President Gerald Ford had fifteen times as much in the bank on that day. If the challenger's campaign had not received $1 million in public money in January and another $1.2 million in February, his advisers have said they could not have continued. Reagan's strong campaign in 1976 fueled his success in 1980.
- *Jimmy Carter (1976)* had $42,000 in cash at the end of 1975. Public funds let him continue through Iowa and New Hampshire, where success propelled him to victory.
- *George H. W. Bush (1980)* was down to his last $75,000 on December 31, when the now favored Reagan had seven times as much cash. Like Edwards in 2004, public money let Bush earn enough votes to get an offer later to run as Vice President.
- *Gary Hart (1984)* had about $2,200 at the end of December 1983, $2,500 in

January 1984, and $3,700 at the end of February. Walter Mondale had $2.1 million in cash on January 31, 1984—more than 800 times as much as his opponent.

- *Jesse Jackson (1988)* was down to $5,700 at the end of 1987 at a time when the front-runner, Michael Dukakis, had $2.1 million.
- *Paul Tsongas (1992)* had $80,000 in cash on January 31, compared to Bill Clinton's $1.4 million.
- *Pat Buchanan (1992)* had $12,000 in cash on January 31 compared to the incumbent President Bush's $8.9 million.
- *John McCain (2000)* was comparatively the richest of these underdogs, with $350,000 in cash on January 31, 2000. His opponent, George W. Bush, had $20.5 million in cash on the same day, spent down from $31 million the previous month.

In each of these cases, the "money primary" without a matching fund system would have settled the race in favor of the front-runner before the official balloting had even begun. In light of 2004, we need to ask what the situations of similar candidates are likely to be in future elections. Underdogs could have a hard time even getting their campaigns started. Imagine how a potential early donor might react if a strong, front-running candidate were to signal an intention to break through the spending limit. The donor might prefer one of the other candidates on the merits. Nevertheless, the donor would have to think twice in that situation before giving: why contribute if you know the spending limit will make it impossible for the candidate to compete in the decisive primaries? To attract early money in the current system, therefore, a candidate probably will have to be willing to reject matching money. Someone who might be a good president need not apply unless he or she can compete in the unlimited money race. Public funds would still be useful for propping up candidates who have no chance to win, but the value to the public would become marginal.

Over the past thirty years only four kinds of candidates have been able to mount viable campaigns without public money:

- Rich candidates who were willing to invest personal funds (Ross Perot, Steve Forbes and, in part, John Kerry);
- A factional candidate with an intense following (Howard Dean);
- A well-connected front-runner, strongly favored by his party's establishment (George W. Bush in 2000); and
- An incumbent President (George W. Bush in 2004).

While these were all worthy candidates, the financial characteristics that let them run without public funds clearly do not capture the full range of potentially good presidents who might deserve the public's attention. The three presidents on the historical list above put the lie to that claim. If others are to have a chance to run as serious candidates in the future, the system needs to change. At a minimum, the spending limit has to permit candidates to campaign realistically against an opponent who is running with no limit.

The CFI Task Force (mentioned previously) recommended a two-pronged approach to resolving this problem. The first was to raise the spending limit for the nomination the same as it is for the general election (about $75 million in 2004). The second was to make sure candidates had an escape hatch: if they take public money and have to run against someone who rejects it, participating candidates should be able to raise as much money as ones who opt out.[4]

The CFI Task Force also recommended that candidates be able to receive public funding early in the year before the election instead of waiting until January of the election year. This would serve two purposes. First, it would make public money available when it is most needed, as campaigns are getting started. Second, it would alter the incentives for candidates who are deciding whether to accept public funds. It would be hard to imagine, for example, that Howard Dean would have rejected public money in April or June of 2003 before he knew that his Internet fundraising would take off, if this set of incentives had been in place.

Two questions arise. First, can candidates run adequate races on $75 million? They can, as long as everyone plays by the same rules. Seventy-five million dollars was a lot more than John Kerry or Howard Dean spent during the contested phase of the nomination contest in 2004—through Super Tuesday—and more than George W. Bush spent through this stage in 2000. Most of the additional money was spent between Super Tuesday and the convention, after the nomination was effectively settled. After Super Tuesday, or whenever the real race is decided, the parties are in a position to pick up the slack for the candidates. If both parties' candidates live by the spending limit, the Supreme Court and Federal Election Commission have made it clear that a party can make unlimited independent expenditures. But if one party's candidate accepts public funding and the other's does not, independent spending for the participating candidate would not be as efficient as the opponent's direct spending. In that situation the CFI Task Force recommended that the party whose candidate stayed in the system be allowed unlimited coordinated spending.

These spending limit proposals, or some others like them, could help to preserve public funding for candidates. By themselves, however, they would not restore one of the system's original and still viable purposes: enhancing the role of small donors. The data showed that except for Dean's supporters, participation by small donors in 2004 was almost entirely a post-Super Tuesday phenomenon. To stimulate greater participation by small donors during the competitive phase of the primary season, the CFI Task Force recommended changing the matching fund from the current one-for-one match for the first $250 to a three-for-one public match on the first $100 in private donations (indexed).[5] This change may not seem major, but because an overwhelming majority of donors still give candidates less than $100 each, this apparently small change could make small donors financially as important collectively as the major donors who now dominate presidential finance. (For the details on this point, see Campaign Finance Institute 2003:39–40.)

Finally, to control costs in a situation where the "escape hatch" creates at least a potential for unlimited spending, the CFI Task Force said that no candidate should need more than $20 million (indexed) in public funds to sustain a viable campaign. To pay for its proposals, the CFI Task Force recommended increasing the income tax checkoff from the currently static $3 ($6 for joint filers) to an indexed $5 ($10 for joint filers.) This would be more than enough to pay the estimated $115 million cost of the Task Force's recommendations.[6]

These specific recommendations may be questioned. However, there can be little doubt that the current public matching fund system is obsolete. A viable system will need an appropriate mix of incentives, addressing both matching funds and spending limits in light of current campaign practices. Without change, we can expect the system to become largely irrelevant. That would be a real loss for the presidency and for the public.

NOTES

1. To prepare for their early starts, these same four candidates also operated political action committees (also known, variously, as "leadership PACs" or "politicians' PACs") during the 2002 election cycle. These PACs could not donate more than $5,000 to the campaign in 2003–2004, but candidates used them to travel during the midterm election year, building up their political networks and donor lists. John Edwards's New American Optimists federal PAC raised $3.0 million in 2001–2002, and his soft money nonfederal PAC of the same name raised $4.6 million. (This was the last pre-BCRA year, when candidates could still raise money for soft money PACs.) Dick Gephardt raised $1.5 million for the Effective Government Committee and $1.4 million for its nonfederal counterpart. John Kerry raised $1.0 million for the hard money version of his Citizen Soldier Fund and $1.4 million for the soft money counterpart. Joseph Lieberman's hard money PAC raised $1.7 million; he did not have a soft money PAC.

2. Of course, to put this in perspective, one should note that all of the Democratic contestants combined raised less money during the second quarter of 2003 than President Bush's campaign did during the month of June alone.

3. The author served on the Task Force and drafted its two reports, from which the remainder of this essay is derived. The full reports, with accompanying evidence, may be found at www.Campaign FinanceInstitute.org. See Campaign Finance Institute Task Force on Financing Presidential Nominations 2003 and 2005.

4. Two major alternatives to the CFI package have been put forward as of this writing. The differences are to some extent over matters of detail. Federal Election Commissioners Scott Thomas and Michael Toner offered recommendations that were not specific as to the spending limit but presented a range that went as high as $250 million (Thomas and Toner 2005). A more complex proposal introduced by Senators McCain and Feingold along with Representatives Shays and Meehan on November 21, 2003 (shortly after the first CFI Task Force report) would also have increased the limit to $75 million if everyone participated, with a ceiling of $150 million if someone opts out (S. 1913 and H.R. 3617, 108th Congress). The CFI Task Force argued (contrary to commissioners Toner and Thomas) that $75 million is more than adequate if all candidates participate in the system. But it also argued, contrary to the McCain-Feingold bill, that a candidate who opts out would have an incentive to blow through any limit, whatever it might be, if it were fixed. Since a fixed limit could

not be recalibrated midcampaign, the Task Force preferred simply to let participating candidates raise as much as the opponent who opts out.

5. The Toner-Thomas proposal would keep the present one-for-one matching ratio and apply it to the first $500 instead of the first $250. This would increase the value of large contributions without enhancing small ones. The McCain-Feingold bill tried to increase the value of small contributions by proposing a four-for-one match for the first $250. However, when the Task Force ran the data, it learned that very few donors give in amounts that fall between $100 and $1,000. The vast majority of donors still give less than $100, while the bulk of early money still comes from those who give $1,000 or more. Therefore, the practical effect of providing a multiple for the first $250 is to increase the value of $1,000–$2,000 contributions and to increase the total cost of the funding package, without improving on CFI's less expensive proposal to increase the role of small donors.

6. The cost estimate assumes a mix of donors identical to those of 2004, with all candidates operating within the relevant spending limit. Under these same assumptions, the McCain-Feingold proposal of 2003 would have cost approximately $194 million and the Toner-Thomas proposal about $205 million (Campaign Finance Institute 2005:16. For a fuller discussion of how to expand use of the checkoff—which is not needed to fund the CFI proposal—see Campaign Finance Institute 2005:18–19.).

APPENDIX 1

The Bipartisan Campaign Reform Act: A Summary

Political Party Soft Money

National Party Committees:
> National party soft money is prohibited. The national parties and their affiliates may only raise and spend money subject to federal contribution limits and source restrictions ("hard" money), no matter how the money is spent.

State and Local Parties:
> State, district, and local party committees must fund "federal election activities" with money subject to federal contribution limits. Federal election activities are defined to include:
> - Voter registration activity within 120 days of the election (whether candidate-specific or generic);
> - Voter identification, get-out-the-vote (GOTV) activity, or generic campaign activity conducted in connection with federal election (whether candidate-specific or generic);
> - Communications naming a federal candidate that promote or attack the candidate (as opposed, for example, to sample ballots).

"Federal election activity" does not include: Communications naming state candidates with no federal candidates; contributions to state candidates; state/local political conventions; state candidate grassroots materials; state/local party office construction/purchase costs.

Levin Amendment Exception—Voter Registration and GOTV may be funded with soft money, limited to $10,000 per source, if such contributions are allowed under state law. Contributors may include corporations and labor unions, if state law permits. Money raised under this exception must meet the following conditions:
- Federal officeholders, candidates, national parties and their agents may not raise "Levin Amendment" funds;
- The funds cannot be used for federal candidate-specific or generic advertising;
- All receipts and disbursements must be disclosed;
- Party committees are prohibited from jointly raising these funds;
- A state party committee cannot raise the money for use in other states;

- The funds cannot be transferred between party committees; and
- The soft money must be matched by hard money under Federal Election Commission (FEC) allocation rules.

Nonparty Electioneering

Definition/Coverage
  An "electioneering communication" is a broadcast, cable, or satellite communication that refers to a clearly identified candidate within 60 days of a general election or 30 days of a primary, and that is "targeted." A communication is targeted if it can be received by 50,000 or more persons in the district or state where the election is being held. Subsequent FEC regulation said this provision was limited to paid advertising.

Corporate/Union "Electioneering" Prohibited
  Corporations and unions are prohibited from directly or indirectly making or financing electioneering communications, although they may still form a registered political action committee (PAC), funded with voluntary, limited, individual contributions ("hard money"), for election communication. The corporate restriction extends to nonprofit corporations and to incorporated political committees (other than PACs, parties and candidates,) as defined by section 527 of the tax code. Subsequent FEC regulation exempted nonprofit charities [501(c)(3)s], which are prohibited from political activity under tax law.

Electioneering Disclosure
  Entities making electioneering communications (individuals and unincorporated associations) must file a disclosure report within 24 hours, once an aggregate of $10,000 is spent, and thereafter each time an additional $10,000 is spent. Disclosure includes the identity of the spender, all persons sharing control over the communication(s), and all donors giving $1,000 or more.

Federal Officeholders, Candidates, Party Officials, and Agents

Federal Election Activity
  Federal officeholders, candidates, national parties, and their agents (as well as entities directly or indirectly established, financed, maintained or controlled by, or acting on behalf of, federal candidates or officials) may not solicit, receive, direct, transfer, or spend any soft money in connection with a federal election, with a limited exception for nonprofit corporations described below. This includes "Levin Amendment" funds for registration and GOTV.

State or Local Election Activity

Any solicitation by federal officials or candidates in connection with a state or local election (e.g., for state or local candidates or parties) must be limited to money consistent with federal contribution and source limitations.

Appearances at State Party Events

Federal officials, candidates, etc., *may* appear at, and be a featured guest or speaker, at a state party event at which the party raises soft money for its purposes. Although the law says the candidate may not solicit money at these events, the FEC said in its subsequent regulations that it would not police formal speeches or informal conversations at such events. Nothing in the law prohibits state party officials from soliciting money at an event at which a federal official speaks.

Fundraising for Nonprofits

- Federal officials and candidates may *solicit* funds *without limit* for the general treasury of any tax-exempt organization described in section 501(c) of the tax code, as long as the principal purpose of the organization is not to conduct certain specified federal election activities.
  - Amounts and sources are limited if the contributions are earmarked for registration or GOTV, but not if they are contributions for general funds and the organization uses some of its general funds for political activity.
- *National Parties* may not contribute to or solicit money for nonprofit corporations or 527 political committees.

Contribution Limits

Individuals

- *To a candidate*: Increased from $1,000 per election (primary, general, runoff) to $2,000 and indexed for inflation.
- *To a single national party committee*: Increased from $20,000 per year to $25,000, within the aggregate limits below.
- *To a state or local party committee*: Changed from $5,000 for a state party's federal account (with no limit for a nonfederal account) to $10,000 for each state, local, or district committee that engages in federal activities, within the aggregate limits below.
- *To a PAC*: $5,000 (no change). Also no change in the limit of $5,000 per election for a contribution by a PAC to a candidate. PAC limits are not indexed.
- *Aggregate Limit*: Increases the maximum an individual can give, in combined contributions, from $25,000 per year ($50,000 for two years), with no sub-limits, to $97,500 for two years with the following sublimits:
  - $37,500 to candidates.
  - $57,500 to all PAC and party committees combined.

- ■ No more than $37,500 to all PACs combined.
- ■ The remainder to party committees. (All $57,500 may go to parties if nothing is given to PACs.)
- • *Indexing*: Limits on individual contributions to candidates and parties and individual aggregate limits are indexed for inflation, as are the limits on coordinated party support for a candidate.
- • *Millionaire Opponent Provision* (Variable Contribution Limit): Increases contribution limits for congressional candidates facing self-financed candidates. These go up on a sliding scale, depending upon the amount of self-financing, with qualifying thresholds and maximum contributions differing for the House and Senate. At its highest, the maximum contribution to Senate candidates may be increased sixfold, and the limits on party support for the candidate are removed. Increased contributions triggered by this provision do not count against a donor's aggregate limits.
  - ○ Self-financed candidates are also prohibited, after any given Election Day, from repaying outstanding loans the candidates make to their own campaigns in excess of $250,000.

Coordination

- • *Coordinated spending as a contribution:* Any expenditure made by a person other than a candidate or party will count as a contribution if it is coordinated with the candidate or party. Coordination is defined as a payment made in cooperation with, at the request or suggestion of, a candidate, candidate's agent or campaign, or party. This reiterates previous statute law. Congress also told the FEC to discard its current regulations and write new ones that do not require agreement or formal collaboration to establish coordination. The FEC's subsequent regulations covered all election-related communications disseminated within 120 days of an election if the person making the communication meets any one of a series of conduct standards, including sharing of a common vendor who makes use of material information about a campaign.

Source: Campaign Finance Institute. This summary was published previously in M. Malbin, ed. *Life After Reform (2003).*

APPENDIX 2

McConnell v. Federal Election Commission
Summary of the U.S. Supreme Court Decision

December 10, 2003
540 U.S. 93

The Bipartisan Campaign Reform Act's constitutionality was challenged by literally dozens of litigants immediately after the bill became law in a case that was consolidated under the name of *McConnell v. Federal Election Commission.* (Senator Mitch McConnell of Kentucky had led opposition to the bill in the U.S. Senate.) On December 10, 2003, the U.S. Supreme Court announced its decision upholding most of the new law. On many of the important issues relating to soft money and electioneering, the division was 5–4. The majority on these issues was made up of Justices Breyer, Ginsburg, O'Connor, Souter, and Stevens. Dissenting were Chief Justice Rehnquist and Justices Kennedy, Scalia, and Thomas.

The following brief summary of the Court's lengthy decision was released the same day by the Campaign Legal Center in Washington, DC. The Center was part of the legal team representing BCRA's congressional sponsors in the case. The summary is reprinted here with the Center's permission. A complete collection of court documents is available on the Center's website.

SUMMARY

The Court upheld the soft money and "electioneering communications" provisions of BCRA, emphasizing the dangers of large contributions to political parties, and of corporate and labor funding of campaign ads. Specifically, the Court upheld:

- The prohibition on the national parties' raising or spending soft money;
- The regulation of state parties' spending soft money on federal election activity;
- The ban on federal officeholders or candidates' raising or spending soft money;
- The prohibition on political parties' transferring or soliciting soft money for politically active, tax-exempt groups (construing this provision to apply only to soft money);
- The ban on state candidates' spending soft money on public communications that promote or attack federal candidates;

- The act's definition of "electioneering communication" as a broadcast;
- Advertisement mentioning a federal candidate, targeted at their electorate, and aired within thirty days of a primary or sixty days of a general election;
- The requirement that corporations and unions use only hard money (instead of soft money treasury funds) to pay for electioneering communications;
- The requirement that individuals disclose their spending on electioneering communications to the FEC;
- The requirement that coordinated electioneering communications be treated as contributions to candidates and parties;
- The statutory definition of "coordination," saying "Congress has always treated expenditures made after a wink or nod as coordinated";
- The new FCC requirements for candidate disclosure.

The Court held the following provisions "nonjusticiable" (that is, the justices declined to rule on the merits of the issue, generally because the issue was not yet ripe for judgment and/or because the plaintiffs lacked standing to sue):

- The increase in "hard money" contribution limits for individuals (lack of standing);
- The "Millionaires' Amendment" (lack of standing);
- The challenge to the FEC's coordination regulations (not ripe for adjudication).

The Court struck down:

- The provision prohibiting minors seventeen years and younger from making political contributions;
- The provision requiring parties to choose between making independent expenditures or coordinated expenditures on behalf of a candidate.

Appendices 3 through 5

The next three tables (3 through 5) are summaries prepared by the Campaign Finance Institute of regulations the Federal Election Commission adopted in 2002 and 2003 to implement the Bipartisan Campaign Reform Act. They include summaries of views about the issues that were expressed to the Federal Election Commission as the regulations were being considered. The regulations subsequently were challenged in court in the case of *Shays v. Federal Election Commission*. In September 2004 the U.S. District Court for the District of Columbia invalidated fifteen of the nineteen regulations challenged in this litigation. As of this writing, the FEC is appealing some of the court's holdings and writing new regulations (or taking other steps) to respond to others. However, the regulations summarized here were in effect for the 2004 election.

Appendix 3

Federal Election Commission Regulations for the Bipartisan Campaign Reform Act of 2002

Soft Money—Issues and Controversies

July 29, 2002

Provision of Law or Issue	Final FEC Regulation & Rationale	BCRA-Sponsors'/ Reform Groups' Views	Impact of FEC's Interpretation?
Restrictions on State & Local Party Soft Money Spending			
The Bipartisan Campaign Finance Reform Act (BCRA) prohibits national party committees from raising soft money. It also prohibits state and local parties (and associations of state and local candidates and officeholders) from spending soft money on federal election activities. These include several different activities each of which must be defined:			
1. Voter registration activity within 120 days of a federal election.	Voter registration is contacting individuals by phone or other individualized means to **assist** registration, including costs of printing and distributing information. (Does not include **encouragement** of registration in order to avoid subjecting small local committees and grassroots groups to Federal regulation.) §100.24(b)(1), §100.24(a)(2)	Should also include encouragement of voter registration by rallies and meetings.	Depends upon extent to which parties spend for activities generally encouraging registration as opposed to individualized contacts with voters to assist registration.

2. Voter identification activity. (Voter-ID)	Voter identification is creating or enhancing voter lists by verifying or adding information about the voter's likelihood of voting or voting for a specific candidate. (Does not include acquiring voter lists because parties also purchase these for fundraising and other party-building activities.)	Should include all voter ID activities, including acquisition of voting lists, to identify registered voters and to determine their preference for a party as well as a candidate.	Depends upon extent to which voter identification activity by state and local candidates is informally coordinated by state and local parties.
	Also does not include a communication (for Voter-ID) by an association of state or local candidates, referring only to state or local candidates, to avoid a "vast federalization of state and local [grassroots] activity without greater direction from Congress." §100.24(a)(4)	Should include communications by associations of state or local candidates. BCRA exempts certain public communications referring only to state or local candidates from the definition of federal election activity, but specifically does not exempt communications for Voter-ID or GOTV.	Depends upon extent to which parties spend on acquiring voting lists and determining party preferences as opposed to verifying or adding information to such lists on likelihood of voting and candidate preferences.
3. Get-out-the-vote (GOTV) activity.	GOTV is contacting registered voters by phone, in person, or other individualized means to assist them in voting. Includes, but not limited to, providing information about the polling process within 72 hours of the election and assisting in transportation to the polls. Does not include encouragement of voting.	Should also include encouragement of voting, and should not be limited to a specific period of time.	Depends upon extent to which parties spend funds on "encouragement" activities as opposed to direct individual assistance for GOTV, and extent to which the FEC limits the time period to which the regulation applies.

Provision of Law or Issue	Final FEC Regulation & Rationale	BCRA-Sponsors'/ Reform Groups' Views	Impact of FEC's Interpretation?
(3. *cont.*)	Also does not include a communication by an association of state or local candidates referring only to state or local candidates (see 2 above). **§100.24(a)(3)**	Should include communications by associations of state and local candidates (see 2 above).	Depends upon extent to which voter GOTV activity by state and local candidates is informally coordinated by state and local parties.
4. Public communication promoting or opposing a federal candidate, or party ("generic campaign activity") by means of broadcast, cable, or satellite communication, newspaper, magazine, outdoor advertising facility, mass mailing, or telephone bank to the general public, or any other form of general public political advertising.	Public communications do not include the Internet. (The Internet is not specified in the BCRA list.) Also, the Internet allows "almost limitless, inexpensive communication" and poses no threat of corruption. **§100.26**	The Internet is similar enough to the listed communications to be included as "any other form of general public political advertising." Could permit a new loophole for soft money as Internet communication develops and requires more funds.	Depends upon future development of Internet as a major source of spending for political communications.
5. Time Period for Voter-ID, GOTV, and Generic Campaign Activity, "in connection with an election in which a candidate for Federal office appears on the ballot."	The time period for these Federal Election Activities is from each State's earliest filing deadline for access to a primary, in some cases as late as the summer of election year, to the general election. (Tracks closely the BCRA's reference to a candidate's "appearance on the ballot.") **§100.24(a)(i), §100.24(b)(2)(I-iii)**	Should span from beginning to end of the two-year election cycle. (Consistent with current FEC policy requiring federal funds to partially finance similar activities over full election cycle.)	Depends upon extent to which parties spend on these kinds of activities during the period of time from the beginning of a two-year election cycle to the primary filing deadline in a state.

Restrictions on Raising Soft Money

The Bipartisan Campaign Reform Act (BCRA) places heavy restrictions on the fundraising activities of national and state/local party officials and federal candidates or officeholders.

6. National party officials and federal candidates or officeholders may not "solicit" or "direct" soft money (except in very limited circumstances) for federal or nonfederal elections. But state and local parties may not raise or spend soft money for federal elections.	Solicit or direct both mean "to ask." (In order to avoid "chilling" inquiry into the millions of innocent private political conversations that make up American politics, there must be no threat of FEC action against ambiguous requests for "support." Therefore, solicit or direct do not include "recommend" or "suggest.") § 300.2 (m, n)	Should also include "recommend" or "suggest" and be applied to a series of conversations to prevent fundraising designed to evade the law. [The FEC General Counsel's draft regulations used the broader phrase "to request or suggest or recommend" based on the Commission's solicitation restrictions on corporations and unions.]	Depends upon how broadly the FEC defines "ask," and on parties' and federal candidates' and officeholders' willingness to risk public criticism of alleged evasions of soft money bans.
7. Federal candidates and officeholders may however attend, speak, or be featured guest at state/local party fundraising events.	There is no restriction on what the candidate or officeholder can say at such events. (This partly reflects "constitutional concerns" regarding freedom of speech.) §300.64	The candidate or officeholder should not be allowed to solicit or direct soft money (as defined in 6 above) at the event.	Depends upon degree to which candidate or officeholder's solicitation or direction attracts additional funds from attendees who mainly pay or pledge in advance.

Provision of Law or Issue	Final FEC Regulation & Rationale	BCRA-Sponsors'/ Reform Groups' Views	Impact of FEC's Interpretation?
	Evading the Soft Money Restrictions		
	Under BCRA, individuals or organizations sponsored by national and State/local parties and Federal candidates and officeholders are subject to the same restriction as the sponsors themselves.		
8. Restrictions on national, state, or local parties and federal candidates and officeholders raising soft money apply to entities "directly or indirectly established, financed, maintained, or controlled" by those sponsors.	Directly or indirectly established, financed, maintained or controlled is determined by adapting the existing 10-factor test which the FEC uses to evaluate whether political committees are "affiliated" with one another to actions of sponsors and their agents. § 300.2 (c) (2)	The 10-factor test is too weak. Federal candidates and officeholders have set up separate federal leadership PACs without the PACs being judged as affiliated to the sponsors' campaign committees. Without a stronger test, including solicitation of funds, soft money leadership PACs might be allowed and "shadow parties" exploiting soft money could emerge.	Depends upon how the 10-factor test is applied in practice. FEC's General Counsel indicated that he agrees with legislative history showing Congress considers soft money leadership PACs to be controlled by federal candidates and officeholders. Commissioner Smith has declared that these groups will not be allowed to raise soft money.
9. Time period to be considered in assessing direct or indirect sponsorship of entities raising soft money.	The determination should be based on sponsor activities after November 6, 2002, the effective date of the law. (Prelegislation activity should not be penalized by retroactive enforcement.) § 300.2 (c) (3)	Permitting surrogates to launch shadow groups right before the law takes effect will make it harder to prevent evasion of the restriction.	Depends upon the FEC's aggressiveness in investigating the actual control of such groups after November 6, 2002.

APPENDIX 4

Federal Election Commission Regulations for the Bipartisan Campaign Reform Act of 2002 "Coordinated and Independent Expenditures"— Issues and Controversies

Under the Federal Election Campaign Act as amended by BCRA, a person who spends money for an election "in cooperation, consultation, or concert with, or at the request or suggestion of," a candidate or political party (or their agent) is deemed to have made a contribution to that candidate or party.

2 U.S.C. §441a(a)(7)(B)(i)-(ii). Unlike expenditures, the law limits the amounts of contributions—and forbids them from certain sources like corporations and labor unions. But what distinguishes such "coordinated" expenditures from independent or uncoordinated ones is the subject of ongoing debate. One side is concerned that too narrow a definition of coordination will permit too much potentially corrupting cooperation to escape from the law's contribution limits, while the other is concerned that too sweeping a definition will reach too much normal and legitimate consultation between officeholders and lobbying groups about legislation having nothing to do with political campaigning.

In 2000, the FEC issued regulations defining "coordinated communications." In BCRA, Congress concluded the rules were excessively narrow. It repealed them and mandated new ones that would no longer require "agreement or formal collaboration" to establish coordination. In addition, BCRA directed the FEC to address: (1) republication of campaign materials; (2) use of common vendors; (3) communications by a former employee of a candidate or political party; and (4) communications made after substantial discussion about the communication with a candidate or party. **Public Law 107-155 § 214(c) (Mar. 27, 2002).**

Issue	FEC Regulation & Rationale	Interested Parties' Views

A communication is "coordinated" with a candidate, party, or their agent, when it is paid for by another person and satisfies: (1) at least one "content standard," and (2) at least one "conduct standard." § 109.21(a).

Issue	FEC Regulation & Rationale	Interested Parties' Views
1. CONTENT: What types of content should be included in the "content standards"?	A public communication satisfies a content standard if it is "reasonably related to an election"; specifically if it:	
Dissemination, distribution, or republication of campaign materials	disseminates, distributes, or republishes campaign materials prepared by a candidate/ agent; **§ 109.21(c)(2)** OR	Outside groups almost unanimously supported this standard as mandated by BCRA's language.
Express advocacy	expressly advocates the election or defeat of a clearly identified candidate for federal office by using words like "vote for" and "vote against"; **§ 109.21(c)(3)** OR	All groups supported "express advocacy" as one of the content standards. (**Business, union,** and **nonprofit groups** generally favored making it the *sole* content standard, because they feared a broader standard would restrict their normal communications with candidates and officials, including lobbying, and be an unconstitutional burden on free speech. **Reform groups** said that making express advocacy the sole standard would ignore other coordinated "campaign ads" that do not use "vote for," "vote against" language, but can be constitutionally regulated to prevent corruption.)

Electioneering communications	is an electioneering communication, *i.e.*, a broadcast, cable, or satellite communication referring to a clearly identified federal candidate, targeting the relevant electorate, and occurring 60 days before a general election or 30 days before a primary; § 109.21(c)(1)	**Reform groups, unions,** and a **business group** maintained that this standard is required by BCRA's language. **Unions,** a **business group,** and some **nonprofits,** however, asserted that this BCRA standard is unconstitutional, given that it goes beyond express advocacy and curbs other speech concerning candidates.
	OR	
Other election-related communications	is another form of communication that: (1) is publicly distributed or disseminated 120 days or fewer before a general election or party primary, convention, or caucus; (2) refers to a political party or a clearly identified candidate for federal office; *and* (3) is directed to voters in the candidate's jurisdiction. § 109.21(c)(4)	**Reform groups** had proposed a broader dual standard covering: (1) communications disseminated within 30 days of a primary or 60 days of a general election and targeted to the relevant electorate (even if the candidate or party were not identified), and (2) communications similar to those in the FEC regulation, but including statements about the record, character, qualifications, and fitness of the candidate, and extending over a much longer time frame of at least 18 months. They argued that the second part of the standard would capture all coordination on likely campaign ads, while allowing legitimate coordination on issue-oriented true "lobbying ads," even if they also mentioned candidates. **Unions, nonprofits, political parties,** and **business groups** opposed the FEC regulation as an unconstitutional limitation on free speech, association, and lobbying of candidates and an invitation for the government to investigate innocent ads, which could chill advocacy.

Issue	FEC Regulation & Rationale	Interested Parties' Views
2. CONDUCT: What types of conduct should be included in the "conduct standards"?	A public communication satisfies a conduct standard (regardless of whether there is agreement or formal collaboration) if it:	
Request or suggestion	is created, produced, or distributed: (1) at the request or suggestion of a candidate/party/agent, or (2) at the suggestion of a person paying for the communication with the assent of the candidate/party/agent; **§ 109.21(d)(1)** OR	**Reform groups** supported this standard and saw inclusion of the second prong (candidate/party assent to others' suggestions) as an indispensable way of preventing circumvention of the first prong (requests or suggestions originated by the candidate/party). **Business groups, some nonprofits, unions, and political parties**, however, expressed concern that the terms "assent" and "suggestion" are vague and subjective, and that their effect would be to discourage citizens' and associations' legitimate contacts with candidates and officials, including lobbying.
Material involvement	reflects "material" involvement (*i.e.*, important to or influencing the communication) by a candidate/party/agent in decisions regarding the communication's content, audience, method, outlet, timing, frequency, size, or duration; **§ 109.21(d)(2)** OR	**Reform groups** thought that material involvement should extend to "discussions" as well as "decisions." They said it would be hard to prove that material involvement influenced "decisions" and argued that "discussions" of communication specifics alone would lead to de facto coordination. On the other side, **business groups, a nonprofit, and unions** wanted "material involvement" defined more narrowly to require control or significant influence over a communication.

Substantial discussion

is created, produced, or distributed after one or more "substantial discussions" about the communication between the person/agent paying for it and the candidate identified in the communication (or his party/agent), wherein information material to the communication about the candidate/party's campaign plans, projects, activities, or needs is conveyed to the spender; § 109.21(d)(3)

OR

Reform groups supported this standard as essential to prevent corrupting coordination. Business groups and a nonprofit maintained that terms such as "substantial" and "material" were vague, likely to inspire unfounded investigations, and liable to chill free speech and legitimate lobbying. Some advocated including language from the D.C. federal district court's *FEC v. Christian Coalition* decision, which requires that such discussions result in the candidate and the spender emerging as "partners or joint venturers."

Former employee or independent contractor

is paid for by a person (or his current employer) who—during the same election cycle—was an employee (or independent contractor) of the candidate identified in the communication (or his opponent/party/agent), *and* who conveys or makes use of information about campaign plans, projects, activities or needs, or used in services provided, that is material to the communication; § 109.21(d)(5)

OR

Reform groups argued that when a communication is paid for by a former employee/independent contractor, coordination should be presumed unless shown otherwise, since it will be practically impossible to prove he "made use of" or "conveyed" material information. They generally favored a defined list of strategic employees/contractors similar to the list of professional services performed by common vendors (see below). On the other hand, business groups, unions, a nonprofit, and political parties thought terms like "made use of" and "conveyed" would chill speech, lead to burdensome investigations, and handicap those seeking employment. They also argued that the applicable time frame of a full election cycle was too long—given the short-term usefulness of political campaign strategies.

Issue	FEC Regulation & Rationale	Interested Parties' Views
Common vendor	is created, produced, or distributed by a commercial vendor after that vendor (including owners, officers, or employees) has—during the same election cycle—provided one or more listed professional services to a candidate identified in the communication (or his opponent/party/agent), *and* the common vendor conveys or makes use of information about campaign plans, projects, activities, or needs that is material to the communication. § 109.21(d)(4) AND	As with former employees/independent contractors, **reform groups** suggested that coordination should be presumed unless shown otherwise in order to ensure adequate enforcement. Some **business, nonprofit, union,** and **political party** groups warned that elements of the rule would trigger baseless intrusive investigations of citizen groups and consultants, deter the latter from offering services to candidates and parties, and chill speech. They also argued that its time frame was unnecessarily long.
"Safe harbor" for responses to inquiries about legislative or policy issues	is not a candidate's or party's response to an inquiry about legislative or policy issues where there is no discussion of campaign plans, projects, activities, or needs. § 109.21(f)	**Unions, business groups,** and **nonprofits** supported this "safe harbor" for noncampaign communications as helpful for groups preparing voter guides and charts, and organizing candidate debates.
3. **AGENT:** What is an "agent" of a candidate or party?	An "agent" is a person with actual authority (either express or implied) given by a candidate or party to engage in any of a list of activities closely parallel to the conduct standards. § 109.3	**Reform groups** found this "actual authority" standard too narrow (as they had previously when the FEC adopted it for the soft money regulations). They maintained that it allows candidates or parties to coordinate communications with an outside spender by using persons without formal authority to sit in on discussions and convey important information to that spender. They wanted

such persons to also be treated as agents, unless they were under explicit instructions not to disclose that information and the candidate/party took reasonable steps to implement such instructions. On the other hand, **business groups**, **unions**, and **party organizations** found the FEC's actual authority standard too broad, because it includes as an agent a person who has authority over relevant activities, but who conveys information "beyond the scope" of his *particular* responsibility.

Restrictions on Coordinated/Independent Expenditures by Political Parties

• BCRA forbids parties from making both coordinated *and* independent expenditures after they have nominated their candidates. The FEC ruled that all national or state-established or maintained parties in a single party group are bound by this restriction. A decision by one member of the group to embark upon either coordinated or independent expenditures on behalf of a candidate restricts subsequent spending by other members. § 109.35. **Party organizations** objected that the regulation does not take into account the significant autonomy of different party committees, which could allow a single state or local party to determine the spending of an entire party group. **Reform groups** supported the regulation as both mandated by BCRA's language and necessary to prevent evasion of the restriction.

• Based on the above provision, the FEC ruled that the national committee of a political party can make independent expenditures in connection with a presidential general election (unless it is the presidential candidate's "authorized committee"). § 109.36. **Reform groups** opposed this regulation, which opens the door for national party committees to make independent expenditures in presidential campaigns, as a major policy change not specifically mandated by BCRA. They maintained that the relatively close relationship between national parties and presidential (as opposed to congressional) candidates, argued against allowing "independent" party spending in those contests.

APPENDIX 5

Federal Election Commission Regulations for the Bipartisan Campaign Reform Act of 2002 "Electioneering Communications"—Issues and Controversies

Under BCRA, funds from corporations (whether nonprofit or for-profit entities) and unions may not be used to pay for "electioneering communications," which are broadcast, cable, or satellite communications that: (1) refer to a clearly identified federal candidate; (2) are broadcast within 60 days before the general election of the candidate or within 30 days before the party primary, convention, or caucus that nominates the candidate; and (3) are targeted to the "relevant electorate," i.e., over 50,000 persons in the state or congressional district that the candidate seeks to represent. Exemptions are provided for news stories, commentaries, editorials, and candidate debates and forums. BCRA gives the FEC authority to make additional exemptions, so long as they do not "promote, support, attack, or oppose a federal candidate." All persons other than corporations or unions who pay more than $10,000 a year to produce and air electioneering communications must publicly disclose not only their spending, but also the names and addresses of all contributors of $1,000 or more.

Issue	FEC Regulation & Rationale	Interested Parties' Views
1. Should unpaid programming be exempt?	Unpaid programming (such as certain public service announcements) is exempt, based primarily on legislative history indicating Congress's focus on ads disseminated for a fee. §100.29(b)(3)(i)	**Nonprofits** and the National Association of Broadcasters supported exempting unpaid communications. **Reform groups** generally opposed the exemption because it would permit corporations that operate broadcast, cable, or satellite systems to distribute public service announcements aiding or damaging candidates, thereby evading the ban on corporate "electioneering."
2. Should communications referring to a law or bill by a "popular name" that includes the name of a candidate be exempt (if that is the sole reference to the candidate)?	Communications containing popular names, e.g., the "Senate McCain-Feingold Campaign Finance Reform Bill," are not exempt, because they may be crafted to promote, support, attack, or oppose a federal candidate. Also, it is unclear which names to include in a "popular name," given that candidates often associate themselves with various bills. Lobbyists can discuss legislation without reference to a federal candidate's name.	**BCRA sponsors** and **reform groups** opposed an exemption due to the lack of an objective standard to determine a bill's "popular name" given the great number of cosponsors for each bill. Advertisers, they argued, often contrive "popular names" linking candidates to popular or unpopular positions, for example, the "Bush tax cut" or the "Clinton health care plan." **Civil liberties groups, nonprofits**, and **unions** supported the creation of a well-defined exemption to preserve the constitutional rights of free speech and association, including effective lobbying.

Issue	FEC Regulation & Rationale	Interested Parties' Views
3. Should lobbying communications on executive or legislative matters, urging the public to contact candidates, be exempt?	Lobbying communications are not exempt. The FEC considered four options for a narrow lobbying exemption. These included communications which did not contain: (1) references to the candidate's past or present positions on policy issues or legislation; (2) references to the candidate's positions, character, and fitness for office and candidacy; (3) explicit "vote for" or "vote against" statements; and (4) statements that "promote, support, attack, or oppose" a candidate. However, all of these alternatives would allow communications that could well be understood to "promote, support, attack, or oppose" a candidate, which are prohibited by the law.	BCRA sponsors and reform groups supported an alternative exemption (even narrower than those proffered by the FEC) for communications where the only reference to a candidate is a statement urging the public to contact "your Senator," "your Congressman," or "your Member of Congress," and ask him or her to take a particular position, without mentioning the candidate's political party. Unions, civil liberties groups, and nonprofits supported certain exemptions they considered consistent with constitutional free speech protections and opposed others they thought hindered effective lobbying. Some business and conservative groups opposed any attempts to create any lobbying exceptions, arguing that the law's curbs on electioneering are inherently unconstitutional.
4. Should communications sponsored by tax-exempt religious, educational, and charitable organizations under § 501(c)(3) of the Internal Revenue Code be exempt?	Communications paid for by 501(c)(3) organizations are exempt, because the IRS already prohibits their engagement in political campaigns, and subjecting them to regulation could discourage their participation in beneficial activities, such as grassroots advocacy. §100.29(c)(6)	Nonprofits supported an exemption, maintaining that the tax code already prohibits 501(c)(3)s from engaging in activities in support of or opposition to a candidate, and feared FEC investigations under BCRA would chill the effectiveness of charitable organization with finite resources. Reform groups opposed a blanket exemption, citing legislative history indicating that BCRA does not treat 501(3)(c)s and for-profit corporations differently and saying that they saw a potential for abuse.

5. Should communications by State and local candidates be exempt?	Communications by state and local candidates that refer to federal candidates are exempt, provided the communications do not promote, support, attack, or oppose a federal candidate. This is consistent with another provision of BCRA that bans corporate and union financing of communications by state and local candidates that promote, support, attack, or oppose federal candidates. §100.29(c)(5)	**BCRA sponsors** and **reform groups** supported this exemption, based on the BCRA provision banning corporate/union financing of communications by state/local candidates promoting, supporting, attacking or opposing federal candidates.
6. Should Internet communications be exempt?	Internet communications, including webcasts (unless simultaneously broadcast over the TV or radio), are exempt because legislative history indicates that Congress did not intend to regulate electioneering communications over the Internet. While some maintain that as the Internet develops, it could come to be used like radio and television, it is premature to craft a regulation responding to unknown future advances. §100.29(c)(1)	**BCRA sponsors** and **reform groups** disagreed with a blanket exemption, stating that it did not give the FEC flexibility to restrict Internet communications, such as webcasting and video streaming, that may someday be the functional equivalent of radio and television broadcasts. **Business, civil liberties,** and some **nonprofit groups** supported a broad exception for the Internet to ensure its unfettered growth by preventing premature regulation.

Issue	FEC Regulation & Rationale	Interested Parties' Views
7. Should presidential candidates be exempt from BCRA's "targeting" requirements, meaning that electioneering communications restrictions apply to them nationwide throughout the yearlong nominating process?	BCRA's targeting requirements apply to presidential, as well as Congressional, candidates. Therefore, restrictions come into play for ads targeted to the relevant state electorate 30 days before a State primary, caucus or convention, and national electorate 30 days before and during a national nominating convention. Although BCRA's language is confusing, a one-year nationwide blackout for all corporate and union financed electioneering ads during a presidential election would raise "constitutional concerns." **§100.29(b)(3)(ii)**	Nearly all groups supported this decision as not inconsistent with the law and necessary to prevent a nationwide advertising blackout during presidential election years.

Other FEC Decisions

- No exemption for communications that refer to a clearly identified candidate in the context of promoting a candidate's business, including a professional practice, because such communications could well be considered to support or oppose the candidate, even if they also served a business purpose.
- No exemption for communications that promote a state or local ballot initiative or referendum because they could well be understood to promote, support, attack, or oppose federal candidates. (Initiatives and referenda have become increasingly linked with the federal candidates who support or oppose them.)
- No exemption for public service announcements for which a distribution fee has been paid because such TV and radio communications could "promote, support, attack, or oppose" candidates, contrary to BCRA.

Works Cited

Abrams, Jim. 2002. "Wide Differences on Likely Effects of Campaign Finance Legislation." *Associated Press State and Local Wire*, 19 March.

Alexander, Herbert E. 1971. "Financing Presidential Campaigns." In *History of American Presidential Elections, 1789–1968*, edited by Arthur M. Schlesinger, Jr. New York: Chelsea House.

———. 1983. *Financing the 1980 Election*. Lexington, MA: D.C. Heath and Company.

———. 1999. "Spending in the 1996 Elections." In *Financing the 1996 Election*, edited by John C. Green. Armonk, NY: M.E. Sharpe.

Alexander, Herbert E., and Brian A. Haggerty. 1987. *Financing the 1984 Election*. Lexington, MA: D.C. Heath and Company.

Anderson, Shea. 2004. "Wanted: Aspiring PAC Campers." AlbuquerqueTribune.com, 19 November. Available from http://www.albuquerquetribune.com.

Annenberg Public Policy Center. 2001. "Issue Advertising in the 1999–2000 Election Cycle." Annenberg Public Policy Center of the University of Pennsylvania.

Armendariz, Agustin. 2004. "The Limits of Charity." Center for Public Integrity, 25 October. Available from http://www.publicintegrity.org/report.asx?aid = 404.

Armendariz, Agustin, and Aron Pilhofer. 2005. "McCain-Feingold Changes State Party Spending: Fundraising Dips, Ad Buys Plummet in First Election After Campaign Reform." Center for Public Integrity, 26 May. Available from http://www.publicintegrity.org/partylines/report.aspx?aid = 690&sid = 300.

Associated Press. 2003. "Democrats Start Presidential Fund." *Associated Press State and Local Wire*, 31 January.

———. 2004. "Nation's Gun Lobby Creating News Corporation." *Associated Press State and Local Wire*, 16 April.

Balz, Dan, and Thomas B. Edsall. 2004. "Unprecedented Efforts to Mobilize Voters Begin." *Washington Post*, 1 November, A1.

Barakat, Matthew. 2004. "Wolf Alleges His Challenger Broke Law." *Richmond Times Dispatch*, 29 October.

Bart, John, and James Meador. 2004. "The More You Spend, the Less They Listen: The South Dakota U.S. Senate Race." In *The Last Hurrah? Soft Money and Issue Advocacy in the 2002 Congressional Election*, edited by David B. Magleby and J. Quin Monson. Washington, DC: Brookings Institution Press.

Barth, Jay, and Janine Parry. 2003. "Provincialism, Personalism, and Politics: Campaign Spending and the 2002 U.S. Senate Race in Arkansas." In *The Noncandidate Campaign*, edited by David B. Magleby and J. Quin Monson: American Political Science Association. Original edition, 30 July.

271

Bedlington, Anne H., and Michael J. Malbin. 2003. "The Party as an Extended Network: Members Giving to Each Other and to Their Parties." In *Life After Reform: When the Bipartisan Campaign Reform Act Meets Politics*, edited by Michael J. Malbin. Lanham, MD: Rowman & Littlefield.

Biersack, Robert [Press Officer, Federal Election Commission]. 2004. Interview by David Magleby, 14 November.

Biersack, Robert S., and Marianne Holt. 2004. "Interest Groups and Federal Campaign Finance: Choices and Consequences in a New Era." In *The Interest Group Connection*, edited by Paul S. Herrnson, Ronald G. Shaiko, and Clyde Wilcox. Washington, DC: Congressional Quarterly.

Billings, Erin P. 2004. "Buoyed DCCC Raises Money Goal." *Roll Call*, 22 June.

Birnbaum, Jeffrey H. 1996. "Political Money: The Rules are Warped, Not Just Bent." *Time*. Available from http://www.cnn.com/ALLPOLITICS/1996/analysis/time/9610/21/main.shtml.

Boatright, Robert G., Michael J. Malbin, Mark J. Rozell, Richard M. Skinner, and Clyde Wilcox. 2003. "BCRA's Impact on Interest Groups and Advocacy Organizations." In *Life After Reform: When the Bipartisan Campaign Reform Act Meets Politics*, edited by Michael J. Malbin. Lanham, MD: Rowman & Littlefield.

Bolton, Alexander. 2004a. "Democrats Feel Pressure to Give More to House Caucus." *The Hill*, 15 July.

———. 2004b. "GOP Leaders Reverse Field, Build a New 527 Network." *The Hill*, 19 May.

———. 2004c. "Meet the Leader, only $25K: Senate Dems Sell Lobbyists Access for the Maximum." *The Hill*, 29 April.

———. 2004d. "The NRCC Closes in on $1M." *The Hill*, 1 April.

Bonaiuto, Dominic, and Anne Keisman. 2004. "Socas Targets Wolf in 10th." *TimesCommunity.com*, 5 October.

Branch-Brioso, Karen. 2003. "Parties will Collect Money but Shift Focus Under Campaign Law." *St. Louis Post-Dispatch*, 11 December.

Brown, Clifford W. Jr., Lynda W. Powell, and Clyde Wilcox. 1995. *Serious Money: Fundraising and Contributing in Presidential Nomination Campaigns*. New York: Cambridge University Press.

Buell, Emmett H. Jr. 1996. "The Invisible Primary." In *In Pursuit of the White House: How We Choose Our Presidential Nominees*, edited by William G. Mayer. Chatham, NJ: Chatham House.

Bumiller, Elizabeth, and Kate Zernike. 2004. "President Urges Outside Groups to Halt All Ads." *New York Times*, 24 August, A5, late edition.

Bush-Cheney Campaign and the Republican National Committee. 2004. "Joint Statement by Bush-Cheney Campaign Chairman Marc Racicot and RNC Chairman Ed Gillespie on Today's FEC Ruling on 527 Groups." Press release. 13 May.

Business Week Online. 2004. "A Union Chief's Bold New Tack," 28 July.

Campaign Finance Institute. 2004a. "CFI Wrap-Up Analysis of Primary Funding: Funds Doubled, Small Donations Quadrupled—But Mostly After Nominations Decided." Press release. Campaign Finance Institute, 4 October. Available from http://www.CFInst.org/pr/100404.html.

———. 2004b. "Money and Politics in the 2004 Primaries" [Transcript of an event held at the National Press Club]. Campaign Finance Institute, 27 February. Available from http://www.CFInst.org/transcripts/022704.html.

Campaign Finance Institute Task Force on Disclosure. 2001. "Issue Ad Disclosure: Recommendations for a New Approach." Campaign Finance Institute. February.

Campaign Finance Institute Task Force on Financing Presidential Nominations. 2003. "Participation, Competition, Engagement: How to Revive and Improve Public Funding for Presidential Nomination Politics." Washington, DC: Campaign Finance Institute.

———. 2005. "So the Voters May Choose: Reviving the Presidential Matching Fund System." Washington, DC: Campaign Finance Institute.

Canon, David T. 1993. "Sacrificial Lambs or Strategic Politicians? Political Amateurs in U.S. House Elections." *American Journal of Political Science*, 37:4; pp. 1119–1141.

Cantwell, Maria. 2002. "Statement of Senator Maria Cantwell (as prepared) on Campaign Finance

Reform." Press release. 20 March. Available from http://cantwell.senate.gov/news/releases/ 2002_03_20_CFR.html.

Carney, Eliza Newlin. 2004a. "The 527 Phenomenon; Big Bucks for Upstairs." *National Journal*, 13 December.

———. 2004b. "In the Money." *National Journal*, 10 July.

———. 2004c. "Truth, Justice, and the 527 Way?" *National Journal*, 24 January.

CBS News Poll. 2003. "One Year Away: The 2004 Presidential Election." CBS News, 10 December. Available from http://www.cbsnews.com/sections/opinion/polls/main500160.shtml.

Center for Responsive Politics. 2004. "2004 Election Outcome: Money Wins." Center for Responsive Politics, 20 November. Available from http://www.opensecrets.org/pressreleases/04results.asp.

China Daily. 2004. "Kerry Dinner Courts Clinton, Carter, Gore." *China Daily*, 26 March. Available from http://www.chinadaily.com.cn/english/doc/2004-03/26/content_318286.htm.

Christensen, Rob. 2004. "Clean-up Clause Bears Fruit." *News & Observer (Raleigh)*, 29 February.

Cillizza, Chris. 2003a. "Critics Slam 'Demzilla.'" *Roll Call*, 5 June.

———. 2003b. "GOP Group Joins Soft Money Fray." *Roll Call*, 24 November.

———. 2003c. "NRCC Raises More, Spends Most of It." *Roll Call*, 16 July.

———. 2004a. "527s Mull New Role in '06." *Roll Call*, 15 November.

———. 2004b. "Gore Steers $6M to '04 Campaign." *Roll Call*, 29 April.

———. 2004c. "Reynolds Creates a 'New' NRCC." *Roll Call*, 4 March.

Clymer, Adam. 2001. "Black Caucus Members Find Themselves Courted Heavily in Soft Money Fight." *New York Times*, 12 July, A1, late edition.

Cochran, John. 2001. "'Rival Campaign Finance Bills' Prospects in House May Hinge on Allaying Black Caucus' Concerns." *Congressional Quarterly Weekly Report*, 23 June.

Common Cause. 2000. "Under the Radar: The Attack of 'Stealth PACs' on Our Nation's Elections." Common Cause.

Congressional Record. 1987a. 100th Cong., 1st sess., vol. 133, issue no. 90, p. S7651, 4 June.

———. 1987b. 100th Cong., 1st sess., vol. 133, issue no. 32, p. S2685, 3 March.

———. 2001. 107th Cong., 1st sess., vol. 147, issue no. 37, p. S2548, 20 March.

———. 2002a. 107th Cong., 2nd sess., vol. 148, issue no. 13, p. H430, 13 February.

———. 2002b. 107th Cong., 2nd sess., vol. 148, issue no. 13, p. H431, 13 February.

Cook, Charlie. 2004. "Color the Presidential Battlefield Light Red." *National Journal*, 18 September.

Cornfield, Michael. 2004. *Politics Moves Online: Campaigning and the Internet.* New York: The Century Foundation Press.

Corrado, Anthony. 1994. "The Politics of Cohesion: The Role of National Party Committees in the 1992 Election." In *The State of the Parties*, edited by John C. Green and Daniel Shea. Lanham, MD: Rowman & Littlefield.

———. 2002. "Party Finance in the 2000 Elections: The Federal Role of Soft Money Financing." *Arizona State Law Journal* 34 (4).

Couch, Mark P. 2004. "Dems Get Boost from the South." *Denver Post*, 3 June.

Cummings, Jeanne. 2003. "A Hard Sell on Soft Money." *Wall Street Journal*, 2 December, A4.

———. 2004a. "Companies Pare Political Donations." *Wall Street Journal*, 7 June, A3.

———. 2004b. "Those 527 Fund-Raisers Prove Resilient." *Wall Street Journal*, 6 December, A4.

Damas, Raul [National Grassroots Director, Republican National Committee], interview by J. Quin Monson and Betsey Gimbel, Washington, DC, 13 December 2004.

Daschle, Tom. 1998. "Speech on the Floor of the Senate, February 25, 1998." News Hour with Jim Lehrer: PBS. Available from http://www.pbs.org/newshour/bb/congress/jan-june98/campaign_ 2-25.html.

Davis, Patrick [NRSC Political Director], interview by J. Quin Monson and Richard Hawkins, Washington, DC, 11 November 2004.

Democratic National Committee. 2004a. "Democratic National Committee Ends Year In Best Financial Shape Ever." Press release. 7 January.

———. 2004b. "Democratic News: 2004 Progress Report." Electronic Newsletter. 10 December.

———. 2004c. "DNC Finance: Patriots 2003–2004." Democratic National Committee. Available from http://www.democrats.org/pdfs/patriots/pdf.

———. 2004d. "DNC Fundraising Continues to Break Records." Press release. 10 May.

Democratic Senatorial Campaign Committee. 2004a. "DSCC Outraises NRSC by Near 2-to-1 Margin in June." Press release. 8 July.

———. 2004b. "DSCC Supporters: Clicking Away to Victory." Press release. 5 October.

Devine, Thomas A. [Senior Strategist, Kerry for President and Partner, Shrum Devine Donilon]. 2005. Telephone interview by Anthony Corrado, 11 January.

Drinkard, Jim. 2004. "Outside Political Group Full of Party Insiders." *USA Today*, 28 June.

Dulio, David A., Candice J. Nelson, and James A. Thurber. 2000. "Introduction." In *Crowded Airways: Campaign Advertising in Elections*, edited by Candice J. Nelson, David A. Dulio, and James A. Thurber. Washington, DC: Brookings Institution Press.

Dwyre, Diana, and Victoria Farrar-Myers. 2001. *Legislative Labyrinth: Congress and Campaign Finance Reform*. Washington, DC: CQ Press.

Dwyre, Diana, and Robin Kolodny. 2002. "Throwing Out the Rule Book: Party Financing of the 2000 Elections." In *Financing the 2000 Election*, edited by David B. Magleby. Washington, DC: Brookings Institution Press.

———. 2003. "National Parties after BCRA." In *Life After Reform: When the Bipartisan Campaign Reform Act Meets Politics*, edited by Michael J. Malbin. Lanham, MD: Rowman & Littlefield.

Dyke, James [Press Secretary of the Republican National Committee]. 2003. Telephone interview by J. Quin Monson, 23 January.

Edsall, Thomas B. 2002. "New Ways to Harness Soft Money in Works." *Washington Post*, 25 August, A1.

———. 2003a. "Dean Taps into Elites in Early Fundraising." *Washington Post*, 5 May.

———. 2003b. "Liberals Meeting to Set '04 Strategy." *Washington Post*, 25 May, A6.

———. 2004a. "GOP Creating Own Groups." *Washington Post*, 25 May.

———. 2004b. "McCain-Feingold Helps GOP." *Washington Post*, 7 February.

———. 2004c. "Republican Soft Money Groups Find Business Reluctant to Give." *Washington Post*, 7 June.

———. 2004d. "Republicans Name 62 Who Raised Big Money." *Washington Post*, 1 July.

———. 2004e. "Swift Boat Group's Tally: $6.7 Million." *Washington Post*, 11 September.

Edsall, Thomas B., and Sarah Cohen. 2003. "Kerry Leads Democratic Hopefuls in Funds Raised." *Washington Post*, 16 April.

Edsall, Thomas B., Sarah Cohen, and James V. Grimaldi. 2004. "Pioneers Fill War Chest, then Capitalize." *Washington Post*, 16 May.

Edsall, Thomas B., and James V. Grimaldi. 2004. "On Nov. 2, GOP Got More Bang for its Billion, Analysis Shows." *Washington Post*, 30 December, A7.

Edsall, Thomas B., and Jim VandeHei. 2004. "Kerry Aims to Accept Public Funding, Reversal Possible if Bush Rejects Money." *Washington Post*, 13 July, A9.

Edsall, Thomas B., and David VonDrehle. 2003. "Republicans Have Huge Edge in Campaign Cash." *Washington Post*, 14 February.

Eilperin, Juilet. 2000. "Secret, Unrestricted Gifts Finance New GOP Groups." *Washington Post*, 8 January, A1.

Espo, David. 2004. "Ad Buying Provides Clues on Competitive House Races." *Associated Press and Local Wire*, 9 September.

Farhi, Paul. 2004a. "Parties Square Off in a Database Duel." *Washington Post*, 20 July.

———. 2004b. "Second Guessing Birds of a Feather Flocking Together." *Washington Post*, 30 July, A21.

———. 2004c. "Small Donors Grow into Big Political Force." *Washington Post*, 3 May.

Federal Election Commission. 1998. "Advisory Opinion," pp. 1997–2021.

———. 2002. "Party Fundraising Reaches $1.1 Billion in 2002 Election Cycle." Press release. 18 December.

———. 2004a. "Campaign Guide—Congressional Candidates and Committees." May.

———. 2004b. "Party Financial Activity Summarized." Press release. 14 December.

———. 2004c. "Party Fundraising Continues to Grow." Press release. 6 August.

———. 2005a. "PAC Activity Increases for 2004 Elections." Press release. 13 April.

———. 2005b. "Party Financial Activity Summarized for the 2004 Election Cycle." Press release. 14 March.

Fournier, Ron. 2003. "Dean Backing Off Spending Limit Promise." *Rutland Herald*, 15 August.

Francia, Peter L., John C. Green, Paul S. Herrnson, Lynda W. Powell, and Clyde Wilcox. 2003. *The Financiers of Congressional Elections*. New York: Columbia University Press.

Freedman, Paul, Michael Franz, and Kenneth Goldstein. 2004. "Campaign Advertising and Democratic Citizenship." *American Journal of Political Science* 48 (3).

Friel, Dennis [Field Director of National Education Association]. 2004. Interview by Kelly D. Patterson, 4 November.

Frontrunner. 2004. "Clinton to Combine Book Tour, Democratic Fundraising Events." *Frontrunner*, 16 June.

Gerber, Robin. 1999. "Building to Win, Building to Last: AFL-CIO Cope Takes on the Republican Congress." In *After the Revolution: PACs, Lobbies, and the Republican Congress*, edited by Robert Biersack, Paul S. Herrnson, and Clyde Wilcox. New York: Longman.

Gerstein, Josh. 2005. "Power Struggle Grips Club for Growth." *New York Sun*, 2 February.

Getter, Lisa. 2004. "With the 527s, New Power Players Take Position." *Los Angeles Times*, 1 November, A16.

Gitell, Seth. 2003. "The Democratic Party Suicide Bill." *Atlantic Monthly* 292 (1): 106–113.

Glover, Mike. 1999. "Bush Says He'll Forgo Matching Funds." *Associated Press State and Local Wire*, 15 July.

Green, Donald. 2003. "The Need for Federal Regulation of State Party Activity." In *Inside the Campaign Finance Battle*, edited by Anthony Corrado, Thomas E. Mann, and Trevor Potter. Washington, DC: Brookings Institution Press.

Green, Donald P., and Alan S. Gerber. 2004. *Get Out the Vote! How to Increase Voter Turnout*. Washington, DC: Brookings Institution Press.

Green, John C., and Nathan S. Bigelow. 2002. "The 2000 Presidential Nominations: The Costs of Innovation." In *Financing the 2000 Election*, edited by David B. Magleby. Washington, DC: Brookings Institution Press.

Greenhouse, Steven. 2002. "Political Director of Labor Federation to Quit Post." *New York Times*, 5 August.

Grimaldi, James V., and Thomas B. Edsall. 2004. "Super Rich Step Into Political Vacuum." *Washington Post*, 17 October, A14.

Haberman, Maggie. 2004. "Clinton Sends Out Fund-Raising E-Mail, Set to Campaign in Pennsylvania." *Daily News*, 21 October.

Hadley, Arthur T. 1976. *The Invisible Primary*. Englewood Cliffs, NJ: Prentice-Hall.

Harshbarger, Scott. 2001. "Statement of Common Cause President Scott Harshbarger on 'Millionaires' Amendment' to McCain-Feingold." Press release. Common Cause, 20 March. Available from http://www.commoncause.org/publications/march01/032001st.htm.

Harwood, David. 2004. "Elections System a Failure." *Denver Post*, 31 October, p. E4.

Harwood, John. 2004. "New Machine: In Fallout from Campaign Law, Liberal Groups Work Together." *Wall Street Journal*, 27 July, p. A1.

Hill, Francis. 2001. "Softer Money: Exempt Organizations and Campaigns." In *The Exempt Organization Tax Review*. April: 50.

Hitt, Greg, and Tom Hamburger. 2002. "New Campaign Finance Law Restores PAC's Appeal." *Wall Street Journal*, 29 July.

Hosenball, Mark, Michael Isikoff, and Holly Bailey. 2004. "The Secret Money War." *Newsweek*, 20 September, p. 22.

Hula, Kevin. 1999. *Lobbying Together: Interest Group Coalitions in Legislative Politics*. Washington, DC: Georgetown University Press.

Jacobson, Gary C. 2001. "Congress: Elections and Stalemate." In *The Elections of 2000*, edited by Michael Nelson. Washington, DC: Congressional Quarterly Press.

———. 2003. "Terror, Terrain, and Turnout: Explaining the 2002 Midterm Elections." *Political Science Quarterly*, 118 (Spring): 21.

———. 2004. *The Politics of Congressional Elections*. 6th ed. New York: Longman.

———. 2005. "The Congress: The Structural Basis of Republican Success." In *The Elections of 2004*, edited by Michael Nelson. Washington, DC: Congressional Quarterly Press.

Jacobson, Gary C., and Samuel Kernell. 1983. *Strategy and Choice in Congressional Elections*. 2nd ed. New Haven: Yale University Press.

Janofsky, Michael. 2003. "Foes of Bush Form PAC in Bid to Defeat Him." *Washington Post*, 8 August, A11.

Jones, Jeffrey M. 2004. "How Americans Voted." Gallup News Service, 5 November. Available from http://gallup.com/poll/content/print.aspx?ci=13957.

Justice, Glen. 2004a. "The 2004 Campaign: Campaign Finance; Republicans Rush to Form New Finance Groups." *New York Times*, 29 May.

———. 2004b. "Advocacy Groups Reflect on Their Role in the Election." *New York Times*, 5 November.

———. 2004c. "Kerry Kept Money Coming with Internet as his ATM." *New York Times*, 6 November, A12.

———. 2005. "Young Bush Fund-Raisers are Courted by the GOP." *New York Times*, 22 January, A11.

Kane, Paul. 2004a. "DSCC Turns to Retiring Senators." *Roll Call*, 4 May.

———. 2004b. "Kerry Transfers Surplus Money." *Roll Call*, 22 September.

Kaplan, Fred. 2002. "Soft Money Watch; It's Apollo Showtime for Democrats." *Boston Globe*, 24 April, A3.

Kaplan, Jonathan. 2004. "RNC Offers 'Super-Ranger' Status." *The Hill*, 18 May.

Katz, David [Director of the Pennsylvania Democratic Coordinated Campaign]. 2004. Telephone interview by Raymond J. La Raja, 11 November.

Keen, Judy, and Richard Bendetto. 2004. "Team Began Planning for Election Soon After 9/11." *USA Today*, 4 November, A5.

Kolodny, Robin, and Diana Dwyre. 1998. "Party-Orchestrated Activities for Legislative Party Goals: Campaigns for Majorities in the U.S. House of Representatives in the 1990s." *Party Politics* 4 (3): 275–295.

Kranish, Michael. 2003. "Kerry Says He Might Exceed Spending Limit, Would Follow Suit if Dean Rejects Public Financing." *Boston Globe*, 11 September.

Krasno, Jonathan S., and Frank Sorauf. 2003. "Why Soft Money Has Not Strengthened Parties." In *Inside the Campaign Finance Battle*, edited by Anthony Corrado, Thomas E. Mann, and Trevor Potter. Washington, DC: Brookings Institution Press.

La Raja, Raymond J. 2002. "Expert Witness Declaration Filed for the Plaintiffs in McConnell v. Federal Election Commission." Washington, DC District Court for the District of Columbia. 23 September.

———. 2003a. "State Parties and Soft Money: How Much Party Building?" In *The State of the Parties: The Changing Role of Contemporary American Parties*, edited by John C. Green and Rick Farmer. Lanham, MD: Rowman & Littlefield.

———. 2003b. "State Political Parties After BCRA." In *Life After Reform: When the Bipartisan Campaign Reform Act Meets Politics*, edited by Michael J. Malbin. Lanham, MD: Rowman & Littlefield.

———. 2003c. "Why Soft Money Has Strengthened Parties." In *Inside the Campaign Finance Battle*, edited by Anthony Corrado, Thomas E. Mann, and Trevor Potter. Washington, DC: Brookings Institution Press.

La Raja, Raymond J., and Elizabeth Jarvis-Shean. 2001. "Assessing the Impact of a Ban on Soft Money: Spending in the 2000 Elections." Berkeley, CA: Institute of Governmental Studies and Citizens Research Foundation, 6 July.

Lakely, James G. 2003. "Clinton, Hip Hop, to Share Billing at DNC Fund-raiser." *Washington Times*, 22 October.

Lane, Charles, and Thomas B. Edsall. 2002. "Campaign Finance Fight Not Over; Having Lost on Hill, Opponents Prepare Court Challenge." *Washington Post*, 22 March.

LaPierre, Wayne. 2002. "Deposition of Plaintiffs, National Rifle Association of America and National Rifle Association Political Victory Fund." Washington, DC, District Court for the District of Columbia, 3 September.

Lawrence, Jill. 2000. "Unions Push Turnout in Key States for Gore." *New York Times*, 30 October, A4.

Magleby, David B. 2000a. "Dictum Without Data: The Myth of Issue Advocacy and Party Building." Center for the Study of Elections and Democracy, Brigham Young University, 13 November.

———, ed. 2000b. *Outside Money: Soft Money and Issue Advocacy in the 1998 Congressional Elections*. Lanham, MD: Rowman & Littlefield.

———. 2002a. "A High-Stakes Election." In *Financing the 2000 Election*, edited by David B. Magleby. Washington, DC: Brookings Institution Press.

———, ed. 2002b. *The Other Campaign: Soft Money and Issue Advocacy in the 2000 Congressional Elections*. Lanham, MD: Rowman & Littlefield.

Magleby, David B., and J. Quin Monson. 2004. "The Consequences of Noncandidate Spending, With a Look to the Future." In *The Last Hurrah? Soft Money and Issue Advocacy in the 2002 Congressional Election*, edited by David B. Magleby and J. Quin Monson. Washington, DC: Brookings Institution Press.

Magleby, David B., and Kelly D. Patterson. 2000. "Consultants and Direct Democracy: The Politics of Citizen Control." In *Campaign Warriors: The Role of Political Consultants in Elections*, edited by James A. Thurber and Candice J. Nelson. Washington, DC: Brookings Institution Press.

Malbin, Michael J. 2004. "Political Parties Under the Post-McConnell Bipartisan Campaign Reform Act." *Election Law Journal* 3 (2): 177–191.

———, ed. 2003. *Life After Reform: When The Bipartisan Campaign Reform Act Meets Politics*. Lanham, MD: Rowman & Littlefield.

Malbin, Michael J., Clyde Wilcox, Mark Rozell, and Richard Skinner. 2002. "New Interest Group Strategies: A Preview of Post McCain-Feingold Politics?" *Election Law Journal* 1 (4): 541–556.

Mann, Thomas E. 2004. "So Far, So Good on Campaign Reform." *Washington Post*, 1 March.

Mann, Thomas E., and Norman J. Ornstein. 2004. "Separating Myth from Reality in McConnell v. FEC." *Election Law Journal* 3 (2): 291–297.

Mayer, Jane. 2004. "The Money Man." *New Yorker*, 18 October, 176.

Mayer, William G., and Andrew E. Busch. 2004. *The Frontloading Problem in Presidential Nominations*. Washington, DC: Brookings Institution Press.

McAuliffe, Terrence [Chairman of the Democratic National Committee]. 2004. Telephone interview by Anthony Corrado, 16 December.

McCain, John, and Russell Feingold. 2004. "A Campaign Finance Law That Works." *Washington Post*, 23 October, p. A22.

McConnell, Mitch. 2003. "Role of Federal Officials in State Party Fund-Raising." In *Inside the Campaign Finance Battle: Court Testimony on the New Reforms*, edited by Anthony Corrado, Thomas E. Mann, and Trevor Potter. Washington, DC: Brookings Institution Press.

McGahn, Donald. 2005. "Comments to the Campaign Finance Institute." National Press Club, Washington, DC, 14 January.

Memmott, Mark. 2004. " 'Tagline' Could Alter Tone of Ad." *USA Today*, 10 March, A4.

Mendelberg, Tali. 2001. *The Race Card: Campaign Strategy, Implicit Messages, and the Norm of Equality.* Princeton: Princeton University Press.

Milkis, Sidney M. 2003. "Parties versus Interest Groups." In *Inside the Campaign Finance Battle,* edited by Anthony Corrado, Thomas E. Mann, and Trevor Potter. Washington, DC: Brookings Institution Press.

Monson, J. Quin. 2004. "Get on TeleVision vs. Get On The Van: GOTV and the Ground War in 2002." In *The Last Hurrah? Soft Money and Issue Advocacy in the 2002 Congressional Elections,* edited by David B. Magleby and J. Quin Monson. Washington, DC: Brookings Institution Press.

Moore, Steven [Club for Growth President]. 2004. Interview by David B. Magleby and Richard Hawkins, Washington, D.C., 5 November.

MoveOn.org. 2003. "No Candidate Wins Majority in MoveOn.org PAC's First-Ever Democratic Online 'Primary.'" Press release. 27 June.

Mullins, Brody. 2004a. "Bush '04 Squeezes GOP 527s." *Roll Call,* 23 June.

———. 2004b. "Greenwood Named President of Biotechnology Association." *Roll Call,* 22 July.

Mutch, Robert E. 1988. *Campaigns, Congress, and Courts: The Making of Federal Campaign Finance Law.* New York: Praeger Publishers.

Nagourney, Adam. 2003. "In the First Mile of a Marathon, Kerry Emerges as a Front-Runner." *New York Times,* 26 February.

Nielsen Monitor-Plus and the University of Wisconsin Advertising Project. 2004. "Over Half a Million TV Spots Have Been Aired in the 2004 Presidential Race." Press release. 27 August.

New York Times. 1912a. "$1,535,000 from Corporations to Colonel in 1904." *New York Times,* 3 October.

———. 1912b. "Bliss Fund List Given at Inquiry." *New York Times,* 19 October.

———. 2004a. "2004 Election Guide." *New York Times.* Available from http://www.nytimes.com/packages/html/politics/2004_ELECTIONGUIDE_GRAPHIC/index_HOUSECQ.html.

———. 2004b. "Campaign Briefing: The Advertising Campaign." *New York Times,* 25 September 2004, A1, p. 13, late edition.

———. 2004c. "Editorial." *New York Times,* 13 December, p. A26.

Nichols, Hans. 2004. "Dems Plan to Redirect DNC Away from Presidential Race." *The Hill,* 1 December.

Oliver, Jack. 2005. "Comments to the Campaign Finance Institute." National Press Club, Washington, DC, 14 January.

Ornstein, Norman J., Thomas E. Mann, and Michael J. Malbin. 2002. *Vital Statistics on Congress, 2001–2002.* Washington, DC: The AEI Press.

Ortiz, Daniel R. 2004. "The Unbearable Lightness of Being *McConnell.*" *Election Law Journal* 3 (2): 299–304.

Podhorzer, Mike, Keith Goodman, and David Boundy [AFL-CIO Director of Political Department, Research Analyst, and Deputy Director of Political Department, respectively]. 2004. Interview by David B. Magleby and Betsey K. Gimbel, Washington, DC, 16 December.

Pollack, James K. 1926. *Party Campaign Funds.* New York: Alfred A. Knopf.

Postman, David. 2004. "State Bush Campaign Betting on Grassroots." *Seattle Times,* 23 May.

Preston, Mark, and Paul Kane. 2004. "Senate GOP Plots Turnout Program." *Roll Call,* 1 October.

Price, David. 2004. "'Stand By Your Ad' Considered A Resounding Success." Press release. 31 January. Available from http://price.house.gov/News/DocumentSingle.aspx?DocumentID=4931.

Public Citizen. 2003. "Dash for Cash Events." Public Citizen, 6 August. Available from http://www.whitehouseforsale.org/dashforcash.

———. 2004. "Kerry Campaign Bankrolled by 564 Big-Money Bundlers." Press release. 16 July. Available from http://www.whitehouseforsale.org/documents/0715PressRel.pdf.

Public Citizen's Congress Watch. 2002. "United Seniors Association: Hired Guns for PhRMA and Other Corporate Interests." Public Citizen. July.

———. 2004. "The New Stealth PACs: Tracking 501(c) Non-Profit Groups Active in Elections." Public Citizen. September.

Reiff, Neil, 2004. Telephone interview by Raymond J. La Raja, 26 August.

Republican National Committee. 2004a. "Donor Information: Super Rangers." Republican National Committee. Available from http://www.gop.com/donorinfo.html.

———. 2004b. "Racing to Victory." *Rising Tide* (summer issue).

Richards, Cecile. 2003. "Comments Made at Take Back America Conference." Washington, DC.

Richardson, Bill. 2004. "Seeking the Latino Vote." January/February 2004. Available from http://www.HispanicMagazine.com.

Riskind, Jonathan. 2004. "Big Gifts to Parties MIA in '04." *Columbus Dispatch*, 8 August.

Rogers, David. 2001. "'Soft Money' Study Shows Concentration of Donations by Wealthy Contributors." *Wall Street Journal*, 16 March.

Rosenthal, Steve. 2003. "Comments to the Campaign Finance Institute." National Press Club, Washington, DC, 2 February.

Roth, Bennett, and John Frank. 2004. "Election 2004: The Home Stretch." *Houston Chronicle*, 30 October, 1.

Rutenberg, Jim. 2003. "Fine Print is Given Full Voice in Campaign Ads." *New York Times*, 8 November.

Rutenberg, Jim, and Glen Justice. 2004a. "A Delegate, a Fund Raiser, and a Very Fine Line." *New York Times*, 29 July.

———. 2004b. "Some Democrats Urge Kerry to Forego Public Campaign Financing." *New York Times*, 9 July.

Samuel, Alexandra. 2004. "Internet Plays Wild Card into U.S. Politics." *Toronto Star*, 18 October, D1.

Savodnik, Peter. 2004. "Democrats Cancel Ad Buy in Colo.-7." *The Hill*, 28 September.

Seeyle, Katherine Q. 2004. "Kerry Pulls Ads From Some States as Spending is Limited." *New York Times*, September 19.

Service Employees International Union. 2004. "Anatomy of an Election Strategy: The Facts in SEIU's Role in Bringing Home a Victory for America's Working Families." Service Employees International Union, 1 November.

Shepard, Scott. 2003a. "Democrats' First Contest is Financial; Big Field, Early Primaries Add Pressure." *Atlanta Journal and Constitution*, 2 February, 18A.

———. 2003b. "Liberal Democrat Energizes Party." *Atlanta Journal and Constitution*, 22 February.

Sidoti, Liz. 2004a. "Bush Team Orchestrates Larger Ad Campaign." *Associated Press State and Local Wire*, 22 September.

———. 2004b. "Kerry Campaign, DNC to Run Joint Ads." *Associated Press State and Local Wire*, 24 September.

Steen, Jennifer A. 2003. "The 'Millionaires' Amendment.'" In *Life After Reform: When The Bipartisan Campaign Reform Act Meets Politics*, edited by Michael J. Malbin. Lanham, MD: Rowman & Littlefield.

———. 2006. *Self-Financed Candidates in Congressional Elections*. Ann Arbor: University of Michigan Press.

Stone, Peter H. 2002. "Hard Questions About Soft Money Groups." *National Journal*, 21 December.

———. 2003. "Inside Two Soft Money Havens." *National Journal*, 20 December.

———. 2004a. "Bill Clinton Helps Ickes' 527 Group." *National Journal*, 6 March.

———. 2004b. "Republican 527s: Full Steam Ahead." *National Journal*, 29 May.

Stone, Peter H., and James A. Barnes. 2003. "Democrats' Money Mavens Unite." *National Journal*, 4 October.

Strom, Stephanie. 2003. "A Deficit of $100 Million is Confronting the NRA." *New York Times*, 21 December.

Strope, Leigh. 2004. "Labor Unions Fail to Deliver Votes for Kerry Candidacy." *Associated Press*, 5 November.

Sweet, Lynn. 2004. "Clinton Brings Fund-Raising Muscle to Chicago." *Chicago Sun-Times*, 1 July.

Sweeting, Rhueheema A. 2004. "Republicans and Democrats Step Up Efforts to Register Millions of Voters." *New York Times*, 6 March.

Tankersley, Jim. 2004. "Coors Aims to Limit Spending; Too Much Campaign Cash Could Backfire and Help Salazar." *Rocky Mountain News*, 1 September, 34A.

Texans for Public Justice. 2004a. "Pioneers and Rangers at a Glance," Available from http://www.tpj.org/docs/pioneers/pioneers_table.jsp.

———. 2004b. "Payola Pioneering: Exposing the Bush Pioneer/Ranger Network" [Report]. Texans for Public Justice, 1 October. Available from http://www.tpj.org/pioneers/pioneers04/index_pio.html.

———. 2004c. "The Bush Pioneer-Ranger Network," Available from http://www.tpj.org/page_view.jsp?pageid = 203&pubid = 85.

Theimer, Sharon. 2003. "Clinton Raising Money for Democrats." *Associated Press State and Local Wire*, 12 October.

———. 2004. "Bush Raises Cash for Senate GOP Members." *Associated Press State and Local Wire*, 2 March.

Thomas, Scott, and Michael Toner. 2005. "Legislative Recommendations Regarding Presidential Public Funding Program." Transmitted by letter addressed to "Congressional Leader," February 9. Available from http://www.fec.gov/members/toner/toner_legrec.html.

Trippi, Joe. 2004. *The Revolution Will Not Be Televised: Democracy, the Internet, and the Overthrow of Everything*. New York: HarperCollins.

Trister, Michael. 2000. "The Rise and Reform of Stealth PACs." *The American Prospect*, September 25–October 9, pp. 32–35.

USA Today. 2003. "GOP Has Gained 1M Donors Since 2001." *USA Today*, 3 October.

U.S. Senate. 1971. Committee on Commerce, Subcommittee on Communications. *Hearings on S.1, S.382, and S.596, Federal Election Campaign Act of 1971*. 92d Cong., 1st sess.

U.S. Senate Committee on Privileges and Elections. 1912–1913. Subcommittee of the Committee on Privileges and Elections. *Hearings on Campaign Contributions*. 62nd Cong., 3rd sess.

Van Natta, Don, Jr., and John M. Broder. 2000. "The Few, The Rich, The Rewarded Donate the Bulk of G.O.P. Gifts." *New York Times*, 2 August.

Van Natta, Don Jr., and Richard A. Oppel Jr. 2002. "Parties Create Ways to Avoid Soft Money Ban." *New York Times*, 2 November.

VandeHei, James. 2002a. "Campaign Finance's New Face." *Washington Post*, 9 July.

———. 2002b. "For Ex-president, a Careful Return to Fray." *Washington Post*, 18 October, A14.

———. 2003. "Two Years After Exit, Clintons Shaping Democratic Party." *Washington Post*, 21 June, A1.

———. 2005. "A Big Push on Social Security." *Washington Post*, 1 January, A1.

Wallison, Ethan. 2004. "Parties Become Major 527 Donors." *Roll Call*, 22 March.

Walsh, Charles. 2004. "Candidates Upfront in Ads no Trend; it's the Law." *Connecticut Post*, 17 September.

Walter, Amy. 2004. "The Final Analysis: The House." *Cook Political Report*, 6 December. Available from http://www.cookpolitical.com/overview/default.php.

Wayne, Steven J. 2000. *The Road to the White House 2000: The Politics of Presidential Elections*. Boston: Bedford/St. Martin's.

Weissman, Steve, and Ruth Hassan. 2004. "The $100 Million Exemption: Soft Money and the 2004 National Party Conventions." Washington, DC: The Campaign Finance Institute. July.

West, Darrell. 2001. *Air Wars: Television Advertising in Election Campaigns 1952–2000*. Washington, DC: Congressional Quarterly Press.

Whittington, Lauren. 2004. "DCCC Expands Beneficiary List; First Round of 'R2B' Deemed a Success." *Roll Call*, 28 September.

Wilcox, Clyde, Alexandra Cooper, Peter Francia, John Green, Paul S. Herrnson, Lynda Powell, Jason Reifler, Mark J. Rozell, and Benjamin A. Webster. 2003. "With Limits Raised, Who Will Give

More? The Impact of BCRA on Individual Donors." In *Life After Reform: When the Bipartisan Campaign Reform Act Meets Politics*, edited by Michael J. Malbin. Lanham, MD: Rowman & Little-field.

Williams, Vanessa. 2004. "Democrats Aim to Organize the Union Vote: Labor Leaders Predict Record Turnout as they Rally Members for Kerry in Battleground States." *Washington Post*, 23 October, p. A8.

Wisconsin Advertising Project. 2004. "Bush, Dem. TV Adv. Near Equal." Press release. Wisconsin Advertising Project, 24 March. Available from http://www.polisci.wisc.edu/tvadvertising/Press %20Releases.htm.

Index

About the Authors

THE EDITOR

Michael J. Malbin is Executive Director of the Campaign Finance Institute (CFI) and Professor of Political Science at the State University of New York at Albany. Before joining SUNY in 1990, he worked for Richard B. Cheney in the House of Representatives and as speechwriter to the Secretary of Defense. He has written and edited numerous books and articles on money in politics including the 2003 CFI/Rowman & Littlefield book, *Life After Reform: When the Bipartisan Campaign Reform Act Meets Politics.*

THE CONTRIBUTORS

Robert G. Boatright is Assistant Professor of Government at Clark University. He is the author of *Expressive Politics: Issue Strategies of Congressional Challengers* (2004) and several articles on congressional politics. He was a research analyst at the Campaign Finance Institute from 2002 to 2004 and is a coauthor of a forth-coming CFI project on interest group adaptations to BCRA.

Anthony Corrado is the Charles A. Dana Professor of Government at Colby College and cochair of the Campaign Finance Institute's Board of Trustees. He is the author or coauthor of numerous studies on political finance, including *The New Campaign Finance Sourcebook, Inside the Campaign Finance Battle,* and *Paying for Presidents.*

Diana Dwyre is Professor of Political Science and department chair at the California State University, Chico. She served as the American Political Science Association Steiger Congressional Fellow in 1998 and worked for Rep. Sander Levin on campaign finance issues. Professor Dwyre has published extensively on political parties and campaign finance and coauthored *Legislative Labyrinth: Congress and Campaign Finance Reform* (2001) with Victoria Farrar-Myers.

Michael M. Franz is Assistant Professor of Government at Bowdoin College. His research interests include interest groups, parties, elections, and campaign advertising. He has published articles in the *American Journal of Political Science, Political Behavior, Political Analysis,* and *Social Science Quarterly.* He is currently working on a book that explores the effects of campaign advertising on voters.

Kenneth Goldstein is Professor of Political Science at the University of Wisconsin, Madison and director of the University of Wisconsin Advertising Project. He is the author of *Interest Groups, Lobbying, and Participation in America,* and recently completed a book on television advertising called *Seeing Spots.*

Ruth Hassan was a research assistant at the Campaign Finance Institute in 2004–2005. She received her B.S. in Political Science and Economics from Northeastern University, summa cum laude, and has recently completed an M.A. in Philosophy and Social Policy at the George Washington University.

Gary C. Jacobson is Professor of Political Science at the University of California, San Diego. He is the author of *Money in Congressional Elections; Strategy and Choice in Congressional Elections; The Politics of Congressional Elections;* and *The Electoral Origins of Divided Government.*

Robin Kolodny is Associate Professor of Political Science at Temple University. She studies political parties, the U.S. Congress, and parties and legislatures in comparative perspective. She is the author of *Pursuing Majorities: Congressional Campaign Committees in American Politics,* published in 1998.

Raymond J. La Raja is Assistant Professor of Political Science at the University of Massachusetts, Amherst. With research interests including political parties, interest groups, elections, political participation, state politics, and public policy, La Raja is the author or coauthor of more than a dozen scholarly articles about campaign finance. He is also the managing editor of *The Forum: A Journal of Applied Research in American Politics.*

David B. Magleby is Dean of the College of Family, Home and Social Sciences, a Distinguished Professor of Political Science, and a Senior Research Fellow at the Center for the Study of Elections and Democracy at Brigham Young University. His recent books include *Outside Money: Soft Money and Issue Advocacy in the 1998 Congressional Elections; The Other Campaign: Soft Money and Issue Advocacy in the 2000 Congressional Elections;* and *The Last Hurrah? Soft Money and Issue Advocacy in the 2002 Congressional Elections.*

Kelly D. Patterson is Associate Professor of Political Science at Brigham Young University where he is also the director of the Center for the Study of Elections and Democracy. Professor Patterson was a Congressional Fellow for the American Political Science Association in 1991–1992. His research interests include campaigns and elections, public opinion, and political parties.

Joel Rivlin is a graduate student at the University of Wisconsin, Madison, and deputy director of the Wisconsin Advertising Project. His research interests include targeting on election messages, political advertising and campaign finance, and the strategic use of negative advertising.

Mark J. Rozell is Professor of Public Policy and director of the Master of Public Policy Program at George Mason University. He is the author of nine books including *Power and Prudence: The Presidency of George H.W. Bush* (with Ryan Barilleaux); *Executive Privilege: Presidential Power, Secrecy, and Accountability* (2nd ed.); and *Interest Groups in American Campaigns: The New Face of Electioneering* (2nd ed., with Clyde Wilcox and David Madland).

Jennifer A. Steen is Assistant Professor of Political Science at Boston College. She is the author of *Self-Financed Candidates in Congressional Elections* (2006). A former political consultant, Ms. Steen has worked for candidates in local, state, and federal elections and served as a precinct captain, national convention delegate, and presidential elector. She received her Ph.D. from the University of California, Berkeley.

Stephen R. Weissman is Associate Director for Policy at the Campaign Finance Institute. Previously, he was legislative representative for Public Citizen's Congress Watch, specializing in campaign finance reform. Weissman is a political scientist (Ph.D., University of Chicago) who has taught at Fordham University, the University of Texas at Dallas, and Howard University. Formerly staff director for the House of Representatives' Subcommittee on Africa, his publications include *A Culture of Deference: Congress's Failure of Leadership in Foreign Policy*.

Clyde Wilcox is Professor of Government at Georgetown University. His books include *Serious Money: Fundraising and Contributing in Presidential Nominating Campaigns; Onward Christian Soldiers: The Christian Right in American Politics; Interest Groups in American Campaigns;* and *The Financiers of Congressional Elections*.

Campaigning American Style

CAMPAIGNING AMERICAN STYLE

Series Editors
Daniel M. Shea, Allegheny College
F. Christopher Arterton, George Washington University

Few areas of American politics have changed as dramatically in recent times as the way in which we choose public officials. Students of politics and political communications are struggling to keep abreast of these developments—and the 2000 and 2004 elections only fed the confusion and concern. *Campaigning American Style* is a new series of books devoted to both the theory and practice of American electoral politics. It offers high-quality work on the conduct of new-style electioneering and how it is transforming our electoral system. Scholars, practitioners, and students of campaigns and elections need new resources to keep pace with the rapid rate of electoral change, and we are pleased to help provide them in this exciting series.

The Election After Reform:
Money, Politics, and the Bipartisan Campaign Reform Act
edited by Michael J. Malbin

Forthcoming

PAC Management for Pros:
Political Action in the Jungle of American Campaign Finance
by Steven Billet

Battle Lines: Power Plays, Redistricting, and Election Laws
by Ronald Keith Gaddie and Charles S. Bullock, III

Dancing Without Partners: How Candidates, Parties, and Interest Groups
Interact in the 2004 Presidential Campaign
edited by David B. Magleby, J. Quin Monson, and Kelly D. Patterson

The Rules: Election Regulations in the American States
by Costas Panagopoulos

Throwing a Better Party: Political Parties and the Mobilization of America's Youth
by Daniel M. Shea and John C. Green

ISSCW   324
         .7809
         73
         E38

THE ELECTION AFTER
    REFORM
CENTRAL LIBRARY
06/07